SEARCH
FOR
MEANING

The Autobiography
of a Nonconformist

By JOHN U. NEF

PUBLIC AFFAIRS PRESS, WASHINGTON, D. C.

For Evie

To whom I want to tell this story

Published by Public Affairs Press
419 New Jersey Avenue, S.E., Washington, D. C. 20003
Printed in the United States of America
Library of Congress Catalog Card No. 73-82014
Copyright 1973 by John U. Nef

SEARCH
FOR
MEANING

CONTENTS

> *O, wonder!*
> *How many goodly creatures are there here!*
> *How beauteous mankind is!*
> —SHAKESPEARE, THE TEMPEST

> *The real duty of the artist [is] to save his dream.*
> —PIERRE SICKLE, MODIGLIANI

PREFACE

The problems confronting humanity today are quite different from those which faced my generation—the generation which grew to maturity during and just after the first World War. Yet I believe that the story I relate in these pages has a relevance to the concerns of the 1970's.

I cannot help being heartened that young people, especially young Americans, are today challenging traditional but outmoded thinking and values, as I have sought to do over the past fifty years. These five decades have been an era of upheaval unequalled in recorded history. Human conditions have changed to an extraordinary degree. Machinery almost everywhere is driven by the force of heat energy; all the earth's peoples are interdependent; humans now have the means of committing collective suicide.

As I suggest in these pages, the failure to recognize the importance of enduring values as the basis for action is a great weakness of contemporary society. Scholarship has done little to overcome this weakness. In fact the gap between action and thought has been widened by major trends in education and intellectual investigation, such as increasing specialization and excessive dependence for guidance, as means of dealing with human relations, upon methods of inquiry derived from the natural sciences. As a non-conforming educational reformer and historian, I have worked against these trends.

The two remarkable women I married have been a dominant influence in my life, in my search for meaning, and in my lasting friendships with Artur Schnabel, T. S. Eliot, and Marc Chagall.

These friendships (combined with others that included Jacques Maritain, Robert Hutchins, and R. H. Tawney) are related to the innovations in my historical publications and in my approaches to the higher learning and to international relations. These innovations have linked me with some idealistic representatives of the younger generation. In ways of the spirit I am closer to them than to my own generation. So I like to think that my *Search for Meaning* is part of theirs.

In my youth the philosophy of Oswald Spengler, who counseled the young to throw away their paint brushes and other instruments of art and to seek instead influence and power, was almost swallowed whole. Fortunately the present pursuit of beauty and even of compassion commands far more respect than the pursuit of influence and power. The appeals which once commanded enthusiasm—Marxism, Normalcy, Two Car Garages, the New Deal, the New Frontier, the Great Society—are no longer satisfying.

The story told in this book suggests that the most stable foundation for happiness rests with a new humanism for a united humanity, rich in diversity but free from the chauvinism, the hatred, the racism and the nationalism which, in their naked power to destroy, have revealed the consequences of evil more clearly than ever before.

My debt to my wife, Evelyn Stefansson Nef, is apparent especially in Part V. I have also benefited by some valuable suggestions from my friend Thomas Hoban Alcock, and my publisher, M. B. Schnapper, who has turned out to be a dedicated editor of a kind I had thought extinct.

It is difficult adequately to acknowledge the assistance I have received from my secretaries, Mrs. Branimir M. Rieger, Mrs. William Scanlin, and Mrs. James J. Hickey, Jr. I compose in longhand and in the course of repeated revisions insertions have sprawled all over the pages. The accuracy and speed of these young women in deciphering my handwriting has greatly facilitated the tasks of composition and revision. Their occasional suggestions also helped me to decide what needed mending. All three are members of the oncoming generation in whom my hopes are centered.

JOHN U. NEF

Washington, D. C.

PART 1

An Adventure of the Heart and Mind

1. A PASSION FOR THOUGHT

In 1923, two years after our marriage, my first wife Elinor Castle Nef and I were living in Paris in a comfortable hotel, the Plaza-Athenée, when I brought back to lunch from the Bibliothèque Nationale, where I was researching, a somewhat older colleague in history who was then expected to have a brilliant administrative career at Harvard. The conversation centered on the historian's calling. He suggested that more than the man of letters, the musician or the painter, the historian needs a tranquil happy life.

Whether or not that is a valid generalization, the fortune that bestowed such a life was good for my work. It helped me obtain direct access to works of art. It helped me form friendships with a number of distinguished men of letters, painters, musicians and other artists. This communion with creators of beauty, a communion shared by both my wives who have had the capacity to delight which exalts, enabled me to embark on the new kind of historical writing that eventually captured my allegiance. Without this "wealth," I could hardly have persisted in efforts to combine what the learned classify as economic history with constitutional history, ecclesiastical history, intellectual history, the history of technology, of science, and the history of the various arts, with a view to the enrichment of history.

Concerned though I have been in some of my books and articles with a few consequences that the pursuit of beauty seems to have had for history, I would not presume to write a treatise on any aspect of painting or sculpture, of music or architecture as such. I am at as distant a remove from Albert Barnes, who appears in one chapter of this book, as it is possible to be.

With my first wife I began to buy pictures a half century ago, out of delight nourished almost every day by visits to museums in off hours from research and composition. As time went on, and the pursuit of historical information extended from documents in European capitals to those in provincial archives, the new search introduced us to many smaller towns, some venerable with municipal buildings, ancient palaces and monasteries, churches, cathedrals and old walls, which carried us back from contemporary Europe to Romanesque and even to Roman times. These monuments often provided examples of what others in days gone by had done with different kinds of materials. I longed to create with documentary information a solid historical edifice after the manner of these monuments.

For many years it hardly occurred to me that the pictures we acquired could have any substantial material value. We kept them modestly insured, hoping that if we lost them we might get back at least part of the small sums we had paid. Such comments about them as came our way did not persuade me that their price might appreciate. Many people, from varied professions and circumstances, visited our home, but few seemed to notice the pictures. Among those who did, the comment that some of the *frames* were *good* was not infrequent. And I remember someone looking at the classic Picasso gouache of a seated woman and, mistaking a shadow for hair, asking rhetorically, "Was he trying to grow a beard on that girl?" This was long before the advent of the "hippies," when sprouting hair, beards and mustaches became so popular among the young.

It was not until after my first wife died in 1953, when most of the pictures had been with us for a quarter of a century, that I was prompted to raise the insurance by an episode in the Chicago apartment where many of them had hung since 1931. The late Robert Strozier, afterwards President of the State University of Florida, was then Dean of Students at the University of Chicago. He sometimes lunched with me to talk over plans for the development of the novel interdisciplinary faculty formed in 1941-42: The Committee on Social Thought. On one occasion, interrupting the flow of our conversation, he turned abruptly to the pictures in the dining and living rooms. "John," he exclaimed, "these are the best investment you ever made!"

I might truthfully have responded with words my friend André Siegfried was fond of ejaculating when someone invited him to do something that attracted him, "Pas d'objection!" The news Strozier volunteered was anything but disagreeable. Yet it was and it is irrelevant to the meaning objects of art have had in my career, save to the extent that Strozier's remark contributed to my confidence that my possession of pictures might represent more than the *eccentricity* of a private individual, that it might reflect, however imperfectly, a response to beauty which has more than personal validity.

A great need in the modern world is to transcend specialties without yielding to superficiality. This requires a realm of free disinterested discourse, on a worldwide scale, among influential and discriminating persons—a realm in which the best works of artists and scholars and pure scientists matter, bear on the ultimate goals of human endeavor. What are these "ultimate goals"? The strengthening of good against evil, of beauty against ugliness, of truth against falsehood, of love against hate. The fact that it is impossible to define these words, and overwhelmingly difficult to choose the right alternatives in the quest for the values they represent, does not diminish the importance of trying to serve those values.[1]

The increasingly minute specialization characteristic of twentieth-century scholarship has done much for the accumulation of knowledge, nowhere perhaps more than in connection with historical information. But the fragmentation of scholarly disciplines, nowhere pushed to greater extremes than in the United States, has contributed to a kind of vacuum in the realm of serious general discourse. Insofar as specialization has come to diminish competence in that realm, and to keep disinterested and informed opinion from counting effectively, it is an evil, for never has the universal been so important as now, on a planet which has become mechanically united by technological progress based in no small part on discoveries in the pure sciences. The dream that has impelled me, ever since I started writing my first book back in 1922, is that my career could contribute a mite to the formation of such a realm of general discourse.

Some writers obtain their most valuable stimuli less from works composed in their own language, than from those they know in foreign languages. I once found myself copying Fielding's style with disastrous results. It would be more difficult for me to be corrupted by Stendhal's, and impossible to be corrupted by Beethoven's. A writer is precluded from copying slavishly the form and style of a work in a foreign tongue (in which the thought and expression are alien to his habits of composition), with the same facility that can beset him in his admiration for a masterpiece in his native tongue. So, if he feels the mission, he is freer to make use as models of what he reads in foreign tongues to the advantage of his message. He can enrich his own idiom by his acquaintance with masterpieces in different idioms.

There is an analogy here to my experience. Works of music and the visual arts have been of value to my historical compositions partly because I understand them most imperfectly in their own idiom, but rejoice in the general impression of beauty they inspire. As a craftsman, works of art and conversations with artists arrest me because of the kinship I recognize them to have with the novel historical compositions which have attracted my labor.

Scholarship has come to be dominated by forms of presentation ill-suited to the unconventional kinds of historical writing which command my allegiance. The quest beyond special and increasingly narrow subjects requires a freedom for the imagination, and a knowledge of many branches of evolution, that specialized scholarship by itself does little to kindle. At the same time to be effectively presented the more general subjects have to be given a substance, a profundity, which the methods of popularization that have become fashionable render almost impossible. Forms derived from artistic models, though not directly applicable to historical composition, help make room both for the freedom that conventional scholarship impedes and for the rigorous discipline that popularization evades.

I had been trained in historical writing since college days. The presence of works of art helped to arouse a larger purpose. It saved me from being smothered by the drudgery imposed by mountains of documents, seemingly endless shelves of books, and quotations extracted on cards. It converted that drudgery into the excitement of trying to build edifices such as I had foolishly imagined I might create by music. Had it not been for the pleasure derived from this transposition of artistic impulses into historical essays, a tendency derived from childhood to depreciate everything connected with myself might have overwhelmed me, driven me from the historian's career and submerged such capabilities as I possessed.

Artists are often alleged to thrive on material adversity. Are not some words that Plato put in the mouth of Socrates applicable to the assertion? "There seem to be two causes of the deterioration of the arts," Socrates tells Adeimantus in *The Republic*. "What are they?" he is asked. "Wealth," he says, "and poverty."

Beauty requires excess, but beyond a point excess destroys beauty. The exact point can never be scientifically established. It varies as between individuals. So does the consequence of material adversity or plenty. As an artistic calling, history may be the one in which poverty is most damaging.

2. A PASSION FOR HISTORY

It was probably at the age of fourteen or so that I had an experience which influenced the direction my writings were to take. We had a remarkable teacher of history in the University of Chicago High School, Arthur F. Barnard. His favorite subject was ancient Greece. When I had to recite in class I was always worried but there was an occasion on which he relieved me of all distress. I can no longer recall what it was I said in answer to a question of his. But when I had finished, he gave me the recognition that is at the disposal only of a generous man of learning. He called the answer "most original." Since this kind of praise was not habitual in his class, it made an indelible impression.

At the time I was living a rather solitary and cloistered hotel life with my widower father. Though he admired his wife's social gifts, he had not shared them and showed no inclination to remarry. He was of Swiss origin, born in Herisau in the canton of Appenzell. At the age of four his parents brought him to the United States where they settled in Housatonic, Massachusetts and threw in their lot with America. He made a fine career and became a leader in the science of chemistry. Founder of the Chemistry Department at the University of Chicago, he presided over it until his death.

I had just passed my sixteenth birthday when he collapsed of a heart attack at Carmel in California in 1915. He had provided for this contingency by appointing his friend and colleague, the philosopher George Herbert Mead, as guardian. Herman Spoehr, scientist of the Carnegie Institution of Washington, who had been my father's favorite pupil, was on hand in Carmel and took me to the Meads in Chicago. A year and a half before I had fallen in love with the girl I eventually married, Helen Mead's niece, Elinor Castle. She was almost five years older than I. When I came into the Mead household, where I was to remain for two years, she was part of it. It was a large household and with my sense of inadequacy, which had not receded during the six years since my mother's death, I was always embarassed when I told a story. Nevertheless stories frequently welled up inside. One came out not long after I arrived at the Meads. It was an account of a battle between the armies of two South American countries. I told my story to a mixed company of about a dozen. They seemed to show no interest. Imagine what it did to me some minutes later to be told privately by the girl in whom all my thoughts were centered, that it

was not only a good story but told in an original way, the very words
Barnard used about my recitation on Greek history. The reassuring
impression his praise had left on my mind and heart was doubled.

This recognition gave me confidence that I might sometimes have
things worth communicating and might be able to tell them. That
confidence, constantly renewed after our marriage by a woman of taste
and discrimination and strong convictions who was highly critical, provided the increasingly personal, often lonely and frequently mis-
understood work I was eventually to undertake with a fortress of
comprehension indispensable to a man so uncertain of himself.

I have always assured persons suffering from sciatica that it is a
childhood malady. It attacked me at sixteen but I recovered and
went into the army at nineteen. The first onslaught came on the eve
of my entrance to college, and George and Helen Mead insisted I stay
in Chicago and spend a year at the University instead of going to
Harvard as planned. During that year I remember writing a "term
paper" on Eleanor of Aquitaine. I chose the subject because I was
in love with the name. The paper was a success with the history instructor, Curtis Walker.[1] He not only gave it a straight "A," but wrote
with contagious enthusiasm, "Gorgeous!" This was most stimulating
for a boy whose father had been continually disappointed by his high
school record.

My experience with "Eleanor" was followed in the spring of 1917
by a long essay written for a rising historical scholar, Conyers Read,
on the political institutions of Alsace-Lorraine before 1789. Read
thought well enough of the paper to urge me to go further with the
subject. So I built up a considerable bibliography. For the better part
of a year I wrote themes treating the history of Alsace-Lorraine. The
merits of the rival claims of Germany and of France to those provinces
were the subject of the first long paper I did in English composition
at Harvard after transferring from Chicago. My inquiry convinced me
that the return to France of these provinces would be just, as President
Wilson suggested in his famous "Fourteen Points." This conviction
helped me to join the army, for my inner life rallied to the President's
pronouncement that we were engaged in "a war to end war."

Later at Harvard I wrote with excitement term papers and other
essays, and made *The Crimson* after hard competition. I was eventually elected editorial chairman of that newspaper, in time to compose
"leaders" concerning the Versailles Treaty. These attracted some
attention among the faculty as well as the students. Charles Town-

send Copeland, an eccentric bachelor who was not without vanity, *asked* me to join his class in English composition, a class officially open only to those who had successfully competed. A much younger friend who had run *The Crimson*, David Little took me aside to caution. He told me that, though not a Jew, my plans for peace and for understanding with Russia as well as with Germany were unwittingly furthering a Jewish plot to take over the world! I cannot remember how Little arrived at his assumption.

In the autumn of 1920, a year of graduate study at Harvard began. I not only served as Manager of the Union, an office in which I succeeded Little, I assisted Arthur N. Holcombe in his course in Government and Frederick J. Turner in his course in American History. I had studied with both in my senior year. Turner's novel ideas about the role of the frontier in the history of the United States (which I had the advantage of absorbing when I used to sit with him in the study at his home while he reviewed, and often raised, the marks I had put on his students' papers) undoubtedly contributed to an interest in the nature of historical causation destined to become a major theme in my lectures and books. At the same time I learned many valuable points about the technical problems of writing history from Charles Homer Haskins' seminar in bibliography and criticism.

My days were overcrowded and I had little opportunity to meditate upon, let alone to develop, the seeds that were being sown. Those seeds were to serve me in good stead during the years that followed. Not least rich in nourishment was the association with these three professors and also with the distinguished economist, Professor Frank Taussig, who admitted me to his graduate course although I had never had an elementary training in the subject. Each of these professors invited me to his home as a guest at small dinners and luncheons. Each followed the directions my life took after Harvard in the greater freedom and leisure which Europe was to provide during what would otherwise have been the five "academic years" 1921 to 1926.

As the crowded academic year 1920-21 was ending, and the Union showed a small profit, the professor of Eastern European history, Archibald Cary Coolidge, long director of the Widener Library, invited me to go in the autumn as his secretary to Russia. At the same time John Cowles promised me rapid advancement in journalism if I came to work for the Des Moines paper published by his father.

I chose instead to marry the girl whose existence gave life to my

work. Unlike many men who share my predilections for the opposite
sex, with the immense scope and variety these can kindle in all aspects
of living and working (predilections which used to be called "frailties"
and which were often linked with Adam's fall), mine has been the
incredible good fortune to have married two of the loveliest and most
interesting women of our times, the second of whom (in addition to
her endless charms and balanced disposition) is gifted as an artist,
has a delightful voice for song, an incredible memory and effective
drive.[2] Both shared my passion for composition and encouraged
me, in every way they found possible, to cultivate it. We have always
rejoiced in each other's accomplishments, I in theirs at least as much
as they in mine.

The late Harold Innis, with whom I formed beginning in 1940 a
warm and enduring friendship, used frequently to discuss problems
of composition. As he probably had the most original ideas of any
Canadian historian of the twentieth century, I was always happy when
we found common ground. I remember our agreeing that it takes
about a decade of continuous labor to do a full length history book.

It had proved so with my first book. The ten years that followed
my marriage to Elinor Castle revolved around the composition of my
massive *Rise of the British Coal Industry*. It was proving so with
my second, *Industry and Government in France and England, 1540-
1640*, which was on the stocks at the time of my meeting with Innis.[3]
It has continued to be so since. My next substantial historical work,
War and Human Progress, which kept me at my last all through the
forties, was published in 1950.

Meanwhile my activities as a university professor, described in Parts
III and IV of this autobiography, were moving from the special
towards the general. My passion for writing, which augmented rather
than diminished, cannot be divorced from those activities. They influenced my approach to history, just as my evolving attitude towards
historical research nourished the reforms in the higher learning that I
was impelled to undertake.

From experiences as researcher, writer and lecturer the limitations
of specialization began to unfold, at a time when scholarship and living everywhere were becoming more specialized. The search for
historical meaning led me to move against the trends. During the
academic year 1941-42 I held frequent luncheon meetings with the
three colleagues I knew at the University of Chicago who sympathized

most with my views: Robert Hutchins, Frank Knight and Robert Redfield. These meetings led to the establishment in 1942 (shortly after the United States entered the Second World War) of an inter-disciplinary faculty, the first fully independent one in any university. Despite the fact (and perhaps also because of it) that the President of the University and the Dean of the Social Sciences were two of the four members of the founding group, we had much trouble in starting this enterprise. It did not seem to the faculty to fit anywhere, which was from my point of view its principal merit. It was as hard to classify as the book I published at the same time, *The United States and Civilization.*[4] And no wonder! For what interested me was and is the whole human being. And how could anything but the whole of scholarship be adequate to serve him or her? What is needed is more rather than less than scholarship can supply. But how can one declare this and gain the support of scores of colleagues who are committed to special subjects and to traditional methods of research?

For reasons of faculty politics, the central administration of the University of Chicago decided to put us under the general rubric of the Division of the Social Sciences, as it was in that division that Knight, Redfield, and I professed, rather than to have us transcend administratively all divisional as well as departmental boundaries. But we called ourselves the Committee on Civilization. From the point of view of what I hoped we might accomplish—to open the way to any creative work of the mind which is seeking a broader base than the increasingly fragmented fields of special scholarship provide—the name was not inappropriate.

Certainly it was more descriptive than the title that was thrust upon us. When negotiations were under way with the chairmen of departments in the Social Science Division to make our group officially a part of the university structure, the Dean Robert Redfield (a friend since childhood) rang me on the telephone. "I can never get this through with the name 'Committee on Civilization,'" he explained in distress. "What name would you suggest?" I asked. "How about 'Committee on Social Thought?'" he ventured. "What does it mean?" I asked. "I haven't the slightest idea," he said, "but I think that title would be accepted, because nowhere in the University are there studies in social thought." The faculty *were* willing to recognize a new specialty but hardly the service of the human being as a whole.

I took the position 'tis better to be than not to be! And despite the title, during a chairmanship lasting some twenty-five years until my retirement, we obtained as a slowly growing group all the authority exercised by departments. We became in effect an institute transcending divisional as well as departmental lines, and could bring distinguished visitors and train students according to our ideas.

The establishment of this faculty, together with the turn taken by my historical compositions, aroused a fresh interest in my work abroad, especially in France. My writing was stimulated by invitations to profess in European academies.[5] The movement in my work from the special to the general found much understanding in France and, to begin with, little in the United States.

That movement led in yet another direction at the end of the fifties. The need for a world conscience and a body of world opinion had pressed upon my mind with intense urgency ever since the explosion in August 1945 of two atomic bombs. My concern resulted in the formation of a small group organized with the participation of several French friends in Paris in 1958, sponsored by the University of Chicago and called a Center for Human Understanding. The enterprise seemed a logical outgrowth of our interdisciplinary faculty, the "Committee on Social Thought." Its deliberations included representatives from Asia, South America and Africa, as well as from the United States and Europe.[6]

Discussions carried on at plenary meetings revealed, to my astonishment, that the problem which has concerned me always in my writings—the roots in Western European history of the mechanized world—is now a major problem confronting all the peoples of the earth. The history that has absorbed me over fifty years has a relevance for everyone because of the questions it raises. Why has human life come to be mechanized? What have been the fruits? What have been the costs? In the light of both, what are the possibilities for achieving "civilization" for the first time in history?

3. A PASSION FOR DELIGHT

As a child I indulged a hidden passion for works of art, partly as a result of my mother's interest in music and partly (after she died) as a result of trips to Europe with my father, between the age of nine and fifteen, when we visited famous galleries and listened to famous orchestras. I speak of this passion as "hidden" because I found it difficult to declare, and still more to discuss, with my schoolmates and playmates.

An only child, my imagination ran riot. I constructed a fresh world of ideal museums which I built and stocked with pictures of extra-ordinary quality by the leading painters to whom I was introduced through these visits to Europe and through guidebooks, particularly Baedekers—then not only the standard but almost the only authoritative guides to travel. I also invented painters and made up imaginary concert programs.

It was all fancy. I created a large ideal country on a distant island. The island existed nowhere on the map, so I conjured up a map of my own. The art galleries inside my head contained such wonderful pictures that Baedeker, when he prepared his guidebook, gave them *triple* stars although hitherto he had never accorded an object or monument more than two.

I knew nothing about contemporary painting. Indeed my father discouraged me from making its acquaintance. He derived much pleasure and excitement from some great paintings, statues and musical compositions. But he was as dogmatic about the graphic arts as he was about the study of alien tongues. One might call his dogmatism about paintings the reverse of his dogmatism concerning language training. In one he had no use whatever for the "living," in the sense of the recent and immediate; in the other it was the "living" alone that commanded his respect. Training in foreign languages had to be in languages that were spoken currently, especially German or French. He considered both Greek and Latin "dead," and he went to the pains of writing to President Abbott Lawrence Lowell in order to be certain that I could get into Harvard (his alma mater) without either. Yet he took no interest in the arts of his time—except in connection with the music of Wagner and Strauss to which he had been conditioned as a graduate student in Munich. In his opinion anything painted or sculptured *since* the sixteenth century was definitely inferior to earlier art. It was almost as if painting began with Leonardo da Vinci's birth in 1452 and ended with the deaths of Michelangelo and Titian little more than a hundred years afterwards. Needless to say he was not likely to introduce me to Ingres or Delacroix. I never heard of either. The only recent artist he mentioned was Corot, and with disparagement.

As his powerful views on all matters were dinned into me, I grew into adolescence taking for granted his opinions were right about painting, sculpture and music, as well as about morals, where he was very strict and unimaginative. Soon after his death in 1915 the United States joined in the First World War. I had no opportunities to visit art galleries for several years, except for an occasional excursion when I was at Harvard to pictures available in Boston. I did not take them very seriously.

It was during the autumn and winter of 1924-25, when Elinor and I were living in Vienna and I had begun *The Rise of the British Coal Industry,* that my childhood interest in art started to flower. We used regularly to visit the Kunsthistoriches Museum, which I still regard as having fewer bad pictures than any other of the finest public galleries in the world. We also visited regularly the Liechtenstein Gallery which has since disappeared, at least as far as Vienna is concerned. The quality of works there put the Liechtenstein as a private gallery in the same unique place which the Kunsthistoriches occupied as a public museum.

The most important event in this period of my life, so far as interest in more recent art is concerned, was the purchase of a Folio issued I think in 1924 under the auspices of *Dial* magazine, then the most distinguished literary review published in the United States. The folio bore the title "Living Art." It contained extraordinarily fine reproductions in color of works by a number of the artists who were then so maligned but who have since become so famous. These reproductions introduced us to Signac, Bonnard and Matisse. They went what was for the time even farther—as far as Picasso, Derain, and Marin to Chagall! In fact, if I remember, the editor justified the word "living" in the title by dismissing two painters not yet dead with the phrase, "Neither Sickert nor Sargent would be in the company of Marc Chagall at home."

"Living Art" first gave me an inkling that something notable and even beautiful was being created by artists I might meet, who were not "dead" even in the sense that, according to the editor, both Sickert and Sargent were. Yet I was inclined not to trust the inner fascination some contemporary paintings evoked. I attributed this fascination to my idiosyncrasies—relating my discoveries to the dream world of childhood invention which had been pricked by my father's discovery that my pretensions at eleven to the art of musical composition were sheer rubbish. He seemed to suffer over the fact that his son was not Beethoven!

In spite of the magic of Vienna, the impression persisted that my wife and I might be sadly misguided in our tastes. It is only recently that I have overcome this feeling of uncertainty.

This tendency to discount my judgment was fanned by the fact that the people we knew, and we met and went out with a considerable number in Vienna (including the later prominent Dorothy Thompson who was then married to a Hungarian named Bard), had little but condescension for the pictures in the Dial Folio. For example, we invited to tea the wife of the American Minister (the United States had then only a legation in Austria), "Pussy" Washburn. We showed her "Living Art." She regarded our interest in that as a kind of fetish of two immature compatriots. Elinor's enthusiasm rose to a high pitch over the reproduction of a Marin. Passionately she told Mrs. Washburn that the picture made her more patriotic than the American flag. The dear lady, who took her official position as an accredited representative of the United States very seriously, almost collapsed with astonishment.

These experiences with an enterprise to reproduce as perfectly as possible contemporary paintings and drawings, led me more and more to concentrate the visits to galleries which I was able to fit in with my demanding work upon examples of visual art by older contemporaries. The world of historical research and the world created by artists merged in my inner life. The one continually filled me with ideas about the other. The overwhelming desire that had beset me since infancy to participate in art, a desire that during my father's lifetime had been no more than a mirage, seemed less impossible of fulfillment. Together the two worlds of composition and delight overcame my sense of solitude. They absorbed the hours of living and of dreaming which fortune gave me in profusion during my formative years from twenty-two to twenty-six. So, even more, did another fulfillment touched upon in the next chapter.

PART II

Love, Art and Scholarship

4. THE MEDITERRANEAN, WOMAN AND MAILLOL

In Europe, according to the records of the weather bureaus, the summer of 1922 was the coldest of this century. During the first winter of our marriage, Elinor and I had gone to Montpellier in southern France to pursue our studies at the university. We had then spent all of April and some of May as newspaper correspondents without pay for the *Des Moines Register* and *Tribune* at the Genoa Conference, the first international assembly after the War of 1914 to which Germany and Russia were invited.

At Genoa we were immersed in paperwork and in public meetings and in private conversations with officials and journalists. We lived mostly in rooms filled with the smoke from batteries of cigarettes. We were sometimes in the streets, but, during a more than six-week Italian sojourn, never in the water or on the beach, except once at the Lido when we went on a short two-day holiday to Venice after the Conference had ended.

Montpellier gave me a taste I have never lost for the French *Midi*. It was taste for a provincial *town*. Our winter had little to do with the Mediterranean Sea, although we were always within a few miles. I cannot remember even seeing the water during the ten-week term at the university, except once from the high walls of Aigues-Mortes where we went for a daytime excursion from Nimes on a weekend when there were no classes.

Coming back from Italy to Paris late in May, on a train that wound along the coast of the Esterel from Cannes to St. Raphael, the oblong window of our sleeping compartment at breakfast briefly framed the Bay of Agay on a cloudless prematurely hot day. That picture of sunny, warm quiet perfection, with what appeared to be a white sandy beach opening on blue sea, kept reappearing to my inward eye during the weeks that followed, and may have helped pull us to the Riviera. But the immediate cause was that we nearly froze first in a Paris June and then in a London July,

14

accustomed as we were to summers in the United States where the temperatures average ten or fifteen degrees warmer than in the northern parts of Europe, which frequently resemble Iceland.

One afternoon we complained of our plight to a knowledgeable Britisher at Cooks Travel Agency in London. He suggested Cannes. We might roast but we could hardly freeze, he said. He also explained that, as one of Henry James' characters said of London in August, "nobody" would be there. That hardly dismayed us for we were self-contained.

We set out forthwith by train from London to Paris and, without stopping for the night, went on to Marseilles and Cannes, where only two smallish hotels were open in this total off-season. One was on the Croisette, the other several streets uptown.

During a long train stop in Marseilles, we read in a local newspaper that in the hotel on the Croisette the only clients, a couple, had performed an agreed murder and suicide. We were relieved to have booked at the other, back about a kilometer from the water.

We soon discovered that there also were only two clients. The man was said to be an American multi-millionaire; his Scottish wife was rarely seen, and then always under a heavy veil and covered with clothes appropriate to 1900. This couple turned out to be dipsomanics and drank themselves into a stupor every few days. This made it worthwhile for the hotel to remain open out of season.

Why? The owner had a villa at Juan-les-Pins, then hardly more frequented in the summer than Cannes. When the couple were dead drunk the chambermaid had instructions to tip off her employer. He would call at their apartment to sell his villa at a high price. A week or so later he would buy it back for next to nothing. The episodes were of sufficiently frequent occurrence to enable him to realize from the spread a handsome profit beyond the expenses of remaining open without other paying guests.

As the train drew into the Cannes station in the mid-July morning, the sun showered us with the warmish dry heat I had sensed in May through the sleeping car window at Agay. The owner of the hotel and his wife took us the very first afternoon in their automobile to see their villa at Juan-les-Pins! Each day after that for a couple of weeks we drove in a fiacre, and took a swim from the long, almost deserted beach west of Cannes harbor. Our companions were a few local people in long cumbersome bathing suits.

Our "cocher" was in luck; his was the only one of nearly fifty horse-drawn carriages, standing in line along the Croisette, which had regular clients.

After a fortnight we decided we would try to locate a place to stay where we could escape the dipsomanics, for when he was drunk the man used to knock on our door at inconvenient times. Without announcing our intentions we told our "cocher," when he came as usual one afternoon, to drive not to the beach but to Juan-les-Pins. That place was then mainly a tiny winter resort for persons threatened with tuberculosis. We got out of the carriage to look around the deserted village, and spied at the end of the Cap d'Antibes a large building rising on a height above the water. "What's that?" I asked the first man we spotted. He thought it was a hotel. "Is it open?" He didn't know. But the "cocher," who had overheard the conversation and suspected our intentions, assured us it was shut. Nevertheless we made him drive out. His horse was obliged to jog another three miles along the empty road that skirted the peninsula. When he mounted the last swing in this road we saw through a large iron gate the entrance to the hotel— an impressive flight of twenty-five vast white stone steps lit by a brilliant afternoon sun.

The doors seemed boarded up. Nevertheless I got out, climbed the steps and rang the bell. After a few minutes a tall, youngish man, about ten years my senior and almost bald, pulled back a door that was shutting out the sun. "Are you open?" I asked. He hesitated and looked through me at my companion in the carriage. He was dazzled. He decided he *was* open. We entered. He showed us the royal suite which had been occupied sometimes in the winters before the war by the King of Belgium and his family. There were two bedrooms with bath, and an enormous salon with three vast doors opening on the porch running the whole length of the hotel. All this, he told us, would be ours. "This is fine," I said. "How much is it?" He named a figure which at the going rate of exchange, following a precipitous fall in the franc, came to about $10 a day for us both *en pension*. Elinor, a good bargainer, said "Will you include tea?" He hardly hesitated with his "Yes." We were "in business."

That is how I became André Sella's oldest client, not in years but in service, for this was none other than he, the son of the old proprietor Antoine Sella, who was away with his wife for the summer holidays.

Father Sella had recognized the possibilities for a summer season on the eve of the 1914 War, long before any other proprietor seems to have thought of this. In February 1914, he had finished building an annex, Eden Roc, below the hotel beside the sea, and he had carved out of the rocks an outdoor swimming pool fed by salt water. Yet even after the war Eden Roc served for some years mainly as a *salon de thé* and auxiliary restaurant for luncheon during the season. That began, as in the nineteenth century, toward the end of autumn and lasted into May. This season wound up in 1932, after which both the hotel and Eden Roc have remained open only during the warmer months.

At the end of the First World War, from October 1918 to May 1919, the property was occupied by the American Red Cross. Some nurses who had come to Europe with the United States Army, accustomed to warm summers at home, used the pool and the sea some twenty-five feet below for bathing, but they soon went home. It was not until our summer of 1922 that, as an experiment without precedent on the coast, young André Sella, encouraged by his father to keep the hotel open with a skeleton staff, formed a small clientele.[1]

Then and there we moved to Cap d'Antibes with its precipitously rocky coast, so propitious a taking off place for the devoted swimmers Elinor and I had become. We found hardly a dozen guests, but there were no dipsomanics among them! We prolonged our stay more than once. Only after ten weeks, in the cool and dark of early October, sometime after the few other guests had gone, were we able to tear ourselves away.

Here began an experience destined to be repeated throughout my life. Lifted from the sea, as on a boat but without the motion, was an ample seemingly unassailable forest garden with Derain-like trunks of trees and penetrating scents of pine and thyme and cultivated flowers, all bound up in a gentle pervasive warmth that I took to as if it were my birthright. From the chateau-like hotel a hundred yards of broad amply pebbled road, forbidden to motor vehicles, descended to the sea (beside Eden Roc), and opened to the eye two islands (the Iles des Lerins), Golfe Juan, Cannes, La Napoule and above that the Esterel.

With the sea all around this garden retreat, whose footpaths then

extended almost a kilometer without fences or houses to the
southernmost tip of the "Cap" (where stood a mosque long since
torn down), it was never too hot for my taste. But rarely in July
and August even at night was it so cold that one missed clothes. I
had always longed to be free of them. Here that was easy and
natural. A city bred child I have often thought, over fifty years
of time, I have never been so close to the beauty of nature and of
beautiful women's bodies.

Later I learned that the summer conditions in southern France
have a similarity to those of the much warmer Peloponnese. The
olive trees and the vineyards, the hot summers, are found all along
the Mediterranean, although never with quite the moderation and
discretion provided at the Cap. The wonders of ancient Greek sculpture and ceramics, which have so overwhelmingly moved Western
artists and travellers, the temples of Attica, whose unique majesty
Renan celebrated in a famous passage, were created thousands
of years ago under climatic conditions resembling those which took
possession of us at Cap d'Antibes.

Mr. Justice Brandeis introduced me later in my mid-twenties to
Alfred Zimmern's *Greek Commonwealth* as one of the books that
meant most to him. In the section on the climate I recognized
what I already knew. In fact during my early days on the faculty
of the University of Chicago I had the temerity, without having
visited Greece, to describe for my students the art economy of
fifth century B. C. Attica in terms of long summers experienced on
the French Riviera. Here was a world, as it seemed, that had
nourished the beauty I had longed from childhood in some mysterious
way to find in company with the girl for whom I had waited almost a
decade, almost as long as Antoine Sella had waited to obtain his first
summer clientele.

What about the years that awakened this Mediterranean idyl?

Without knowing of the other's existence, Elinor and I had met in
an entrance hall on the ground floor of a late nineteenth-century
Chicago flat building on Sixtieth Street overlooking the Midway,
and a vacant lot distant from Jackson Park. The "Hunter Building" it was called. There the Meads lived in two apartments, each
with numerous small rooms, on the fourth and fifth floors under-
neath Clarence Darrow the celebrated lawyer who once debated
Genesis with William Jennings Bryan.

What brought Elinor was her aunt—Helen Castle Mead—who had invited her from a finishing school in Connecticut for the Christmas holidays that ended 1913. She was never to return to the school and was destined to spend the next four years at the Meads as a University of Chicago undergraduate. What brought me was the errand of collecting the fresh butter my father purchased every week from the Meads, in a rather feeble effort to repair the dreary fare of the nearby Hotel Del Prado, to which we were condemned after the death of my mother, a delicate gourmet.

Because of its six floors, the Hunter Building had an elevator operated by the janitor. Elinor was waiting for it. We entered together and discovered ourselves getting off together. Someone must have answered the bell at the Mead apartment. Someone must have introduced us. Yet I remember no one.

So it was from that day forth. In her presence, which became very frequent after my father died a year and a half later and I entered the same household, she alone existed. She became the constant companion of my inner consciousness, whether she was present or not. Everything I did and thought was influenced by her.

She was just nineteen; I six months past my fourteenth birthday. Since my mother's death five years before, several girls my own age had drawn me towards them briefly. For reasons I hardly understood; although, on one of our summers in Switzerland, my father had explained the sex act. "For marriage only!" was the label he stamped upon it.

I may have had a premonition that December night that Elinor would deliver me from the third-rate life of a boy living in a family hotel, would draw me close to the island of delight that my inner thoughts were building. But marriage at fourteen with a girl of nineteen hardly seemed a practical proposition! She certainly never thought of it in those days.

From almost the start of her sojourn at the Meads she had a succession of what then were called beaux. All were old enough to seem eligible; a few were much older than she. In varying degrees each precipitated feelings of excruciating jealousy. These increased as I became conscious of the beauty of those parts of her I was able to see. The first occasion was when I again came for Mead butter. She was dressing to go out with one of her beaux. A lone child without a father,[2] Elinor, liking me from the outset, had begun to treat me as a younger brother. On this occasion she asked me to hook the back of her dress. The beauty of her neck was unique; Lorado Taft, the Chicago sculptor, called it the most exquisite young woman's in the world. As it descended into her shoulders, I saw these dotted with freckles. In other women freckles repelled me; hers were pure gold and added something the rarest jewel could not have conferred.

A few months later, in June, a capital event occurred which fixed my taste for Woman. Elinor's mother, who was keeping house for her own father in Lexington, Massachusetts, decided to take her daughter to Europe for the Summer of 1914. They were to sail on a Dutch boat, booked to leave New York the day my father and I embarked for Le Havre and Paris. That was still a time of chaperons, and the Meads hit on the idea of having my father chaperon Elinor on the train journey. Given my father's puritanical disposition, this involved no risk. But for his son the exposure proved fatal. Elinor had a lower berth, and, after she'd prepared for sleep behind the curtains, she pulled one of them back to say "good nite." There she was, reclining against the pillows in a low-cut night gown showing the essential curves of her breasts which I had never noticed before. Breasts on other women had rather shocked me. The beauty of hers captured my senses.

That was when I first wanted to go to bed with a girl. But not with any girl; with *thi*s girl. Although the wait extended more than seven years, my condition was such as to admit no substitute. Perhaps that's one of the reasons she waited about marrying till I grew up, for she had in the interval a number of enthusiastic and persistent suitors, several of whom have had distinguished careers and one of whom became a very great astronomer. The next morning, as the train was speeding down the east bank of the Hudson, her enthusiasm over the prospect of meeting her mother after some months separation, led my father, who wasn't given to such declarations, to tell me he'd never met a child so devoted to a parent. This loyalty for those they love, of which a few women have the secret, she was destined to lavish on me.

That moment of the lower berth gave Pullman cars a promise which was eventually fulfilled on many occasions in private drawing rooms with Elinor. I was only weaned from such conveyances by the jet plane after she had gone.

The vision on the train led my imagination to undress her. Increasing material was supplied by almost innumerable peeps during the two years I lived at the Meads, and finally, when I was about to leave for Harvard after the summer of 1917, during six weeks in Wyoming where I contrived to share with her and her mother a guest cottage part of a "dude ranch." Always eager to draw as close as possible, I managed to catch frequent glimpses of her at least partly nude. Sometimes these were reflected in the glass of her transom, when she left that open, as I had a room on the same corridor in the apartment in the Hunter Building. These impressions were also snatched outdoors, sometimes in the shrubbery of Jackson Park, sometimes in the Wyoming woods, when in the innocence of her four-story seclusion or of a still deserted wilderness beyond the ranch, she forgot to pull down the shade. And, closest of all, in the bathroom at the Meads when she bathed, through the glazed window commanded from a deserted inner stairway I visited without detection late at night after she had come home from a party. There I repeatedly witnessed, but dimly, the curve of her back descending to her lovely hips and bottoms.

Such impressions might have supplied content for paintings had I the gift to paint. Instead they gave substance to Elinor's presence on that island I had begun in solitude to sketch before we met. As a child I acutely wanted a sister and after my mother's death a mother. At first Elinor, who had a mother, became my older sister. Increasingly the stolen sight of her body combined with fantasies of sex that pursued me since childhood. These were now converted into fancies relating to Elinor and to the intimacies of *her* childhood. About that I absorbed information sometimes from bits of conversation with her and her mother, sometimes from overheard conversations with her close girl friends. As manhood approached and I was about to leave Chicago these fancies matured. They merged into a hope which I found my father's brief instruction in Switzerland helped me to visualize, and which I carried with me into the four years at Harvard following the Wyoming trip. In the summer of 1918 my decision to enlist for Officers Training School gave me courage to propose. Her refusal was clothed in tender kindness—she said it was the best proposal she had had. This enabled me to declare I would never marry anyone else.

Elinor ceased being a sister on that island of the blessed. She was transformed into what I supremely needed: a mistress and a wife.

Eventually she became both at one swoop. She played the two roles with complete conviction, one to the perfection of the other, over thirty-one years that separated our marriage late in 1921 from her death in February 1953. After an early morning breakfast in our suite at the New York Plaza, union began in glowing wonder betrayed, after she took off her dressing gown, by the thinnest of night gowns. As she turned towards the bed, that night gown provided much flimsier protection than the glazed window of the bathroom in the Hunter Building. Two dimples peered above and revealed her bottoms. Then she turned again and the veil lifted.

The recollection of the cold November air on a New York street, an hour afterwards, never failed to return at every late autumn season. The Plaza experience, frequently renewed and always fresh, became a habit, ever nearer perfection, during the three months winter stay in our small hotel room in Montpellier. That room contained all the facilities. Separated completely from the life we had formerly known, without any of the surveillance which pursued us till we left Chicago hours after a private civil ceremony, it permitted those total intimacies in the ways of living, eating, waking, loving, and sleeping which are possible between two persons of different sex drawn together by the overwhelming gift of love.

No recollection is stronger than the feeling that came on a walk alone one winter afternoon after my class in finance at the University of Montpellier, where Rabelais had studied, along the Grand Rue, the street leading back to our room and her. In a drizzling foggy rain (that tends usually to chill my thoughts) the knowledge captured both body and mind that I was happy, that this gift would always diffuse a benediction hitherto missing, would make the completion of every honest experience worth any effort it demanded. She felt something complementary. Complete agnostic that her death was later to prove her she spoke nevertheless of the finger of God. Our unions became so natural and so varied with the years and decades that what we were granted could be taken for granted.[3]

Little wonder when her body gave me endlessly such exquisite joy that my pleasure in the sight of other women's bodies clothed and partly clothed (and almost unclothed as they came to be at Cap d'Antibes) took on added attractions. What had sometimes repelled me as a child soon had an increasing fascination. This did not require the possession of other bodies. Nor did it come only from the realities of Elinor's and my private happiness. It came also from the experience with art, from the increasingly frequent presence during those years abroad and after of examples of what great art has done for Woman and for the delight she radiates.

Elinor and I came together at a time when clothes were still very complicated especially for women. On the beaches near Santa Monica in California, where I had gone in pursuit of her in the summer of 1921 before she decided on the train back to marry me, she and I had talked about the tendency already visible to shed clothing. She was pleased to find I was open-minded enough to welcome that. During the years that followed our descent on the Riviera the movement for lighter covering was instrumental in bringing vacationists in Europe south in the summer.

Excess, however, is an enemy of happiness as of art. And even nudity can become excessive. My adventure with it was rendered magical by a gradual approach. Even later the magic was protected by an instinct acquired in childhood to avert my eyes sometimes in order to fill my imagination.

Elinor's body was very beautiful, in spite of a short left arm of which I was never aware but which caused *her* acute neurotic concern. Betsy Swing (sister of the late Raymond Swing the commentator who was George Mead's nephew) was studying in Chicago to be an artist and living at the Meads when I joined their household.[4] She pronounced Elinor's the most beautiful body she had seen and as an art student she must have seen many.

Yet for all its lure, which no art can reproduce, the nude body never has the perfection great art is capable of conferring. The artist can purify the reality and therewith enhance the joy that life alone is capable of giving. And in our contemporary world—as I was later to discover after many visits to the Mediterranean paradise on which we had stumbled—no artist has managed to give beauty to Woman more happily than Aristide Maillol.

He was born farther west than Antibes, near the shore of this same sea close to the Spanish frontier at Banyuls-sur-mer. Always an artist, he had started by designing and weaving tapestries. He was forced at forty to give up the loom because of its demands on his eyes. He found he might go blind.

It was in weaving that he first externalized, for others to share, his varied visions of the body as he found that expressed in lovely women. His early tapestries gained the admiration of two older artists, Renoir and Gauguin. Gauguin was horrified when the news came that Maillol had married, for Gauguin regarded marriage as a deplorable institution. But it did not seem to harm Maillol's art. It was this young girl of Banyuls (one of half a dozen whose mysterious charms he had made into a vision and had woven into his tapestries) who became the model for his early statues. Renoir in later life achieved his greatness in the sculptor's art after he had moved to the Riviera, where he sculpted as well as painted among those olive groves between Cagnes-sur-Mer and Cap d'Antibes which I got to know after he was dead. They have now been almost obliterated by the summer invasions, until the Cap itself, with its private homes and gardens and especially its hotel, remains the last defense of the old order on the coast.

I cannot remember when it was I saw a statue by Maillol. It may well have been in Mannheim, where for the first time we saw Lehmbrucks, to whose sculpture the Dial Folio introduced me. The greatest Lehmbrucks are as moving for me as any Maillol. But his statues generally give me less consistent delight. And those of Renoir, which also greatly please me, are never quite as convincing as the best Maillols.

Most Maillols, like the best Lehmbrucks, have a happiness and a humanity hardly equalled since the ancient art of Greece. That first overwhelmed me some weeks after I started my researches in the British Museum during the autumn of 1922 after leaving Cap d'Antibes. To catch my breath for further work, I left the Reading Room for a stroll and suddenly came on the Elgin marbles.

So I found most fully in Maillol what I instinctively sought in modern sculpture. His "living art" had that absolute simplicity, vouchsafed me in love, which I needed in writing.

How did it happen that Evelyn and I, forty years later, acquired a Maillol? It never occurred to me in my youthful days of buying pictures I could possibly possess one. I discovered that Evelyn's late husband, Vilhjalmur Stefansson, the great explorer, had inscribed a book on Maillol to her in 1944, an expensive book he had bought because of the love she had for Maillol's work as representative of the art of sculpture she has been tempted to try herself. On the front of the book is a replica apparently of the very statue in wood that we now have in bronze. How did that come our way?

In the late spring of 1967 three years after our marriage, when we were about to leave Washington for a European summer, Evelyn went a day ahead to shop in New York. When I arrived she told me she had seen at Knoedler's Art Gallery a Maillol she thought we might love, less expensive than we had supposed one would be. I was immediately captured by what she had unearthed. Yet we both felt we had better wait, especially as we were on our way to Paris and could see again the numerous Maillols planted in the gardens, once occupied by the Palais des Tuileries, where they had surprised us on our honeymoon. So we told the man who had shown us this small statue we would like time to decide. He was not a salesman. "That's all right. Take as much time as you like," he said. "No one has seen it. It has been in a back room for years and I just brought it out to look at yesterday before Mrs. Nef happened in." "We will be back on the 31st of August," I said. "That's my birthday," he remarked, "I will lock it up till then."

In the meantime we visited the shop of Madame Dina Vierny on the rue Jacob in Paris. She had been Maillol's model and as pupil and friend had helped him with his work during the last ten years of his life. She was the person chosen by André Malraux, when Minister of Culture, to place those statues—almost forty— that had already captured Evelyn and me.

We talked with Dina Vierny about Maillol. She showed us some twelve statues that were for sale. None suited our house and purse as well as the one in New York. We showed her a photograph. "It is authentic," she said. "I shall not persuade you to buy one of these."

When we saw our statue again we were confirmed in our love. Our friend at Knoedler's suggested sending it to Washington so we could see it in our house at leisure. It has been there ever since.

What drew me towards Maillol was his return in an age of growing storm and strife to the natural in art. I wanted to return with new material to the natural in history, so generally abandoned for the tortuous ways of specialization and rigid slavery to documentary evidence often dogmatically interpreted and erected into a goal, a goal wherein the human side of the subject is often forgotten.

Rodin deals with tortured action. The serenity necessary even in treating tragedy is lacking. I was always troubled by the enthusiasm manifested in our times for an artist more tortured than Rodin, for Joyce, an enthusiasm I found early in some of my American contemporaries, particularly one youth in Vienna in 1924-25. He used to reiterate that there had been only two great writers, Shakespeare and Joyce.

I was never drawn in the fashionable direction Joyce represented.

I felt instead the need for writing as simple prose as possible and for making the subject as concrete and important as it deserves. This feeling has been strengthened by the simplicity and inevitability of the sculpture of Renoir, of some statues by Lehmbruck and above all by those of Maillol.

They have given us women we can see as first cousins to that woman of Peplos Kore, probably the creation of the sculptor Phaidimos about 530 B.C., one of the glories of the Acropolis Museum. In the visions that he realized Maillol retained what may be called the thin, firm cord of human sameness which unites his works not only to those of the Greeks but to those of the ancient Egyptians and the Chinese.

This natural perfection came to him, without straining partly from sources that nourished the Greeks. In the isolation his origins provided (for it is since his death that Banyuls has been invaded by hordes of ill-dressed summer tourists and hurried bathers) Maillol had two assets which he absorbed to the advantage of his art, two assets denied Lehmbruck. The first was the French tradition. The second was the Mediterranean inspiration.

The French tradition, as it came from the late seventeenth and eighteenth centuries, provided Maillol with universality and humanity when these values were increasingly threatened. Over-specialization and unmitigated nationalism were enemies of both. France is far from having escaped these endemic diseases. But during Maillol's lifetime (which lasted until 1944), the French had remained receptive to those general ideas in the arts which are our universal patrimony.

Concentration must not be confused with overspecialization. One is indispensable, the other a handicap, to beauty. All great artists concentrate. Our concern is upon what and how. Maillol concentrated on the beauty of women. For the artist her body can be an inexhaustible source. The practice of treating it as such came to Maillol with less strain than to his foreign contemporaries because of the French tradition, as that is fulfilled in visions realized by such artists as Watteau and Fragonard. As the Goncourt brothers wrote, Watteau found "le rien qui habille la femme d'un agréement, d'une coquetterie, *d'un beau au-delà du beau physique.*" ("The secret which clothes a nude woman with a barely existent veil, with dalliance, *with beauty surpassing physical beauty.*") That was the way my fancy clothed Elinor.

What made it easier for Maillol than for most of his contemporaries to renew this tradition was his Mediterranean experience. It never deserted him. It was not interrupted by the Franco-Prussian War, which came when he was a child, nor by the First World War, which came when he was over fifty.

Maillol's Mediterranean experience united him to the eternal Greece, for the unity that students of geography like the late André Siegfried have found in that inland sea exists. After my marriage to Evelyn when I first went to Greece, I had a feeling of returning from whence I came. The descriptions of Greek summers that I had been giving my students during the thirties and forties seemed authentic. I was so frightened lest the Acropolis should disappoint us after my descriptions of its wonders, that we didn't dare lift our eyes for several days in Athens; only to discover (after we had climbed it and had been so moved we cried) that we had a perfect view from the balcony of our hotel bedroom. When Maillol made *his* first journey to Greece a half century earlier, in the company of Count Kessler (his German patron), he felt that *he* had come home.

When free from tourist invasions and protected from the worst humidity, long Mediterranean summers are an endless source of renewal for the artist. They combine an inducement to quiet and relaxation, necessary to the restraint the artist must possess, with an incitement to brave execution through the exaltation indispensable to greatness. The violent winds described by Homer occur everywhere on occasions. The Mistral issuing from the lower Rhone Valley in all directions often seems discouraging to the spirit. But if one can face that wind, in the teeth of it one's excitement can be raised to the point of glory. Thus the Mediterranean offers a strange combination for the human psyche. If that psyche is able to combine the sedative with the stimulant in proportions that heighten the creative effects of both, the striving artist is endowed with conditions favorable to enduring results.

These opportunities have come my way on the occasions when I have undertaken to compose there. In 1934, under pressure, I had to write an article for M. M. Postan, who had just taken over the editorship of *The Economic History Review*. It is called "The Progress of Technology and the Growth of Large-Scale Industry, 1540-1640," and it has been not infrequently reprinted.[5]

To be nourished to the full by the Mediterranean the artist has to be born into it as Maillol was. But firsthand experience with that inland sea during many happy summers has helped me to appreciate the art of Greece and the art of Maillol. So far as form is concerned both have guided me throughout life. What led to Maillol as to Greece, was the haven the Mediterranean provided from the cold during the summer of 1922.

5. FREEDOM FROM COMPULSION

In Vienna during the autumn of 1924 and most of the winter of 1925 I began to write *The Rise of the British Coal Industry* in what turned out to be the roughest of drafts. I had collected masses of information during two years of prolonged research. How was I to evaluate this information and weave it into a coherent story?

Searching for data at the Public Record Office in London I had tumbled (among other nuggets) on manuscript Port Book entries of English trade coastwise as well as overseas (for coastwise shipments frequently paid taxes). These entries were made by customs officials from the mid-sixteenth to the early eighteenth century. Here were unexploited records of shipments of coal and other commodities to and from most English ports. In the hours after the archives and the libraries were closed, and in the agreeable seclusion of hotel rooms, I added up the amounts entered port by port and year by year.

The statistics arrived at revealed a rapid growth in the British coal trade and also in the trade in salt and glass, unknown to those who had been writing economic history, but in accord with enthusiastic statements by contemporaries of Elizabeth I, James I and Charles I. During several decades preceding the English Civil War, a few Englishmen and Scots were aware of the phenomenal spurt in industry and trade. But they had been without the support of figures. These showed there had been an increase in British coal carried by sea of about twenty-five fold between 1560 and 1700. From 1560 to 1640 the *rate of growth* in the coal trade was comparable to that from 1760 to 1840, then regarded as the first period of phenomenal industrial progress in Great Britain—the period in English history to which the phrase "industrial revolution," apparently coined in early nineteenth-century France, has stuck.

This discovery was made before "economic growth" became a central theme for economists and economic historians. It is ironical to reflect that my early research may have contributed a mite to the quantitative mindedness of twentieth-century Western scholarship, for that seems to have become a fetish in the sense that much intellectual effort is now focused upon problems of "economic growth" measured statistically, to the exclusion of more human developments.

Investigation has shown there is hardly a limit to the materials available in European archives for weaving figures into the most complicated webs congenial to mathematical and scientific scholars in their abstract constructions. These do not help, however, to relate the knowledge of expansion, which I derived from figures, to a host of other non-quantitative discoveries that came my way, for example the most varied pictures of English and Scottish life that peered out from the proceedings (preserved in manuscript) of many sixteenth and seventeenth-century law courts.

What kind of book should I write? I came to realize that a concrete knowledge of many sides of history (derived not at secondhand but from more direct contact with the past through source materials) was necessary to understand the particular history of coal. Few aspects of English and Scottish experience during the late Elizabethan and Stuart periods seemed unrelated to the mining, transportation and utilization of this hitherto little exploited fuel. Moreover knowledge of what happened in Great Britain could be satisfactory only if it were compared with what happened in other European countries during the same periods. And also, as I was later to learn, with what had happened in other parts of the world even earlier.

Statistics, no matter how elaborate, hardly enable one to create a work of art. I was confronted with a choice between the procedures derived from the application to history of scientific methods (which were alone to become fully respectable in the academic world) and an imaginative treatment of the effects of coal on human evolution. Unlike most graduate students of my time who were under academic supervision, I was free to choose.

Upon the choices I made almost subconsciously my growing associations with beauty, and not least with contemporary works of art and with artists, had an ever increasing influence. In the throes of composition in Vienna, I enjoyed for the first time in my education freedom from any time limit or external compulsion. Delight helped determine my route.

The experience of Central Europe was in a way a diversion from the mainstream of my artistic formation. Yet it was in Vienna that my life took the course it was destined to reaffirm immediately afterwards in the France we had already begun to explore, but where the choice between art and science had remained open.

What was life in Vienna like? I used to write and rewrite six or seven hours a day—the maximum dose I have been able to manage steadily and continuously. After those hours we were available for all sorts of artistic diversions and conversations which the Central European capital offered, in spite of its notorious poverty after the 1914 War and the reputation then attached to it as an expiring city. Elinor and I were immersed in each other, in the music at the Opera, at the Redoutensaal of the old imperial palace, at the Volksoper and at small concert halls; we were also immersed in the theatre of Max Reinhardt, Moissi and foreign troups, including the Russian Pitoeffs who came from Paris on a visit. Partly under the spell of great theatre, we began to think there might be contemporaries who were contributing to artistic history. In March 1925 we began to look at recent paintings, including those of contemporaries, on short visits to Munich, Mannheim and Berlin.

Germany has acquired some of the finest paintings of the period from 1850 to 1920. Lieberman the famous court painter and father-in-law of the philosopher Kurt Riezler (later my colleague at the University of Chicago when I was developing the "Committee on Social Thought"), acquired and housed a fine collection of modern pictures in his fabulous mansion on the Pariser Platz across from the Adlon Hotel. A generation afterwards I saw some of those pictures in the Riezler apartment in New York on my way to an assignment at the Collège de France in Paris in 1953.

Our closest friends in Vienna were a couple named Dillon. He was I believe (although this will sound incredible) the British *naval* attaché. (I say incredible, because little Austria hardly had a Navy!) As the 1914-18 War was ending Dillon had come to Vienna. There he had met, as she sat on a table in an office the British had commandeered, one of the most dazzlingly beautiful Hungarian girls that I have ever seen, and such Hungarian women had for me after Vienna, a unique fascination. Finally one married me and I learned why.

Mrs. Dillon was the daughter of Baron Bornemisza, an Hungarian officer of the old Central European nobility. At about the turn of the century he had taken as his bride an American woman who came from Philadelphia. The Baron died young. We sometimes saw his widow who also lived in Vienna and came to dinner in Paris in our apartment in the Avenue de Saxe. She had not the amazingly mysterious beauty which her daughter derived from this mixed marriage. Another daughter, almost as beautiful as Mrs. Dillon and who frequently came to Vienna, was married to the famous German steel magnate Baron von Thyssen.

The Dillons had a place in society and many local connections. They shared both with us. A trifle older, Dillon was as fascinated with my wife as I with his. They made charming companions whether we were together as a foursome or in company with others. We even timed a brief excursion to Budapest so that we could meet Dillon there when he went on diplomatic business. Our friendship waxed all through those months of late autumn and winter. It culminated in a ball in their ample Vienna apartment attended by some of the most attractive representatives of the diplomatic corps and the old Austro-Hungarian nobility which, at its best, was unequalled for grace and charm that the contemporary world will slough off at its peril.

We used to go with the Dillons, after the opera or the theatre, to Sacher's for supper. One never ate before the performances, for those always began between six and seven-thirty. Frau Sacher, who had reportedly been the mistress of Franz Josef, would always show us to the small inner sanctum. It had only a few tables, most of them for four persons, and was barren of all pictures save two. One was Franz Josef, the last Emperor of Austria-Hungary; the other his younger contemporary Kaiser Wilhelm II. These were placed conspicuously at each end of the room. The food was delicious, though never copious— just what was needed for a late collation on the eve of another day of composition, always a difficult task in spite of my growing addiction to it. Frau Sacher guarded this sanctum with great pains. She didn't care a bit if most of the tables remained unoccupied and so admitted only a few persons. She always refused the so-called "Schieber" (the pushers), the new rich in Austria and Germany, persons who were reputed to have made their money from the war the Germans were so conscious of having "lost."

Those who got into the sanctum sometimes had the dignity of being waited on by Frau Sacher herself. One night when we were with the

Dillons she appeared with an extraordinary delicacy and offered this to our wives, saying, as it seemed, a trifle ostentatiously. "Nur für die damen" (For Ladies only). I cannot remember what this delicacy was, as I never tasted it, but Frau Sacher's words pleased me by suggesting she shared my predilections for women, essential to my work as an historian who writes under the influence of art.

Social relations with the Dillons were combined with others at the American legation, where we had a pleasant association not only with the Washburns but with a secretary named Edwin Wilson whose father had once been ambassador to Mexico. We met several other interesting people, but not so many as to interfere with the work which filled our lives, for my wife had her own writing to do. Nor did we meet so many as to interfere with the artistic education and the love which so profoundly affected my work.

During these Vienna months I discovered Beethoven, Mozart and Bach. As a child my father had taught me I *ought* to admire their music. Now I did. It became an open sesame to all the arts.

One usually speaks of music as composed and of history as written. Yet I find myself speaking of *composing* history. Perhaps this habit is derived from my childhood dream of becoming a musician, a dream later transposed into my career as historian. The structure of "classical" music suggested ways of piecing together harmoniously discoveries from several realms of specialized historical investigation hitherto unrelated. Finding how much great music meant showed me how the pursuit of beauty in composition could complete life however long that should last. This helped me to feel at home in the world, to believe in the peace of which there has often been so little during the times I have lived through.

When we moved on in March 1925 for brief stays in the three German cities I have mentioned, we went not only to concerts, to opera and to famous picture galleries but also, partly through family connections both my wife and I had with Germans,[1] to private exhibitions. Eventually we visited a Berlin dealer who had a small exhibit of watercolors by Paul Signac. One of his watercolors—a fine picture of the harbor of La Rochelle [2]—was reproduced in that *Dial* folio *Living Art*. It had been one of my favorites when we used to study those reproductions in our large hotel sitting room with its balcony overlooking the Opera House in Vienna.

And now at the Berlin dealer's we had almost our pick of about twenty small Signacs that were real. They enchanted me. Without being fully aware of the act, we bought the one we liked most for about a hundred dollars. That then seemed a large sum.

The picture shows a bend in the river Seine at Les Andelys near Giverny, with the famous old twelfth-century castle of Richard Coeur de Lion built into the hill above. It delights now more than forty-five years ago. Its subject makes it a piece of history, and so not an inappropriate purchase as the first step towards the small home of art we were to assemble. Nourished henceforth by the continuous presence of original pictures, the kinship I already felt for the artist's calling strengthened my desire to become a non-conforming historian.

6. THE VEXATIOUS GERMAN PROBLEM

I had arrived in Vienna with a romantic notion of the Germans. I supposed they had been misled in the First World War and were ripe for peace, an impression which could legitimately be derived from the times of Schiller and Goethe, Leibnitz and Kant, Bach, Mozart and Beethoven.

Such optimism could hardly have been a consequence of childhood memories.[1] It came rather from gratitude for deliverance from the mass slaughters of 1914-18. I glossed over childhood memories and interpreted the Armistice in the spirit of Woodrow Wilson's leadership. Victory seemed to imply a mandate to bring war forever to an end. Why should not all the world's peoples, including the Germans, welcome that goal? When the difficulties in the way of establishing peace became apparent, I tended, under the influence especially of J. M. Keynes' *Economic Consequences of the Peace*, to blame these difficulties on the Versailles Treaty (which I had defended in the Harvard *Crimson* when the terms were announced).

Later, during the French occupation of the Ruhr, we had been often asked to dine in Paris by new friends: Edouard Champion, who had inherited his father's famous bookshop, and his American born wife. On one of these occasions we met an American couple who were living in France, where the husband had been sent by his business firm. At that time I regarded Poincaré's policy as anti-German, as contrary to the Wilsonian spirit, and I was so hurt to have these two Americans ardently defend it that I jabbed my fruit knife into my finger and had to be given first aid by Julie Champion.

My optimistic view of German post-war intentions came partly from family connections, particularly Elinor's. Her father, Henry Northrup Castle, had studied philosophy in Germany in the 1880's when he met and eventually married a Leipzig girl he brought back to the Hawaiian Islands where he was given, as the son of S. N. Castle, founder of the firm of Castle and Cooke, the editorship of the chief local newspaper, *The Honolulu Advertiser*. Shortly after the birth of a daughter, his wife was thrown out of a carriage she was driving at Waikiki and killed.

Henry Castle remarried two years later. His second wife, a school-teacher, Mabel Wing, had joined the Punahoe Academy Faculty in Honolulu. Two years after his remarriage Elinor was born. But her father had been so anxious to show the first girl to her German relatives that, two months before his wife's confinement, to the stupe-faction of his family and friends, he hurried to Germany for a pro-longed stay. He decided to return to *The Advertiser* only because of a revolutionary movement in Oahu on behalf of the Hawaiian mon-archy. Intending to join forces with his family in Philadelphia, where his second child had been born two months before, he took passage on the North German Lloyd steamer "Elbe." With his older daughter he was drowned in the North Sea when the ship collided in a fog with a smaller boat and sank, leaving almost no survivors.

Elinor and her mother had kept up the relations with her father's numerous German family. We saw them at Mannheim on our German trip. My father's great success as a graduate student of chemistry, also in the eighteen-eighties, and his subsequent publication of his scientific papers in the German tongue, provided different kinds of connections especially in Munich.

Shortly after we had reached Vienna, I remember being told by Edwin Wilson, the young diplomat whom we met at the American Legation, that I was misreading the German mentality. Before his assignment to Austria, Wilson had been a third secretary at the U. S. Embassy in Berlin. That was when Alanson B. Houghton of Corning Glass was Ambassador. His son Amory Houghton (a generation later Ambassador to France) had been a friend at Harvard and we had marched for weeks in the same squad at the training school for infantry officers in Camp Lee, Virginia. During discussions following the Armistice of 1918 young Houghton and I advocated as against most of our fellow soldiers, several of them Harvard class-mates, a generous peace. I was pleased later to find in his father's pronouncements as Ambassador to Germany what I then regarded as a "liberal" outlook similar to that of his son. I suggested to Wilson that he must have been happy working with such a broadminded chief but he answered that Houghton was not a good ambassador to send to *Germany* because he is "much too pro-German." Wilson went on to tell us that the Germans were more callous than other peoples when it came to human life.

At first I attributed Wilson's view[2] to chauvinism derived from the war. But as time went on I had disquieting encounters with the Germanic spirit. On one occasion a German with whom we were having tea in Vienna pompously instructed us that the French language was rich in ideas but poor in words, while English was rich in words but poor in ideas. German alone, he explained, was rich in both. Mentally I placed these remarks beside the title of a volume then continually displayed in the Viennese bookstores, "The French Language: a German Dialect." I also associated his arrogance with the anti-semitism then rife in Austria.

The assassination of German foreign minister Walter Rathenau, shortly after we had heard him at the Genoa Conference make a most moving appeal, in *French,* for peace, was still fresh in our minds. Doubts began to accumulate as to whether all the blame for the misunderstandings among the powers once allied against Germany should be blamed on French post-war policy.

In the shelter of marriage and the joys of discovering Europe anew with comfort and steady work, I had come to a belief, which may well have been inherited from my mother, that violence and, above all, war were anachronistic. The roots of my reviving consciousness of the ruthlessly expansive consequence of human nature, especially as exhibited in Germany, went back to my childhood trips abroad with my widower father. Before the First World War I was taken to Europe five times. My father had received the doctor's degree, *summa cum laude,* from the University of Munich in 1887 as the result of his preliminary researches in the chemistry of the carbon atom. Whenever we went to Munich he visited his old teacher, Adolf von Baeyer, who before the 1914 War occupied the famous chair of chemistry once held by Liebig, perhaps the plum academic post of the old German Empire. The holder of that chair enjoyed a prestige and an influence unknown to professors in the U. S.

We used to go to Baeyer's summer residence on the Starnberger See. We spent a day there and several in Munich in 1911 at the time of the crisis over Morocco which came close to precipitating the First World War. I was struck at the time by the cruel manners of Baeyer's grandchildren. Their apparent pleasure in inflicting pain for its own sake whenever they found a pretext, contrasted with the manners of my childhood contemporaries in the United States, although the latter's were not always tender. And while I played with these grandchildren, my father was shocked by Baeyer's enthusiasm for German military preparedness.

News of impending war came a few days later, when we were still in Munich. The Germans began to mobilize and I saw and *felt* their troops marching through the streets. One sensed the lust for war and the wild hope for fulfillment in victory or death. Young men were not only eager to go, they seemed to be irretrievably frustrated when war failed to materialize. This contrasts strongly, and happily, with the recent reluctance of American youth to be mobilized for service in Vietnam.

Much later, as a student of history, I found the outlook of these soldiers was in the German tradition. I learned Nietzsche had written with deep insight that the Germans were eager for war because it offered an opportunity to commit suicide with a good conscience.

This enthusiasm for battle as a means of liquidating earthly obligations jibes with information provided by a comparative study of the sport of mountaineering as pursued by different peoples. A book on that subject (whose author and title I have forgotten) appeared in the nineteen-thirties. It contrasted the outlook of climbers of several nationalities. The author found that the Germans were preeminent for undertaking climbs virtually impossible of accomplishment, where the chance of dying is so great as to make the attempt suicidal. Mountaineering in the twentieth century became for German adepts less a sport than a call, like war, to premature death. I was able to compare this with my memory of a British mountaineer named Ryan who had given me instruction in rock climbing at the Montanvert, above Chamonix, a few weeks before the outbreak of the 1914 War. He was making first ascents but he always chose a route which he and his mountain guides had carefully studied and believed *feasible*. It was life, not death, that great English climbers like Edward Whymper and Mummery sought, as did this twentieth-century successor.

During adolescence my childhood impressions of the German mentality, derived from visits to Munich before 1914, had been forgotten In the relief brought on by the Armistice of 1918 from the overwhelming yet almost subconscious danger that faced each boy of my generation, I became convinced that, if the victors in the First World War were good sports, they could appeal effectively by generosity to the "good German." That would lead to a good Germany, the Germany of Schiller's "Ode to Joy." Hearing Beethoven's Ninth Symphony just after our arrival in Vienna, Schiller's words, combined with the magnificent music, moved me as I have seldom been moved.

Episodes in Vienna had prepared me for a change in attitude towards the Germans, but it was the trip to Germany that proved decisive. In Munich, Mannheim and Berlin we met not just with opinions about the Germans like those of our American friend Wilson; there Germans spoke for themselves. What did they say?

We reached Munich in late winter 1925. A light snow covered the ground. Getting up early for a walk in the park the morning after our arrival, I was amazed by the crunch of marching feet. Around the corner came a squad of Germans in civilian clothes, carrying wooden guns, the only "weapons" then available to them. They were training with a gusto which brought out of my subconscious the moment in 1911 that had been forgotten.

The next day, eager to become better acquainted with modern painting, we paid a visit to a leading art shop. As we were admiring some great canvasses by Cézanne, Renoir, Degas and Pissarro, the Jewish owner joined us and, learning of our interests, gave us a brief tour. He was amiable and talked about the pictures. Then, just as we were about to leave and were shaking hands, he wheeled and, showing strong emotions, burst out with these words: "Why did *you* come into the war? We would have won if you had stayed out!"

A similar impression of the preoccupations of the "good Germans" came the next day. My first wife had studied in Munich in a high school for girls (höhere Töchter-schule). The headmistress was alive and active; so we called on her. She recognized her former pupil instantly, throwing her arms enthusiastically around Elinor. Then without the slightest preamble, she led into another room and confronted us with a large photograph of a German in helmet and uniform covered with decorations. "That is my brother," she said. "He was a general in the German army. Do you know what I teach my students? I teach them hatred. I teach them to hate the French."

We went to the University of Munich and engaged, for a small fee, a youngish student to have tea every afternoon at the hotel. He was working for his doctor's degree and was glad to earn a little extra money. By conversing with him we aimed to revive our German which had had less practice than we should have liked in Vienna, where almost everyone in diplomatic circles was eager to talk English or more often still French. Here in Munich the hotel menus were always in German and "Poire Hélène" became "Eisbäcker Richard Strauss."

Hitler spent time in a nearby prison. One hardly thought of his party as a serious element in German politics, about which we read a fair amount in the newspapers and magazines. Yet in the course of very pleasant conversations with the "graduate student" we sought his political opinions. He said flatly that the Germans could not put up much longer with the ignominies they were exposed to under the Republic that had been established after the war. "We are going to have a strong man," he explained, "and then in ten years we shall get our *revenge!*"

This multiplying evidence of emotional violence in the daily life of Munich startled me into controversy from which I had hitherto desisted. "Look here, my friend," I said to our tea guest in response to his declaration, "Germany has led Europe into terrible wars twice in a half-century, in 1870 and in 1914. What sense does it make to repeat this slaughter in each generation? What is gained?"

Our guest looked at me with a kind of pity and remarked very earnestly, "You don't understand these things. You are ignorant . . . almost unintelligent . . . Sometimes it is good to kill. I got into the war for a while and I have killed men. I know how well that tastes."

As I recite these episodes I remember how my father and I were introduced to the First World War. We had been staying at the Riffelalp Hotel above Zermatt since early July. When we arrived the hotel was filled with European guests, many of them German, but well before the first of August all the Germans and the Germans alone had disappeared. Sichel, in his biography of Modigliani, and Nina Hamnett, in her *Laughing Torso,* record the same experience in connection with Germans in Paris. They vanished in anticipation of "The Day" Germany awaited.

My father, nearly all of whose European cultural and scientific associations were with Germany, blamed the war on the Germans from the outset. It is small wonder that he was comforted to be mistaken for an Englishman on the eve of the first Battle of the Marne, when we were en route from Switzerland to America.

I am reminded too, as I recall Elinor's and my journey into Germany in 1925, of a talk I had years later in 1938 with our friend the late Edwin Hubble about the German attitude towards war. By that time Germany had got its strong man, and he was rattling his sword without even a touch of the equivocation which the discredited Kaiser occasionally permitted himself, and without any of the good manners Bismarck had managed to retain before that Kaiser dropped him as pilot.

Hubble was a poor boy from the Midwest. He had won a Rhodes Scholarship which brought him to Oxford for three years well before 1914. There were, of course, German Rhodes scholars and Hubble formed an acquaintance with one. On what the English call the "long vacation," Hubble set out to see something of the Continent and to stop in Germany. He had made a date to visit this German in Kiel. His fellow Rhodes scholar hospitably came to the station *in uniform.* After polite salutations he whisked Hubble to the drill ground, as preemptorially as the headmistress was to whisk Elinor and me to look at the photograph of her brother. The German then summoned two squads of fellow soldiers and stood Hubble against a brick wall. "Here," he remarked to his comrades, "I have brought this man for you to look over carefully. He is a good specimen of Anglo-American manhood. I want you to fix him in your minds because this is the kind of man you are going to kill."

That experience of Hubble's jibed with an account which the late Professor Louis Massignon, a famous Islamic scholar, gave me. As a young man he went to Athens around 1900 for a Congress of his specialty. There he met a young German with whom he conversed learnedly over problems of Islam and its history. A decade afterwards Massignon went to another learned Congress of Islamic scholars in Holland. Finding this same German, he set out to renew what had been a pleasant scholarly association. But the German was now concerned only with international politics. He could talk of little other than the coming war. He made plain that the possession of Alsace-Lorraine was

not enough for Germany. "Look here," he said in the deepest seriousness, "We are going to have a war and we are certain to win. Why
doesn't France surrender in advance and become a German province?
That would simplify matters and diminish bloodshed. We shall con-
quor you anyhow. The French will have a fine future as part of Germany. As subjects of our Empire they will thrive. Give up." "But we
couldn't," Massignon responded. "We are an old people; an independent people; we value freedom." "Do you mean to say that if there is a
war *you* would go into the army?" the German asked. "I should have
no choice," Massignon replied. The German persisted, "If you found
yourself in the firing line opposite me, would you shoot to kill me?"
"Alas, that would be my duty," Massignon observed. The German got
up and strode pretentiously across the room. Clasping Massignon's
hand vigorously, he could only express his admiration with the words
"You should have been a German!"

My father had taught me the greatness of the music of Brahms, of
Wagner and of Mahler, at the same time that he decried the worthless-
ness of all contemporary painting and sculpture. And it was in the
German speaking countries that Elinor and I were discovering from
fine examples the merit of *contemporary* art. Though few of the recent
works we were admiring were by German born artists, we were disposed, after our experience with galleries and dealers in Munich and
Berlin, to find the Germans gifted connoisseurs of all the graphic arts.
Wasn't there something incongruous and deeply disturbing about
these expressions of warlike violence side by side with the German cult
of culture? Yet the two were associated with one another not only in
Munich, Mannheim and Berlin, but also in Austria where (combined
with anti-semitism) they were partly hidden by courtly manners.
These incongruities led me through the following years to the conclusion that the pursuit of culture by itself is not enough. It must not
be separated from the whole human experience. The tortuous and the
obscene so prevalent in some contemporary art had a common source
in the cult of violence and the gluttony over pain, especially prevalent
in the German mentality as it developed during the early twentieth
century. The beauty I sought in the writing of history needed the puri-
fication and discipline that only humanity and love for another (which
is the contrary of self-love) can supply. Love for another is incompati-
ble with hatred of the human race.

At a seminar held in 1968 with some federal executives in Washington, several of the participants asked why I regarded the mentality of the Chinese and the Russians at the present time as less belligerent than that of the Germans (and even the Japanese who so admired the Germans) before the World Wars. No doubt there are several reasons. One is the pleasure the Germans have taken in killing and in dying for their country, their exaltation in patriotic violence unlimited. This is something for which neither the Russian nor the Chinese peoples have had the same preparation.

Yet it would be unfair and untrue, indeed it would be ridiculous, to suggest that either violence or nationalism—pushed to an extreme in Germany—are of German origin, that their ugly manifestations are peculiar to the Germans. They are alas common to the human race. And they are contagious.

The ideal world created, first in my childhood dreams and then on a long European honeymoon, had no room for either. During the five decades that have followed, what was once true only of my ideal world was to become true of the real world too. With the invention and the proliferation of nuclear weapons, the pursuit of nationalism for its own sake and the unleashing of unlimited violence have become the ultimate danger for all humankind. The need to divert murderous and suicidal impulses into other less dangerous and more constructive channels than nationalism and war has become overwhelming.

The gratitude I felt as far back as 1921-22 in the glow of early marriage for my good fortune, had led me to wish that my work might help to transfer great striving from war to peace. But by 1925 I was committed to the writing of history. Was this commitment reconcilable with the obligation I felt to serve the cause of humanity? Art suggested that the "scientific" study of history was an imperfect means of revealing what has been. In order to tell "exactly what happened" (an impossible objective which must nevertheless be the historian's purpose) he should be guided by a search closely akin to that of the imaginative writer, the poet, the musical composer, the painter, the architect and the sculptor. It is the essence of what happened that the historian should seek.

Another question arose out of "the German problem." Does the historian discharge his conscience adequately by revealing the essence of *what has been?* I began to doubt it. Under the inspiration of a hunger for beauty, I felt that the career of historian now calls for more. He must try to relate the essence of what has been to what *ought to be*.

7. FRENCH CITY LIFE

My first purchase of an original work of art had occurred on the eve of our return to France in the early spring of 1925. One of our earliest moves on reaching Paris was to write to the artist who had drawn in beautiful colors that bend in the river Seine which had captured us in Berlin.

When we met Paul Signac he was among the oldest "living" artists, older than Matisse, Rouault or Bonnard. His art was very different from theirs. He is thought of, with Seurat and Cross, as forming a school to which the name "pointilliste" is attached. Touched by our interest and youth, Signac helped with our education. He seemed to take more pleasure in talking about his predecessors the day we visited him in Passy, than in showing his own pictures. He expressed special admiration for Delacroix and insisted we must see his murals in the Church of St. Sulpice, giving us instructions how to find and look at them.

Signac drew attention especially to several remarkable drawings in his apartment by nineteenth century artists—among others Cézanne and Seurat. Signac's purpose was to show that both were as good draftsmen as the greatest masters of any age. He stressed the lines in one drawing, referring to a famous remark which had become a cliché, "La ligne d'Ingres vaut celle de Léonard" (Ingres' draftsmanship equals Leonardo da Vinci's.) He suggested that this could be said even more emphatically of Cézanne or Seurat than of Ingres. While few would have made such a comparison in 1925, it has now become standard. A recent critic puts Seurat's *Grande Jatte* in a class with the greatest results achieved by Giorgione.

This lesson from Signac went far to shatter the last prejudice carried away from the artistic upbringing of my father: that modern pictures were inferior to those of the past. I found it easier to recognize the stature of Cézanne's pictures and of some Seurats than of the Delacroix murals Signac so admired. Nevertheless he helped me to recognize the important place occupied by Delacroix, along with Gericault, in the history of painting. Delacroix's "Journal,"

which I read years later, became one of my favorite books and a
source of material for my histories.

We showed Signac the watercolor bought in Berlin and asked if
we could see some of his other watercolors. Then and there we chose
a small landscape of the harbor of St. Tropez. Signac had a country house near that little town; this was long before tourists treated
it as a summer resort. Our picture shows only one sailing vessel in
the port where today a thousand or so small ships are crammed
together at anchor all through the months of July and August.

Signac is not perhaps a great painter, but he is a great follower
of Cézanne as well as Seurat. An authentic artist, his watercolors
have always delighted me. Watercolor seems the medium best
suited to his special gifts.

Madame Signac was a trifle annoyed by the attention we gave
to his watercolors. "You know," she said, "my husband is not *only*
a watercolorist." Perhaps she was thinking that his oils brought
more money. This may well have been a consideration *for us,* but it
was not the main consideration; I have never regretted our choice.

We did not see Signac again. Some months later when we were
lunching at what was then a favorite Parisian restaurant, called
(after Anatole France) "La Rotisserie de la Reine Pédauque," we
found Madame Signac at the next table with Bonnard. She introduced us and we had a most agreeable conversation. He was a
charming man, but his pictures never held me as firmly as those of
Chagall and Derain. I even preferred Pascin, Signac, Segonzac,
Matisse and Picasso, and later Dufy.

Our two Signacs, a pair about 9"x12", and our conversation with
the artist who had created them, whetted our appetite for contemporary graphic works. The purchases committed me to a lifelong direct experience with original pictures that paralleled in time
and intensity my commitment to a kind of historical composition
that was hardly less a matter of choice. It seemed natural to bring
the two commitments together. Our return to Paris, for a long
stretch of keeping house in two attractive apartments, provided a
setting where I was able to do so more fully and continuously than
had been possible when we lived in the Bristol Hotel in Vienna.

We were well prepared for French city living. While I had come
to Europe intending to be an economist, and had planned to work at

the London School of Economics, a doctor advised me to avoid the
rigor of an English winter, and to go to London later. Harvard
economist Allyn A. Young, who was to die prematurely while on the
staff of the London School, had recommended starting at the University of Montpellier, a famous center of learning since the Middle
Ages. He told me it had also a reputable Law School. The study of
economics was part of the law school curriculum in France, not the
subject of a separate department as in the United States. So I
could begin my preparation in economics at Montpellier immediately
after Christmas in 1921.

The Hotel de la Métropole, where we found that private room (so
perfect for learning to know one another), was favored mainly by
French businessmen who came to purchase the abundant *vins ordi-
naires* of Languedoc. The Métropole was also an inn where famous
visitors occasionally stopped for a night or two; both Marshal Foch,
whose brother was a local priest, and Lord Harding, the British
Ambassador, came during our stay.

We soon became deeply attached to a Greek couple who were,
like ourselves, living in the hotel and whose associations were with
the worlds of politics and literature rather than with academic life.
Their son Georges Katsimbalis, exactly my age, was my fellow student in the law school. He used to come to the hotel almost every
evening for meetings with his parents in which we were asked more
and more frequently to join. Twenty years afterwards Georges became celebrated because Henry Miller named a book after him.
Georges is "The Colossus of Maroussi." Those who have read that
rather wonderful philosophic account of Miller's visit under Katsimbalis guidance to the mainland of Greece at the outbreak of the Second World War, will know what a compelling *raconteur* Georges is.

Throughout the European years we frequently shared his stories.
One of the first was about the reception for students at the École de
Droit, given by the Dean, whose name was Valéry, on the occasion
of the "rentrée solennelle," which took place, as was always the
case in French universities, in the autumn; consequently before we
reached Montpellier, indeed before we landed in France.

Georges Katsimbalis was obliged to matriculate in the law school
largely against his will, because his father wanted to punish him into
becoming a lawyer and thereby help to recoup the family fortunes.
Georges had a passionate interest in literature, especially poetry.
He used to recite poems aloud in French and English, as well as in

ancient and modern Greek. We could understand neither, but he made them sound beautiful.

Shortly before coming to Montpellier, during a stay in Alexandria, he had picked up a small paperbound volume of Paul Valéry's poetry. It will be difficult for some today to realize that in 1921 almost no one in the United States, few persons outside France, and only "connoisseurs" in France itself had heard of Valéry. He was as obscure then, in public and in academic French society, as the contemporary painters we were to admire soon afterwards. He became a generally recognized figure in literature only after the death of Anatole France, whom he succeeded as a member of the French Academy in 1925.

When Georges Katsimbalis, with his "avant-garde" interest in letters, confronted the Dean in the receiving line at the Faculté de Droit, he reverted to his literary interests and asked if his host was related to *Paul* Valéry. The Dean did not like the way the question was put. He muttered unenthusiastically: "Yes, he's my brother. Why do you ask?" Georges said he had been reading a book of Valéry's poems bought in Egypt. This hardly diminished the Dean's annoyance. "Yes," he said, "it seems my brother sometimes writes verses. Maybe they're read in the Orient."

Several years later I related this episode to one of the Dean's colleagues, Marcel Moye. Moye had become our friend and counselor in Montpellier, where he was professor of public finance in the law school and a frequent contributor to the local newspaper. A hunchback, he was a man of remarkable intelligence who lectured with great facility and clarity. He was an idol of the students and belied the assumption that French professors never met with them socially, for he dined with us more than once.

Moye's malformation had precluded him from youthful diversions and he was so precocious that he received his degree in law three years before reaching the age at which he could present himself for a faculty post. Realizing that intellectual work is a habit easily lost, and that he had no genius for a writer's career, he studied successfully for two more higher degrees, one in medicine and the other in letters, in order to retain the discipline of steady application he had acquired. No doubt the pursuit of two additional degrees contributed to his broad interests. His lectures were always preceded by a brief period during which the students could write on the blackboard questions on general subjects unrelated to the course he gave. "What does the professor think of the present situation in China?" was one such question.

Our friendship grew until his death on the eve of the Second World War. By that time I was a professor at the University of Chicago and Moye devoted one of his last newspaper articles to an essay of mine that had just appeared in an American journal. In it I expressed concern over the limitations of growing academic specialization, and the lack of a genuine exchange of general ideas between professors and students. Since Moye shared this concern, he documented his column about my essay from his own experiences. Such support from a reputable scholar of my father's generation, at a critical turning point in my career, fortified my purpose to found two years afterwards, in 1941-42, an interdisciplinary faculty with more personal relationships between professors and students than had become readily possible in most universities.

My talk with Moye about the brothers Valéry occurred when I was in no position to think about such a faculty. Yet Moye's account of his colleague *Professor* Valéry's indifference to the poetic art, of his lack of pride in his brother's genius, may have contributed subconsciously to the formation I was already seeking for others as well as myself when I entered the academic profession. Moye explained how, as an educator, the Dean was insensitive to the world of imaginative insight which absorbed his brother. That was the world which gave me *enthusiasm* for writing history. I never really settled into the economics I had come abroad to study. Unintentionally Marcel Moye, a professor of finance, aided and abetted me to abandon the intention.

Our evenings with the Katsimbalis in the Montpellier hotel were many and fascinating. The difficulty was that Costaki, Georges' father, was himself a copious storyteller. He regarded his own capacities as superior to those of his son, whose gifts he sought to curb in the interest of a conventional career. Katsimbalis père died before the Second World War, before Henry Miller came on the scene, so Miller did not have to contend with the kind of competition we met. Georges and his father talked simultaneously, ignoring one another. Listening to both of them was a difficult experience.

These almost nightly conversations contributed to my education, which like that of my first wife had been prepared for by childhood experiences in Europe. The Katsimbalis, like all the close friends we made during the four years that followed, were cultivated Europeans. We began to learn something of European habits of thought and action, in many ways different from those we were accustomed to in the United States, particularly in the Middle West.

Before taking to the long days of regular writing, which became habitual in Vienna, I acquired a habit of spending all the daylight hours at work in libraries and archives. When in Paris most of this time was devoted to the Bibliothèque Nationale (with a brief interlude towards one o'clock for a small collation with Elinor at some nearby café). When I first worked in that famous library, its administrative officers had not yet abandoned the old-fashioned ways of the pre-electric era. In autumn and winter the library opened after sunrise and closed at sunset. There was no artificial light. What seemed to me no less quaint were the catalogues of authors and titles. They started with Z and ran backwards to A. One day I grumbled over this "inconvenience" to the attendant who was accustomed to supply me with my materials and with whom I had a pleasant acquaintance. His surprise took the form of saying that the French system of cataloging was the only one intelligible to *him*.

A number of similar contrasts between different European countries and between these and earlier experiences of Chicago and Harvard made it impossible to *condescend* to the past because of its different ways. Thus foundations were laid for an approach to other nations, present as well as past, on *their* terms independent of nationalism.

The first European winter, before I found my career the next autumn, was passed in a regular program of study—mostly lecture courses—at the University of Montpellier, and in excursions to the towns and sites—Carcassonne, Aigues-Mortes, Nimes, the Pont du Gard, Orange, Avignon, Les Baux, St. Remy-en-Provence, Arles— that unite Languedoc and Provence to a distant human past. Enriched more than we then realized, Elinor and I had gone at the end of March to the political conference at Genoa which some hoped might heal wounds of the 1914-1918 war.

We supposed we were saying good-bye to the Katsimbalis forever. Imagine our surprise and pleasure, therefore, when on the second evening after our arrival in Paris in June we went to the Grand Guignol and stumbled on Georges with his father in the audience. During our remaining four years in Europe we were never separated for more than a few days from the Katsimbalis when we lived in Paris, as we did for long stretches and after our return from Vienna for a solid year.

Like all my intellectual friendships, this one has endured. Decades afterwards I had the joy of a reunion with Georges and the pleasure of introducing him and the wife he married long after those years in Paris to Evelyn and to an even older friend of mine than Georges, to James Douglas, who, together with his wife Elinor, were staying with us at the Grande Bretagne Hotel a few weeks before the military revolution of 1967. The Grande Bretagne is just across Constitution Square from the house, long since torn down, where Georges was brought up. That belonged to his grandfather who around 1900 was one of those Greek millionaires of whom it has become so fashionable now to read in the newspapers. By the time we knew Katsimbalis, the family was less affluent. For political reasons, as close friends and supporters of Venizelos, they found it desirable to live abroad. For Georges, as well as for his parents, Paris was the world capital of arts and letters.

We came to know several of the Katsimbalis' political friends, especially through Costaki's brother-in-law Micalacopoulos, who had already been Venizelos' minister of finance and was later for a brief spell prime minister. He gave me the warmest of welcomes into his political circle as a "budding economist," introducing us to Venizelos himself at Lausanne late in December 1922.

By that time, however, I had begun to taste the sweets, not only of historical research, but of the arts and letters to which I had introduced myself as a child. That interest was more congenial to Georges Katsimbalis than to his uncle. Nevertheless Micalacopoulos kept a sympathetic eye on my career. He saw enough promise in the turn my interests were taking to recommend me for a decoration by the Greek government. That is how I became a Chevalier of the Order of the Phoenix.

Later we were appalled when Micalacopoulos was banished by his political rivals to die on an Aegean island, after having surrendered the premiership under duress. He is reported to have said he did not wish to be responsible for a drop of blood even if it were "shed through the nose." Would that his ilk now occupied *all* the "summits."

The associations I had through Georges with three other young

Greeks were of help in that union of art with historical composition to which I was increasingly drawn. Georges' closest friend was Theodor Stephanides, who had been his comrade at the front after Greece had joined in the 1914-18 War. Stephanides had an English mother and was almost tri-lingual, in Greek, French and English. He was exactly Georges and my age, twenty-two or twenty-three when we met. But he wanted to appear older because he thought that would help him pass the examinations for a medical degree. With this in view he had grown a beard, in a time, unlike the present, when beards were most unfashionable among youth. Like Georges, Stephanides was more interested in literature, especially poetry, than in the career he was preparing. Unlike Georges, he was determined to succeed in his career. Realizing that he might not find the enthusiasm to apply all his talents to medical studies, he wanted to arrange matters so that the jury of physicians would think he was already advanced in years and treat his candidacy with a leniency bordering on favoritism. I never knew whether the ruse had anything to do with his success. In any event he passed his examinations and later became the physician on the island of Corfu. There he was able to pursue his deeper literary interests through friendships with the Durells, Henry Miller and others, as well as with Georges.

Both Stephanides and Katsimbalis used to come frequently to our apartment, especially after we moved in October 1925 from the avenue de Saxe to the rue de Lille. While our conversations were primarily literary, they ranged over the entire realm of art.

The Katsimbalis were generous. Both father and son did everything in their power to enlarge the European education we were finding for ourselves. Observing our inclination after our return from Central Europe to draw closer to contemporary visual art, Georges introduced us to two more of his Greek friends whose primary concern was painting. One, Vasilakis Photiadès, *was* a painter; he was a trifle younger than Georges. The other, Nico Mazaraki, somewhat older, made most of his living at the time by dealing in pictures. He had numerous connections but no shop, and was accustomed to display his wares in his apartment in the rue Notre-Dame-des-Champs.

Photiadès was the fruit of a late marriage. His father, Constantin Photiadès, had published in 1910 what is still the standard life of George Meredith—*George Meredith, sa vie, son imagination, son art, sa doctrine* (a book immediately recognized and translated into

English). His mother, who long survived her husband, was of French origin and somehow related to Renan. She was almost fifty when their son was born. He and she were well off. He had no need to earn his living by the pictures he painted, still less by the poems he wrote. Yet his devotion to the arts seemed genuine, it was that of a professional participant not of an amateur in the depreciatory American meaning of the word.

Photiadès lived with his mother on the Square du Trocadéro (a *cul de sac* off the rue Scheffer). In the small entry hall of their apartment the only ornament was an almost life-size Picasso etching of a woman's head from the now famous 1905 series. Again and again I was arrested by this picture. With the exception of "The Frugal Repast," etched in 1904, of which I had then never seen an original, it seemed far greater than any of the works of Picasso reproduced in the Dial "Living Art," or even the actual paintings of his that we were beginning to see in Paris, particularly at the Rosenberg Gallery. In fact, I remember asking who had done this etching and being surprised when Photiadès told me it was Picasso. It appeared to my inexperienced sensibility more like an old master, like a Dürer or a Holbein.

I remember also asking Photiadès what he felt about Picasso in general. This etching aroused his enthusiasm, but he regarded Picasso as inferior to Derain as a *painter*. That coincided with my impression during the years 1925 and 1926, when Elinor and I were exposed to many works of both.

In Photiadès I met for the first time a man of my age who was working under similar conditions. It was not as an instructor but as a comrade in arms that he helped me. His example confirmed a conviction that I might find my own way as an historical writer, with the help of the rich data supplied not only by the documents I was discovering in archives and libraries, but by the works of art which filled leisure hours. There was no need to please a professor by reciting on these works, according to his conception which would have differed from mine. I was free to find myself in them.

Not surprisingly our absorbing interest in graphic art led to a desire to own more contemporary pictures. Photiadès made no direct contribution to this new turn in our lives. It never occurred to us to buy *his* pictures; he had no others to sell.

Mazaraki did. Our association with him provided a source we were able to draw upon during the last two years of our European sojourn for some of the pictures that have been with me ever since. Other connections we made on our own insured that we would return to America with tangible examples of European genius.

Our artistic education advanced during the spring and early summer of 1925, after we moved into the apartment building in the Avenue de Saxe. The flat we occupied belonged to a French businessman named Ingres. (It was a name he had assumed; he was no relative of the painter.) He had once taught French language and literature in Canada and at the University of Chicago, where he had been brought through the good offices of my guardian, George Mead. He had returned to Paris with a Canadian wife. When she left on a long visit to America we leased their flat from April until October. It was on the sixth, the highest floor, with small balconies overlooking the broad Avenue de Saxe, in the center of which once a week was an open air market where Elinor loved to buy supplies. After Madame Ingres (who in ten years had learned very little French) returned, we were able to sublease for another six months an apartment at 9 rue de Lille from a Buffalo couple, the Livingston Fryers, who then lived half the year in Paris. It was larger than the one in the Avenue de Saxe and on the ground floor was a garden. It had its kitchen and storerooms in the basement. Edith Wharton's secretary had chosen it for the Fryers. They had a long lease with what had become, as the value of the franc fell in terms of dollars, a ridiculously small rent. The eighteenth-century furniture in the main rooms was a continual delight. While living here our first pictures began to accumulate.

The routine of daily writing, begun in Vienna, was carried out even more rigorously in Paris. I worked the whole of every morning, with an extra dividend in the late afternoon lasting till dinner time, then about eight. It is a routine that has persisted for more than fifty years.

A writer has an advantage over a shopkeeper or a clerk in that his business is portable; it can be practiced in Cap d'Antibes no less than in Vienna, Paris, Chicago, Los Angeles, Honolulu or Washington. This made possible that combination of work with travel which became habitual.

During this youthful year in Paris work was combined with daily visits to pictures. Immediately after lunch (and before the afternoon stint of writing began at four or five) Elinor and I always went to the Louvre or the Luxembourg, or to the gallery of some dealer.

At the Louvre we saw the classics of course, but the more we saw the more we returned to a special collection which began with Courbet and ran through Cézanne. This was the famous Camondo Collection which M. Camondo, an affluent financier, had left to France in 1908. He had specified the collection be kept together for a period of some forty years. There were precedents for such abundant private gifts to the Louvre, notably in the pictures received in 1869 at the death of Louis La Caze, that very rich assemblage with its Watteaus, Chardins, Fragonards and Bouchers, its Velazquez and Rembrandts—one of these a very great example by that painter of painters. But most of the works in the La Caze collection were altogether respectable to the academic critics of art before the State acquired them. Not so the nineteenth century pictures when Camondo made his gift.

Although the state did not refuse it, and although Isaac de Camondo added further pictures in 1911, the officials banished the collection to an upper floor of the Louvre, reached by a staircase few were enterprising enough to climb. It was a marvelous collection and seeing it day after day helped provide the foundation on which my taste has rested ever since.

The greatest pictures were three Cézannes which are now among the most famous works of the nineteenth century. One is the small *Card Players*, recently stolen while on tour, to be happily recovered soon afterwards. This was a theme Cézanne repeatedly treated. There is another example now beautifully shown with a half dozen of his other masterpieces in the Courtauld collection in London, which I saw for the first time on my honeymoon with Evelyn in 1964. And there is a much larger canvas in the Barnes Collection outside Philadelphia. Barnes regarded all Cézanne's other "card players" as preparations for the picture he owned, but it would be difficult to support that contention. The Camondo *Card Players* is a masterpiece in its own right, and has now become one of the glories of the Musée du Jeu de Paume on the Place de la Concorde, where the great French State Collection of recent paintings came to be housed. There also are the two other great Cézannes from the Camondo Collection: the *Maison du Pendu* and the *Vase de Fleurs*.

Daily during these months in the rue de Lille, just across the river from the Louvre, we were nourished by the beauty of these paintings. We also filled our imaginations with works of Degas, Manet, Monet, Renoir, Pissarro, Sisley, Seurat, Van Gogh and

Gauguin, works which were then exhibited in the Luxembourg Museum as well as in the Salle Camondo. We examined again and again those that came up for sale at auction, as in the immense Gangnat sale of June 1925 which included 160 Renoirs. I still have the catalogue wherein we noted down the prices most of the pictures fetched. Twenty, fifteen or even ten thousand dollars was then regarded as a satisfactory return for a fine Renoir.

During that year in Paris from early 1925 to early 1926 these pictures of countrysides, vases of flowers, balconies, theatre stages, street scenes, salons and bedrooms with men or women in various stages of dress and undress, entered my consciousness so deeply that I found myself inevitably comparing them with the life and the still life that was all about us everyday in our own home, in the homes we visited and in the country where we penetrated on Sundays. Each comparison added charm and meaning to the painting or the watercolor of which it reminded us. And no less inevitably each return to a painting or watercolor enhanced the beauty of the actual scenes and experiences it evoked. From this enhancement of reality I dimly perceived that the rearrangement of historical materials according to the requirements of beauty, as the artist sees those requirements, might enhance the realities of history, might give the story a permanence that the strict scientific handling of documentary evidence does not achieve.

This daily communion with works of art also prepared us for decisions as to pictures we wanted to acquire, among those of younger painters whose works were not out of range of our purse as were those of Renoir and his contemporaries.

8. ENCOUNTERS WITH CHAGALL

The next purchase after the Signacs came months later, in the autumn of 1925. I was responsible, independent of Elinor, independent of Signac, independent of our Greek friends and acquaintances.

As the fourth anniversary of our marriage approached, Elinor and I were installed in the attractive apartment in the rue de Lille, a block from the river Seine. One afternoon I wandered along the quai past the bookshop our friend Edouard Champion had inherited from his father. On Paris streets in those days one's eyes often encountered unexpectedly in a show window a painting for which a collector now would give his teeth. Slowly I mounted the rue de Seine and halted in front of a picture shop belonging to Pierre Loeb, one of the best supplied smaller dealers of the period.

I entered Loeb's shop determined not to leave empty-handed. Among the fine pictures that were for sale was an oblong nude of Modigliani's, now regarded as a masterpiece. I was no stranger to delight in nude women, but what attracted me most were two Chagall gouaches, done between 1915 and 1917, after the artist's return from Paris to Russia on the eve of the First World War. One is a woman in a scanty dressing gown, bathing her baby. The other he calls "Fête," an imaginative portrait of the Jewish holiday "purim." I gave Pierre Loeb what he asked for both and carried them home.

I had made no mistake. Elinor loved them. They are now the glory of the Salle Chagall, Evelyn's and my bedroom in Georgetown. Whenever I wake my eyes fall on them. I rejoice in the wonderful red and yellow and green colors that seem stronger after forty-six years. Only the other day when I was feeling hungry a desire beset me to taste the cake the peasant woman is carrying in "Fête."

Knowledge of Chagall's work had come first in Vienna through his now famous green and yellow rabbi reproduced in the *Dial* Folio. Then in Germany we had seen a few of his pictures and many reproductions. His paintings and gouaches made a deep impression for I had never before seen a work of art anything like them. They lured me by their wonderful colors and their fantasy. Here unspoiled by fate was the authentic world of a child. The pictures evoked an echo of my own childhood dreaming, which like his has never come to an end. Unlike mine, *his* was often Biblical; mine was related to a never-never land of perfection. Both of us were filled by illusions concerning the possibilities of life in the world. Both had had the complete fulfillment that love of a woman who returns it can confer. Perhaps one thing that brought us together with decisive firmness long years afterwards, was the hope that, since we were capable of dreaming things that are beyond what can be seen, these things might possibly (counter to previous experience) be made for the first time accessible to other human beings if they were to want them enough. How can all the love and color that Chagall conjures up, and has expressed over seventy years in so many artistic media, be nonexistent?

Chagall had returned to Paris (his home for three years on the eve of the 1914 War) after ten years in his native Russia, where he had married his childhood sweetheart Bella. Those had been years of revolutionary change, more violent in Russia than anywhere else.

It never occurred to me when I bought his pictures that I should ever meet him, though I knew he lived in Paris. But violence pursued him in the France he had adopted and that was adopting him. Violence in its Nazi form drove him out of Paris and then out of southern France. With Bella, he was cast up in June, 1941, on the western shores of the Atlantic in New York like many other refugees.[1] Then in the autumn of 1944, as the Second World War was coming to an end, Bella died.

On the eve of the United States entry into the war, and during the American participation, the interdisciplinary faculty at the University of Chicago was being established under circumstances to be described in Part IV. In the plans for its development following the defeat of Germany, my colleagues and I arranged a series of weekly lectures by men of great distinction in different fields of creative endeavor. Our intention was to illustrate the common ground of inspiration and achievement in all creative work. The series opened in February, 1946. We chose Chagall to speak for the artist.[2]

His turn came in April. He had never travelled west of the Hudson and he had never travelled by air. Since his marriage in Russia he had never travelled without Bella.

To help in facing what was difficult for his sensitive personality and his dependent habits, he called on the companionship of a New York friend, the late Louis Stern, whose extensive art collection included several Chagalls. We had asked them to start their three days in Chicago by coming directly from the plane for dinner. Four or five of our friends, among them Frederick Sweet one of the curators of the Art Institute of Chicago, had assembled to meet them. The plane was late, but they arrived just before dusk when there was still enough light for them to peer from the street into the living room of our ground floor apartment.

What did Chagall see as he got out of the taxi to find his host emerging from the front door to greet him? He saw to his astonishment two pictures he had created thirty years before in Russia. For him the Middle West had loomed as an unknown and alien land. He dreaded this journey to a city recently the site of Indian wigwams and now, according to newspaper reports, full of gangsters. He dreaded the ordeal of speaking in public for the first time. He missed Bella. But now he was conscious he was already the companion of his hosts. He was not a foreigner in a strange house. He was at home. Those two gouaches, purchased twenty-two years before, told Chagall that he had been recognized much earlier not through fame but through love. This made a deep impression to which he was to refer repeatedly afterwards. It unloosened his tongue, never very taut.

Some ask how his English was then and now. The answer is non-existent then, after five years in the United States, and the same now. Yet like De Gaulle he understands a great deal of what is said when others converse in English. And after all he found a medium other than language in which to communicate. That evening examples of his speech in the graphic medium were on hand to reassure him. He talks fluently not only in Russian but in French, a tongue in which all of us that evening were at home.

We listened while he was impelled to tell the story of his childhood, to evoke a few of his early fancies that bore an analogy to mine, the same fantasies and colors that had first drawn me to his pictures. Since this occasion I have heard him tell several times of his early days. But he never told of them better. What struck me most in his account that first evening were the words: "Every decision in my life has been determined by my art."

9. THE FANCY OF DUFY

Through his personal connections Nico Mazaraki had in his possession pictures by several of the foremost "living" artists, among them Derain and Utrillo and especially Raoul Dufy. His enthusiasm for Dufy's paintings and watercolors sometimes reached a high pitch of emotion. On one occasion, he confronted us with two brilliantly colored landscapes, exclaiming "C'est le Claude Lorrain de nos jours!" At the time this struck me as an absurd and wholly incongruous comparison. It still seems rather far-fetched, but I now realize that some of Dufy's results could be represented as coming, as Claude's had come, from the inspiration derived from land- or sea-scapes. That may have been the thought behind Mazaraki's exclamation. I still question any close similarity of intention or of style. Dufy seems above all a great imaginative decorator and, at his best, a marvelous colorist in a class in that respect not with Claude but with Van Gogh. But I no longer think there is anything absurd in treating Dufy as an artist who will endure. Nor do I now regard as fabricated Mazaraki's enthusiasm for his pictures. I am grateful that he persisted in his determination to interest us in Dufy.

How was it that I came to delight in and to profit from Dufy's work? This appreciation was probably a slow process going on subconsciously ever since I had become aware of his characteristic style. Yet the realization that his was a dazzling charm hit me all at once many months after my first acquaintance with his work. One day Mazaraki phoned that he had acquired some new watercolors Dufy had just finished while working on the Riviera. Not waiting for Elinor, I hurried to the rue Notre-Dame-des-Champs in much the same frame of mind as when, a few weeks before, I had gone to Pierre Loeb's shop in the rue de Seine. And with a similar result.

Mazaraki brought out two large acquarelles, each in marvelous colors, which seemed on this gray Paris afternoon to fill the dingy room with light. One was the "Blue Train" puffing white smoke as it started out of Antibes station on its way to Nice. The port of Antibes, the Vauban fortifications and the old walled town were captured with original fancy and unified in typical Dufy style, while the Mediterranean beyond the breakwaters provided a blue background with a ship in full sail. All overhead was the Mediterranean sky of endless blue characteristic of the Riviera especially as we had come to know it in July and August.

The other watercolor, in the same spirit, is of a different scene in its way no less stunning. It is a symphony of Dufy greens and reds, inspired by a Provencal landscape. I have never been able to identify the place where Dufy derived this inspiration, but I assume it is back from the coast in the hills near Antibes.

The two pictures complement one another. Placed side by side that afternoon without competing ornaments or colors, they evoked that mysterious devotion to the Mediterranean awakened three years before. They gave me a sense of protection and well being missing from the chilly Parisian winter. "Le Train Bleu" filled me with memories of a journey south in the early spring of 1923, just after that very train had been christened and we had occupied overnight two connecting "singles," with a third discreetly distant for my mother-in-law, Mabel Wing Castle, to whom I was always much attached. She joined us that spring for a three week vacation at the Hotel du Cap, where we had escaped after a long spell of research in the damp and fog of London.

The moment Mazaraki confronted me with those pictures, I knew I was going home with them no matter what the price. He didn't ask much, a trifle more than a hundred dollars (possibly two hundred) a piece, as nearly as I can remember. Gathering these large pictures under my arms, whence they trailed to the ground, I climbed into a taxi and made in excitement for the rue de Lille.

Hundreds of times since I have driven past the spot along the old road leaving Antibes for Nice where Dufy created the "Blue Train," and never without thinking of his picture. I see that much more often, and it evokes the scene. One enhances the plenty of the other, as we were learning contemporary art can do from our experiences in the Camondo Collection.

The fancy in the Dufys is different from that in works of his predecessors. Like the Chagalls, but unlike the Cézannes or the Monets, it is not so much that reality is given a new dimension by art as that a new world, a fresh reality derived from fancy, has been created.

These pictures from the Riviera were the beginning of our Dufy acquisitions. Before the winter of 1925-26 ended, four more that had belonged temporarily to Mazaraki were installed in our apartment.

A picture that I did not buy, but which Mazaraki assured us was a masterpiece was a "Venus"—a nude woman on a shell, all in blue. The color *was* stunning but the work as a whole left me ill at ease. This must have come from a feeling that Dufy's fancies lend themselves best to landscapes, seascapes and to imaginative transpositions of music, of circuses, of horseraces, rather than to the direct portrayal of women or men however fancifully conceived.

We soon bought two more remarkable Dufys, both watercolors. "Longchamps" portrays the famous races, though less representationally than the "Blue Train" does its subject. "The Circus" is in blue, like the Venus, but with many figures, none direct portraits. This large watercolor provides a totally different impression from the famous "Cirque" by Seurat, once owned by John Quinn and given at his death to the French state at about the time we were making these purchases. Of its kind, a lesser kind, Dufy's "Circus" is an equally inspired vision of a modern spectacle to which as a child I had been introduced and which had put me into a fright. By this time that fear had left and Dufy's creation was not designed to revive it.

Our fifth Dufy is a landscape like the first two. The setting may be Morocco, which I have never visited. But the whereabouts are unimportant. It is a lovely warm watercolor of about the same size as the "Blue Train" and just as satisfactory to live with.

There was a sixth large watercolor of the harbor of Marseilles. To my regret we obliged ourselves to part with it soon after our return to the United States.

Our Dufys aroused much merriment among the visitors we entertained in our rue de Lille apartment, especially the American visitors. No doubt they found it disconcerting to see modern pictures in a setting of French furniture from the period of Claude Lorrain. While I was becoming more charitable to the comparison Mazaraki had drawn between Claude and Dufy, such a rapprochment between past and contemporary art was then unthinkable for conventional "collectors." The reaction of an American lady of substance, then in her sixties, was characteristic. She was brought to call by a friend from Hawaii. When she saw the Dufys and the Chagalls she could hardly have been more scornful. "What rubbish," she observed. "A child, with no training in drawing or in mixing colors, who played with watercolors, could do quite as well. How absurd for you to have bought such trash. Come round to my hotel suite. I'll show you some really good contemporary art." We did. I cannot remember anything about her paintings, except that their authors are now unknown.

The occasion for parting with the Marseilles picture was prompted, however, not by such episodes, but by an obligation felt to Elinor's aunt, Helen Castle Mead, and to her husband. We had no children. When we returned to the United States their son, an only child, had three, with a fourth on the way. So as a token of gratitude to the Meads for taking me into their home as a youth we gave their son this Dufy picture. What could be more appropriate as decoration for his children's playroom!

I don't know what has become of this large watercolor. I should envy the owner were it not for the good fortune life has brought me.

By "good fortune" I do not mean "worldly goods" or the means of acquiring them. The "good fortune" came from the help for my career which the pictures we acquired—and particularly these Chagalls and Dufys—have increasingly provided. The childlike fancy which shone in their work was not a limitation but a quality. That fancy is "most

original." Remembering the confidence Arthur Barnard had expressed
in his young pupil, I hoped my inclinations to break away from the
conventional treatment of history might prove as justifiable as the
break Chagall and Dufy had made from the conventional treatment
of artistic subjects.

The nature of their innovations differs fundamentally in character
from that of earlier remarkable innovations such as Bosch or still more
Grünewald, who was a greater painter than Bosch. (He is perhaps
among the greatest painters of all times.) Besides other remarkable
qualities, Grünewald's imagination anticipates features of twentieth-
century art. But notwithstanding the radiant and compassionate
quality of his Christ, it is Picasso, with his harsh and relentless results,
or Rouault, with his worldly despair, that he anticipates. It is not
the childlike dreams of Chagall, devoid of all cruelty, or the serenity
and joy of Dufy.

Chagall and Dufy are fundamentally optimists. They provide two
fairy lands, two refuges in an age of unprecedentedly rapid mechanization, filled as that age is with unprecedentedly frequent nervous
shocks. There is perhaps no precedent in art for the fancy of these two
artists, who are so different and so independent of one another.
Daily access to their pictures helped give me confidence in my own
optimism. Many years later in *The United States and Civilization*
I drew a utopian blueprint. Cynical voices everywhere were saying
that the time for Utopias was over. The happiness Chagall and Dufy
have managed to embody in their pictures contributed to the vision
of a happier world my book expresses. The example of their pictures
strengthened me too in starting a Center for Human Understanding
in the hope that world community may become more than a dream.
Chagall was so drawn to this effort to win humanity by means of love,
that he asked to participate and became a member of the Center, as
he is now of the Nef Foundation that has succeeded it.[1]

During the last eighteen months of our sojourn in Europe I was
haunted by a poetic summons derived from two very famous verses,
one by Baudelaire, the other by Keats. The first is from *Le Voyage*:
"Au fond de l'inconnu pour trouver du nouveau." The other is the
first line of the *Last Sonnet*, "Bright star! Would I were steadfast as
thou art." Together these verses issued a call that has never died
away, to find in the careers of historian, professor and educational
reformer new ways of building with exalted human hopes, hopes so

readily deformed by surrenders to the conventional procedures followed in these careers.

I was fascinated by causation as a theme and by historical comparisons that revealed historical causes. Fresh ways had to be found for treating those causes. Experiences with works of art and with artists gave me the courage to experiment.

The Dufys, like the first Chagalls, were acquired without acquaintance with the artist. We had no idea what manner of men Chagall and Dufy might be. Elinor and I met Dufy when we were returning home on the "Queen Mary" from what proved to be the last of a series of summer visits to Europe in the thirties before the Second World War.[2] Dufy was enroute to Pittsburgh where he had been appointed one of the judges for the annual Carnegie show of art. He was a charming man, completely unassuming. We shared some congenial conversation. On one occasion Elinor led him to a private dining room on the ship to show him a painting by Vanessa Bell, the sister of Virginia Woolf whom we had come to know in 1933. The reason Elinor knew its whereabouts and wanted to have Dufy's opinion of it was that she had bought from Mrs. Bell (Clive Bell's wife) a small version of the same scene, executed in preparation for this very painting.

Dufy knew nothing of Vanessa Bell. But unlike many artists who can see no good in works of their contemporaries, he spoke with pleasure of this picture and praised the way it was painted. *"C'est bien,"* he said, "the only good thing on the ship. It is strong. It has individuality. The colors are like Flandrin's but not his false academism, and well painted—*La peinture est bien."* It escaped the faults of English painting that stared him in the face, Dufy said, in other pictures on the ship.[3]

Modesty and openness of mind were, we found, characteristic of Dufy. Decades later, after his death, a new friend, Gerard Gaussen, then a counselor of the French Embassy in Washington, told of a similar experience he had had with Dufy in Venice on an occasion when another well-known painter had shown much less generosity towards his contemporaries.

Dufy was nearly sixty when we met. Like Chagall, but in a different way, he was an enchanting human being, graced as is Chagall by more than a minimum of decency.[4] This helps me to understand why I was so drawn to his art, for while an artist's works, once finished, are separate from their author, they bear resemblances to their parents.

10. PASCIN'S WOMEN

Not long after the visit to Pierre Loeb's shop we bought from him three small watercolors that Jules Pascin had done some years before in America. One was called "The Handsome Barber"; it was from his New Orleans period during the First World War or just after. When we met him we found he attached some importance to this picture. It is a fine example of his style. In a sense this style is derivative of Cézanne's adventures in the same medium, but Pascin's creamy watercolors could never be legitimately mistaken for anyone's but his own.

The second watercolor depicts two alluring black women (one a nursemaid) with a child at play. The third is a cart drawn by two donkeys in Havana, with several workmen in summer costume, one perched on another cart.

Wherever they have been placed these pictures have provided three warm spots of beauty. The one of Havana introduced me to the Caribbean long before I went there, first to Antigua in 1954.

I am not sure of the circumstances under which we met Pascin. It was some weeks after we had acquired these watercolors and at a party which included another painter, Geneviève Gallibert (of whose pictures more later), and André Salmon, the critic who had been closely associated with the remarkable group of artists congregated in Paris since the early years of this century.

Pascin's real name was Pincus. He pronounced his assumed name "Pass-*keen*" and so did his friends. He would have appreciated it if these random remarks could do something to restore his pronounciation. At the time of our meeting he was in his early forties, a man of moderate height, clean shaven and modestly dressed, with no trace of aggressiveness or assertiveness. He inspired confidence by the integrity of his knowledge of the *métier* he had mastered. He knew much about human nature, particularly the feminine kind with its strengths, weaknesses and great beauties.

We gave a small dinner for him at the Trianon, a restaurant on the Left Bank by the old Gare Montparnasse, frequented by men of letters such as Paul Bourget as well as by painters. He came with his mistress, Lucy Per Krogh.

Pascin's conversation had an extraordinary fascination enhanced by the animated movements of his hands. These were always about to draw. He was a very fine draftsman and drawing was so much second nature that when he conversed one never forgot it. His marvelous lines appeared in conversation in the form of gestures—long and wavy, curved or straight—whatever was required to accompany the words. His speech enriched his drawing, much as I was to discover long afterwards that Stravinsky's accented the rhythm of his music.

We asked Pascin what the United States was like, for he had lived there since we had left almost five years before and many changes had taken place. He had gone to America with his first wife, Hermine David, who was also a painter. Through the good offices of Alfred Stieglitz he had become a citizen of the United States, although he was born in Bulgaria and had spent most of his adult life among the artists of Paris. There before the First World War he had already become part of the movement represented by Picasso, Derain, Matisse, Chagall, Braque, Segonzac, Vlaminck and many others.

During our dinner at the Trianon he expressed himself about the United States both in conversation and with his pencil on the back of the menu card. He portrayed the life of New York by drawing a speakeasy, with a heavy-set, bloated, millionaire client clandestinely advancing a dollar bill through a small opening, to be poured, in return, a glass of strong water. Much of what he told us was happening in our country anticipated the account Frederick Lewis Allen gave years later in his book, *Only Yesterday*. Pascin prepared us for the return to New York even better than that watercolor of his prepared me for the Caribbean.

He told of experiences in New Orleans during the First War. Then and later he continued to have, as some of his pictures show, a pronounced pleasure in associating with black people. To the consternation of the neighbors in New Orleans, he and Hermine David received them as friends in their home—a practice which caused some scandal, for it was very much less common in the United States then than now and unheard of then in the South.

Before we parted at the Trianon he invited us to spend an evening with *him*. This occurred on a beautifully warm summer night of a kind which now seems rarer in Paris than one imagines it was then. When we arrived towards eight o'clock, light was still pouring into his ample studio in the large apartment building in Montmartre where he lived and worked. Here we met not only Lucy but also for the first time his black cook-housekeeper and a couple of other friendly female retainers. The walls of the rooms were covered with his drawings, paintings and watercolors; making an impressive scene of "living" art such as no carefully tended museum provides with the same natural charm. Apart from the master, almost nothing was to be seen but women in all stages of dress and undress, those who were with him as well as those he had created.

Recently I conversed with Chagall about Pascin, whom he knew when they were both starting work in Paris. Chagall was talking about a man in that artist's world who had somewhat dubious *moeurs*. I asked Chagall whether Pascin "aimait les femmes" (loved women). Without hesitation he answered, "Uniquement" (exclusively). This was evident in the setting of people and pictures in his studio-home.

We were attracted by the women who were there—dark as well as white—and in an important way even more (because of their permanence) by the women he had made alive on paper and canvas. It was difficult to be sure where the "real" ones left off and the "living" ones began. Before Pascin took us to dinner, we bought two of the latter. One is a pastel of a reclining woman with her clothes pulled back. My mother-in-law found it so shocking that she begged us never to hang it. But I on the contrary could find therein nothing but sheer delight. The other is of two "living" women who are younger, whose clothes are too scanty to need pulling back. "Two Girls on a Couch" is no less shocking to some eyes than our reclining woman was to my mother-in-law's. Pascin used it as a sketch for at least two of his best oils, one of which hangs in the Art Museum in Grenoble, with its fine collection of modern and contemporary art. The drawing we bought is a perfect example of Pascin's remarkable draftsmanship. He winced that evening when Elinor spotted it. He didn't want to part with it, and asked very nearly as much as for the pastel.[1]

About the time this meeting with Pascin occurred, Albert Barnes, against his original inclinations but under the persistent prodding of Paul Guillaume, had begun to buy Pascins for his gallery in Merion, Pennsylvania. Pascin told us how Barnes, accompanied by John Dewey, had recently swept through his apartment studio and gone off with several pictures for which he paid cash, as we had just done. Pascin was incredibly generous. It was notorious that he could never hold onto money. As soon as he got some, he immediately spent almost all of it on his friends.

So it was that evening. All of us, including his female entourage, went off to a restaurant where Pascin ordered a ravishing repast. Afterwards we went on to a nightclub. His housekeeper and most of the others were dancing when she suddenly shrieked, halting the music and gaiety. Like the others in our party, I was mystified as to the cause. It bothered Pascin to find she thought someone had insulted her color. When I asked her to dance the episode subsided. Later a tall man—possibly the very one who had pinched her—came over and whispered, "You shouldn't take that *au tragique* (so seriously); nobody ever approaches me in that sector except to pick my pocket."

Although we were about to return to the United States, Pascin wished to retain the relationship. He gave us a letter that proved an open sesame to Dr. Barnes' exclusive collection, with its numerous small Pascins. Later still we almost met our new friend again. Pascin used to come over periodically to the States for short visits. This was partly to retain his American citizenship but also because he liked the people. On one occasion in 1928, we got in touch with him because the colors of his pastel of the reclining woman showed a tendency to run. We were about to leave Swarthmore College, where I had been teaching a year, for another European visit before settling at the University of Chicago (as will be related in its place.) We wrote to Pascin, who was in New York, asking if he would fix the colors. "Please leave picture with Weythe," he telegraphed on May 22, 1928. "Leave in two weeks for Paris. Hope to see you. Coming back early fall." The picture was returned to us in beautiful condition after having been restored by his own hand. But alas we never saw Pascin again. Hardly three years later he chose death by suicide, leaving the message written in blood "Pardon, Lucy."

Decades afterwards, in 1964, when Evelyn and I were in Paris on our honeymoon, we wandered into a small shop in the rue de Seine, not far from the place once occupied by Pierre Loeb. We had seen announced a small retrospective Pascin exhibition. The exhibition turned out to be what might be called scrapings of Pascin's art, a few meagre unfinished drawings and watercolors. There was only one other visitor, a small bent elderly lady. Seated in a corner, she hovered over a table, neither speaking nor reading nor changing her position— seemingly a part of these remains, all lacking the life that had been so strikingly present in Pascin's home on that summer evening of 1926.

After we had looked at the pictures, something prompted me to ask the proprietor of the shop "What has become of Lucy Per Krogh?" He pointed silently to the still figure in the corner.

11. "READING MAKETH A FULL MAN"

Graham Wallas, author of *The Great Society* (a book I read at
Harvard), had gone to Oxford as a scholarship boy in the later nineteenth century when students who depended on scholarships were still
rare at the two most famous English universities. After a number of
stimulating meetings with his tutor during the first terms, the "long
vacation" loomed. The don provided Wallas with a list of books.
He was expected to give an account of them in the autumn.

"How did the reading go?" his tutor asked at their next meeting.
Poor Wallas had not cracked a book. "Well, sir," he mumbled, "I
haven't read much, but I've *thought* a lot."

Actually a *university* education *can* get in the way of reading
and even of thinking. During our five years in Europe freed from
university obligations, I found it possible to indulge a desire to read
to an extent previously impossible, but for which I had acquired a
passion that has never left me when, barely eighteen, I was alone on
that Wyoming ranch waiting for Elinor and her mother with nothing
to occupy me except *War and Peace*. No book has ever more completely absorbed life. The need for a new kind of history, to which
Tolstoy devotes the Epilogue, filled my mind long afterwards and
influenced the course my historical writings took.

The desire to read had been awakened even earlier by a grandmother who, when I was eleven or so, stuffed me with Shakespeare.
She used to quote one of her contemporaries who insisted that "a
person well read in Shakespeare is well read."

From 1922 through 1926 the countries to which we had access in
Europe were mending from the world war. No imminent crises
threatened a young man's career. As the partner of a woman addicted
to reading, it became easy and natural to read. We used to read
each other to sleep. I felt a growing enthusiasm to fill any empty hours
and even minutes with books, creative reviews and serious newspapers.
There were more of those than there are now. I soon found appetizers
to stimulate my literary appetite: the *Nouvelle Revue Francaise*, *The
Criterion*, *The Dial*, *The Nation*, *The New Statesman*, *The Times
Literary Supplement*, *Le Temps* and *The Manchester Guardian*.

Instead of diverting me from good books, these journals led me
to them, for I discovered that no review, however competent and
full, can be a *substitute* for the book itself. *The Adelphi* introduced
me to Katherine Mansfield; it reintroduced me to D. H. Lawrence

and stressed the importance of Chekhov. It was even helpful for economic history: H. G. Wells (whose books I had enjoyed as a youth)
wrote a letter to the editor asking if some reader would recommend
a guide to the economic development of France and Germany in the
nineteenth century. From the response to Wells' letter I learned
about J. H. Clapham, whose work I came to admire and in whom
I later found a supporter for mine. In consequence I was never left—
on railway journeys, boat trips, in bed, on the underground, in buses
and even in cabs and taxis—without reading to absorb my thoughts.

Soon after reaching Montpellier, Elinor and I had found a list published by André Gide (whose uncle was an economist) of the ten
greatest French novels. This led me soon, after our journalistic es-
capades at Genoa, not only to read but to ponder and to live over
the adventures related in *La Princesse de Clèves, La Vie de Marianne,*
Manon Lescaut, Les Liaisons dangereuses, La Chartreuse de Parme,
Adolphe, La Cousine Bette, Madame Bovary, Dominique, and
Germinal. That last novel took me into the early coal mines of
northern France at a time when I had committed myself to a history of the still earlier British coal industry. *Germinal* helped me to
discover the value, for a study of historical causes, of comparisons
between the histories of different countries at a time when economic
historians were increasingly specializing, not only in particular subjects and periods, but in particular countries and regions.

The classic French novels led to the classic English, American,
Russian and German novels. And these led to classics of other kinds.
At the time these literary excursions began the French writer,
Valéry Larbaux, published a book entitled *Ce Vice impuni; la lecture.*
Reading was the major vice in which I became entrenched during
my five years abroad. It was not the gravest of the vices that
attracted young Americans of my generation who lived in Europe.
The vice led me when a professor, to seek reforms in university
study that might provide for those students who sought opportunities to read on their own, and thus to break away from the rigid
specialization towards which higher education was oriented.

During our first nine months abroad my reading centered on economics and politics. But once I embarked upon a daily routine of
historical research and writing and abandoned the idea of acquiring
knowledge by systematically following university lecture courses,
I found myself drawn to philosophers, particularly French, such as

Montaigne, Rousseau, Pascal, Montesquieu, Voltaire, to historians
such as Taine, to Diderot's letters, and above all to the classics
of literature, including great poetry and drama. I returned to
Shakespeare and took up Bernard Shaw and Molière. The reading
of plays proved essential to a full appreciation of the theatres and
operas we frequented in London, Paris, Vienna and (very briefly)
Berlin. There we had the opportunity of comparing Shaw's *Saint
Joan* as acted in London by Sybyl Thorndike and in Paris by
Madame Pitoeff, with Elizabeth Bergner. After her German version
ended the audience filed out talking in astonishment over Shaw's
strictures on Joan's executioners, repeating to each other a trifle
inaccurately, "Aber er *ist* Engländer" (But Shaw *is* English).

The directions my general reading took, independent of special
courses of study such as universities provided, was determined by
those years abroad. Reading affected the organization of my life.
The letters of Diderot to Sophie Volland, for instance, in which he
describes his routine of daily work, conversation and exercise in the
chateaux he frequented—particularly the one at Grandval (the estate
of the Baron d'Holbach)—reassured me of the stimulus to a full life
which my newly acquired habits of alternate concentration and diversion could provide. Much later, when I was a widower, I was already prepared to make use to advantage of visits to chateaux where
kind French friends generously invited me.[1]

Love of literature was an important ingredient in the sense of
fulfillment I felt during the early years abroad. In no small part that
love grew out of friendships with the Champion and the Katsimbalis.

Edouard Champion lived with his wife Julie on the Avenue
Pierre I de Serbie in a large apartment full of valuable books. They
often invited us to dinner or lunch with writers such as Blasco
Ibanez, Valéry Larbaux, the Tharaud brothers, Jacques Boulanger. . .
and conversations with them suggested new ideas that encouraged
me, in exchange for their observations, to express thoughts for *their*
comment and criticism.

Most of the fine books which lined the walls of the Champion apartment apparently went unread, but their presence was felt. It helped
us to be at home with the books Elinor and I were reading, not a
few purchased at Edouard's suggestion from his family bookshop on
the quai which now bears his father's name. There Anatole France,
whom we also read and discussed, got his apprenticeship. Edouard
was prompted by this early association with France to publish a series

of small volumes in memory of the encouragement this famous man
of letters had given him. France had apparently told the little boy:
"The friends of Edouard are the best friends in the world." So
Edouard published a small paperback by a distinguished author
(Claudel or Valéry for example) for each letter in this sentence.
He prolonged the series by adding the words "Anatole France to
Edouard Champion, friend of letters and of women." He generously
gave us copies of these booklets as they appeared.

The Katsimbalis' major cultural interests were in literature too.
This was true of the father who had translated "Omar Khayyam"
into Greek and who knew Madame de Noailles, the French poet of
Romanian origin. It was even truer of Georges Katsimbalis and
of Theodor Stephanides, who had contacts in Paris with famous contemporary writers. We spent evening after evening with the two
Greeks, especially in our apartments in the Avenue de Saxe and the
Rue de Lille. Our ardent discussions were more often related to
literary values, to lines of verse, than to politics and economics.

T. S. Eliot was a continuous subject of controversy. We had
read "The Waste Land" first in *The Dial*. But "Prufrock" was my
favorite; its lines were always running in my head like those of
"L'Horloge" and "L'Invitation au Voyage," and those of the Odes
"To a Nightingale" and "To a Grecian Urn." I also devoured Eliot's
first two books of essays, *The Sacred Wood* and *Hommage to Dryden*.
It was these that turned me to Marvell and later to Donne.

Our Greek friends, with one exception, did not share our taste
for Eliot. The exception was Photiadès, who wrote verse himself
and who, I seem to remember, had known Eliot briefly at a sanitarium
in Switzerland. His championship of Eliot's poetry, like his enthusiasm for Derain's painting, helped to reinforce strong inclinations of mine.[2] And Katsimbalis and Stephanides encouraged my
interest in Eliot by their opposition to his verse. They asked us with
vehemence how a *poet* could sing of "the bloody wood. When
Agamemnon cried aloud," they asked how a *poet* could compare the
evening to a "patient etherized upon a table."

Their opposition taught me that genuine disagreement can be more
constructive for an artistically inclined historian than easy agreement
derived from superficial acquaintance with works of art. "Soft soap"
is valueless; it is seldom based on inner experience; it contains little
or nothing of substance. In the circles of the Champion or the
Katsimbalis the vigorous disagreement stung me into reconsiderations

of ideas derived from my new literary experiences. It had the further
merit of confirming my prejudice that such experiences are important.

In respect to literature Paris was more nourishing than Vienna. But
it was an English experience that taught me once and for all the
fundamental need to take nothing at second-hand. I discovered it is no
less vital to read literature in the original than to seek out *source*
materials in connection with historical research. Later as a professor
I tried to convey this lesson to students who are prone, instead of
finding their own way, to want someone to *tell* them the meaning
of a philosophical work or even of a novel or a poem.

I learned this lesson in the following way. Elinor had a close
kinship with Henry James, Dorothy Richardson and Virginia Woolf,
against a rich background she had acquired earlier through her
mastery of classical English, French and Russian stories. Most of
all she had a kinship with Proust. She read with tremendous caring
(partly because she would have liked to be a professional writer)
Proust's famous novel *A la Recherche du temps perdu* as it came out
in installments before and after Proust's death late in 1922. Perhaps
as compensation for the fact that she was never able to finish any
of the stories she began during the early years of marriage, she was
continually describing with enthusiasm episodes from Proust in her
conversations with me and literary friends of ours like Malcolm
Cowley, whom we often saw in Montpellier before *he* had read a line of
Proust and when he was mistaken about the pronunciation of that
writer's name. Elinor made the episodes so vivid that I felt for some
time no need to read Proust. Busy with research and writing, I
persuaded myself my wife's accounts were the equivalent of the
source. (Indeed I am not sure Elinor did not make a similar impression with her Proust on Malcolm Cowley.)

In the summer of 1923 in London we met a charming old bachelor
named Ball, then in his seventies. The Cima di Ball, a difficult
climb in the Dolomites above San Martino di Castrozza, had been
named for his father. After our meeting with the son, he used to
entertain us whenever we were in town. On one occasion at the old
Carlton Hotel where the famous Escoffier was in charge of the
kitchen, I was put next to a fascinating English spinster Miss
Trevelyan, twice my age. The dinner was worthy—as I later discovered—of the dinners Proust describes in his novel, and my con-

versation with this lady centered on his book. I did my best to keep
abreast of her. But my second-hand resources proved inadequate
and I found the going harder and harder, at the same time that my
dinner partner's intelligence and charm made me wish to converse on
equal terms. When finally this lady said that reading Proust had
been "the greatest experience of her life," I realized that *I* too must
regain the time lost.

Thus I came to discover Proust. The task required concentration.
It was facilitated by heavy colds in the head to which I was subject
at least twice a year. Each cold provided an uninterrupted stretch
of time. Proust's impact (after Balzac and Stendhal) was tremendous; the Grande-Hôtel de Balbec at Balbec-Plage was almost more
real than most of the hotels we stayed in. And I was so captivated
by the style that I tried translating into English the pages where
the Marquis de Norpois, French minister to Berlin in 1870, describes
the moves on the eve of the Franco-Prussian War.[3]

This experience with Proust helped me to read the great books to
which our life abroad attracted me with an attention and a thorough-
ness that had been missing from my studies during my previous
years at Harvard. I read for purposes determined by the needs of
my inner life as a writer-historian. My married life also relieved me
from the vacant day dreaming into which I used to drift during
and before my years at Harvard. A total attentiveness was born.
I became so convulsed with laughter over *Humphry Clinker,* while
waiting to see the Livingston Fryer's solicitor about a theft in a
room of their apartment they had locked up, that I attracted the
attention of the other waiting clients. And my dread of coming to
the end of *Tom Jones,* read in snatches on the bus from Knightsbridge to the British Museum, was equal to my earlier dread of an
emptiness that would come after I finished *War and Peace.* What
I absorbed became part of me, good in itself, not small change acquired
for some utilitarian purpose such as passing a college examination.
I began to read "for keeps."

The value of this attentiveness would be difficult to overstate. It
awakened the concentration vital to a man of letters. Faced with an
endless sea of information in the sixteenth and seventeenth-century
manuscripts I examined in archives and libraries, my research into
the British coal industry had led me to the simplifying expedient
of focusing my attention on the word "coal." It became second
nature to scan page after page of documents and books, spot that

word, or find it in the index when there was one, and then take notes that seemed relevant to the subject. In my hurry to finish, I frequently read too hastily. This led me into many a small error which I was fortunately able to correct by a thorough reexamination of the sources when the book was in proof from 1929 to 1932.

The discipline of concentration needed for the consecutive thinking that helped me to concern myself with the whole was acquired less from my historical research than from my general reading in subjects that had nothing directly to do with my book. This discipline could not have been acquired if I had read the books with a view to passing examinations. For then I should have been searching for particular facts somewhat as I searched documents for statements relating to coal, facts which in the case of answers to examination questions would have been related to someone else's mind.

By wide but intensive reading I learned to be thorough and careful. Books of my choosing not only taught me how to concentrate, reading them also had much to do with the conviction that grew before and after my first book was published that, for its full fruition, special knowledge must be put in the context of more general truths. Self-acquired fascination over literature, no less than self-acquired fascination over music and over pictures shaped my life.

12. LONDON AND ENGLISH CULTURE

This book has probably given an impression that the compelling European influences in our lives were continental and especially French. That is so. But lest the reader suppose that we were always escaping from the damp English climate, I hasten to add that actually Great Britain and, above all, London played a hardly less important role in my academic formation than France. After all my major subject of concern was the rise of the British coal industry. I had to discover where this coal was mined, through what villages and towns it was transported and whence it was shipped. On old maps of the British Isles I was able to spot these places as they had existed during the spread of the new fuel in the sixteenth and seventeenth centuries. In consequence I gained a more extensive knowledge of English and Scottish place names (often spelled differently in Tudor and Stuart times) than many an English geographer.

The basic materials for my coal history came from manuscripts in the English and Scottish archives, plus some in the Archives Nationales and the Bibliothèque Nationale in Paris. My researches were before the times of ready microfilming and xeroxing, and it never occurred to me to feed the statistical data from the port books into an adding machine. So we were much in England and learned much from the English people.

From the beginning my work interested R. H. Tawney, then the chief economic historian at the London School of Economics. He was known not only for his tract *The Acquisitive Society,* but also for his part in the so-called Sankey Commission which had conducted a thorough inquiry into Britain's contemporary coal mining industry. Our relations, begun by correspondence in 1922, ripened into friendship. In 1926 Tawney's enthusiasm for a draft of Part III of my book, brought him, with his wife, to spend some days in our apartment in Paris. When they arrived we were packing to go to London, where we had already leased a furnished flat refashioned out of a garage in Rutland Gardens off Knightsbridge. The composition of my book, begun during five months in Vienna and pursued daily during the year in Paris, continued with unabated intensity during the months that followed.

Thanks to the Tawneys and to other English friends, some of whom we had met at the Genoa Conference in 1922, I was no stranger to London's rich intellectual and literary resources. After our first summer at Cap d'Antibes we had passed three extended spells in that fascinating city. We lived in subleased flats, once in North Gate overlooking Regent's Park. There we entertained relatives and friends including the charming and patient Micalacopoulos in whose face my mother-in-law once fell asleep without his taking offense.

One consideration that had led to the early British coal industry was the abundant references to it in manuscripts of the Elizabethan and early Stuart periods. I taught myself to read Elizabethan handwriting and found seemingly endless data on coal and allied subjects in the Archives of London, first and foremost those of the Public Record Office, then those of the British Museum and the Guildhall. It soon became plain that there was also much to learn from collections outside the city. So we began to visit other places. We travelled to Newcastle-on-Tyne, to Durham and to Edinburgh, making "finds" beyond our expectations, and once, in the cause of comparisons with coal mining in continental countries, to Aachen, where the files of an obscure local newspaper showed that coal was dug in the German Wurmrevier at least as far back as the late twelfth century, when the great cathedrals were under construction.

It is perhaps fortunate that my researches were interrupted in the late winter of 1924 when Elinor was taken ill with gall stones. As she recovered slowly from the operation, our physician advised an extended summer vacation for both of us. We spent six weeks on Lake Como, first at a hotel in Bellagio and then more briefly at the Villa d'Este. We used to read More's *Utopia* aloud on rowboat excursions.

It was in the quiet of study in agreeable hotel rooms that I became aware that mere collecting of material was an inadequate preparation for making a book. I must set about to write. Vienna seemed a suitable place to begin, for there I would not be tempted to go back to the archives for further material.

By the time the Tawneys came to Paris, fairly advanced drafts existed for what eventually became the first volume of *The Rise of the British Coal Industry*. My delight in poems, plays, novels and essays (particularly Montaigne's *Essais,* which Katsimbalis' father used to insist should be read only after forty) had never been so strong as at that time. My love of music, born in Vienna, had been nourished and extended by hearing choice performances in Paris. Finally thanks to the purchases we were making, the visual arts had become as essential in our existence as they were in my childhood dreams of a more civilized abode than any found in the guidebooks.

This tripartite nourishment reached its peak just before our departure for London in company with the Tawneys. At about this time there arose throughout Europe optimistic hopes of a renewal of "civilization." [1]

In the Spring of 1926 London gave us the sense of a world that had a place for us. A decade later, shortly before the Second World War, I remember talking with Edwin Hubble about the gift England was capable of bestowing on a young American attracted by a creative career. He spoke with warmth of his three years as a Rhodes Scholar. He put in one word what he found at Oxford that he had missed in the United States. The word was "recognition."

Thanks primarily to Tawney, London made me that gift in 1926. He vouched for me as a coming man of talent with an exceptionally attractive and gifted wife. Those were our credentials. They were accepted generously by a number of distinguished persons who offered us spiritual as well as material hospitality, persons from the academic domain such as Wallas, Salvemini, Clapham, Beveridge, the Hammonds, persons with Manchester Guardian connections such as Wadsworth and Hobson. We had fleeting contacts in the political domain with Lord Sankey, who was then Lord Chancellor, and with Ramsay MacDonald, who had been and was again to be Prime Minister.

These men did not simply grant us meetings in response to conventional introductions; they did not merely allow us to interview them, as Eduard Benes had at the Genoa Conference. They accepted us as younger equals and allowed us to experience a healing sense of intimate communication, without taint of competition, such as is possible between an older generation which has arrived and a younger generation accorded the confidence that it will. When no sense of nationalism intervenes, as was the case at the time, the fact that the young are from a foreign country can contribute to the richness of the relationship.

We found in these eminent men and women an enthusiasm for letters that made my recent reading of Voltaire, *Humphry Clinker*, *Tom Jones* and other absorbing books comprehensible media of exchange. One day at a small dinner in Rutland House, given by our aristocratic neighbor Lady Anstruther, the principal subject MacDonald discussed was Hogarth's place in the history of painting and drawing. Fielding's words—"Oh Shakespeare for thy pen, oh Hogarth for thy pencil"—prepared me for the discussion.

Since our arrival in Europe we had been daily readers of *The Manchester Guardian*. Those were years when C. P. Scott was still issuing his thundering editorials, as he had been doing for half a century. Early on, before we had set foot in England, he came out with a forthright condemnation of Fascism the day after Mussolini's famed march on Rome aboard a railroad carriage. Unequivocally *The Guardian* took the position that il Duce's seizure of power was profoundly dangerous for the future of democracy, a cause to which Wilson had committed the United States in the First World War.

I was struck by Scott's conviction. Such integrity was a kind of passport for distinguished Englishmen, as these appeared in our lives during those four London months. Shortly after we arrived the famous General Strike was declared. While it was still on, a handful of persons came to dinner in our garage-flat. Among them was J. A.

Hobson, a most unorthodox and prolific writer, whom the "economists" would not accept as respectable. He had an American wife and his daughter had married Scott's son. The others were Tawney and A. P. Wadsworth, then labour correspondent and later, years after C. P. Scott's death, editor of *The Manchester Guardian*.

With his liberal background, Hobson was regarded as sympathetic to the Labour Party, then out of office. The Executive Committee of that party bore major responsibility for calling the General Strike and I was surprised when Hobson expressed firm opposition to it. He pointed out that the working people from other trade unions, who had stopped their labor to demonstrate solidarity with the striking coal miners, had *broken their contracts*. The fabric of "civilization," he said, had been woven out of respect for contracts. The issue of honoring an agreement, freely entered into, ought to take precedence over all other issues.

Not long afterwards I witnessed a demonstration of the essential gentleness and humanity of the English character at its best. At a dinner Lord Sankey and his sister gave for about a dozen people, most of them active in politics, he told a story that only one with confidence and hope in the importance of tender manners could have related. He spoke of a visit he had made to Wales as a judge on circuit. The local authorities brought before him a ten year-old culprit, and set about to impress the judge with the basic iniquity of this lad. They said he deserved the harshest of sentences. "He's a thief," they told Sankey. "What has he stolen?" asked the judge. Then, with an air that the enormity of the crime must speak for itself, "Why, Sir," one of them declared, "he stole a pheasant's egg!" Here was a reminder that the effort of spreading the tender manners of the few to the customs of the many is essential to the future of "civilization."

Later the Lord Chancellor, whose house was in Westminster, took us privately into his beautiful garden. It was a mild July evening. He talked of the great Greeks of the fifth and fourth centuries B.C., perhaps the richest period in history for its philosophers, dramatists and historians, whose works I was to appreciate fully some years afterwards. The words "whom the gods love die young," he said, had not for these ancient Greeks the meaning usually attached to them. Whom the gods love die young, however heavy they may be with years.

This idea made a deep impression. It helped me to recognize that a good life could count more not less the older one grows, that, within limits, humans are offered the opportunity to grow younger in spirit the longer they last.

How does one live one's career to the full? Mainly by finding one's last, when it provides an inspiring goal, and sticking to it. If one is to do this one has to make the right refusals. In Europe we had a good training in those. In order not to interfere with scholarly routine in Paris, we refused in the winter of 1926 the invitation to visit Greece at the behest of Micalacopoulos who had become Prime Minister. In order not to interrupt this same routine I renounced in the spring in London, with Tawney's approbation, an attractive invitation to go with Mrs. Tawney to collect money for the wives and children of the striking miners, on a trip that included the tempting prospect of a night in the country with Beatrice and Sidney Webb.

Lest the reader think me "uncharitable," I should add that Elinor accompanied Mrs. Tawney and participated in the collection. Unlike reading, this was a sphere in which my wife *could* do my work. At a tea the Tawneys gave so we would meet older members of the academic profession, I had an opportunity to compare my working habits with theirs. Salvemini and Beveridge were there; they were established authors like the others, including the host. All were in agreement that (as with Trollope in Victorian times) the optimum daily stint of composition over long stretches of time is about four uninterrupted hours. As chairman of a Royal Commission, Beveridge said he had once put in seven hours daily for six weeks and so exhausted himself mentally that it took him nearly six weeks to recover. For my part composition consisted in combining steady hours of writing with intellectual refreshment of the kinds touched upon in these recollections and with short periods when the body takes moderate exercise—such as walking—conducive to leaving the mind fallow. I was finding more time is required for composition than for research. When I started on the history of coal, Tawney asked when I expected to finish. I hazarded a guess, "In six months." "More like six years," he suggested. He was nearer the mark, but even his number turned out to be an underestimate. It took *ten* years! Invariably the problem of dividing time between the search for material and actual composition is a delicate one. It cannot be settled according to a fixed formula; it differs according to the gifts and temperament of the writer, the subjects treated and the conditions under which the materials are gathered. It is the work itself, not the time supposedly available, that must determine the duration.

Years afterwards, when I became a professor, I had a young woman student who chose to read a paper in one of my seminars on Tocqueville. She surprised me by saying he was not a good historian. Why had she passed this judgment? "He tells us so himself," she replied. "Where?" "In his letters," she explained. She said that Tocqueville had worked for only four weeks in the departmental archives at Tours and then had spent three years writing his *L'Ancien Régime et la Révolution*. For this student it was axiomatic that his book could not be very useful if it was derived from such a negligible amount of research.

If a history is to approach a work of art, it is vital to concentrate on the composition and not to allow one's material, particularly one's notes, to get in the way of the story. This does not mean that one has a right to be inaccurate or to rest descriptions on inadequate materials. It does mean that the content and the form are determined by the requirements of the imagination.

Two years of almost exclusive concentration on research concerning the coal industry was probably too long. Fortunately before my book was published I learned to return to the original sources for fresh inquiry such as can be effectively undertaken only after a book has been partly written. Historical composition acquires a dialectic of its own, so that the questions that demand an answer, and the facts required to answer them, frequently cannot be anticipated.

But there is a danger of going to the opposite extreme. Following my research, composition became so habitual that I gave myself no chance during the remainder of those years of European living to reexamine the source materials. In consequence I later had to return to Europe and, with the help of an expert researcher Tawney kindly found for me, reexamine the material after most of the book was in galleys. My own financial resources plus the indulgence of an old publisher, Mr. Stallybrass of Routledge, enabled me to rewrite large portions of the text while it was in proof, as Marcel Proust had done with his novel. Ideally this is not a bad way to prepare a book, for opportunities of improving a text that escape one when it is in typescript appear after it is in proof. But publishers no longer permit such revisions. The cost has become prohibitive and they have lost the patience some once possessed.

Our months in London, full of academic riches and relieved from the teaching routine and the course examinations that often bury the neophite struggling for a degree, were an investment that paid dividends for the rest of my life. Those months also enabled us to continue the purchases of small works of art that have provided so much additional capital. We continued to buy during our last London sojourn, and, after that was over we went in for a buying spree during a final month in Paris.

A contemporary artist whose works danced in my consciousness— along with those of Signac, Derain, Picasso, Matisse, Chagall, Pascin and Dufy—was Dunoyer de Segonzac. It was in those last months in London that we acquired what we have of his.

Among many kindnesses the Tawneys introduced us to Sir Michael Sadler who then presided over University College at Oxford. Tawney had learned of our interest in contemporary art during his stay in our Paris apartment. All four of us had spent a day in Chartres. While Tawney was not primarily a man of artistic tastes, he valued them. He came along with us to the Salle Camondo in the Louvre, and expressed a healthy preference for Cézanne in whose works he found a substance lacking in most other recent painters.

Tawney was pleased to arrange a visit to Oxford to see Sadler's collection. Accompanied by Mrs. Tawney we went up for the day and lunched with Sir Michael and his wife.

We were impressed by their Courbets, a painter we had long admired in French museums. To my confusion I mistook one for a Segonzac. The mistake was pardonable for Sadler's favorite *contemporary* painter *was* Segonzac, who was well represented in his collection. There is, moreover, a kinship between the two masters. My taste for Segonzac, especially for his landscapes, was part of my predilection for those contemporary innovators in the visual arts whose strength lies in their power to translate the novelty of their fancies into forms related to the greatest artistic traditions. That is what I hoped I might manage in a different medium: discover in such original views of the nature of historical evolution as came my way (for the concepts that darted in my mind) forms of historical expression with the cohesion and the substance indispensable to a work of art. Although embarrassed at first over having mistaken a Courbet for a Segonzac, the fact that the confusion had been possible, increased my pleasure in the work of Segonzac.

Not long after this inspection of Sadler's paintings we visited a London dealer, F. M. Turner, at his "Independent Gallery" in Grafton Street. He had some Segonzacs for sale. Our principal purchase was an oil, a moderate-sized canvas called "Green Trees." We also bought a largish drawing of a scene from the Ile de France, and an enchanting series of some fourteen etchings.

Segonzac's oil paintings frequently seem unsatisfactory compared with his drawings and etchings and some of his watercolors. But "Green Trees" does combine, with taste, the living qualities of the landscape with the abstract qualities of paint. It achieves a result which some contemporaries have belligerently sought by suppressing the representational at the cost of human qualities indispensable to beauty.

Cézanne is a supreme master of the kind of perfection in oil painting which combines both. So, hardly less miraculously, is Monet. Dunoyer de Segonzac pursued similar ends in his own way, often with success. A work such as "Green Trees" could never be mistaken for a Cézanne oil, any more than a Pascin could be mistaken for a Cézanne watercolor. "Green Trees" is an authentic and charming picture in a style personal to Segonzac.

Just before the financial crash of 1929 we were coming back from Europe again, where I had spent six months revising my coal book with the help of original documents, and we met Segonzac. This was on one of the last voyages of the famous old Cunard Liner "Mauritania." Segonzac was about to visit the United States to judge the annual Carnegie Show in Pittsburgh and we were introduced. He was most cordial and was pleased to know we had a few of his works. We used to talk at length after lunch with him and an Italian painter colleague also on his way to Pittsburgh.

On the crossing too was a professor of art whom I had known in 1920 and 1921 as a much older fellow member of the Signet Society at Harvard. He was now at New York University and talked the first morning out about academic politics. When he discovered I had been appointed to the University of Chicago, he remarked that Chicago had dealt his university a body blow by taking away the most noted member of their art department, John Shapley, brother of the celebrated astronomer Harlow Shapley.

On one occasion when we were talking to Segonzac and the Italian painter, I became aware that this art professor was continually circling the deck at a brisk pace and rather pointedly, as it seemed, scraping

us as he passed. I assumed he was anxious to be introduced to the
French artist. Eager to be agreeable I stepped aside on his eleventh
or twelfth turn, leaving Elinor with the two painters, and said, "Would
you like to meet Segonzac?" He said, "Who?" "Oh," I replied with
some surprise, "Dunoyer de Segonzac, you know. He is a contemporary French painter of distinction." "John," he said, "my
subject is fifteenth-century Spanish art"—a perfect illustration of
the limitations of specialization.

It should be remarked, however, that this New York professor's
ignorance of contemporary painters was more understandable in 1929
than it would be today. In the twenties Segonzac was still treated
by the conventional French art connoisseurs as hardly less outrageous
than Picasso, or any of the other "living" artists of the Paris school.

In 1960 I tried an experiment to demonstrate the change which
had taken place in the views of French critics over forty years. There
was then a large retrospective exhibition of Dunoyer de Segonzac at
Charpentier, a famous art dealer on the rue du Faubourg Saint
Honoré in Paris. The dealer had assembled something like a hundred
of his works. My friend the late Jean Désy, who had retired as
Canadian ambassador to France, gave a dinner in his apartment in
Neuilly. Among my fellow guests were the head of the Musée de
l'Homme, Roger Hein, and André Chanson, curator of the Petit
Palais who is a member of the French Academy.

The dinner had nothing to do with the Segonzac show, although
that was being discussed in Paris art circles. In the midst of the
splendid food and wines Désy always provided, and during a lull in
the conversation, I asked with the innocence of a boy from the country whether Dunoyer de Segonzac was a good painter. The two
curators of art gazed with surprise mingled with scorn and con-
desension. "He is a *great* painter," they exclaimed in unison.

The contrast with conditions forty years before could hardly
have been more glaring. If at a similar gathering of potentates
I had posed the same question in 1921, or even 1926, the scorn might
have been directed not at me but at Dunoyer de Segonzac!

13. DERAIN'S CALL TO ORDER

Soon after meeting art critic André Salmon, I found that he considered Derain "le regulateur" of the whole movement in con-

temporary painting. Almost from the beginning of the twentieth
century Salmon had been on friendly terms with the group of
artists, living in or near Paris, who knew each other well and influenced each other's work. His judgment of the special place
occupied by Derain was made in a book he published in 1920. The
book set out to evaluate the contributions to beauty of the artists
Salmon had appreciated during the previous twenty years, and
few of distinction had escaped his notice. He called his work
L'Art vivant. (The Dial Folio "Living Art," which had played such
a part in our artistic education, may have borrowed the title.) His
argument, that Derain's leadership had helped the contemporary
painters of the Paris school to achieve more substance and order
than their revolutionary innovations might otherwise have possessed,
carried weight because of Salmon's growing reputation as a critic.

The place Salmon accorded Derain had a special significance for
me. The substance and order I sometimes missed in contemporary
art was what I sought in my own medium. With Derain's canvasses
I felt on safe ground. Might not his leadership be the leadership
I coveted, a leadership I found also in Eliot's poetry and later in
Stravinsky's music and Schnabel's playing of Beethoven, Mozart
and Schubert?

Derain's position as "regulator" had been strengthened by his
work from 1919 to 1926, perhaps the best of his periods. His painting
then took fresh directions which stemmed naturally from some of
his greatest realizations on the eve of the 1914 War, such as the
"Joueur de Cornemuse" and his less known "Last Supper." Frances
Crane Lillie purchased that at the time of her conversion to Roman
Catholicism early in the nineteen-twenties, thereby taking it out of
the channels which bestow publicity on a painting for her interest was
not so much in a work of art as in a contribution to her church.

My preference for Derain's canvasses of the early post-war
period was reinforced by another authority with a wider scholarly
audience than Salmon, a prominent historian of art, Elie Faure.
His pamphlet on Derain, parts of which I set about to translate,
had been published in 1924. This essay told of the struggle Derain
waged within himself to keep in leash his extraordinary facility. That
might have led him (as some find it did later, after the early
nineteen-twenties) to obtain cheap, superficial results. According to
Faure it was as if Derain, during the years of his struggle just before
1914 and just after 1918, tied his hands behind his back to achieve

the depth beyond technique much twentieth-century painting lacks. As a young man he destroyed many pictures he could have sold to advantage. Unlike most of the artists who were his contemporaries, he stopped painting for seven years when he was a soldier, first during his military service at the turn of the century, and then during the war from 1914 to 1918. He did not even sketch for four years, according to Faure. "But the war helped him make discoveries in painting because it helped him make discoveries in himself."

In the same essay Faure wrote: "He does not fear to undergo and even to acknowledge the influence that the masters, including recent masters, have had upon his sensibility." Derain sought a *synthesis* of great painting, not unrelated to my jejune but nevertheless genuine childhood hopes for an ideal art of the future situated in a new found land.

How did we come on our Derains? Now more than forty years later I am told by Marc Chagall that Mazaraki had some fine examples of the post 1918 period. I cannot remember seeing any, though Mazaraki should have known of my special enthusiasm for this painter. He did show, and I bought, a small Derain canvas of a woman's head. While it is interesting it is more an exercise in oil than a work of art, and is probably a sketch for a portrait Derain did later of Madame Moise Kisling.

I used to see occasional examples of Derain's current work in the windows of Paris dealers and in the "Salon des Independants," where many artists later recognized as great then exhibited each year. There in the autumn of 1925 was a beautiful "Vase of Flowers," about twenty by twenty-one inches, Derain had framed as his contribution to that year's show. It struck me as a classic which like all classics, as Sainte-Beuve tells us, breaks from tradition only to reestablish that with fresh authority. At the same time I formed the impression, from some paintings by Derain in dealers' windows, that no contemporary artist could paint a woman as well as he. Since I always preferred women's bodies to men's, these pictures made a great impression on me. It was to his still lifes and his nudes that I was especially drawn, though I have since come to consider some of his landscapes as no less remarkable. Perhaps the finest of these is a late work, a view of Amiens, that took him eight years to complete.[1]

I found it impossible to return to the United States without Derain.

In addition to the one from Mazaraki, we bought five more Derains.

One sunny afternoon during a casual visit to the gallery of Bernheim Jeune in the rue du Faubourg Saint-Honoré, I came almost by accident on the very picture I had been hoping to find. It is the portrait of a woman naked to the waist with beautiful breasts. It is among the most living of all the nudes in oil I have seen across fifty years of time in museums, dealers' shops and private homes in Europe or the United States. Derain appropriately set this extraordinary picture in a massive, magnificent old frame before releasing it for sale.

As with my first purchase of two large Dufy watercolors, it was love at first sight. That is how I bought "Buste de femme," the title given this work. I directed the salesman at Bernheim to deliver it to Potier, the famous packer, to be carefully crated for shipment to the United States.

It is an allusive and mysterious painting, allusive in that it arouses all sorts of delights that are suggested but hardly stated, not least by the background which has a Rembrandt-like quality; mysterious because its effects are radically different as seen from different positions in a room and in different lights. This woman changes her mood as you watch her. It is true of this picture (as it tends to be of Derains in general): either you like what you see greatly or you reject it wholly. Seen to advantage, "Buste de femme" can and has evoked enthusiasm from discriminating judges.

Marc Chagall is by no means a Derain enthusiast but does respect his best works, particularly those prior to the nineteen-thirties. He had seen our six Derains in Chicago on two occasions, but he reassessed them, and reassessed Derain as a painter, when he came recently, in 1968, on his first visit to Evelyn's and my Georgetown house. There he and his wife spent many quiet hours alone with us. One afternoon as he was moving about the large drawing room as he likes to move according to his fancy, he focused his attention on "Buste de femme" with something close to reverence. As he drank in what he saw he muttered to himself, "C'est un chef d'oeuvre" (it's a masterpiece), an expression he has rarely used in the course of our long friendship about the work of a contemporary, and never about a work of his own, whatever may sometimes be his inner satisfaction over some result he has achieved.

The dealer who had supposedly something approaching a monopoly of Derains in the twenties was Paul Guillaume. Some days after the discovery at Bernheim Jeune's I set out for Guillaume's gallery, forgetting what August meant in Paris. His shop was boarded up.

But I refused to abandon the search.[2] I entered a covered alleyway next to the shop, looking for a concierge. In the semi-darkness I was filled with sudden, but brief, dismay by the fall of a heavy squirming object on my back. It turned out to be a huge cat, who clutched fortunately without vicious intent. The scuffle brought the concierge's wife up in a jiffy. I told her we were leaving for America at the beginning of September. She was instantly sympathetic. She gave me Guillaume's address at the Golf Hotel in Beauvallon, and he arranged by correspondence to have us shown all the Derains in his shop by a person later identified as "Madame Castel." He also authorized her to show us the large personal collection of paintings by various recent masters then hung in his apartment at 20, avenue de Messine.

In his shop, to my astonished delight, I found the "Vase de Fleurs" from the 1925 Salon des Indépendants. Next to that was a startingly impressive lifesized bust called "La Grecque." It is painted on wood, another evidence of Derain's profound respect for the ancient masters, manifested early in his career by copies of works by Ghirlandaio. Oil was first used in later medieval times. But through the time of Ghirlandaio (1449-1494) much oil painting was done on wood. Canvas came in extensively only at the very end of the fifteenth century.

These two pictures in Guillaume's gallery so fulfilled my hopes that we decided then and there we would own them. Elinor helped pick out two additional paintings, exquisite but smaller, and both on canvas. One is a portrait of a lady, "Madame C.", with the back of her head resting against the wooden rim of a chair. The other is a singularly harmonious and economical still life of a bowl and pitcher, in browns perfectly blended with creamy waves of white, vibrating with life. We made a bid for all four pictures by telegraph, and the purchase was soon consummated to Paul Guillaume's satisfaction as well as ours.

Concerning the quality of these Derains Guillaume wrote glowingly just after we had departed for New York in September. "You have made a happy choice, and I congratulate you. Le buste (the one on wood) est un des plus beaux et des plus interessants tableaux de Derain, les fleurs sont une rareté. Les deux autres sont delicats . . ." (The bust on wood "is one of the most beautiful and most interesting pictures of Derain, the flowers a rare gem. The two others are delicate.") His words may seem the interested comments of a salesman. That interpretation could be reinforced by the piquant fact that the letter is written on stationary of The Barnes Foundation. Guillaume's influence on the collector and self-appointed critic, **Dr. Albert Barnes,** is suspected to have been often compelling; in any event it was sufficiently strong so that the doctor named one of the rooms in his museum at Merion, Pennsylvania, for this dealer. But Guillaume also managed Derain's affairs, and Barnes apparently detested Derain and all his works. Later after we had visited the Barnes Foundation (as is related in its place), I saw Guillaume for the first time. I spoke of Barnes' attitude towards Derain and he said "it hasn't the slightest significance." Which may suggest that Guillaume was adept at reconciling the irreconcilable.

Nevertheless he *was* more than a salesman. He had serious ideas about aesthetic values, as his earlier association with Guillaume Apollinaire and other artists certifies.[3] Evelyn and I had occasion recently to verify the objectivity of the words Paul Guillaume used in his letter of 1926. His widow later married one of the richest French financiers, Jean Walter. After Walter's death she gave most of what was once Paul Guillaume's personal collection to the French state. It was on exhibition at the Orangerie in 1966. A good deal was familiar from my visit to the apartment in the rue de Messine in 1926. Evelyn shared my impression that our Derains are finer than those Guillaume retained. Indeed we came away wondering whether that personal collection, with many works of famous contemporary artists besides Derain, was not made up of pictures Guillaume had found difficult to sell before his early death.

Derain apparently attached importance to the oils we had acquired. On our way through Paris in 1928 for a summer of work in the village of Les Aldudes (in the Lower Pyrenees) on the last chapters of my coal industry, I wrote to him about them. His reply is dated July 25, 1928. "Je ferai donc pour le mieux pour réparer les tableaux," he wrote in his own hand, "Si vous voulez faites les parvenir à Mr. Paul Guillaume, 59 rue la Boetie, qui s'occupe de toutes mes affaires, qui me les apportera à l'endroit ou je travaille. Vous n'aurez donc rien à vous occuper et je les reparerai selon votre désir." (I will do my best to repair the pictures if you will kindly send them to Mr. Paul Guillaume who takes care of all my business and will bring them to my studio. So there's no need for you to trouble about them and I will mend them in accordance with your wishes.)

Perhaps the pictures or their frames had been slightly damaged in shipping from Paris to Washington.[4] It is not clear in retrospect why I wrote to Derain or why we never availed ourselves of the opportunity provided by his reply. At the time of our correspondence the Derains and some of our other pictures were on exhibit at the Philadelphia Museum of Art. They remained there until early in 1929, when the Philadelphia Museum shipped them to Chicago after I had started professing at the University, and the problem of getting them to Paris and back may have seemed too difficult to cope with.

The motives that prompted my choice of Derain as a *painter* resemble those which led me decades later to buy with Evelyn a Maillol bronze. Both artists succeed in creating "living" art that is original without ceasing to seem natural, inevitable and in the tradition to which great artists have always paid homage. If as is sometimes supposed Derain's was a tortured life, there is nothing in his best works to torture the lover of beauty.

14. FELLOWSHIP WITH VOLLARD

Among the picture dealers of the late nineteenth and twentieth century none has equalled Ambroise Vollard in distinction and fascination. He amassed hundreds of Cézannes when they could be had for next to nothing. He held the first exhibition of that great master's works. Cézanne and Picasso and other first-rate artists found him interesting enough to paint, and Cézanne kept him sitting in a chair on a pedestal so often and for such long stretches that he was always falling asleep and once tumbled—body, chair and pedestal—to the floor. On that occasion Cézanne is said to have ejaculated: "J'aime mieux les pommes; les pommes ne bougent pas." (I prefer apples; apples don't budge.)

Vollard's shop was in the rue Laffitte. But before 1926 he had given up the profession of picture dealing, and had established himself along with his treasures in a large mansion on the Left Bank, across from the nineteenth-century church of Sainte-Clotilde, at 28 rue de Martignac. He was willing to sell items from his bountiful, casually-arranged collection, but according to his humors. These were not lacking in justification nor sometimes in eccentricity. As he could now live handsomely for a year on the proceeds of two or three sales, he was never in a hurry. He took three months to clear the small payment on a Paris bank we were to make him. When I called the delay to his attention he asked, "Do you imagine that every time I get a check I clamp on my bowler and head for the bank?"

He had been a material supporter of a number of struggling artists of genius and talent who came of age around 1900. He advanced them enough money to live, against a portion of their work. Some of these artists—notably Rouault—left Vollard with paintings, water-colors and plates on the understanding that these should remain in his hands for them to retouch. And Rouault was often in even less of a hurry to finish than Vollard was to sell. He held back for something like forty years what became his *Miserère* Album. Rouault was in his eighties when the prints were finally run off and released. The huge volume weighed about seventy pounds as I know from first-hand experience. A copy designated for Rouault's old friends, the Jacques Maritains, was entrusted to me. Rouault's daughter, Isabelle, brought it to my hotel in Paris and I carried it by boat and auto-mobile all the way to Princeton, where the Maritains were living.

Early in the century Vollard had many dealings with Picasso. As I have never met Picasso the best way I have of introducing such a formidable figure in the history of art is through my acquaintance with Vollard. Picasso had done, independently of Vollard and for another dealer, what has become the most famous of all series of twentieth-century etchings, fifteen or so in all. The first and prob-ably the greatest of the series, "Le Repas frugal," was etched in 1904; the others in 1905. After Picasso had finished the plates, prints were pulled and signed by the artist, a few of the signatures etched into the plates. Vollard soon bought the plates. After almost a decade he had further prints run off in 1913. These are not numbered and no one seems to know how many examples exist.

The series has become legendary. A book devoted mainly to it and published early in the nineteen-thirties was soon out of print. The book eventually sold for much more than Vollard asked us for the set of fourteen original etchings in 1926.

Months before we had begun to look at Picasso oils. But our means were small and the prices asked always disproportionately large com-pared with those we were paying for other acquisitions, and even compared with the sums we were later to pay for Segonzacs and Derains. So we were disposed, in one way, to put Picasso's paintings

in the realm with those of Cézanne and Renoir: works of art we
would have treasured if we could have afforded them. Yet, in another
way, I was unable to put Picasso's oils in the same class as Cézanne's,
or even (which will no doubt shock many readers) as Renoir's.
Actually I preferred Derain's or even Segonzac's best oils to those of
Picasso, except for some of his very early period, 1903-1906, which
were already practically unobtainable.

I remember a short expedition Elinor and I made earlier to a
gallery in the rue la Boetie where the dealer was supposed to have a
monopoly of Picasso's output. As we entered the shop my mind was
not on painting. As usual pictures of historical development were
going round in my head as the result of a morning of composition.

We looked at some recent oils by "the Spaniard," as Chagall calls
him. They were most entrancing episodes in color as well as line.
As we looked we became aware someone was standing behind us. It
turned out to be the famous dealer who owned the shop.

Paul Rosenberg began to expatiate on Picasso's genius. He said,
"You know Picasso is the greatest genius of our times." I now
recognize that for some serious critics this remark is defensible. Yet it
struck me that afternoon as hopelessly excessive. "He does these
things in an hour," said the dealer, pointing to the beautifully colored
canvasses we were looking at. "He works only a few hours a day and
turns out a stupendous number of pictures." "What does he do
the rest of the time?" I asked. "He thinks," Rosenberg answered.

The answer now seems a good one. It should have seemed so
then, for I was already experiencing the refreshment that can come
when the mind lies fallow. Nevertheless, that day the dealer's reply
struck me as fatuous. We asked the price of the two oils and excused
ourselves for leaving the gallery.

So it was with no idea of buying Picassos that we gained admittance to Vollard's house on that August day in 1926. We wanted
to meet Vollard, to learn from him more about "living art" and
about artists, living and recently dead, whose work had come to
fascinate us, work which he knew as a whole perhaps better than
anyone alive. How Elinor gained access I cannot remember, but
I remember vividly our entrance from the street into the spacious
ground floor that apparently served as a kind of storeroom. The first
impression of rather ill-lit disorder was immediately forgotten in the
wonder of several beautiful statues by Renoir. Until that moment

I had not known he was a sculptor but instantly recognized his sculpture from an extensive acquaintance with his paintings.

Another feature of that ground floor was a finely polished "batterie de cuisine," a display of kitchen utensils such as might appear in a Chardin or a Derain. We learned later that Vollard was an inveterate gourmet of the kind that were born and raised only in France. We learned at once he was a charming and accommodating host. But since we had entered without an invitation and unannounced, he asked us to return the next afternoon. He then showed pleasure in our youth and our interests. So far as I remember almost all his pictures were stowed away instead of hung on walls. He seemed always to have to go and fetch from some hidden depository such canvasses as he chose to show. He was reported to have paintings by all the great masters of the late nineteenth century, many scores of Cézannes and dozens of Renoirs, at that time the two modern artists whose works excited us most. He freely showed some of their masterpieces, remarking that he did so only because he knew we couldn't afford them.

The conversation waxed. Vollard told stories about Cézanne, and his early problem of selling that great artist's pictures thirty years or so before, when people with our means could have afforded to buy some of the best canvasses. One story concerned a German collector who came to the shop in the rue Laffitte asking to see some Cézanne watercolors. He fixed on one and asked the price. After reflecting about an hour he decided not to buy, declaring the picture was "unfinished." "Why do you think so?" Vollard asked, for he saw no reason to suppose that Cézanne had abandoned the work prematurely. "Il y a trop de blanc" (There's too much white), the collector observed.

Some six years later during a trip to Berlin not long before 1914, Vollard called on this client in his apartment. He was surprised to find among the pictures the very watercolor the man had rejected. Vollard remembered he had sold it to a dealer a couple of years after that rejection for three times the sum he had asked this client. But he did not betray his recognition. He remarked instead that it was a fine watercolor. "How did you get it?" he inquired. With a show of pride the German told him and named the price—ten times what it would have cost if he had bought it from Vollard in the first place.

Vollard gave us a sense of participating in his world. Learning I was an historian and that my wife too was something of a writer, he picked out and inscribed to us several paper covered books which he had written and published. One was his account of Cézanne which I was to read and treasure.

We became anxious not to leave without making a purchase. Elinor asked Vollard if we could see the Rouault etchings he was reported to have. He explained he couldn't sell them because he had promised Rouault not to.

Later we introduced the subject of those early Picasso etchings. We could see instantly that Vollard had decided to let us have them. A tall, large boned man, well filled out as became a gourmet, he rose from his chair and strode from the room. After some minutes he returned with a large album. Laying this on a table he began examining the prints. He tore one to shreds and threw the scraps in the fire before we could remonstrate. "What are you doing?" was our startled question as the flames consumed the paper. "Je ne vends pas ça" (that's one I don't sell) was all Vollard said and I have never known what he chose to suppress. This is why I spoke of *fifteen* etchings. And that is how we came to own *fourteen*.

The set we purchased seems to be complete. Though I have seen in museums and private homes and in the retrospective of Picasso's original prints exhibited at the Bibliothèque Nationale a decade ago, etchings pulled from the 1904-1905 plates, I cannot remember any which is missing in our set.

During the years immediately following, we purchased further black and white Picassos. The most remarkable was a drawing relieved with white gouache on blue paper, entitled "Femme Assise." Elinor bought it in New York from Felix Wildenstein shortly after I had taken my first academic post at Swarthmore College and was learning to teach and to combine teaching with working. Wildenstein was about to hold at Paul Rosenberg's shop on Fifth Avenue an exhibition of many Picasso drawings. In New York for only a day, Elinor persuaded Wildenstein to let her see them before the opening. She had her pick and chose well—a kind of female Moses seated in an ample armchair. It was probably done in 1923,[1] a fine example of what has sometimes been called Picasso's classical period.

One morning more than thirty years later, after Elinor had died, T. S. Eliot and his wife Valerie were sitting on the sofa in my Chicago apartment facing a battery of newspaper reporters firing questions.[2] One of the few amiable ones, prompted presumably by the presence of this classic drawing on the wall behind the sofa, was "What do you think of Picasso, Mr. Eliot?" That picture perfectly illustrated his reply: "Picasso is a great artist," Eliot said. "But before taking liberties, he was a superb draftsman."

This draftsmanship appears too in the other original prints added after our return to Chicago, mostly purchased in the late twenties or early thirties from Alice Roullier.[3] She then had a fine gallery of contemporary art. She used to replenish her prints every year on trips to Paris where she had excellent connections with the dealers. It was in this way that we acquired a cubist "L'Homme à la guitare" and a "Gravure au burin sur cuivre," done in 1915. There are two versions of this and we have the second. Also two beautiful classical prints—"Les trois baigneuses III," an etching done in 1922-23, and a lithograph of 1924—"Femme couchée." Finally we also bought Picasso's etching of a woman's head of 1925 and a "collage" ("Abstraction en Noir") of uncertain date.

While we loved these pictures from the start, I could not bring myself for some years to regard Picasso as one of the great artists of the past two centuries. My mind suddenly changed in 1932, when in the midst of the Great Depression Elinor and I took a summer trip to France. On the road to Paris we learned that there were two special exhibitions that summer, an official one, a retrospective of Manet held in the Orangerie, and a private enterprise. Some Paris dealers had arranged a Picasso retrospective of about 150 pictures in the Galerie Georges Petit. There were almost no tourists in Paris at this depressed time and so no crowding. I went to both exhibits supposing that Manet was a *great* artist and Picasso was not.

The experience brought an unexpected reversal more convincing than surprising. Picasso seemed much the greater artist of the two. I remain a strong admirer in spite of some revulsion over his cheap works. But not a blind admirer. Rather a shocked admirer. Evelyn and I recently saw an exhibit of the canvasses Picasso had just provided for the town of Colmar and thought them totally unworthy.

Among Picasso's most ardent admirers is Madame Marie Cuttoli, long a leading patron of painters who were her contemporaries for she has reached a great age. Elinor and I had entertained her in Chicago when she was a refugee during the 1939 War and had got to know and like her. Evelyn and I renewed the acquaintance after our marriage. Since the war she has lived with Professor Henri Laugier, who worked under UNESCO on behalf of human rights and whom I also knew. They had a magnificent collection of nineteenth and twentieth century paintings, many now given to the State. Most of their collection once hung in the house she used to own in the rue de Babylon in Paris, but some pictures remained in the villa they still have at Cap d'Antibes. There the principal works are Picassos. One day in 1966, when Evelyn and I were lunching with them, Laugier declared with the enthusiastic violence characteristic of his conversation that Picasso is unequivocally the greatest artist who ever lived. I looked somewhat dubious and said, "I would not go quite so far." "Who is greater?" he shot back. I thought a bit and said, "Well, Rembrandt." "Oh, he is not even in the same class," Laugier answered decisively.

I could never be so decisive over anything. I *have* sensed, through my own experience and through the experience of my two wives, an enormously powerful strain in Picasso. For me, nevertheless, above greatness are humanity and love. Picasso has been touched by both, but too often he has evaded them.

Neither had escaped Vollard.

15. FINALE TO THE EUROPEAN ADVENTURE

For a short while during the summer of 1926 we lived in a pleasant upper-story apartment at 5 Square du Trocadéro, a *cul de sac* on a hill in Passy above the valley of the Seine.

Our apartment offered excellent facilities for assembling and packing the belongings we had acquired. These included household linen, silver and ornaments. But the main thing was the pictures that were becoming an essential part of life. In addition to those mentioned already, others less substantial had come into our hands at almost no cost. We had a lithograph of Matisse, two lithographs of Dufy, a Boilly print of three men shaving, and also two exquisite small colored lithographs of Marie Laurencin. We had an additional drawing of a girl by Pascin and one of his lithographs, both acquired from Pierre Loeb, as is attested by a receipt scribbled in Loeb's handwriting August 24, 1926, on the stationary of the Grand Café de la Rade in Toulon. ("Earlybirds," like Loeb and Paul Guillaume, were now moving south for their summers.)

We had also an etching by Pascin's first wife, Hermine David, a night club scene of the then glamorously notorious *Boeuf sur le toit*[1] in the rue Boissy d'Anglas, a haunt of Jean Cocteau. In addition there were a number of pictures we had bought mainly to please our Greek friends, especially Mazaraki, and without making any consequential outlay. On one occasion Georges Katsimbalis took us to visit a Greek artist of the period named Galanis, who had asked to meet us. He was knowledgeable, a man of taste. "A good engraver," Chagall calls him. We carried away a number of his charming woodcuts. I often wish we had pursued this acquaintance for that afternoon was memorable. It gave me, as did my meetings with Photiadès, the feeling of sympathetic kinship with artists, at a time when my longing to be an artist had begun.

A favorite painter of Mazaraki's at that period was a Central European named Menkès. Elinor and I never saw him, but Mazaraki was always putting his canvasses under our noses. Finally getting no response, he gave us one in desperation.

As a result of Mazaraki's friendship with Geneviève Gallibert, we used frequently to see her. In the course of our last year in Paris we bought several small pictures of hers. Later Mazaraki was to live his last years with her in a stunningly situated villa overlooking the Riviera from Vence. Gallibert is now apparently coming into her own. A large book devoted to her works has just been published. In it we find the portrait in watercolor of a stalwart peasant, a portrait I have owned for forty-five years. We have several other watercolors, particularly those of Paris scenes. Gallibert caught the old French taxicabs of my youth as no other artist was able to do. These had played a considerable rôle in my artistic education. Huddled in a rug given us for our marriage by a concerned Irish couple in Chicago, who thought (not inaccurately) that we might freeze in Europe, Elinor and I used them frequently both in Montpellier and later in Paris. On some of these excursions I was reminded of the midnight sorties Proust used to make when Paris was in bed. Heavily bundled he had his taxi drive to the Ile de la Cité so he could peer at the spires of Notre Dame Cathedral, that "ship anchored in the Seine." [2]

Our Galliberts were the purchases of youthful friendship. She has an attractive way that makes her work unmistakable. Few critics would deny her talent, even if you regard it as small. She has pursued steadily and consistently the *métier* she adopted, along with her slightly older and greater contemporaries.

The pictures were available for reexamination in that Passy apartment. Through each purchase and acquisition, whether minor or the fruit of long consideration, we could recapitulate the adventures of five years abroad.

There were too many pictures to hang. Potier packed them into a series of boxes. Along with other baggage, these were confided to the French Line and loaded at Le Havre in the hold of the *Paris*, the ship that had carried us from New York in 1921.

On the boat train we found ourselves in the same compartment with a middle-aged Frenchman who introduced himself as Pierre Aubert. He was in the iron and steel business, a man of progressive ideas who had already conceived and was doing all he could to bring about what became, much later, the Common Market. Aubert adopted us then and there. He was our constant companion on the ship. Also aboard the *Paris* was a group of distinguished French academics. Their journey to participate in an international convention of philosophy scholars in Cambridge, Massachusetts, was being sponsored by the French government. In the delegation were Monsieur Lapie, then President of the University of Paris, Lévy-Bruhl, the anthropologist with a world-wide reputation for his study of the primitive mentality, and Célestin Bouglé, the Director of the leading Paris institute for training in the higher learning, the Ecole Normale Supérieure.

Aubert had the idea of bringing the two "promising" young Americans as he regarded us, into communion with these ripened French scholars. So he gave a dinner. The only place secluded enough was the "salle à manger des enfants." Few children were crossing and those who were dined early. So the small room reserved for them was empty from eight till midnight. It provided a setting for new associations. Bouglé became a steady acquaintance; we entertained him three years later when he came to the University of Chicago to receive an honorary degree, and thereafter we used to call on him in Paris.

Lévy-Bruhl came to see us in our small flat in Washington, where we lived almost a year. He exuded scholarship and good will. The only trouble was that he insisted on conversing in *English*, a language in which he classed himself as adept. While my French was more imperfect then than now, Elinor had gone to school as a child in Lausanne and had taught French in two high schools. She handled the language with immense facility and intuitive comprehension. Lévy-Bruhl, whose English was not unintelligible, proved totally incapable of grasping our meaning when we put our ideas and views before him in English as he insisted. He didn't demonstrate the cliché of understanding better than he spoke. He spoke better than he understood.

Someone has said that to acquire a second language is to acquire a new soul. That can be true provided one thinks and even dreams in the second language and provided one approaches matters of concern (whether large or small) in terms of one's adopted country no less readily than in terms of one's own. Fortune enabled me to return many times to France with these assets, and with a third even more important to the international understanding humanity so needs today. I went not as a representative of any particular interest, but as a private person invited by French scholars. No one who is sent abroad as a diplomat or financed by a university of his own country can acquire as readily a world point of view.

Our pictures were naturally part of our conversation that night on the *Paris*. We suggested to the Frenchmen that they might see them on the dock where we expected the boxes would be opened by the customs officials. As it turned out we were unable to share this pleasure with these French "philosophers." They had diplomatic passports and were hustled off the ship ahead of the rest of us.

We had heard dreadful tales about customs inspection and feared the worst. We declared everything. Imagine our relief when the inspector informed us that the pictures, as original works of art for which we had vouchers, were not subject to duty. This added to our pleasure in seeing them for the first time since they had been packed. The culminating joy was the expression on that inspector's face when he opened the crate which Potier had fashioned for Derain's "Buste de femme" in its antique frame. He was not prepared for what he saw.

The painting is always changing its impact. The effect of surprise can be staggering, as it was on Chagall more than forty years later. This was such an occasion. The picture captured the best in that inspector, and I found this confirmation by another human altogether untutored in the contemplation of works of art most reassuring. It gave me confidence in the country to which we were returning.

The confidence was compromised, however, by what we learned long afterwards from Pierre Aubert. He had not been allowed to land until the next morning, and so missed our exhibition on the dock. The immigration officials who went aboard invoked a rule to the effect that if a ship docked after 8 p.m., all foreign passengers must spend the night on board. The *Paris* actually docked at 7:50 p.m.

This was the Prohibition Era, with its "speakeasies," that Pascin had described by a few pencil strokes on the back of the menu at the Trianon. According to Aubert the immigration officers insisted on having the best brandy the ship's cellar could provide. They drank themselves into an unpleasant state, and some foreign passengers took to their rooms to avoid incidents.

Our friendship with Aubert was renewed twelve months after that disembarkation. He came to stay with us for a weekend in Swarthmore, Pennsylvania, and saw our pictures for the first time. On that occasion he was again disillusioned. When he went to mass Sunday morning in the adjoining town of Chester, the service seemed to him to lack the enriching reverence he expected. He was shocked in the most sensitive part of his being, the spiritual part.

Happily he kept his faith in us, for we admired his ideas. He was certainly a man of the future insofar as the Common Market is concerned; a "Jean Monnet manqué" (a premature Jean Monnet).

We entered a strange country when we disembarked. Sensitive, gifted Elinor was never able to adjust herself. She expressed her distress on the very first night in a New York hotel, where we lost no time before sleeping together. In becoming part of one another for the first time after our return, we found all the magic Europe had accustomed us to receive, the repeated magic that had had so much to do with the rich lives we had led everywhere we settled.

She expressed astonishment that this could happen in America. "Do people feel happy like this over here? Do they sleep together?" she asked incredulously as we lay entwined in the aftermath of our joy. The contrast between the atmosphere of Europe in that tranquil summer of 1926, and the noisy, hustling United States seemed to her overwhelmingly tragic.

The sad impression from this first contact was never erased, although she threw herself into the life we were to make together in America with all the zeal and charm and intelligence that were part of her nature. Her gifts for writing and entertaining and conversing (for which she had a kind of genius) seemed to grow. Our life became in essential ways even sweeter; our unions often more wondrous, as this first night of lovemaking foreshadowed. Yet she never managed to recover the inner hope and assurance that years abroad had bred.

As time passed a form of paranoia entrenched itself in her inner life. It led her eventually to take extreme precautions to protect our food, to insure that her increasingly voluminous writings were not read, to assure that our intimate conversation was not captured by sound recorders and that we were not both asphyxiated during sleep. The origins of this illness went back to her girlhood before we had met, as I discovered after her death from a terrified letter in her correspondence—a letter written in San Francisco when she was fifteen or less.

The months and years after our return much increased the hidden terrors she felt for many of her contemporaries and extended the terrors far beyond the borders of the United States. Nowhere she soon believed could either of us be safe. Except for myself and a few others whom she drew to her heart, she trusted no one. Her trust in me was greater even than it had become abroad and she also extended the circle of the "honest people" (as she called them) to include new friends we were destined to make. She trusted us partly because she saw our eyes as closed. None of us were sharp enough to grasp the extent of the evil intention of "the others," so obvious to her. She found us simply too naive, too hopeful, to recognize the plot against all "honest people" that stared her in the face.

She was too cautious openly to betray these convictions. They were confided fully only to me, and on bits of paper which she immediately burned. She lived a most active life and it was not difficult for me, who held the key, to forget her suffering and, because of it, to take comfort in the lucidity of her mind, the delicate sensitiveness of her heart, and in her total loyalty to those she trusted, first and foremost to me. She was absolutely sure of her ground and completely convinced of the "dishonesty" of anyone who suggested she needed psychiatric treatment.

In a symbolic sense, her dismay stemmed from the mechanized world humanity was entering; evidence of this was then more obvious in the United States than in Europe. Her dismay contained premonitions of the new terrors that have come to threaten humankind before my time is up. Indeed the very conditions she tried to protect us from existed already in Soviet Russia and Fascist Italy; they were soon to entrench themselves in especially revolting forms in Nazi Germany and most of Central Europe. Other countries, including the United States, especially in the so-called "McCarthy Era" of the early 'fifties, were not to escape the threat of such horrors.

If that threat seems to have receded during the late 'fifties and much of the 'sixties, nevertheless the world is faced as we enter the 'seventies with dangers to human existence such as our ancestors (for all their overwhelming trials) never confronted. Elinor used to whisper, "after I am gone you will see that I was right." If we regard what she dreaded as symbolic, her fears *were* prophetic. While the "plot" against "the honest people" has not succeeded in the United States in ways she depicted long before Orwell, the need to have "honest people" more effective than they have ever been before has now become overwhelming.

16. HUSBANDING RESOURCES

Some years ago when Deborah Trzyna (then our secretary and the exceptionally bright young wife of a State Department officer) began taking down notes which became a sketch for these early chapters, what puzzled her was whence came the money to sustain all this activity abroad? She finally asked the question point blank.

It reminded me that my compatriots are often less interested in the nature of things they encounter than in the ways of finding the means which makes it possible to provide these things. Products which are unclassifiable, as well as standardized commodities which supply mass markets, frequently excite curiosity less for themselves than for the ways they are paid for. These ways affect the value society attaches to the products of the mind and even to those of the heart.

Plenty of examples of this state of opinion came before Mrs. Trzyna asked her question. Some years after Elinor and I returned from Europe we were spending an evening with old friends in Honolulu. Over the desk in the husband's study was a large photograph of the Cathedral of Notre Dame. This marvelous building had a fascination for me since childhood. With its walls, flying buttresses and towers, seen from the rear with the Seine flowing past, it resembled a vast ship waiting to hoist anchor. I told my friend how I felt. He heard me out patiently and then declared: "What would interest *me* is how was it financed?"

A generation afterwards I was invited by the College of St. Thomas in Houston, Texas, to deliver the annual Smith Lecture in history. In his introduction Father Murphy, the President of the College, mentioned that my first book had been *The Rise of the British Coal*

Industry. He said quite a lot of flattering things and referred to other books of mine. My lecture was devoted to the importance of religion in the evolution of "civilization." [1]

Passing through Washington some weeks later I was stopped in the Mayflower Hotel by a man I had never seen. He said he had been in the audience in Houston and would like to talk about the lecture. Delighted I turned a willing ear. But all that weighed on this gentleman's mind was that book on the British coal industry. "What I want to know is this:" he said, "did John L. Lewis pay for it?"

The reply to his question, and to Mrs. Trzyna's, is that the money came from inherited wealth; from stocks and some bonds. I was not left destitute by my father: he willed me enough to cover the expense of my education, and I actually earned what was for those times a tidy amount during my first year of graduate study at Harvard. I married an heiress to one of many small fortunes acquired in the Hawaiian Islands by the few men who, beginning in the mid-nineteenth century, had founded the principal business firms that are still operating. With headquarters in Honolulu these have expanded and prospered and some have many subsidiaries. In her case the parent companies were Castle and Cooke, a firm founded by her grandfather, and Alexander and Baldwin, in which the once large Castle family had substantial interests.

It was Elinor's wish that I share her wealth and I had no prejudice against doing so. Far from preventing me from setting to work, the increased income enabled me to become an enthusiastic and daily writer before and also after I became a professor. Beginning in September 1927, when I was given my first teaching appointment I received, in addition to what is classified by the tax regulations as "unearned income," a modest university salary every month until my retirement in 1965. I was then granted the small pension professors emeritus are entitled to.

Although she had a good head for business when she put her mind to it, Elinor had no sustained interest in financial affairs. She was an observer and writer. It was her wish that I should manage her money as well as mine without the advice of investment counselors. So I took care of these holdings as best I could. Down to the late nineteen-forties I managed with little professional help. Then I met, in 1948, a brilliant Chicago attorney, Thomas Hoban Alcock, who has become an increasingly staunch friend and advisor. While I always made, until my marriage to Evelyn, the financial decisions, I never gave major

attention to them and certainly never let the management of invest-
ments interfere with my work.

A good deal has been heard in recent decades in the United States
of the value of a "free society." Among the liberties envisaged, one
might suppose, would be the opportunity inherited wealth provides for
the choice of an independent career not determined by the give and
take of the market place. The past is not without examples to suggest
that such independence can be constructive for society. Certainly in
the matter of creative art, not least of literature and particularly of
poetry, the need to sell in order to make a living has often been more
of a handicap than a help. Both Virginia Woolf and E. M. Forster
tell us that most earlier English writers (and practically all English
poets) had at least small independent incomes to sustain them. It was
so sometimes in connection with the art of painting. Cézanne could
never have lived on the sale of his pictures; he might have been forced
to abandon his career had it not been for the "rentes" (government
bonds) his father provided during an age of stable prices.

When we became friends, T. S. Eliot told me he had recognized early
that if he were obliged to live on such income as he could derive from
his poems and essays, he would be forced to release work unworthy
of him. (It is well known that much of his writing required relentless
revision.) That was why he got a job in Lloyds Bank and later a post
with the publishing house of Faber and Faber. These assignments enabled him to sustain himself and his first wife. What is more important for his art they enabled him to write as his inner summons demanded. Lady Rothermere subsidized *The Criterion,* which he made
one of the most creatively influential magazines of this century.

What has puzzled me, in view of the immense resources in profits,
dividends and interest, is why it should be so frequently assumed in the
United States that in the creative life what can be sold or supported by
large foundations alone has value. One is only a professional worker
with the mind when what one turns out is paid for by publishers and
other dealers, by business or labor enterprises, by foundations or by
government departments and agencies. When the author pays for his
own work he is working, as was once suggested to me by an income tax
employee, "for his own edification." When my first wife, who never
received money for writing, died with a book on the stocks, a local
reviewer in Chicago made much of the argument that the book (part

of which I edited and published) should never be reviewed because Elinor was not a "professional writer."

Money has freed me to do work I believe in. This advantage became apparent during my five year apprenticeship abroad. It continued in the choice of subjects and the manner of composing all the books and articles I have since published.[2]

The same freedom helped me to found an interdisciplinary department at the University of Chicago, and the still more recently established Center for Human Understanding. The University largely financed the interdisciplinary faculty, but, apart from its help, money for these adventures was not forthcoming from any of the usual channels, academic, foundational or governmental; it came from inherited wealth, my own and that of a few friends.

The routes I was impelled to follow never found a place on established maps for a career in the higher learning. It is perhaps suggestive that I matriculated at Harvard as an "*unclassified* student." My apprenticeship in Europe again unclassified me. After I entered the academic profession with a doctors degree from an unconventional school—the Robert Brookings Graduate School—I was once more unclassified: an unorthodox historian who became a member of an economics department. I unclassified myself, for good and all, by founding and managing the first interdisciplinary faculty in any university.

My old friend, the late André Siegfried, used to define a "vacation" as the condition under which one works at what one likes. External recognition is an important even a vital stimulus. But without the inner fire of profound desire it cannot sustain the non-conforming initiative that independent resources protect in a truly "free society."

PART III

Discoveries

17. RETURN TO THE UNITED STATES

Why did we come back?

Our return was not caused by material necessity. Still less by disillusionment with life abroad. We had never been so well off—materially, physically, intellectually, socially and spiritually—as when we loaded our cargo, hoisted anchor and steamed back to the States. The answer to this capital question has a bearing on this entire autobiography for it was not the first time, nor was it the last, I changed route in the midst of what seems, looking back, like a high road to comfortable "success."

There was little in the advice received at Harvard before our departure for Europe late in 1921 to prompt our return. Among those I consulted was Archibald Cary Coolidge, "Archie" as he used to be affectionately called, the rich middle-aged bachelor who directed the Widener Library and covered eastern Europe in the History Department. He enthusiastically applauded my plan to marry and study in Europe. "Go abwaad," he urged with the attractive lisp characteristic of the Boston Coolidges of his generation, "and stay as long as you can. I stayed ten years. I should pwobably never have weeturned if an uncle hadn't come and forced me to pack."

Unlike Coolidge I had no family and Elinor's family sent no representative in pursuit. There were American precedents for a writing career abroad. Henry James, Edith Wharton, T. S. Eliot all achieved a secure reputation in the United States partly because of advantages that residence in Europe provided.

One may wonder whether Eliot would have held a commanding position in letters so soon if he had returned to America before 1920 when *The Sacred Wood* was first published and he entered his thirty-second year. After all *Poetry* magazine printed "Prufrock" in 1915 mainly because Ezra Pound, who admired it, had a reputation with the Editor, Harriet Monroe. Little was made of the poem in the United States in those days. Afterwards "The Death of Saint

Narcissus," another of Eliot's early poems, the first lines of which anticipate "The Waste Land," was "killed" in proof by the editors of *Poetry*.[1]

In the early encounters we had with art and scholarship, however, I never dared think of myself as a man of letters and would easily have swallowed the income tax collector's view that I was working "for my own edification." The decision to return to the United States was not sudden. Actually neither of us had ever thought of staying permanently abroad. The only question was when we should come back. Elinor wanted me to be a professor and I wanted to be one.

I had an exalted idea of what being a professor could mean. It appeared as an opportunity to serve humankind. My father used to talk about a consideration that led him into chemistry—the opportunity he saw to reduce human suffering through the discovery of new knowledge. He had gone from Harvard to graduate research in Munich in the eighteen-eighties with the intention of being a physician, but had come to think he could be of greater service as an experimental scientist. Instead, for example, of treating as a doctor particular cases of pneumonia, he aimed, as a scientist, to uncover some hidden principle of chemical behavior that would lead to the conquest of the disease destined to kill my mother prematurely at the age of 49.

While I had no such specific objective as the conquest of pneumonia, I assumed that a university was where one searched for basic truths about society the discovery of which would lead to better relations among human beings. This assumption was strengthened by encounters with a special kind of Englishman of whom Tawney, Hobson and Wallas were personifications.

After our return to the States a stalwart moral force of Wallas' generation, the then prominent sociologist L. T. Hobhouse died. In connection with his going Tawney wrote: "Knowledge is such an excellent thing in itself that one has no right to ask for more." The words suggest a confidence that existing conditions lead towards the increasing use of knowledge for good. That confidence was still in evidence as late as the nineteen-twenties. Yet at this very time it was being undermined by the influence of such brilliant Bloomsbury figures as Maynard Keynes, whose sense of moral values was nearer that of a Renaissance Italian than of some Victorian Englishman, and by materialists, like another Englishman I met in Washington in

1927, who remarked that moral values were no doubt worthy ornaments but you couldn't eat them.

The period in Western Europe and North America during which faith prevailed in man's capacity to guide societies in the direction of the good, so that scientific discoveries would be used to construct rather than to destroy, was shortlived. Our ancestors down to the sixteenth and seventeenth centuries had hardly possessed that faith. It developed during the seventeenth and eighteenth centuries and was already beginning to wane in the early twentieth century.

Not long after our return we had dinner in Baltimore with a Boston couple. I had known the husband at Harvard. He was interning at Johns Hopkins on his way into medical practice. Remembering the reason my father had given for studying medicine, I asked if it wasn't a satisfaction to be serving humans as a doctor, and was astonished to learn that such a motive had nothing to do with his choice of a profession. The idea had never occurred to him. As we soon discovered the assurance of a certain income was likelier to be the motivating force behind any career, including an academic one.

Many will find me naive in believing that contributions to knowledge could have moral value, as well as in supposing that the First World War could have been (indeed still could be) "a war to end war." The twin ideas were my guiding stars.

In 1926 the first seemed to point the way back to the United States. What I remembered of my relations at Harvard with distinguished professors and even more of our connections at the University of Chicago through both our families, suggested the pursuit of knowledge for its own sake would count for good more in the United States than elsewhere. Chance offered an exceptional opportunity. The Robert Brookings Graduate School was a new venture in higher education where red tape had not yet had time to impede indepen'dent study and writing.

Fortune helped us to achieve rapidly a respectable niche in the American academic structure. The small Brookings Graduate faculty in Washington, all of whom professed in a small residential house almost next door to the home of Justice Holmes, encouraged me to present as a thesis my developing book on the British coal industry. It was unfinished in the sense that the pictures Rouault left with Vollard were unfinished. The Brookings faculty manifested a confidence in this work analogous to that Vollard showed in Rouault's. They enthusiastically accepted as a dissertation the draft that was then available.

My final examination for the doctor's degree came in the spring of 1927, hardly nine months after our arrival in New York harbor. Harold Moulton, who had left the Economics Department of the University of Chicago to direct Robert Brookings' educational enterprises (transferred soon after his appointment from St. Louis to Washington) had a weakness for my attractive wife which did me no harm. She had been a pupil in one of his classes at Chicago, and he was enthusiastic about our career abroad. He was president of what became the Brookings Institution, and though not a practicing member of the staff at the Graduate School, participated as was his privilege in my examination. By good luck he got into a controversy with another examiner, an economist from Columbia University, over a point in economic theory that had nothing to do with the questions addressed to me. They thrashed over the matter for almost an hour to their mutual satisfaction. And to mine. I sat back, caught my breath, and eventually acquired a relaxed confidence and pleasure in finding I had for the first time a captive audience of seven who were obliged to listen attentively to what I wanted to say about European history.

The ceremonies awarding the degree were postponed that year from June until September. In the meantime I was free to buckle down wholly to rewriting my coal book. The boiling Washington heat (when we lived in a top floor apartment before there was air-conditioning) drove us to Cape Cod for six weeks. There I was able to write five or six hours each day with comfort.

The Brookings faculty were anxious to find me an academic post as soon as possible. Before the summer one of the four regular teachers at Brookings, Walton Hamilton (who later joined the Yale law faculty and still later became associated in Washington with the firm of Arnold and Fortas) staked out a job for me in the Department of Economics at Swarthmore. I had never heard of Swarthmore when I went to be looked over by its President, Frank Aydelotte, who was later the first Director of the Institute for Advanced Study at Princeton. I was successful in gaining two important points; a part time appointment that would allow some hours each day for my work, and the privilege of introducing students to a few classic writers—such as Adam Smith, Rousseau and Montesquieu—in addition to half a year of Bye's textbook in economics.[2] We were obliged to use that because of an agreement the chairman of the department had made with Bye to sell his book at Swarthmore in return for having Pennsylvania students use the textbook the chairman at Swarthmore had recently published on international trade.

Aydelotte was trying to put into effect what some students called the "Bally-ole System." That was their way of pronouncing Balliol, the famous Oxford college where Aydelotte had discovered the tutorial instruction that prepared our better students for examinations administered by outside examiners. The name "honors course" had also an English ring. Aydelotte had been a Rhodes scholar at Oxford before the 1914 War. He was head of the American branch of the Rhodes Trust and his initiative at Swarthmore was causing considerable friction within the faculty, among those who clung to the habitual instruction, and opposition among football-minded students and alumni, who put sport first in the hierarchy of learning.

This might have become a serious concern had I remained at Swarthmore. But the Brookings support continued. When Harold Moulton came from Washington to spend the night in our house, he offered to take over the next morning my class in finance. He loved the subject and in its teaching was a dynamic whiz. His arrival and enthusiasm bolstered my morale because, along with Walton Hamilton, he was negotiating for a post at the University of Chicago better suited to my scholarly interests.

Their success was complete. The normal procedure would have been to find a position in the History Department. William E. Dodd, later United States Ambassador to Germany, was at the time chairman of that department. Like his wife, he was a close friend of my mother-in-law, Mabel Wing Castle. But he was timid and worried lest he be charged with what (out of the closeness of the Dodds' friendship for my in-laws including George Mead) he imagined might be regarded as a form of nepotism. So when their overtures for a place in *history* were lukewarmly received, Moulton and Hamilton, who had both been members of the Economics Department at Chicago, turned to Leon C. Marshall, then head of the department as well as of the Business School. He didn't have Dodd's inhibitions and as it turned out was about to leave Chicago. So he appointed me to the Economics Department. This suited Dodd. He was pleased that Elinor and her mother were brought back as neighbors without imposing the slightest academic responsibility on him.

There is no way of telling now whether Moulton still thought of me as a future "economist" in 1928. In any event he showed no annoyance over the fact that in all our five years abroad, I had never delivered, perhaps out of an instinctive sense that Keynes' view of ethics and mine were fundamentally at variance, the letter of introduction he had given me to that famous man.

The appointment Moulton obtained (with Hamilton's help) proved a stroke of incredible luck. For the next decade it gave me freedom to continue and intensify a concern with artistically-oriented teaching and research. I gradually discovered a path into history that was untrodden and suited to the creation of a kind of historical edifice which offered room for a growing communion with beauty—in music and literature and above all in the visual arts.

Things might easily have taken an opposite turn. Marshall had appointed me after consulting only one of his colleagues and had washed his hands of the appointment by leaving for Baltimore. The president of the University of Chicago, the physicist Max Mason, who had sanctioned the appointment, left equally suddenly and unexpectedly for a post with the Rockefeller Foundation.

The colleague Marshall had consulted was Chester Wright, who had long professed the economic history of the United States. Although not a sparkling figure he was an honest man with ideals at once Puritan and humane, who shared my ethical views. He had joined the economics faculty nearly thirty years earlier. He was a New Englander, Harvard trained and trusted by all his colleagues. As he had the interests of "the department" almost painfully at heart, he carried weight in departmental decisions.

A position in European economic history, as a possible addition to the economics faculty at Chicago, had been under discussion for some time. In view of Wright's concern with the American side of the subject, an appointment congenial to him was wanted. Wright and I took to one another from the outset. It was not that our views of either teaching or research were similar (let alone identical). But Wright had no stake in *European* economic history, apart from the purchase of books in that subject for the University library—a matter with which I was able to help. He was the kind of magnanimous person, rare even in universities, in no way troubled that the study of European economic history was being turned in directions that would never have occurred to him. He liked me, he liked my wife who trusted him, he liked my wide knowledge of Europe, and he liked what he heard from the students about the character of my instruction. I was blessed in consequence with a freedom hardly equalled in any other department of the University of Chicago, or perhaps of any university.

This gave me a strategic position I could have never attained in the History Department. Having a considerable capacity for editorial work, I became helpful to the economists in publishing their journal, *The Journal of Political Economy*, then edited by Jacob Viner and Frank Knight. Making no claims to be an economist, having no ambition to become one, I appeared to other members of the Economics Department neither as judge nor competitor, the two kinds of associate least agreeable to most scholars and teachers. Art and ethics and even the kinds of economic considerations which commanded my interest were outside my economic colleagues' fields and so outside their concern.

The Economics Department of the University of Chicago was regarded as the best in the country, with the possible exception of its Harvard rival. Its reputation went from strength to strength during the nineteen-thirties. But within the charmed circle, where I was made to feel at home as a fellow scholar by men who valued serious scholarship more than it was valued at Swarthmore, the department was divided into opposing factions. They disagreed sharply on points of economic theory. But these issues were not of a kind that mattered to me, nor had I any competence to take sides when, as sometimes happened, the disputes turned bitter. And in the area of history where my concern was deep and where my emotions as well as my mind were engaged, there was only Wright. His singularly self-effacing temperament made it easy for us to resolve differences without the injured feelings such differences are likely to arouse. It also put us at ease that, out of very different approaches to scholarship, we invariably agreed about the qualifications of students for degrees.

Increasingly I broadened my view of history into a great sweep extending from Homeric times in the Mediterranean lands to the contemporary industrialization of Europe in the late nineteenth and twentieth centuries. Summers spent in European archives and in establishing relations with European historians added greatly to the first-hand knowledge of industrial development I had acquired abroad during the twenties. In the mild climate at my mother-in-law's house in Los Angeles, I was able to work effectively during the three coldest months of each year, thanks partly to the nearby presence of

the Huntington Library in San Marino. Its first director, Max
Farrand, had offered me full-time employment as part of the
Huntington staff after I had already accepted an appointment at the
University of Chicago. So he always welcomed me in pursuing further
research that seemed relevant to my work. That was done under most
favorable conditions in a house hardly twenty minutes drive distant.

Economic history was being treated increasingly as unrelated to
surrounding problems. Such treatment seemed insufficient. From
the outset at Chicago, therefore, I tried to discover and describe
relationships between the growth of economic output, changes in
technology and in the forms of industrial enterprise, agrarian evolution and changes in the price levels. The search for more subtle
and profound explanations of all these changes had to be pursued,
I discovered, in ecclesiastical history, for example in the confiscation
of monastic properties, as well as in the evolution of religious thought.
The search for explanations had also to be pursued in connection with
constitutional, political and military history, the history of science,
the history of philosophical and political thought and the history
of the various arts: architecture, music, painting and sculpture. Myriad
historical interrelationships were the substance of my lectures.

The best students often responded with excitement. It is not clear
whether they understood what I was driving towards. Looking back,
after recent meetings with former students, I have the impression
most of them did not understand. But they liked the subjects, few of
which were treated by their other professors, they liked my manner
and enthusiasm, the stories I told and the pains I took in reading their
papers and in listening to their problems.

Their views about my lecturing may have been similar to those
expressed by a student about my guardian. This young woman was
in the habit of telling her friends she adored listening to George Mead
as he spoke in a warm throaty voice through a well-tended beard of
a kind then rare and considered full of distinction. One day a friend
tried to pin her down. "But what is George Mead saying?" the friend
asked. Taken aback, the woman burst out: "I don't know. But he
sounds like a fresh wind blowing in the forest!"

The success of many popular professional lecturers at the University of Chicago, not concerned with training students for some
specific discipline or branch of government service, has rested on
little more concrete comprehension than this woman was able to
muster. My success among the students was partly of that variety,

and was provided in no small measure by a captive audience which the Economics Department obtained from the outset by their decision, under Wright's influence, to make a lecture course in European economic history compulsory.

During those halcyon years of the thirties, I gained a small but highly esteemed reputation among a few distinguished scholars in Great Britain, France and Belgium, as well as Harvard where the three leading economic historians—Gay, Usher and Gras—all became my champions. The result was inevitable. Bids from other universities arrived. Yale and a couple of lesser academies invited me to join their faculties. Chicago wanted to keep me. As a result, by the time I was thirty-six, I was made a professor, with a courtesy seat in the History Department in addition to my secure position as a non-economist among the famous Chicago economists.

The unconventional subject matter of my lectures turned my mind in the direction of academic reform. But why it might be asked didn't I follow the respectable path of accepting positions of some small power? On the threshold of the forties, and before making an irrevocable choice, I was offered the editorship of the University of Chicago Press, the chairmanship of the Department of Economics, and more than once the deanship of the Division of the Social Sciences. In the eyes of the academic profession any of these offices, and especially the deanship, were for a man not forty stepping stones towards the kind of authority that conventionally can be employed to influence the course of the higher learning. Yet such offices struck me as disproportionately unimportant to the needs of our times.

The dreams I had nourished of a peaceful world, and hoped others would realize, were dissolving more and more in the realities of power politics. Everywhere people collectively and in the persons of the finest individuals were faced by Japanese and Italian imperialism, and above all by the brutal dictatorship of Nazi Germany, projected as it seemed into the West European peninsula by the Spanish Civil War. The first printed expression of the need I came to feel for resistance to the political dangers that beset humankind took the form of an article, "In Defense of Democracy," for which, after some difficulty and on the eve of the 1939 war, I found a publisher in the graduate magazine of the University of Pennsylvania. Before the war started I sent an offprint to Winston Churchill, inscribed to the "First defender of democracy." I doubt that he even saw it. But to me the world crisis seemed more than a political problem for which direct and even military resistance to tyranny, though no doubt vital, would not be enough. In spite of agreeable conditions for work, I had become profoundly disturbed by the state of higher learning and of educational institutions generally, not only in Chicago, but throughout the United States. In spite of the applause of the specialist, I felt increasingly lonely because the larger meaning of history seemed to find no comprehension from the American public or even from immediate colleagues in the university itself. I had been told by one of my teachers at the Brookings that the publication of my coal book "would put me on the map." It had not occurred to me this would be the map of only a tiny group in a new specialty. It had not occurred to me that little or nothing would be done (even among that tiny group) to pursue the new lines of inquiry this book opened up; that great sections, such as the five chapters on the interrelations between the history of mineral law and agrarian history, would go unexploited.[3]

If I offered any of my publications to a friend to read, he (or more often she) would always shy away saying "It would be way over my head" or "I couldn't possibly understand it." This was disconcerting for an artistically-minded historian, who was trying to write clearly and simply and who was hungry for an audience.

My experiences as a scholar led me to question the methods of graduate instruction and particularly of academic specialization. A concern over the state of the learned professions found expression in an article called "A Social Science Objective." It was printed in the local *University of Chicago Magazine* under a photograph not of me, but of an old man, a double "f" Neff, of German origin, who had taught French in my father's time.

My concern grew over more constructive ways of imparting knowledge and training children, as well as under-graduates and graduate students. I became increasingly impressed by the limitations of economic history. It was the discipline that had offered me my first opportunity, but artistic leanings, derived from our European adventure, led me to question the assumptions underlying economic history as a specialized field. I began to realize with something of a shock that, even among those practitioners who were least Marxian in their political allegiances, the outlook that governed their teaching and writing was an *economic* interpretation of history. Among theoretical economists the most conservative non-Marxists believed that the major difficulties besetting the world could be solved by adopting the "right" economics. They were Marxists in reverse. For them Marx had the wrong economics, but he was right in finding economics the key to salvation.

History suggested "a plague on both your houses." Neither Marxian nor anti-Marxian economics, neither a socialistic nor a "free enterprise" approach to society, had a sufficiently broad philosophical and cultural basis to serve as a foundation for building on the civilized experiences of man's recent past.

Was it not perhaps my duty not simply to comment on Marx, as my colleagues in economic history were inclined to do, most often unwittingly, but to replace him as an influence in the interpretation of the past. That idea, dimly present as far back as 1939, added to my sense of loneliness in the specialty I had embraced with such profound hope. A year later, when my essay, *Industry and Government in France and England, 1540-1640,* was published, a Marxist reviewer reproached me for having had a perfect Marxist case and then having thrown it away. In practically all quarters it almost seemed to be compulsory to fit one's ideas into an existing category or belief. But what if one's findings fitted none of the recognized categories or beliefs? It was not to gain the backing of any special group of scholars, of any university or locality, of any particular creed that I had become a professor.

The conditions present in the learned disciplines and in university discussions led me to strike out along untrodden ways both in scholarship and administration. At the same time fresh experiences outside the academic world, in the worlds of art and letters, drew me towards this unorthodox career.

18. THE PRETENTIOUS BARNES COLLECTION

Our first American residence was in a Washington apartment building across the street from the Duncan Phillips Gallery, one of the most exquisite private collections of contemporary paintings to be found anywhere in the world. In the 1920's there was virtually nothing else in the city on public view to complement the pictures in our small apartment and I missed the frequent and often unexpected encounters with new masterpieces so common in Paris. Habits acquired abroad were strong and after lunch we would often visit the Phillips Gallery to look at a fine Daumier, or Corot, or Courbet, or Matisse, or Rouault, and especially the great Renoir "La Canotière" (The Luncheon of the Boating Party).

These visits were instructive as well as refreshing for the historical work in hand. The pictures emphasized, by analogy, as had the Camondo Collection in Paris, the value of an orderly presentation of diverse concrete materials.

The Phillips never seem to have separated at all rigidly the paintings they have on public view from those they enjoy and share with friends in the privacy of their home. This has continued to be true since they built a new family residence on Foxhall Road and ceased to reside in their house opposite the Fairfax, thenceforth used more exclusively for exhibition purposes. This blending of the informal with the formal in their lives gives a humanity to all their treasures that one too frequently misses (as is suggested later in these recollections) in private collections on public view.

I never had the advantage of knowing any of the family until after Duncan Phillips' death, but recently, when she invited Evelyn and me to a small dinner, had the pleasure of seeing at leisure the pictures Mrs. Phillips retains at her home. There we found the finest Bonnards I have seen. Unlike the late Duncan Phillips, I am far from regarding Bonnard as the greatest painter since Cézanne, but I was captivated by the bright charm of these works of his, so beautifully placed. What captured me still more were two oils—one by Cézanne, the other by Picasso—in the dining room. The first was a most luminous mountain range that made the south of France seem (as it had seemed to Petrarch when he ascended the Mont Ventoux five centuries ago) a stepping stone to Heaven. The other was a Picasso of 1903, at the point he became independent of the influence of Toulouse-Lautrec.

Seeing the pictures in the Phillips Gallery over and over again whetted our appetite for private collections. Dr. Albert Barnes had built a museum beside his home near Philadelphia. So in March 1927 I forwarded the letter Pascin had written for us asking Barnes permission to visit his Foundation in Merion.

Barnes was acquiring a bad reputation among museum officials and other collectors. He was said to have a terrible temper and to outdo himself in barring persons from his pictures. Therefore it may surprise the reader to learn that in answer to our inquiry there came immediately a cordial reply signed by his secretary, Miss Mullin, who was to become hardly less of an ogre by reputation than her employer. She said they would be glad to have us visit the collection without giving notice any day except Friday.

I never made weekday dates from Washington, because they broke my routine of writing and study. So we set forth for Philadelphia on a rainy Saturday a couple of weeks later. We reached the grounds in Merion and were admitted, to find the museum closed. We were told to ring the bell at Dr. Barnes' adjacent house. When we did a maid appeared who seemed to want to keep us out. Elinor quickly placed her foot in the door so that it could not be closed and handed the maid Miss Mullin's letter. In due course a middle-aged woman descended the stairs and said she would show us the museum but we would have to wait. Elinor asked if we might sit in the living room, for it was raining. Somewhat reluctantly she admitted us.

While waiting we saw some of Barnes' private collection. I remember fine works by impressionists and post-impressionists. They were a pleasure to see, although not the equal in beauty or in tasteful arrangement of those Mrs. Duncan Phillips now has at home.

Soon the middle-aged lady returned and led us to the Museum. She unlocked the doors, and in her company we spent some three hours going over the whole collection, taking as much time as we liked to enjoy the pictures that arrested us.

A few months later, after my appointment at Swarthmore only a score of miles from Merion, I wrote Barnes again, asking to bring my wife and this time my mother-in-law as well. The response was more cordial than the first had been. We were given the run of the gallery as before and eventually Dr. Barnes himself joined us and conducted us around, explaining some of the pictures.

He seemed to be enjoying our presence and suggested he would be glad if I came over regularly to follow one or more of his classes. I declined as graciously as possible on the ground that, just entering the academic profession, I already had more work than I could manage in teaching at Swarthmore College and in finishing my "thesis" for publication. One sensed his displeasure.

Whether it was this refusal or whether Dr. Barnes (who was reputed to keep sound-recorders to spy on persons who visited the gallery) reviewed the somewhat disparaging remarks my mother-in-law made about one of his then avant-garde pictures, the next time we applied for entrance, about six months later, we were refused. Perhaps it was because we asked to bring our houseguests, my mother's old Chicago friend Frances Crane Lillie and her sister, Emily Chadbourne, both of whom wanted to see the Barnes Collection. I have been told that Dr. Barnes objected to having well-known Americans come, and the Cranes were both wealthy and prominent, for their brother Charles had been Minister to China. Barnes had no objection to persons who were unknown and who were introduced by an artist like Pascin whose work he was collecting. But bringing Chadbourne and Lillie was a different matter.

The refusal was not a serious blow. Twice we had seen this collection, with its dozens of Renoirs and almost equally numerous Cézannes, its Prendergasts and Eakins, its abundant recent works including an especially fine large Matisse of the Fauve period. The gallery also contained many Picassos, Soutines, Pascins and almost equally numerous little pictures by Jean Hugo a grandson of the great Hugo. The visits to Merion left lasting impressions. Whether I should have profited as an historian from formal instruction from Dr. Barnes and his staff seems doubtful. Judging from their published works his was not the kind of teaching I sought. I felt the need to find my own way among masterpieces and among books on aesthetic history and criticism. The time it would have cost to visit that Merion Museum regularly would have interfered with what had now become a strict routine of teaching, nourished by mornings of research and writing which provided opportunities for using my impressions of beauty and delight in my calling.

There are innumerable stories about Barnes' bad manners and his mistreatment of distinguished and ordinary persons. No doubt there is some truth in all these stories and much truth in some. The doctor's side of his relations with perhaps the most illustrious associate he ever employed, Bertrand Russell, was given in a pamphlet "The Strange Case of Bertrand Russell," published years later.[1]

Before considering the possible significance of this and other squabbles as they reveal Dr. Barnes, I want to add a further story about him. Unlike most, it was told without hostile intent.

My friend William Wood-Prince asked me to dinner at the Chicago stockyards in the late summer of 1953. Just returned from the half year in Paris that followed Elinor's death, I was working up for publication the lectures I had given at the Collège de France. Prince, then president of the Union Stockyard and Transit Company, was a principal member of the Saddle and Sirloin Club and had a private dining room at his disposal.

It was a stag dinner. F. W. Specht, whom Prince was soon to succeed as President of Armour and Company, was a fellow guest and somehow Barnes' name came up. It evoked much interest in Specht, although he hardly shared Prince's enthusiasm for art. A poor boy, he had gone to work in his hometown of Philadelphia and had earned his living for years as a butcher before coming to Chicago and rising to the top position at Armour's. He related how he used to visit among black friends, long before this was a common occurrence. One evening in a suburb along what is fashionably called "the main line," he found himself the only white man except for another Philadelphian. The two men were introduced but Specht didn't catch the other's name. When the party broke up, this man asked "Where are you going?" and, on hearing he was returning to Philadelphia, said "I'm going your way," and offered a lift. To Specht's astonishment, he found himself in a spacious limousine with a chauffeur. When they got to Merion, the man said, "This is where I live. I will have my driver take you on to your home, but wouldn't you like to come in first and have a nightcap?" That is how Specht found himself in the house where Elinor and I had landed briefly on that rainy Saturday afternoon in 1927.

It was Specht's impression that Barnes was most at home with black people. He certainly met them at Pascin's in Paris. He was a complicated man whose weakness for hating (which is attested by many stories) had probably much to do with his serious concern with art. His aesthetic views often conflicted with those of professional interlocutors. Holding his own position with strong emotions, he was likely to fly off the handle. Moreover his exploitation of the invention of argyrol, then widely used in treating syphilis and upper respiratory complaints, may have been partly responsible for making him aggressively defensive in his "public relations." Argyrol was hardly an elegant mainstay for an enormous collection of contemporary art, but that was how *his* work was partly financed. He bought hundreds of pictures in a short space of years, becoming a collector on such a scale that he convinced himself he had no rival in the field.

He seems to have regarded most other collectors, as well as most museum directors (many of whom might be called public collectors), with contempt. And he had little tolerance for the time-consuming sightseer whose motives in looking at pictures are often frivolous and even revolting to a person who cares for beauty, and still more for one who has pretensions to being creative himself. Barnes certainly cared, and believed that he was creative. He set out with the idea that he would use his pictures to educate the public. One assumes this was the basis for his long friendship with John Dewey, regarded by many in Barnes' time as the leading American philosopher. Part of Dewey's philosophical instruction and writing were devoted to a theory of aesthetics. It was Barnes' notion that, helped by Dewey's knowledge and friendship, he could evolve an original explanation of the principles that govern the visual, or at least the graphic arts.

In short while Barnes started as a collector, his life became a revolt against collectors, public as well as private. He may have imagined he was making a collection to end collections!

His life also became a revolt against himself. For his objective of educating the American public to a better understanding of aesthetic values, he was perhaps his own worst enemy. He apparently wanted to become creative in the sense that a great artist is. But the medium in which he sought to excel was the *analysis* of works of art. And it is well in analysing works of art to be reminded—as Turner is said to have once reminded Ruskin—that "Art's a rum thing." No one near to Barnes would have dared to remind him of that. Nor was he quite Ruskin. He didn't try to find inspiration from the visual arts for the pursuit of another art, as Ruskin did for the art of letters. Instead he assumed the role of critic, choosing the major portion of his examples from his own collection.

Whether he succeeded as a critic is questionable. He was sometimes a good judge but highly erratic. He laid down aesthetic principles and then insisted on forcing pictures within the frame of the principles. As a critic he not only missed being Aristotle II; he was not even a *first-rate* writer whose critical prose is a pleasure to read, like Vasari or Fromentin, both of whom were, unlike Barnes, practicing artists. Among recent critics of the graphic arts, his stature is certainly below that of Roger Fry, Kenneth Clark, even Clive Bell, Philipp Fehl or Edgar Wind. All of them are more illuminating for the amateur of art than Barnes. Too often, he permitted arrogance to get the upper hand. Unlike Socrates he supposed he had found wisdom; that he had a monopoly on truth.

Barnes' weaknesses are reflected in the Foundation itself. Following his death and after much litigation, access is now by law allowed anyone who applies, although the number admitted is limited. Revisiting the collection forty years later with Evelyn in 1965, it struck me as less nourishing than I had once supposed. No doubt my pleasure was hampered by the presence everywhere in the grounds, along the path leading from the entrance and especially in the Museum itself, of police guards armed with revolvers. But after discounting for the effect of these security regulations, the gallery seemed too overpoweringly stuffed with pictures, and with various other individual artistic impedimenta such as Spanish iron handicrafts or Pennsylvania Dutch dower chests. The pictures were more crowded than I remembered. The galleries reminded one of the museums in French provincial towns, as they were before the efforts of the new ministry of culture succeeded in clearing away some of the deadwood. Chez Barnes there are too many works for the admirer to see the best happily. Not infrequently one has to crane one's neck to catch an inadequate glimpse of a small Hugo or Pascin or even a small Cézanne. Many bad as well as good canvasses clutter up the walls, detracting from the fulfillment which the masterpieces could offer if given more space. For all its marvels, and the collection has many, the total impression is depressing.

Barnes did not succeed in providing a private museum of contemporary art that relegated all others to a secondary place. He did not succeed, as he hoped, in dethroning the public museums by substituting a gallery capable of revealing the artistic principles alleged to govern beauty. Insofar as his furious efforts had a positive influence on the cultural scene in the United States, the influence ran counter to his intention. By puffing up his own collection he became in spite of himself the proud possessor. Thereby he stimulated a whole tribe of rich persons, who lacked his talents, to assemble pictures competitively *en masse*. He gave all collections whether private or public, some even finer than his, a value *as collections* that outshines the individual works of art which are present only by the grace of the geniuses who created them, persons often as modest and inconspicuous as Barnes had become arrogant and prominent. His efforts on behalf of the artist were no doubt sincere but, as he practiced them, they were more often crushing than elevating.

In lecturing at the University of Chicago soon after we arrived in 1929, on the eve of the Great Depression, I acquired the habit of making the history of various arts in Europe an integral part of my story. Not long after I had started, and as the Depression was ending, Chicago had another world's fair to rival the famous one that had been held in 1893 to commemorate the four hundredth anniversary of the discovery of America. Nineteen thirty-four was the hundredth anniversary of the founding of Chicago and the organizers of this new world's fair decided to include an extensive exhibition of art, especially of paintings. Local collectors were invited to lend their pictures and these were assembled with fanfare in a building on Lake Michigan.

The name given the fair was "A Century of Progress," and the organizers of the picture exhibition proposed to dub this "A Century of Progress in Art Collecting." In one of my lectures I mentioned their intention. The words, "A Century of Progress in Art Collecting," were greeted by a roar of more genuine and louder laughter than I remembered encountering before from students, although laughter was by no means infrequent in my classes. It was a fine tonic, for few greater dangers can beset the individual than those of forgetting how to laugh and how to cry—two responses to our human lot which are near twins.

I had not realized to what extent the students would share my reaction to the title for the proposed exhibition. They recognized how ridiculous it could be to speak of "progress" in art *collecting*, an aspect of confused values that beset the American scene.

The student response emphasized a point about evolving American culture that calls for critical examination. The ludicrous element in the title mingled with a tragic condition, for the ludicrous and the tragic are as near twins as the laughter and tears they provoke. The collecting of works of art has tended to be treated as more important than art itself. The careers of the collector and museum director carry more prestige than the career of creator. This condition is truer now than when Barnes started to collect. Unintentionally his career helped bring it about.

There is nothing necessarily wrong with carefully tended, clinically clean museums. The conveniences and the cleanliness introduced with the help of modern technological progress can be good for art. But on a condition. "Progress" must not enthrone the care-taking mentality at the expense of the dust and sweat and earthiness that are indispensable to the pursuit of beauty itself.

I found a good example of such misplaced enthusiasm the first time I visited the Huntington Library in San Marino, California, where the Director had given me permission to work. I was checking references in my still unpublished coal book and asked the librarian if I could see a copy of Defoe's *Complete English Tradesman*. Did I want the second edition? she inquired. That would serve my purpose, I told her. "All right," she said, "I'll send for it, but you must not cut the pages."

As the years passed the precedence given, both in academic and civic affairs, to new buildings, to collecting, classifying and caretaking, over that given to the creative life of individuals came to trouble me increasingly. For generations in Europe and America, as in some places in the Near East and Asia, the careful preservation and systematic presentation of manuscripts and books, and of all kinds of objects of craftsmanship from beautiful locks and keys to musical instruments, have been providing the artist and the scholar (and the simple observer) with materials unrivaled in the past in quantity, variety and accessibility. Their value will depend ultimately upon man's capacity to use them to lift the human spirit and to ennoble the human experience. And that will depend on the cultivation of man's imaginative faculties to serve the causes of delight and love.

As my acquaintance with classical history grew I was impressed, as others have been, by the analogies between the contemporary Western World and the Roman Empire. In connection with beauty, I fondly reminded students of words that Anatole France, in one of his novels, attributes to a citizen of the Roman Empire who was contemplating a statue by Phidias. "That's a fine work," he says, "but who would want to be Phidias?"

Yet as history began to take a personal form, with the help of artistic experiences, I refused to believe that man's fate is inevitably determined by inexorable historical forces. My inner life created a faith that human beings themselves partly determine the future of societies, and that they are not *fated* to follow the path of the Roman Empire.

That faith moved me to become a reformer. It also convinced me that attempts at reform would be inadequate if they were left to the conventional channels, such as, in the realm of collecting, Barnes represented in spite of himself.

19. THE MIDWESTERN DESERT

Hamlin Garland, the midwestern writer who lived his last years in Los Angeles, became our friend during our annual winter visits to Elinor's mother in the 1930's. We had first met him, with his wife and two daughters, in London in 1923 at the home of an elderly American spinster, Miss Douglas, who owned what had once been Whistler's house in Chelsea. Garland's books interested Elinor as authentic expressions of the American scene, and she often made him and his work a subject in her writings.

Garland had passed part of his formative years during the 1880's and 1890's as a young author in Chicago. Some critics think his best work was done then. He became the leader of a group of talented local writers and other artists, including his brother-in-law, Lorado Taft. Garland was founder and first president of the Cliff Dwellers Club. It was originally intended as a meeting place for artists. But by the time I joined the University of Chicago faculty it had become no more than a convenient place for increasingly numerous non-professional members to get a hurried meal on the way to the Thursday evening or Friday afternoon symphony concerts in Orchestra Hall. During the same stretch of decades the small circle of artists who had direct personal relations with one another (and who had gathered as "cliff dwellers") was inflated into the Society of Midland Authors, a kind of registration bureau for persons who qualified with its executive committee as "professional."

Garland was bitter in his later years about Chicago as a home for writers. He had fled to New York some time during the first decade of this century. On more than one occasion I remember his speaking of Chicago as an artistic desert. He was not alone in thinking so. One Chicago woman, Catherine Dudley, considerably younger than he and who came from an old society family, agreed with him and moved to Europe about 1932 never to return. She explained she could not stand the prevailing lack of taste.

Then too there were the New York visitors, fond of telling you what a dreadful place Chicago was and how much better was New York. They advised anyone with creative talent whose work might count, to evacuate the midwest, and Garland may have been seduced by such talk. There is an element of truth in his description of Chicago. Yet I cannot truthfully say that the city was a desert for the highly personal career on which I embarked.

Chicago had a vigorous creative tradition, running back to the days of Jane Addams. She died at 75 in 1934. In her early years the city had a number of talented writers besides Garland, and some of the most sensitive and perceptive art collectors in the United States. There was Martin Ryerson, who was the first Chairman of the Board of Trustees of the University of Chicago and also of the Art Institute, and the second Potter Palmer, who eventually succeeded him at the Art Institute and with whose wife we felt at home. She had not quite the public glamour of her world famous mother-in-law but she was a beautiful woman. There was also Mrs. Lewis Larned Coburn, who had perhaps the most wonderful Toulouse-Lautrecs to be found anywhere. And, a little later, there were Frederick Bartlett (a painter of distinction), Chauncy and Marion McCormick (who was good to me when I was a widower) and Leola Epstein. Her husband was a resourceful and successful man of business and his widow became one of my (and later Evelyn's) closest friends. She was my principal supporter for the work of both the Committee on Social Thought and the Center for Human Understanding, whose history forms an essential part of this story. In memory of his second wife, Helen Birch, Bartlett left a stunning collection of contemporary paintings to the Art Institute, at a time in the mid-twenties when that museum might not have accepted them if the Bartletts had not been so *socially* acceptable. On one occasion when Marion McCormick was away and the Chagalls were visiting me, she gave directions to take them to see the pictures in her Chicago apartment overlooking Lincoln Park, and Chagall, pleased with those he saw, said they expressed the taste and love of the owners, unlike so many of the recent collections assembled on the advice of dealers. The Epsteins had a unique collection of works by old masters, among them perhaps the finest picture François Clouet ever painted.

These persons felt the struggle upstream that taste imposed on a Chicagoan. I remember Martin Ryerson's widow saying: "Martin and I frequently told each other when we reminisced about our experiences, 'Well, anyway, nobody can take those away from us!' " They missed the opportunities they longed for to share these experiences.

When we returned to Chicago there were other persons who had interesting experiences with contemporary art that were worth sharing. Among them one in particular, Alice Roullier, helped us to add to our original prints. Her father, a Frenchman, had established a shop in Chicago. He died before we reached the city, but his daughter took over the shop. She had good taste, particularly in prints. In addition to some Picasso etchings which we bought from her, we acquired a number of small, delightful and original examples of graphic art by Matisse, Rouault, Braque, Kandinski and Renoir. We also acquired two exquisite etchings by John Sloan and one barnyard scene by Adolf Dehn. In our early days in Chicago, we and Alice Roullier more or less adopted each other, eager for the knowledge about modern art we were able to exchange.

Another woman who took a serious interest in pictures was Inez Cunningham. That was her name when we met. She was then married to an insurance man who, like some others fearing destitution, jumped out of a window during the Depression. She had been an art critic for a Chicago newspaper, later married a man named Stark and still later another named Bolton. While I was far from sharing most of her tastes and opinions, she and Elinor found each other congenial and we saw her frequently and talked seriously about art before she moved to Washington in 1939. With the growing craze for organization, the group that surrounded her formed a specialized society just before she left Chicago—the Society for (Collecting) Contemporary Art (of which I was once offered the presidency). It ceased to provide the creative sustenance that existed before the group had organized and set about finding members.

Something similar happened to the Renaissance Society, which had been formed during the First World War by persons within the University of Chicago with artistic interests. The animator was the American wife of a German colleague of my father's, Martin Schütze, and Elinor spent much time in helping her with exhibitions and lectures. Eve Watson Schütze was herself a talented artistic photographer and an amateur painter, who had done two delicate photographs of Elinor as a girl before we met in the Hunter Building. She died on the eve of the Second World War, and something of the artistic vitality she had managed to evoke in others disappeared from the Renaissance Society and the university. Yet in the period before the Second World War, our relations with the three women art lovers—Alice Roullier, Inez Cunningham and Eve Schütze—provided a measure of helpful conversation about contemporary art. And then there was Harrington Shortall, a musician, who was somewhat suspicious of our enthusiasm for

Stendhal until he discovered that this had the support of reputable contemporary French critics. These associations helped us to retain in Chicago something of the atmosphere that had surrounded us in Paris in the twenties, through informal discussions of arts and letters. Related as these were to my work, this atmosphere helped give it zest.

In my case the dehumanization of artistic stimuli which followed the disappearance of the three just mentioned was to be replaced later, with interest after the War of 1939-45, by friendships that came my way with several practicing artists: with Martyl wife of the physicist Alexander Lansdorf, with Sylvia Judson the sculptress, and with Ivan Albright who moved me by a gift of one of his major etchings. But in the period after Elinor died when I came to know the work of these artists best and to need their comradeship most, they all lived at long distances from the University in that spread-out agglomeration, the Chicago area. Communication became increasingly difficult, though I had as compensation during this sad period the devoted friendship of an older artist, the painter Laura van Pappelendam (who had been Elinor's trusted friend for many years) and whose enthusiasm for the visual arts, especially painting, was strong, authentic and total. Also I had from a distance the enthusiastic support in my efforts at educational reform of Alfeo Faggi, a fine sculptor whose work is underrated, and who had left Chicago before we settled there.

During the thirties support looking towards the educational reforms I was destined to undertake came especially from several colleagues. They used their influence on my behalf when I set about to try to alter the nature of graduate studies. What was even more valuable, their friendship sustained me in my unorthodox ideas.

One of these friends was Robert Hutchins, who had been chosen President of the University of Chicago in 1929, less than a year after my appointment. Hutchins had no flare for the musical or the graphic arts and he was disarmingly aware of it. But his first wife considered herself a distinguished artist and he, in his role of "good husband," supported her as best he could. In the late thirties we were much drawn to each other's ideas and Hutchins encouraged me to talk about these and about my artist friends and artistic interests. We lunched together frequently and out of our meetings a new kind of graduate department was destined to grow. His was a meaningful friendship.

Beardsley Ruml was a friend of Hutchins before Hutchins and I became friends. At the beginning of his presidency Hutchins had made Ruml Dean of the Social Science Division in which the Department of Economics was located. Ruml welcomed my reforming urge, but what I most value in the relationship Elinor and I had with him and his beautiful wife Lois, was the enthusiasm for Hutchins it helped to generate. "You know," Ruml once said, "Bob has been touched by the divine fire." There was a measure of truth in those words. An important element in the early years of my friendship with Hutchins was spiritual. I owed him a part of my enthusiasm for the reform work I soon undertook. This speaks well for his generosity, since the directions of my reforms were in many ways different in their implications from his. One test of an educational leader in a position of some authority is that he be able to recognize what is good in others different from himself. Bob Hutchins' friendship reassured me over a long and difficult period and I have never ceased being grateful.

Another friend from whose enthusiasm I derived moral support that helped me break with rigid academic tradition was Robert Ezra Park, the sociologist. He was brought up in a small town at the head of Lake Pipin in the northern Mississippi valley, Red Wing, Minnesota, which had hardly seven thousand inhabitants in the late nineteenth century. At that time his father became a modestly successful local businessman and eventually bequeathed Park a steady income, giving him a freedom similar to mine. Elinor and I got into the habit, beginning in 1940, of renting a summer cottage the Parks owned at a resort in northern Michigan called Roaring Brook. Hardly a summer day went by without long and stimulating conversations. On one of the innumerable hikes Park and I used to take, he described an event in his adolescence that changed the character of his inner life. When he was about twelve, on an early morning walk along the banks of the Mississippi's upper reaches he happened to look across at the opposite bank. There for the first time in his life his eyes met three young girls bathing in the nude and unconscious of being observed. Park described their lovely long hair which was hanging loosely and reached down beyond their waists, as the early morning sun played about their bodies, and played also on the water and tall trees. The girls never saw Park, but for the first time, he said, he realized the meaning of beauty.

That hold on one of the bases of creativity, which I had discovered at much the same age as he, never deserted him in a well-filled life of eighty years. It enabled him to understand and appreciate my search for beauty. Park's sympathy led him to recognize the need I had to find some place for art in my work at the University of Chicago. Disillusioned as he was becoming with the course taken by sociological studies, he felt an increasing interest in my plans for reforms.

We had met first in Hawaii when we were guests at the house of one of Elinor's aunts, Carrie Castle Westerfelt, on the famous beach at Waikiki then sparsely settled and for me full of the wonder my romance had brought. It was the winter of 1930. Park and I found we could converse to our mutual enrichment about the academic world and also about conditions all over the planet, not least the problem of color, for he was one of the chief authorities on the Negro problem. I was 30, he 65 and about to retire from the University of Chicago's Sociology Department.

He had started his career as a newspaperman in Detroit and had married a Michigan girl from Lansing. They had then spent several years abroad, mostly in Germany and particularly Strasbourg, at the time incorporated in the German Reich.

Park joined the academic profession early in the 1914 War at the behest of William I. Thomas, the well-known American sociologist who, like the John Deweys and the George Meads, lived next door to my parents when I was a child. But it was Park's long and meaningful experience with black people, which began when he went around the world with Booker T. Washington before coming to Chicago, that turned out to be his finest academic asset.

He was able to take a completely independent view of the Negro problem. The color barriers so strong and prevalent in his time had long ceased to exist for him. While still a newspaperman in Detroit he had come to spend a weekend in Chicago, furnished with the address of a moderately priced boarding house. When he checked in he discovered the clientele was all Negro. That was agreeable enough to him. He had a somewhat swarthy skin and the first morning when he was returning from his shower in an abbreviated dressing gown, he encountered a jet black lodger who looked him over with admiration and exclaimed, "Ya'll won't have no trouble passin' in 'dis town!"

Like Park, I was without racial prejudice and have always felt at home with persons of all colors. Park confirmed me in the feeling that the great blessing for Negroes, as well as whites, would be not to separate them ideologically or in any other way or to ask special privileges. The ideal is to give all men and women equal opportunities based on *qualities*. There would be no such thing as black assets or white assets. There would be only human assets.

There were two other university men, much older than I, with whom I often discussed world problems and intellectual conditions on long walks in Jackson Park. One Frank R. Lillie had been a colleague of my father, first at Clark University in Worcester, Massachusetts, and then for many years at Chicago, where as a child I had played with his children. Lillie was a zoologist and was made Dean of the Biological Sciences Division soon after I came to the Economics Department. When he retired he became President of the National Academy of Sciences.

The other, Dallas B. Phemister, had come from Carbondale in southern Illinois to attain at an early age a great and deserved reputation as a Chicago surgeon. Later his interest in the theoretical foundations of surgery and in the history of the subject led him, at considerable financial sacrifice, to found and develop the Department of Surgery in the new University of Chicago Medical School. As a medical student in Paris, he had acquired a habit (as Elinor and I did later) of paying an hour's visit to great pictures each day after lunch.

Perhaps I was prepared subconsciously for Lillie's and Phemister's sympathetic response to my aesthetic approach to social and humanistic studies by a youthful experience with another University of Chicago scientist. On the eve of my first marriage, I paid a call on the man who had succeeded my father as head of the Chemistry Department, Julius Stieglitz. I had known him and his children from infancy. He had always seemed rather dry and forbidding.

When he heard of my plans, pointing momentarily towards the study of economics, he felt a duty to issue a warning to the son of his dead colleague. He had, he explained, no respect for the social *sciences*. The notion which was spreading, that human subjects could be treated by methods directly derived from the experimental sciences, struck him as misguided. Those efforts to imitate science would lead, he said, to little truth. They lent a misleading and farfetched stability to shaky results. He hoped I would not be taken in by what he seemed to regard as a dreadful heresy.

A number of things Stieglitz said stick in my memory fifty years afterwards. It may have been that his distrust of the scientific study of man provided me with reassurance when I found little taste for scientific methods in connection with economic phenomena, particularly for discussions of human motivation in mathematical terms.

Whether Julius Stieglitz would have approved of the use I have made of artistic inspirations, in writing history and in educational reform, is another question. There was in his family more than a streak of artistic appreciation. His brother, Alfred, was not only the father of artistic photography in the United States, he married the painter Georgia O'Keeffe and was a leader in introducing contemporary art to New York.

Lillie and Phemister were sympathetic colleagues and close friends. But both were committed to the existing conditions of graduate study and research to a degree that I was not. This was much less true of Park and Hutchins. Park did not enter the university profession until he was a man of fifty, with a successful career of thirty years in journalism behind him. Hutchins had, in a sense, never entered the *ranks* of the academic order; he had been summoned to an administrative post as assistant to the President of Yale only two years after his graduation from college, and he had become the effective Dean of the Yale Law School soon after he took his law degree in 1925 at the age of twenty-six.

Both Park and Hutchins were disturbed by the directions academic studies and research, especially outside the experimental sciences, were moving. While neither shared my enthusiasm for music and the graphic arts, both had a taste for literature which led them to recognize and sympathize with the forces that moved me to draw on the resources of art more than of science in my work as teacher and writer of history, and eventually as founder and chairman of a small interdisciplinary faculty. They were not only ready, as Lillie and Phemister were, to give such a faculty their blessing, they were disposed to provide all the active support that their positions enabled them to muster.

The desire to set a fresh example in writing and in graduate instruction came strictly from my experiences. No one else was responsible. But Hutchins and Park gave me the impression that the effort ought to be made and that it might not be hopeless. So from the point of view of my work during and after the thirties, Chicago was anything but a desert. It was a land of unique opportunity.

20. THIN AND SANDY SOIL

During our five formative years we had chosen to live and work outside the academic enclosures. Now we were part of them. The faculty atmosphere was essentially hostile to imaginative thinking, let alone to flights of fancy and their realization in works of art. One of the surest ways to belittle the scholarly reputation of a colleague was to call him a "poet."

Such a state of mind might seem to resemble that of Dean Valéry in Montpellier concerning his brother Paul, and no doubt constraints of a somewhat similar kind would have existed if I had joined a French Faculté de droit or Faculté des lettres. Yet the difference in the atmosphere encountered in Chicago as contrasted with Europe cannot be explained merely in terms of a change in *milieux*. The American — particularly the midwestern — scene was partly responsible. In the twenties and thirties "pragmatism" as a philosophy pervaded educational institutions to a much greater extent in the United States than in Europe. Nowhere was this more noticeable and telling than at the University of Chicago, where John Dewey had launched a full-fledged pragmatist philosophy faculty at the end of the nineteenth century. Pragmatist concepts were audible in both the social sciences and the humanities. The artistic imagination was not simply left out of the orbit of scholarship as was partly true also in Europe. Scholars adopted kinds of dogmatism with respect to art and artists which were at that time less prevalent abroad, or at any rate carried less weight.

American dogmatism took two contradictory forms. One was especially prominent when I joined the University of Chicago faculty. It denied objective standards in connection with works of art. Colleagues treated as axiomatic that beauty for one society or one country or one person is ugliness for a different society, country or person. Taste is determined by the genes and the environment. It has no validity in its own right.

During the nineteen-thirties this form of dogmatism was in the process of begetting a counter dogmatism. Scholars sought, and sometimes claimed they had found, rules to enable anyone to agree on what is a work of art and what is not. The matter could be settled by dialectics.

I was by no means inclined in the direction of the counter-dogmatism that took temporary hold at Chicago. Its advocates were seeking standards for judging poetry or prose resembling the criteria Albert Barnes was striving to formulate for the graphic arts. Nevertheless with my predilection for beauty and delight, I found distasteful the declarations that there is no such thing as artistic taste. For me, unlike Hamlin Garland, this midwestern atmosphere was more a challenge than a summons to flight. The important matter was to try to change the atmosphere.

This problem of artistic discrimination was by no means directly related to the matters of educational reform on behalf of which in the nineteen-forties I was impelled to act. The idea of a relationship between beauty and scholarship, moreover, was unintelligible to most colleagues whether they favored or opposed the numerous reforms then under discussion at the University of Chicago. It concerned me for I saw (what was later to become a fashionable criticism of academia) that science and art were sundered into non-communicating areas. This sharp separation seemed unhealthy for the understanding that was becoming more vital for all humankind than ever before. I recognized the need for a haven where the search for artistic beauty and certitude would be protected, a haven where good taste would be treated as an independent value. I thought of the haven as accessible to the scientist as well as to the creative artist. I thought of it as a haven providing *general* subjects of discussion arising out of their specialties but of interest to both.

A concern with art had little interest for some of the colleagues who were to join our interdisciplinary faculty. But for them, as for many others, the growing specialization between subjects was a fact no academic could escape whether or not he was disposed to regard it as desirable. Such colleagues usually agreed specialization was being carried too far. They witnessed an enormous proliferation of fields of study in each academic center and the projection of these local developments onto the national scene. The proliferation was accompanied by the founding of new learned societies, each with its complement of officers, secretariats and scholarly journals.

I was not unaware of the value of fresh specialized exploration, nor was I against it in principle. I had benefited from the recognition of economic history as an intelligible field of study. This had provided facilities for developing ideas independent of the conventional study of history as well as independent of economics.

What was disappointing in the push towards specialization was the absence of alternative objectives of unification, of parallel investigations designed to uncover, and to bring together intelligibly, the implications of fresh knowledge in many fields, the old as well as the new, for strengthening the individual, complicated, integrated, human being as a whole. When colleagues in economics came up against some overlapping question beyond the scope of their study, they invariably treated it as a deadend. "That is for the political science department, this is for the philosophy department," they would say. Fellow academics were busily evading vital questions connected with their discoveries. My approach to "economic history" convinced me that, with increased specialization, there was a greater need than before for common denominators which would help relate fresh *special* knowledge to a *broader* view of man and his problems.

This process of doubt concerning the academic trends most colleagues regarded as inevitable, developed during a period of years. My concern went back to Swarthmore. There a scientific colleague kept deploring the schizophrenic tendencies but at the same time insisting they were bound to go farther and farther. He used to say that nothing could *possibly* offset the trend. I found it difficult to see the necessity for ceaseless fragmentation, if it blocked a broadening of the basic body of knowledge. I felt also the lack of recognized goals for human improvement, such as might provide specialists in different fields with inspiring common objectives.

Most of the manifestations of the mind encountered outside the university were disappointing. In American letters and art there was little constructive to offset, much to abet, the overspecialization, the materialism and the relativism that beset the scholar. Little was emerging from American literature, painting or music helpful in bridging the gaps that the expansion of the higher learning was leaving in its wake.

The distance separating writers from scholars was strikingly brought to my attention by Garland. Vernon Parrington's *Main Currents in American Thought* had seemed the most revealing historical work by an American scholar since Turner's essay on the frontier, Veblen's *Imperial Germany and the Industrial Revolution,* and Henry Adams' accounts of himself and of *Mont Saint Michel and Chartres.* Through Parrington's third volume I had become familiar with Garland and his slight but definite significance for letters, before our friendship began and before I had read a line he had written.

One evening when he was dining at my mother-in-law's, we asked him whether Parrington had got some of the material for his Garland chapter from personal acquaintance. It emerged that not only had Garland never met Parrington but had never until this moment heard of his book. Elinor had the pleasure of showing him the pages devoted to him.

In addition to Parrington's interest in the political implications of American thought—a subject stimulated by his friendship with his colleague J. Allen Smith—he had a considerable taste for literature and gifts for writing. He had developed his talent inconspicuously over some two or three decades, mainly as a member of the English Department at the University of Washington, before the first two volumes of *Main Currents in American Thought* appeared. Garland's ignorance showed how little fruitful communication existed between letters and scholarship, even when scholarship was imaginatively concerned with letters.

We found a movement towards proliferation in the arts comparable to the one in scholarly pursuits. The main travelled roads were leading to the rapid multiplication of specialities and to a prodigious increase in the number of participants in each specialty. New societies were being formed. Many were concerned with the collection or the classification of artistic works. Such societies provided a kind of equivalent in the artistic sphere for the library sciences which were becoming so comprehensive and efficient in the academic sphere. The damage to general understanding and to the deeper human affections, for which the trends in the higher learning were partly responsible, was not being repaired by the multiplication of societies of art collectors or classifiers.

In contrast with French, American writers and artists were too frequently regarded and treated as second class citizens. A French wholesale dealer in vegetables who came originally from Marseilles and who had been one of our fellow guests at Cap d'Antibes during the first summer season, told me a decade later he was not at all envious of a politician's career; what he admired and honored above all else was a great thinker, writer or painter. This trader was rather gross as a man, he was by no means a connoisseur. It is difficult to imagine an American businessman with a similar background taking such a position.

Traditionally in France the status of the poet had been higher than that of other men. The Valois kings would have agreed with Ronsard in his claim that his verses would long outlive their reputations. So it remained for many generations. Louis XIV, whose grandeur as head of a state has hardly been equalled, spoke of Racine as "le premier homme de France" before adding slyly, "après moi" (the finest man in France . . . after me). The traditional French conception of the superior value of the artist was alien to the American scene. For prestige in the United States the President is without a peer.

Henry James once drew a comparison between France and England with respect to the career open to the artist. "In France," he wrote, "the artist finds himself, *ex officio*, a member of a large and various society of fellow-workers; whatever may be his individual value, his basis or platform is a large and solid one, resting upon social position and public opinion. He has to make his work a success, but he has not as happens in England, where the vivacity of the artistic instinct appears to have been checked in a mysterious manner by the influence of Protestantism, to justify and defend his point of view. His point of view is taken for granted, and it may be said that his starting-place is the point at which, after much superfluity of effort, the artist in other countries arrives."

If the artist's starting-place in France was on higher ground than in other countries, it is natural to assume that his contribution to history has been weightier there. In *Les Origines de la France contemporaine*, Taine portrayed the French Revolution as mainly the work of a few great men of letters, first among them Voltaire, Montesquieu, Rousseau and Diderot. As late as the Second World War, French writers and other artists retained positions of priority in the minds of an articulate public. They derived this both from their more elevated starting-place and from the greater influence they were believed to have on institutions and events.

Had James made his comparison with the United States, he could hardly have found conditions *more* congenial for the artist there than in England. In literary art he would have found them less congenial. The Victorian British inherited a pride in their poets and men of letters which Americans were inclined to reserve only for statesmen and judges, after presidents. The considered recognition of the mind which Hubble had felt in England has been harder to achieve in the United States. In speaking of the place of the writer in this country, Hamlin Garland out of his experience remarked early in the course of our friendship, "The American soil is thin and sandy." When asked why he could only add, "It always was so."

Between the two world wars a view came to prevail that the search for knowledge is its own reward; that scholarship can thrive without a general audience through the multiplication of learned specialities, each with its small group of fellow workers who are, as it were, "in the know." George Ellery Hale, the astronomer who was so successful in raising money for the Carnegie Institution of Washington (an oasis for scientists), took this line in conversation at his home in Pasadena when we paid him a call in 1931. He had been my father's colleague at the end of the nineteenth century, and he seemed to feel (as my father did too) that insofar as the public were concerned, all that was needed to nourish the scientist was adequate funds to experiment.

Whatever the case of experimental scientists, artists and men of letters need a comprehending response from a considerable number of individuals who are part of a general audience. To provide an artist with money can be helpful. But it is inadequate.

Artur Schnabel used to say that the artist may be compared to a mountaineer seeking an echo. He will keep calling for a time, but if a response never comes he eventually gets discouraged. Discouragement dampens the forces of artistic inspiration, although no doubt to different degrees in each artist. The artist's creativeness depends, in no small measure, on an inner conviction that his works have power to move minds and hearts in directions that matter. (The loving mother feels that way about her child.) The greater the artist, the stronger is likely to be his hope for such a miracle. If that hope seems to be denied, his inner resources are depleted or turned into neurotic channels at best irrelevant and often harmful to his art.

Such irrelevancy was a handicap even to the great American architect Frank Lloyd Wright. His was a powerful genius supported by an exceptional physique which carried him into his ninetieth year. His early struggles in search of a responsive comprehending public hardly exhausted him. Nevertheless his mind was sometimes warped in directions unworthy of and unrewarding to his best self. Disappointed by the absence of the echo he sought, he would occasionally lose not only restraint but discernment. He would pump up his ego to an extent which would have depleted the creative energy of a man with a less robust nervous constitution. I knew him only under pleasant conditions when his best sides shone brightly. Even then he could seldom resist praising himself to blot out the insecurity that lingered at the height of his career.

In connection with the founding of the "Committee on Social Thought," Wright came to the University of Chicago to speak for the architect in a series of lectures called *The Works of the Mind*,[1] the series which also brought Chagall, Schoenberg, Alfeo Faggi, John von Neumann and Senator Fulbright. He arrived in Chicago with his attractive young wife, telephoned and, finding us out, told my mother-in-law that he was dumbfounded to be met at the downtown hotel, where he was known, with a refusal of appropriate rooms. My mother-in-law calmed him, and found them a large suite in a hotel near the University of Chicago. This warm welcome put him in a gracious mood. Dining with us on the evening of his lecture a more charming and creatively informative dinner companion would be difficult to find. After dinner, as we walked the short distance to Mandel Hall, I remarked that never had so many people been milling about on 57th Street since the University abolished football. "It's the same everywhere," Wright felt impelled to say. "Last week, when I talked in San Francisco, the building was so packed that they could get me in only by breaking a window and hoisting me through."

This kind of crashing response to celebrities, whether artistic, political or literary, was a commonplace in the United States even before the Second World War. But it seldom produced the kind of echo nourishing to a creative artist. What he most needs is a sheltered harbor of quiet reassurance. Fanfare and publicity fail to provide it. Deafening applause and the awarding of widely advertised prizes have frequently been mistaken for recognition of artistic

achievement. Genuine understanding, the kind that helps an artist
to fulfill himself, needs to be provided in small and stimulating,
rather than in heavy and intoxicating doses. Garland might more
appropriately have called the American soil "thin and noisy."

It has been suggested recently by a researcher into the matter,
that the granting of Nobel Prizes has dampened rather than maintained the genius of the recipients. It is questionable whether more
American artists of promise have not withered under the weight of
the kind of acclaim that is accorded the few than from the neglect to
which everyone of them is subject at the beginning of his career.
Two things drown American artists: failure and success.

Despite the solid income from stocks, bonds and royalties which
made Ernest Hemingway a millionaire, for all his awards and for
all the enthusiasm his person generated when he appeared in public,
he spent his last years in a state of merciless emotional disintegration.
Before he was sixty he was unable to write. The plight of Scott
Fitzgerald, as he told it in "The Crack-up," was partly a result of inadequate recognition. Towards the end of his life, Thomas Wolfe, like
Hemingway later, suffered from misplaced adulation.

Elinor was a staunch admirer of Wolfe's long novels and left
several unpublished treatises on them. She once looked him up in
New York when I was there to give a history lecture. We were
staying in an uptown hotel and Elinor had brought our maid, a
young and not unattractive Irish girl of about 22. The meeting with
Wolfe, who was a non-stop talker, began before lunch. As the day
waxed he became more stimulated and his conversation kept pace
with his mood. Words *poured* from his vast frame. His major
theme was how unbearable he found life in New York. He complained that he was asked out ceaselessly by persons with whom he
had nothing in common and denied communion with others who
could help him in his work. He was obliged to spend so much time
wining and dining and "bull slinging," as the phrase then was,
that he had almost no time to think or even write, for he was
capable of writing without much reflection. It never seems to have
occurred to him that he could say "no."

When lunch was served in our suite by the Irish girl, his eyes
moved longingly over her ample person as she hovered about.
"God," he muttered, "I want to get out of this. I'd like to be
married and move to some small town in the middle west. Do you
think she'd marry me?" he half-seriously asked.

Enjoying himself and not wanting the fun to end, Wolfe insisted on taking us for tea to his famous editor Maxwell Perkins, (though he left the Irish girl behind!). The three of us spent a couple of hours in Perkins' home with his wife and five daughters. Finally Wolfe parted with us reluctantly. He seemed in a fever induced by what the French call "abattement," beaten-downness, attributable to "success." A summer or so later, when we were in Georgia, we read in the paper of his death.

Problems connected with a lack of public attention, alternating with a plethora, damage not only artists but also middlemen, publishers and dealers in works of art who represent artists and their work for the sake of profit. Unlike Ambroise Vollard, they too often lack comprehension of the creative imagination that must sustain the artist if he is to approach his goals.

The role played by these middlemen raises the question to what extent it is helpful to guide creative minds in their work. At the time of our meeting with Wolfe he was on terms of easy and congenial intimacy with Maxwell Perkins, whose role as a kind of mentor of prominent writers is said to have been second to none during the thirties. Wolfe is supposed to owe Perkins a heavy debt for the quality achieved in his best books. Perkins took the manuscripts and cut them relentlessly, often more than by half. There is no doubt Wolfe needed cutting. It was enough to hear the words sputtering from his person to be sure of that.

I don't know whether Perkins overstepped the bounds of helpful criticism in his dealings with Wolfe or other American writers, as some of them have alleged. To form an opinion on the merit of the quarrels they had with this widely known editor would require an investigation of voluminous materials such as I have not undertaken, and a personal knowledge of the contestants that I do not possess. But, in the case of Wolfe, it is usually conceded that Perkins did little to damage, and much to improve, *Of Time and the River* and *Look Homeward, Angel*.

Nevertheless it is necessary to inquire whether the activities of publishers and art dealers in general have been mainly constructive. The value for the writer of a critic—indeed of a relentless critic— is difficult to overstate. With the discovery in 1968 of the original copy of T. S. Eliot's *The Waste Land* we know how Ezra Pound's useful role of severe critic improved the poem. Few honest writers are unaware that they owe much to friends, editors, research associates and assistants, and to some publisher's readers, for corrections, compressions and suggestions.

The only valid object of such interventions must be to bring out better the *intentions* of the artist. He must have the final decision as to what revisions do that. Unless he *has* intentions that are original and vital, his contributions can hardly be taken seriously. The constructive critic respects those intentions. It would never have occurred to Vollard to tell an artist how to paint or to etch in order to *sell*. In recent decades in the United States there have certainly been many cases (my impression is of a rapidly increasing number) in which publishers and dealers have overstepped the limits they ought to impose on themselves.

In the thirties a French novelist commented in one of his books that in the United States nobility has been replaced by publicity. An American of my father's generation, Shailer Mathews, long dean of the University of Chicago Divinity School, devoted a small part of his life to reading books in his field for publishers. He told me in 1938 that there had been a great change in their directives during the previous half century. When he began, the dean said, the only thing that concerned them was the quality of the books. By the thirties they had almost lost interest in quality as such and were concerned only with the question "Would the book sell?"

Since then I have encountered again and again persons who have tried to change the kind of work done by writers and artists in order to fit the market. For example, long ago I wrote some impressions of France which took on the proportions of a small book. When submitted to a publisher in the middle west, he said it was not the kind of book he wanted. He then described the sort of book about France he would be willing to publish and suggested I write it. The single, dampening consequence of our meeting was to prevent me from ever trying to improve the book to carry out my intentions.

A similar experience came to a close friend, a leading physicist who is now a member of the French Academy. He has diversified talents and throughout most of his life has been an amateur painter. When we met in Paris some years ago, after an absence of three or four years, he asked me to look at his latest canvases. I was astonished to find he had changed his style and commented on this. He said, "Yes, you are right. An American dealer promised me a one-man show in New York if I painted the way she wanted." He asked whether I preferred his present to his old style. I said frankly I did not. He agreed.

Such interference, by no means confined to America or to our times, has its origin in a lack of respect for artists and for art. It reminds me of an occasion in Chicago when Stravinsky was to lecture for the Committee on Social Thought. The students who were managing the evening kept him waiting unnecessarily and someone said to them, "What do you mean by such discourtesy to one of the greatest living musicians?" "He had better learn that this is a *democratic* country!" was the reply.

The man of genius has been beset at all times and places by misunderstanding, nonsense and disrespect. The artist has almost always had to struggle against adversity. But stupidity and nonsense have perhaps never been as prevalent or as influential as in recent times. The vulgar and irrelevant have perhaps never before so completely drowned the voices of discrimination as since discrimination has become scarcer and consequently more valuable.

An old newspaper clipping contains quotations from the acceptance speech Hemingway wrote when he was given the Nobel Prize in literature. He was too ill to go to Sweden to receive it. What he stressed in his remarks was the artist's loneliness. Of course loneliness is the lot of artists in every land and in every age. But to that loneliness is added the loneliness which comes from the public state of mind in the United States, where the creative person either receives almost no attention or the most debilitating kinds of over-attention.

An awareness of these limitations of the American scene for artists was one of the contributing factors to my new idea: that it might be possible to provide a place within a university where they can hope for an echo when they call. Such a haven might help fertilize the American soil for art. It might give a new dimension to scholarship such as could help artists and scientists to communicate.

My desire for such a center in an American university arose not only from concern over the conditions we found in the United States during the decade before the Second World War. It arose also from experiences during trips to Europe.

Chicago was far from the centers of major disturbance in the later thirties, when the storms of war were gathering and the sense of moral values was distintegrating all over the world. Our store of European memories was replenished from time to time by summers abroad and, increasingly, as the Second World War loomed, by the rising stream of refugees escaping into the United States.

21. THREATENING CLOUDS OVERSEAS

Americans remember 1932 as the year when the Great Depression touched bottom. Herbert Hoover, who had talked in 1928 about a car or more to each family and of Prohibition as "a noble experiment," was dismissed from office when the voters elected Franklin Roosevelt by large popular and electoral majorities.

For me 1932 generated a kind of magic. The seemingly endless coal book was finally in page proof. The formidable index which, even with help from an expert indexer, took two months to complete, was sent to Routledge in June and finished copies of the two volumes were promised for Christmas. The Nazis had not yet come to power; some persons over-optimistically believed that threat was over. I had recovered from a throat illness that had given Elinor and me much concern in 1929, and we were ready to go abroad again. For the first time since we married, Elinor had decided to have a baby. That decision eventually led to three miscarriages but we were still happily unaware of this sad outcome.

Someone once said of my father that he *had* to be an optimist because pessimism would have killed him. Apparently I inherited this trait. Pleasurable impressions flooded my inner life as we set out on our Atlantic journey. Inwardly I formulated words similar to those Franklin Roosevelt was to utter, with thrilling effect, months later in his first Inaugural: all we had to fear was fear itself.

As warmth and sun declared themselves after a cool June, we piled luggage into the trunk and back seat of a new Buick (which Virginia Woolf later spoke of as "your vast car") and departed from our Chicago apartment. It will be difficult for an American whose outlook is derived from the prosperous sixties to believe that in 1932 the old and often winding roads from Chicago to New York were almost empty of automobiles. Occasionally one even saw a horse-drawn wagon. I could relax while driving at a leisurely pace in a way no longer possible.

We were four days on the road, three nights in hotels almost without clients. When at Hoboken we drove the automobile onto the "Berengaria" for shipment to Cherbourg and presented our stateroom ticket, the purser moved us (without our asking and at no extra charge) into the magnificently appointed bedroom of a suite. He could afford this amiable gesture because few cabins were occupied. He provided a marvelous place for lovemaking.

The sea was a millpoint as it had been on that happy journey back on the "Paris" six years before. The joy, promise and freedom from tension which an ocean voyage can offer had full play.

Ours was one of two automobiles unloaded at Cherbourg. European motoring started in bliss. It continued and ended as perfectly as it began. There were even fewer cars on French roads than on those in the unprecedentedly depressed United States. The daily distances we needed to cover were much shorter, and there were almost endless riches along the way. Without pressure we found ourselves going wherever we felt impelled. We had never owned and driven a car in Europe before, and for the next five summers, this proved an easy and endlessly fascinating experience.

In 1932 we renewed our old friendships: with the Champions at Le Touquet, where Edouard had been made "maire adjoint" (deputy mayor), and with Cap d'Antibes, where we invited the Siegfrieds and where André Siegfried began to share the swimming with us. We had met the Siegfrieds in 1926 when they came to tea in our apartment in the rue de Lille, while the Tawneys were visiting and Siegfried described in his idiom the United States we were about to enter as interestingly as had Pascin in his.

Hitherto our experiences in scholar's homes in Europe had been limited to England. Now we established refreshing and durable connections with a number of French-speaking scholars and their families: the Siegfrieds in Vence, the Henri Sées in Rennes, the George Bourgins in Paris and the George Espinas in Montfort-l'Amaury.

Thanks to our command of a car and growing knowledge, we discovered and made friends with provincial towns and villages and some of their inhabitants, in a manner that became impossible with the spread of automobiles in Europe after the thirties and forties. These excursions brought us close to the spirit of French townspeople and villagers. Our automobile crept lovingly through crowds that appreciated the delicacy of the intention. One warm sunny Sunday afternoon, when near Cahors people thronged the broad road in front, a beauty of a girl walking in a party of six turned her head and, discovering the oncoming car, asked to their delight and mine, "Why don't you honk your horn, my friend?" One felt as if the French people had made some progress in humanity and tenderness, since the grim cruelties of the Revolution which for years soiled the faces of the expiring Ancien Régime and even more of its opponents.

In such towns and villages we explored ancient houses and castles, narrow streets and water-driven mills from the seventeenth and sixteenth centuries. Here was a world which had already begun to take on reality in my lectures. We gathered new documentary and archeological evidence of its existence.

The climax of the 1932 summer was a motor journey through northeastern France into Belgium, a week's trip on which we embarked from Paris with the Espinas. He was about to retire as archivist at the French Ministry of Foreign Affairs after publishing an immensely erudite four volumes on medieval municipal life in the rather gloomy little town of Douai. He had also collaborated with his friend Henri Pirenne in collecting and interpreting masses of documents on the medieval textile industry.

Pirenne was considered by many the greatest living historian. The Espinas introduced us at a historical congress in Liége, the ancient city with its surrounding coal mines about whose history I had learned many details from documents. Liége was not far from the village in the Ardennes where the Pirennes had a summer place and where we called on them in 1935 a few months before his death.

In 1932 we stayed several days in Liége and became friends not only with Pirenne, but with two younger Belgian historians, François Ganshof and Paul Harsin. The Congress ended in a blaze of oratory with Pirenne proposing, because we were visitors from the United States, the health of the American President.[1] This toast enabled me to respond with a toast to Pirenne that ended the banquet.

The next day a few of us—the Espinas, Harsin and Pirenne—went to the small inn then reputed to serve the best meals in town. In his priestly robes the local monsignor of this ancient prince-bishopric came too. He assumed the appearance of being shocked when Pirenne, full of zest and charm and on the crest of good burgundy, told of a stay he and his wife had made at the White House. He claimed he had caught a glimpse of Madame Hoover "toute nue." He later settled for "clothed in a dressing gown." The good Monsignor lost and never recovered his fountain pen, which he had lent so that every guest could sign the menus. Then we said good-bye to the scholars including the Espinas, and started back to France by way of Charleroi and Mons, with their mounds of coal and slag.

Once during that summer in a new Paris restaurant, we had a prolonged talk with the proprietor about the French political scene. Our attention turned to Raymond Poincaré whose career was ending. Along with Briand and the young Herriot, Poincaré had been the principal force in formulating policy since the First World War. The proprietor explained there was little with which one could justifiably reproach this former prime minister and president. He had led an impeccable life at home and as a politician, but, alas, one missed something essential. The proprietor kept insisting, "Il n'est pas complet" (He is not complete.)

Pirenne was. In manifesting the graces of understanding and politeness, sensing the fact that it is no less essential in writing history to bring art and wit as well as science to bear on the infinitely varied subject matter, Pirenne seemed whole in a sense that no member of a history department we had met in the United States was complete. The best of them just missed this remarkable historian's combination of profundity, taste and universality.

Pirenne had not believed in the coming of the First World War. Yet his enthusiasms had survived the shock in spite of the years he had spent in a German prison, deprived of books, of communion with the learned, and even for a time of pen and ink. His wholeness was part of the armor that saved him. This leads one to wonder, across the forty years of revolutionary technological and scientific progress that have intervened since 1932, whether wholeness may not be the single human ingredient most necessary for meeting the future.

For me 1932 was the first of six richly filled summers spent in Europe. That was when my historical writing turned to comparisons of the history of France with that of England during the sixteenth and seventeenth centuries, and especially to the differences between developments in the two countries which marked the century following the Reformation, the hundred years from about 1540 to 1640.

Our motor trips provided firsthand insights for making these comparisons. The remains of the world I was trying to understand and describe were to be seen everywhere we went as I examined, with the help of local archivists, documents bearing on past conditions.

During our earlier years in Europe in the nineteen-twenties, we had been barely introduced to local archives, and only in England. Now the vastly rich French resources were spread out for inquiry within easy distance of our automobile.

In France documents are divided between the national archives in Paris and the almost innumerable departmental and communal archives in provincial towns. With the help of printed inventories as well as of letters which I exchanged with local archivists, it was possible to spot in advance manuscripts relevant to the history I planned to write. I could then read and have them copied on the scene of the conditions they revealed.

Breadth of outlook extended even to the archivists, trained in the Ecole Nationale des Chartes, several of whom worked with me during these summers. Some took an easy interest in other aspects of life than the keeping and ordering of documents, a broader interest than I encountered in the Public Record Office or the MS division of the British Museum. These wider interests of French archivists were rarely at the expense of the assignment they were obliged to shoulder, that of sorting, cataloging and publishing inventories of the manu-scripts entrusted to their administration.

Perhaps this breadth of view is a singularly French characteristic. As the years passed I encountered it also in French generals, busi-nessmen, politicians and even engineers.

The provincial collections which yielded the juiciest materials were at Bordeaux and Marseilles. In each place we came to know the principal archivist. In Bordeaux I took him, along with my wife and our two traveling companions, to lunch at the Chapon Fin. That famous restaurant no longer exists. It had been a favorite resort for King Edward VII on his way to and from Biarritz, and was regarded in the early twentieth century as unexcelled—in a class with Voisin, Foyot and Larue in Paris. I had ordered in advance a fine bottle of Chateau Latour and was disappointed when the archivist said nothing about it. As we were leaving I asked whether the wine had pleased him, "Yes," he said, "it was very good. But," he added, wishing apparently to contribute to my education, "you know Mr. Nef the *true* claret is Chateau Lafite." Lest the reader may not think knowl-edge of wine a component of wholeness, let me add that at Marseilles the great archivist of the thirties, Monsieur Bosquet, combined his prodigious labor of assembling, caring for and presenting documents with the writing of rather good novels. He did not separate the professions of archivist and man of letters; they were two aspects of a single career, each enriching the other.

Both my wives have had an intense admiration for the work of Virginia Woolf. Elinor began to read her as the First World War was ending, years before she had a public in the United States. Mrs. Woolf had published only *The Voyage Out* and *Day and Night* when Elinor's enthusiasm started. Her literary experiences had led her to discover and admire Dorothy Richardson and Marcel Proust. Virginia Woolf, as another "stream of consciousness" pioneer, appealed to Elinor's perceptive and passionate appreciation. While we lived in Europe and afterwards, Virginia Woolf's books (like Proust's) came into our library and experience as soon as they were published.

Elinor had horrified Mrs. R. H. Tawney, when the Tawneys did so much to make us at home in London, by saying the person she would like most to know was Mrs. Woolf. Mrs. Tawney's displeasure was another symptom of the sharp separation between the world of letters and the world of scholarship. That widened after the twenties even among persons in England who occupied university chairs.

During our second summer in Europe, in 1933, Elinor, who had begun a long piece of writing, part of which I published after her death,[2] took it to Mrs. Woolf. She read it carefully and treated Elinor with much kindness. She then asked us to tea in the Woolf house (Monk House) at Lewes in Sussex. We spent an interesting afternoon. I screwed up my courage to the point of sending her a copy of *The Rise of the British Coal Industry*.

Mrs. Woolf wrote a most amiable letter of acknowledgment. She had evidently at least scanned some chapters and had been impressed by the extensive documentation. But it never occurred to her to treat those two volumes, the way I hoped she might, as an effort with different subject matter to achieve a unity in four parts comparable to a long symphony in four movements! Much later I explained this intention to Artur Schnabel, and he recognized its validity. To Mrs. Woolf, however, the fields of art and scholarship were separated by a gulf. My wife's work belonged on one side, mine on the other.

From 1933 on Elinor knew that, as a writer, she could approach Mrs. Woolf without difficulty. She never abused her entrée. Four years later we saw the Woolfs again. They asked us to tea in their London flat with Lady Sybil Colfax (the famous hostess who is often mentioned in Harold Nicholson's *Diary*) and a young British lord whose name I cannot remember. Elinor described that occasion in *Letters and Notes, Volume I*.[3] There was a strange communion between the suffering of the two women, which can easily be detected if one compares Elinor's unpublished writings (preserved in the Archives of the University of Chicago) with Leonard Woolf's accounts of his wife in his autobiography. Both suffered illnesses very different in manifestation but similarly ineradicable, and similarly emotional in origin.[4]

It was in that same summer of 1937, for us the last in Europe before the Second World War, that Mrs. Woolf arranged a meeting for Elinor with her sister, Vanessa Bell. As a result, we bought the small oil painting of an English garden, a sketch for the larger picture which Mrs. Bell had painted for one of the private dining rooms on the "Queen Mary." [5]

This visit to London was darkened by the imminence of war. I remember Lady Colfax comparing the state of mind of the English on the eve of 1914 with their state of mind in 1937. "Then," she remarked, "no one thought of war. Now no one thinks of anything else."

Directly after Hitler came to power in Germany in 1933, an English colleague discussed our prospects as historians. "It's all very well for you to plan," he said, "but what future is there for a man of my generation in England? We are doomed." By that time I already rated America's chances of remaining aloof much lower than he.

On the boat going back in 1933 we found James McLaughlin, then a forty year-old professor in the Harvard Law School, whose father, Andrew C. McLaughlin, had been my father's colleague at Chicago and whose family had known the Castles, the Meads and the Nefs closely since the beginning of this century. McLaughlin had been an artillery captain in the United States Army and had fought in France. He was on his way home to Cambridge, Massachusetts after spending several weeks in Germany. He saw the German problem as it had revealed itself to me eight years before. Now all the pent up desire to kill and conquer was ready for release. It had found its "leader."

Philipp Fehl (a graduate of our interdisciplinary faculty at Chicago who has become Professor of Art in the University of Illinois) has pointed out recently that German expressionist art was suited to the war posters of the First World War as "Art Nouveau" was not. Fehl writes out of a central European childhood. Expressionist art came into its own as never before with the rise and triumph of the Nazis, which Fehl witnessed. It screamed forth the "beauty" of desperate acts of aggression, which our student tutor in Munich in 1925 had explained in a lower key but with the same fiendish conviction. There was only one way to meet it, Jim McLaughlin kept telling us on that Atlantic crossing. Alas, after my experience with Germans how could I doubt that he was right? But I averted my eyes as I have instinctively done since childhood. Elinor could not avert hers. What she saw rising in Germany during the six years following 1933 shattered her already weakened spiritual defenses as Nazi genocide was to shatter the physical defenses of millions during the war that came.

One's heart went out to those on the other side, especially to the French, who did not want to fight as obviously as the Germans wanted to. France seemed already surrounded. Mussolini began to shout "Corsica, Nice and Savoy" and soon afterwards embarked on the conquest of Abyssinia. We crossed the channel from Folkstone in July 1936 driving from Boulogne, with Jim McLaughlin's sister (Constance McLaughlin Green, who later became a Pulitzer Prize winner for her history of Washington) and her daughter Lois. We spent the night in comfortable hotel rooms at Lille as the Spanish Civil War burst on the world, creating what one feared would be a third front for France. The French Royalist newspaper *Action Française* and other right wing organs set about to forestall an engagement against the Franco revolution by the French government under the Socialist prime minister, Léon Blum. During the twenties, when the "incomplete" Poincaré had been trying to build defenses against Germany with the royalists' blessing, the left press in Paris referred to him as "Poincaré la guerre" (Poincaré means War). Now headlines, under royalist inspiration, screamed "Blum la guerre!"—a slogan ill suited to Blum's intelligent and finely cultivated mind.

Before going to Paris to be greeted by these headlines, we drove in search of documents to Arras and Cambrai. At Arras we were rewarded by a most attractive and cultured archivist, who made transcripts of many local documents enabling me to work out the production of beer in the town over a stretch of years in the sixteenth and seventeenth centuries. I used these materials in my comparison of economic growth in France and England from 1540 to 1640.[6] As we were leaving Arras, the archivist advised us to visit Vimy Ridge, scene of a shortlived Canadian victory against the German army in the First World War. The trenches dug by the Canadians had been preserved for interested visitors.

We had already tasted the conditions of that war at Cambrai. I had a list of documents, culled from the printed inventories, to be examined in the communal archives. When he saw the list, the concierge, who replaced the local archivist on vacation with his large family, said not a single one of these items remained. When they retreated, the Germans had set fire to the Archives. Those manuscripts which had not been burned had been drowned by the advancing Canadians in their efforts to put out the fire.

The effect of the old trenches twenty years after, on a man who might have lived and died in them if he had been a trifle older, was devastating. It seemed inconceivable that men could bear the mud and the horror of "going over the top," after the freezing cold, the drenching dampness ten and twenty yards under the soil. All one's instincts, all one's hopes, cried "Never again!"

And yet what was to come was worse. Atrocities in plenty there had been, no doubt, during the First World War. Being in those trenches seemed itself atrocious. But there at least one would have been with fellow soldiers, there would have been some spirit of comradeship with a prospect of furloughs, even if one hadn't the luck to get a light wound nicknamed by the French poilus "la bonne blessure" (the happy wound). There would have been the possibility of nights spent in the arms of a girl willing to give all to a soldier defending her country. Danger and the prospect of a short life could and did heighten the comfort and consolation of sensitive men and women whose romantic senses were awakened. Alan Seeger sang for many of his generation and the generation that followed in *I Have a Rendezvous With Death*.

The war that loomed in 1936 spared many the ordeal of the trenches. But in its place every horror we had been brought up to think of as medieval was revived: reintroduction of relentless physical torture, herding into buildings innocent women and children to be burned alive when the soldiers deliberately set them on fire. In addition came mass destruction from the air, and infliction of limitless shame, pain, disgrace and incineration in boxcars and gas chambers for millions of both sexes and all ages accused of no crime other than their race or their refusal to hail Hitler.

Medieval cruelties and horrors past belief had been inflicted with at least some pretense that higher goals were being served, such as the saving of souls from damnation. The object of the concentration camps, with their millions of victims without benefit of martyrdom, was the dehumanization of man and especially of woman.

After our 1936 visit to the First War battlefields, we moved on to Paris where I could work among the documents in the **Archives** Nationales. Some days later we set out for Poitiers, Bordeaux, Agen, Moissac and Toulouse. Then, on a most beautiful evening, we drove over one of the artificially restored drawbridges that spanned the moat surrounding old Carcassonne. To our astonishment the area about the Hôtel de la Cité was choked with dozens of splendid Hispano-Suizas. After the four of us had changed clothes, we found the dining hall full of well-dressed Spaniards, mostly women and little girls and boys with their nannies. They were the wives, children and servants of the principal officials of the Hispano-Suiza enterprise at Barcelona, escaping in company automobiles.

Everywhere in France that summer and the next we were confronted in the newspapers and magazines with news of battles on the other side of the Pyrenees. The French sensed that the Spanish Civil War was only a prelude to the degradation of Europe under Nazi leadership. The obliteration from the air of the small town of Guernica, in Spain, was a rehearsal for later destruction of villages, towns and cities all over the world.

During the Second World War a story came out of France about Picasso. Perhaps it is apocryphal, but it reveals a side of that great artist that should not be lost in the presence of some of his cheaper work. In German-occupied Paris little heat was to be had. Picasso apparently found it less uncomfortable to sketch and paint in his small apartment on an upper story overlooking the rue La Boetie than to work across the Seine in his studio in the rue Jacob on lower, damper ground. One winter afternoon he was as usual at work, with friends gathered about him, huddled close together to keep warm.

In occupied Paris there were no automobiles moving save those of the Conqueror. All was still in the Picasso apartment, when suddenly the visitors detected the noise of a motorcar stopping in front of the building. A couple of minutes later there was a knock at the door. One of Picasso's friends opened it. There, in morning coat and high silk hat, stood a German. Picasso paid no attention. The Nazi approached him in some embarrassment. "Master," he said, "I am Otto Abetz, the German Ambassador. I don't know if you are aware of it, but I have always been one of your greatest admirers, not least because as a young man it was my supreme ambition to become a painter. Since I have come to Paris, there hasn't been a night when I haven't thought of you. I have kept saying to myself, 'Has the

Master enough to eat? Has he adequate means of keeping warm?'
I couldn't bear not to come and see. I will arrange, if you permit, to
provide you first with coal and then with some delicacies of which I
know you are now deprived."

Picasso simply said, "I need nothing," and went on painting. After
several unfruitful attempts at conversation Abetz tried another tack.
"Master," he said, "it would mean much to me if I could see some of
your latest work."

At that Picasso put down his brush and went into an adjacent
room. He returned with a large photograph of *Guernica*. That immense canvas had been on exhibition in the United States when war
was declared, and it was destined to remain in New York as part of
the collection of the Museum of Modern Art. Picasso handed the
photograph to Abetz, who held it in his hands and gave it careful
study. At length he said, "Master, it's a wonderful work. Perhaps it
is the greatest picture you have made. As a person who tried once to
paint himself, I am filled with admiration. I find myself wanting to
have you tell me how you did it." Picasso answered: "I didn't; you did."

22. BONDS WITH EUROPEANS

Even when we were unable to go abroad our connections with
Europeans were never summarily cut off. We were blessed continually
with visitors who shared our susceptibility to works of the imagination. Without encouragement I might never have founded the Committee on Social Thought or the Center of Human Understanding.

Two distinguished scholars whom we had met in England arrived
on the scene while I was a graduate student in Washington. Both
entered our family circle on terms of intimacy, one over a period of
months, the other briefly but intensively.

The first was Graham Wallas. Brookings School brought him as a
visiting member of its small graduate faculty for a semester. He had a
room at the old Cosmos Club on Lafayette Square and complained
that the radiators thundered too early in the morning a summons
to awake. He was frequently our dinner companion, alone or with
other friends. His lectures were few, delightfully informal and discursive. His dinner conversation often seemed a continuation of his
lectures as his lectures seemed a continuation of his dinner talk. Both

were variations on themes that were fresh in his mind because of books he had written or was planning to write. Norman Hapgood (the well-known magazine editor of the age of Wilson and Brandeis), who loved to talk with the vocabulary of a journalistic drama critic about the theatre, letters and art, and who when in Washington joined us on these occasions, used rather unkindly to attribute Wallas' relaxed meanderings to "anecdotitis." Hapgood meant presumably that the old gentleman, then in his seventies, had entered his anecdotage. Yet this seems a superficial diagnosis. One wonders if Wallas' mind had not always worked in much the same discursive way—as a reflection of inwardly darting thoughts which were far from systematic, but to which he managed nevertheless to give respectable form in his major works. His habit of carrying a tiny notebook in his vest pocket, and stopping in the midst of his lecture to bring it out and record some notion that had suddenly lit up inside him, was certainly nothing new. Thirty years before, at the end of the nineteenth century, when the Wallas and the Webbs, as fellow Fabians, were frequently together *en famille* the habit is said to have annoyed Sidney Webb. Mrs. Wallas tried to smooth it over by explaining to Beatrice: "Graham isn't putting down what Sidney says; he's putting down what he thinks about what Sidney says."

The *Art of Thought* was a subject dear to Wallas. His notion that the most seminal and original ideas often come when we are relaxed away from our last, can be traced back at least as far as Aubrey's *Life of Hobbes* and down through Archbishop Temple, who, in his Gifford Lectures, *Nature, Man, and God* (1934), speaks of it as characteristic of his experience. For those who have this kind of mind, creative thought *is* an art. I remember feeling nonplussed later at the University of Chicago when a young German colleague asked me to deliver a lecture (I think for the sociological club) on *my* historical method. I could only exclaim, "I haven't one!"

Wallas helped to give me confidence in the ways my mind evolved. He also strengthened a conviction that works based on intuition at their best, are more enduring than treatises that simply set forth factual propositions. His failure to organize his materials systematically, as the Webbs did, seemed a virtue.

Wallas was a great teacher. Whether in class, conference or social communion, the absence of inhibitions, formalities and forbidding restraints, often associated with the English, was most engaging. Of all Englishmen I have known, Wallas found it easiest to like Americans. For others this required effort; it was a duty. His liking was intuitive.

It was through Wallas that we came to know Gaetano Salvemini. He had been a professor of history at the University of Florence and a principal opponent of Mussolini in the Italian Chamber of Deputies to such a point that he broke with the new regime soon after the march on Rome. He took refuge first in England and during most of the twenties was probably Mussolini's most effective English-speaking opponent. His prominence in the United States was derived less from his scholarly publications (which then existed mainly in Italian) than from his political stance. For American lecture bureaus he became *the* leading anti-fascist. Later he was made a professor at Harvard.

Before our return from Europe, Wallas had read us a letter of Salvemini's written from the States. In it he described the standard arrangements made for his appearance on lecture platforms. To guard against charges of partiality (after the fashion of the apocryphal English lord-mayor who, newly elected, promised his constituents to administer justice without partiality or impartiality) lecture agents invariably billed Salvemini with a fascist partner. This rival was accorded equal time. Towards the end of their joint program, Salvemini explained in his letter, the discussion came to resemble "una partita di box" (a boxing match).

The Tawneys also knew Salvemini as a welcome opponent of dictatorship. Not long after our arrival in Washington a letter from Mrs. Tawney told us Salvemini was coming to America again. We invited him to stay with us and managed to get him a scholarly lecture at the Brookings Graduate School on "Florence in the Time of Dante." In addition his lecture agent arranged a meeting so he could present his case against fascism.

Already in those days the United States government took elaborate steps for the security of political refugees. It was impressed upon us that, in addition to the police protection provided, we should be wary of dangerous characters who might lurk about while Salvemini was our guest. I decided to scrutinize carefully the audience for his Brookings lecture. Standing at the entrance to the building on I Street I saw advancing an ill-dressed foreigner. I accosted him for credentials. My embarrassment was considerable when he handed

me a letter from Salvemini referring to him as a close friend. This
brought an end to these guard activities for which I was obviously
ill-equipped.

Salvemini was a delightful guest. We invited several local scholars
to come in for meals and our conversation almost invariably led into
questions of letters and of art. In return for our hospitality Harold
Moulton organized a stag dinner with the then small staff at Brookings. These social scientists were in another world of discourse from
the political battle that concerned Salvemini in his public appear-
ances; they were still farther from the world of artistic scholarship
offered him in our Fairfax apartment surrounded by pictures.

At the Brookings dinner the program concentrated on questions
of economic theory and statistics. There was no light moment until
after the desert. Then Salvemini told a story about a poor atheist
in the thirteenth century condemned to death by the Pope. Before
handing the culprit over to the civil authorities for burning, the
Pope offered him a stay of execution on condition he would tell how
much water there was in the Mediterranean Sea. Without hesitation,
the man answered: "There are nine trillion, four hundred and ninety
billion, eight hundred million, six hundred and twenty thousand,
seventy-two and a half buckets. And," he added, "if your Holiness
doesn't believe me, he can measure them himself."

"He was," Salvemini concluded, "the first statistician." No one
smiled and soon afterward the members of the Brookings staff said
good night in preparation for another day of scientific research.

After Washington and Swarthmore came Chicago. In the autumn
of 1931 we moved from a small into a large apartment on Dorchester
Avenue near the university buildings and lecture halls. This was
my home for thirty years. It gave us space for the two things we
loved most, people and paintings. There was also a study, which we
lined to the ceiling with books, and where I worked in the mornings.

Henceforth we received a parade of Europeans, some of whom became fast friends. Their visits ranged from a tea time rendezvous to
a stay of weeks. Among those who merely flitted by were Le Corbusier and Fernand Léger.

Three young local architects brought Le Corbusier out for the
evening. The conversation about architecture and the graphic arts
was most animated. The great architect was drawn to us and to the
pictures that surrounded us, many of them by friends of his. He

sent us, in thanks for that evening, one of his colored gouaches.

Léger first came to Chicago with a mistress, to the horror of some good society folk. He was feted by Rue Carpenter, founder of the Chicago Arts Club and first wife of the businessman-composer John Alden Carpenter. She arranged an evening so Léger could show slides of his pictures in a lecture hall of the University Hospital. I sat just in front of Léger. Soon after the opening, one of the slides was thrown on the screen upside down. Léger's immediate ejaculation was "On croira que c'est voulu" (They'll think that's the way I painted it.)

He spent most of the war years in the United States. When the Institute of Design invited him to Chicago again, he delivered a lecture in the rooms of the Arts Club, then in the Wrigley Building just north of the Chicago River. As he had never learned English, I translated for the audience. In return, Léger gave Elinor first choice among his pictures assembled for exhibit and sale. She bought a small abstract, brilliant watercolor.

I had met Léger at the train and we discussed his text during our long drive from South Chicago to the Wrigley Building. His attitude towards art was part of a grand plan he had of a total architecture for working class quarters, in which his pictures would provide color and light and give the working man pleasure in the mechanized labor and the dingy surroundings of the industrialized society that was taking over existence. Léger's position seemed logical. It made his works understandable. For my taste his work always seemed rather too mechanistic. But he was a serious artist and in many compositions he put colors together with much charm and style.

The relationship of a new architecture to my hope of creating a Center for scholars and artists was taking form at the time of Léger's second visit. During the war it seemed that new ideas relating to reconstruction and rebuilding could become more than dreams. Both Le Corbusier and Léger attracted my attention to architecture. But the hope that the Committee on Social Thought might participate in the rebuilding of Chicago came from friendships formed with two men from Central Europe. Both already had great reputations over there when the Nazis came to power. One, Ludwig Mies van der Rohe, was of Dutch origin; the other, Laszlo Moholy Nagy, was Hungarian. Though neither was Jewish, both left Germany soon after the tyranny was established and settled in Chicago for Central Europe ceased to be livable for true artists.

The rising Nazi threat to the peace of the world and to human decency took graphic form in connection with pictures which were added to those we had brought from Europe. One day, about 1935, Elinor came home with two pen and ink drawings by George Grosz. She must have realized they would shock me and so she had bought them on her own for next to nothing, from Alice Roullier I seem to remember. The smaller is a street scene with a man who looks rather like Hitler. The other, "The Art Critics," is a cruel portrayal of a group having after dinner coffee in a salon. Their shortcomings are so relentlessly revealed that a sensitive mind suffers even more acutely than over photographs of atrocities or obscenities perpetrated in concentration camps.

At first I couldn't confront the creatures in those drawings without discomfort. But now, decades later, when almost in spite of myself I have some inkling of what the human character at its most cynical can be; now after the contemporary cruelties and horrors of the war years in Europe have become history these pictures seem in an inverted sense superb. A Chicago lady, who was one of the White House advisers on art during the Kennedy régime and who is a talented decorator herself, told me she regarded "The Art Critics" as among the greatest of Grosz's drawings.

One evening over dinner, sometime around 1937, a student guest told me he was studying architecture with a master at what was then the Armour Institute of Technology. "He is the greatest man in Chicago or for that matter in this country; his name is Mies van der Rohe," the student said. That was the first time I heard of the great architect. This genius actually sought me out because he agreed with my academic ideas and initiative. A mutual friend, another architect, Alfred Shaw, brought us together. Shaw had married the first Mrs. Carpenter's niece and namesake, Rue Winterbotham. Mrs. Shaw eventually became the third President of the Arts Club her aunt had founded and got Mies van der Rohe to do the building in which it is now housed.

Before Mies had begun to have many orders, which is to say during the war, Shaw and he and I used to lunch or dine together on an average of once a month. We met sometimes in the Shaw, sometimes in the Nef apartment, sometimes at a restaurant or club.

Our object was to consider how we might help one another in our work, and how this might contribute to a better United States.

Historical exploration had led me to believe that all sides of a society's or a country's development are interrelated. The architecture of an epoch—for instance the Romanesque and Gothic in Europe or the Baroque—is both a reflection of its history and an influence upon that history. Mies and Shaw asked me to give my views on these interrelations in a lecture (one of a series) sponsored by the American Institute of Architects with support from the Sociology Department of the University of Chicago.[1]

Mies recognized in my view on the place of architecture in society and the need for reforms in education, ideas that supported and dove-tailed with his for rebuilding the city of Chicago along new lines. He was surprisingly timid in the use of words, indeed he appeared to some as inarticulate. The word that most attracted him was "Order."

Despite his reticence, he eventually evoked in our conversations a grandiose scheme for doing over the waterfront for many miles along Lake Michigan. He envisaged a series of causeways running parallel to the shore about two miles out. These would relieve traffic congestion and provide a setting for buildings in his characteristic style.

I had thought, even before I met Mies, that the chaotic illness of urban life, which was revealing itself then and was destined more recently to disgrace our cities, might be healed by some overall conception of architectural genius. For example in Los Angeles, where we went in the winter, were three or four fine houses Frank Lloyd Wright had been commissioned to build. They were lost in a sea of cardboardish constructions and cluttered vacant lots. How wonderful it would be to have an entire city the expression of one or better still of all the innovators, among whom Wright and Mies were prominent. For Mies the Committee on Social Thought, as a university creation designed to bring together many scholarly disciplines and to bridge the gulf between the sciences and the arts, was an ideal institutional base for a plan to rebuild Chicago he imagined. If it worked, the plan could be used by other cities. The decentralization we recognized as a need for American life could be carried through under the aegis of great art. Financial support might come from rich business interests and from the Chicago city government. With enthusiasm born of these dreams, Shaw endeavored to draw a few businessmen and municipal officials into our small meetings of three. Alas nary a businessman came and only one local politician, an alderman who was then out of office and has never since got back.

At the time, during the war, Mies was virtually unknown in Chicago circles as a practicing architect. A few years later he found a financial backer who helped this modest unobtrusive genius get orders. Thereafter Mies was paid to construct individual buildings here and there, in other cities as well as Chicago, for instance in New York, in Houston, in Washington. But the idea of an entire city laid out artistically, with architecture as its unifying theme and appropriately supported by municipal planners, who would conform their wishes to the projects of the artist, was never considered.

There are of course precedents in history for unified cities. Ledoux's small town not far from Dole in Franche Comté at Arc-et-Senans, built originally in Louis XV's reign to facilitate the manufacture of salt, remains an impressive example of such an effort. Other creations are in the air today especially since the building of Brasilia.

Perhaps the idea discussed at those meetings with Mies and Shaw will be taken up in the future and extended to many cities all over the world. A civilized humanity such as has never existed on this planet, can hardly be achieved unless men are able to master the powers of destruction science and technology have placed in their hands. The realization of such a scheme as Mies had for Chicago could help to divert labor and materials on a vast scale from destructive to constructive industry. Its success would depend upon a widespread revival of craftsmanship, for both Wright and Mies encountered frustrating difficulties in fulfilling even the small orders they received because no craftsmen were available for carrying through their designs and furnishing their buildings. Think what would be needed in the way of craftsmanship if much of America and other parts of the world were rebuilt under the inspiration of beauty.

This prospect of having to train a substantial minority of the population in craftsmanship will dismay only those whose careers are determined by the trends, those who climb aboard trains headed for what is likely to be, rather than for what ought to be. Perhaps nothing is more needed for future human welfare than a revival of craftsmanship, for new and interesting opportunities to work with the hands. The kind of architectural world that concerned Mies and Shaw, combined with my dream for an interdisciplinary faculty extended to many universities,[2] could do much to create and nourish new artists and craftsmen. It could revive inventive workmanship. It could awaken individual men and women to a creative purpose.[3]

Many today feel the need for just that. They now have, in amateur pastimes, only pusillanimous means of fulfillment. Their artistic instincts may be obliterated, even without a nuclear holocaust, if high rise buildings, mechanical engines and computors become, not our servants, but our mentors.

In Chicago when the Committee on Social Thought was starting I found another supporter in Moholy Nagy. He had come as a youth from Hungary to Berlin, drawn by the group of distinguished architects and artists who formed the Bauhaus in the interval between the end of the First World War and the establishment of the Nazi regime. Our friendship developed as the war was ending.

When Moholy left Germany in the thirties and settled in Chicago he was faced with the problem of making a living and taking care of a wife and two small daughters, in a place where very few valued or even knew about his reputation as a versatile artist. In the tradition of the Bauhaus he had added to his knowledge of architecture and painting a familiarity with crafts which, though they seemed to be dying everywhere in the world, were necessary for making furniture and other objects for new houses.

Elinor's and my meetings with Moholy became frequent; it was at his house that we were introduced to Gropius, another great architect, and Giedion, the Swiss writer on architecture. I discovered that Giedion had made an extensive use of *The Rise of the British Coal Industry* in one of his books on architecture—of course without acknowledging in print the debt of which he spoke freely on meeting me.

Moholy always had a hard struggle obtaining money. A group of Chicagoans led by Walter Paepcke, head of the Container Corporation and later (with his wife) founder of Aspen, gave him financial help in starting the Institute of Design, where he set about training students in the arts and crafts. As the Second World War was ending, and the "Committee on Social Thought" was about to develop, he looked forward to cooperation with us. Elinor had long taken much interest in his work. In his turn he recognized her extraordinary taste. He asked me to lecture at the Institute of Design. At the time I was developing an historical thesis concerning the renewal in Europe following the awful struggles of the Reformation and the religious wars. He found a validity in the analogies I drew to the epoch through which we were living. I remember with gratitude and emotion the way he introduced me to his students for the opening lecture. When a week later it was time for the second, he was in the hospital stricken with leukemia. Although he rallied, went to New York, and came back to sit in a small room adjoining the lecture hall to discuss one of my later lectures, he died before the series was completed.

Like the ideas of Mies van der Rohe, those of Moholy concerning the crafts are suited to the epoch ahead, if peaceful relations can be established throughout the world and the overwhelmingly destructive weapons put aside for keeps. Although from different backgrounds, both men recognized the connection between their plans and mine, and the validity of both plans for the future. I dimly recognized their bearing on the future in 1941 when *The United States and Civilization* was finished. It was clearer in 1967 when the second rewritten edition appeared.[4]

A third artist from Central Europe, who joined forces with me morally on the eve of the Second World War, was Victor Hammer. A Viennese, he sought asylum when the Germans entered Austria, because of deep opposition to the Nazi dictatorship, although it presented no immediate threat to his life as an over-age gentile.

Thanks to his work he had friends outside Central Europe. He had much to do with the decoration of the castle and built the chapel at Kolbsheim, near Strasbourg. Kolbsheim is owned by Alexis Grunelius and Hammer had painted the portrait of the proprietor's wife, a granddaughter of Guizot, Antoinette Schlumberger Grunelius. After the war we were to know the Grunelius through Jacques Maritain and to visit them.

When Hammer came as a refugee to the United States, he found a post as teacher of printing at Wells College for young women, not far from Cornell. He was not only a painter and architect, but also a printer-craftsman, who set type by hand most beautifully and operated a small hand press. He continued inconspicuously and frugally at this work and managed, after his retirement from Wells, to find some small financial support in Lexington, Kentucky, as artist-in-residence at Translyvania University. His first wife died in 1954 and a year later he remarried. His second wife was one of his pupils, Carolyn Reading.

Hammer was a man of many talents, an artist of the old academic nineteenth-century school. No one could think of him as avant-garde.

He was not touched by genius in the way that Mies van der Rohe, and even perhaps Moholy were. Yet unobtrusively he was a more stalwart pillar for what would be creative innovations than either. He was more uncompromising as a craftsman.

He used to spend days going over published books and articles of mine, marking and then discussing the passages that he considered aesthetically felicitous, as well as others that called for improvement. His hero was a neglected nineteenth-century philosopher and patron of art, Conrad Fiedler (1841-1895), whom he regarded as one of the most gifted men of letters of modern times. He found me potentially Fielder's equal and recognized my hope of finding a place in letters as legitimate. He also recognized the need that existed in the universities for transcending scholarship in the cause of art.

So, not unnaturally, as the idea of founding a faculty both for scholars and creative artists claimed my imagination, I drew strength from my growing friendship with Hammer. He invited me to lecture at Wells and offered me an opportunity to demonstrate how the barriers between departments of knowledge could be pierced to the advantage of learning as well as of art. I chose to treat the interrelations between great Elizabethan and Jacobean literature and music and the industrial and technological innovations of that age in Great Britain.[5] As we both wished, the entire student body and faculty attended. Here was an effort on behalf of the creation of the general public for the *art* of scholarship we both sought.

This visit to Wells also introduced me to Hammer's family and his printer's shop. Thereafter we had frequent meetings in Chicago. We retained to the end of his life our artistic communion.

Among other foreign visitors who came to us in Chicago before the war were a remarkably engaging English don from Cambridge, H. S. Bennett, and a French gentleman, Charles Du Bos, whom Jacques Maritain sent with an introduction. Both were sympathetic to the unorthodox approach to university instruction and research that impelled me towards educational reform.

Bennett (whom his wife and friends always call Stanley) was at the beginning of the twentieth century one of those stunningly handsome young Englishmen whom the oncoming German soldiers were being trained to kill. He never lost his fine presence. While he did not die in the First World War as Rupert Brooke did, like

Tawney he was terribly smashed up, losing one of his legs. I never heard him speak of that though we met frequently over forty years.

We became friends when he spent a semester as visiting member of the English Department at the University of Chicago in 1930. And in 1939 I had the pleasure of being delegated to invite him to take a permanent chair in the Department of History. He declined partly because he felt, like Tawney, a duty to remain in Great Britain during the onslaught upon his country that the Germans under Hitler were obviously about to unleash. After the war he came on three separate occasions under the aegis of the Committee. He stayed for a whole quarter year in 1948, along with Tawney and the Oxford trained Italian scholar and political thinker, Alesandro d'Entreves. He came twice later with his wife, Joan Bennett, who was also a member of the Cambridge faculty.

Bennett became a syndic and then the chairman of the Board of Syndics of the Cambridge University Press. It was his wide cultural interests, and his association of creative art—especially poetry and the novel—with scholarship which made him naturally a part, whenever he came to Chicago after it had been founded in 1942, of our interdisciplinary faculty. Bennett's deep and learned understanding of medieval economic and literary history and his penetrating inquiry into the English reading public during the early period of printing, never submerged his interest in the literary life of our era. He was as far as possible in outlook from that professor of art on the "Mauritania" who, because his subject was fifteenth century Spanish art, had no interest in meeting Segonzac.

Bennett had been recommended as a Chaucer scholar in 1930 to my father's old colleague John Manly, who specialized in Chaucer and was long head of the English Department at Chicago. Manly had planned to bring G. G. Coulton, the eccentric medievalist, but Coulton, being unable to come at that time, persuaded Manly to take in his stead his younger colleague and friend. Bennett, had none of the prejudices which led the old gentleman into polemics. He revealed at once his independence of the specialization that was becoming so prevalent in graduate teaching and scholarship. We used to converse animatedly over luncheon at the round table in the Quadrangle Club, reserved for the faculty in the "Social Sciences." It was suggestive of his broad interests that he chose that table when there was another for the humanities faculty.

He used to describe, as he saw it in 1930, the English literary scene particularly as represented by novelists. "Never," he said, "had so many technically competent novels been written, excellent in style and even in structure." Their weakness was that most of their authors had "nothing to say."

Those words struck a chord that brought us forever into the same orbit. Soon afterwards he came home to meet Elinor. And then we made friends with his wife during our summers abroad.

Somewhere Pascal, in describing a contemporary, remarks "on s'attendait un auteur et on trouvait un homme." (One was prepared for an author and one found a man.) The description has always seemed to suit Bennett. If he failed to fit easily into any scholarly niche, that is precisely because he had the quality of completeness that our French restaurant proprietor missed in Poincaré. In our effort to serve the whole human being, Bennett was always an incomparable ally.

Du Bos came to the Midwest later than Bennett, in the late thirties, and what might have become a long friendship was cut short by his death in Paris on the eve of the War. He had taken part actively in the French literary movements of his time and revealed a stunning talent for criticism displayed better in speech than in print. Author of many books and articles, he never found a respectable position in the academic setup. He had neglected to work for the kind of degree that would have entitled him to teach in a French university or even a lycée. The only place for him would have been the Collège de France. That great institution, of which more later, has welcomed some men of letters, among them Paul Valéry, who have not the necessary degree. But so far as I know, Du Bos never thought of presenting himself as a candidate. And the only way of getting in is to announce your candidacy when there is a vacancy and then call on all the surviving members to solicit their votes.

Du Bos had come to America at the invitation of Sister Madeleva, President of Saint Mary's College in South Bend, Indiana, (the female Notre Dame). A gifted poet familiar with the French literary scene, Sister Madeleva appreciated Du Bos' remarkable range and the depth of his literary and philosophic, as well as his religious, understanding. He soon became a frequent visitor to the Dorchester Avenue apartment, where he was at home among the pictures and the conversation, particularly Elinor's. He was the only person I have known, and my acquaintance is rather extensive, who was completely bi-lingual. He had an English mother and a French father and could deliver a technically perfect lecture in either English or French. He did this not infrequently, as we Americans say, "out of school." He was quite capable, when simply a guest, of improvising a lecture. All one had to do was to raise some question that interested him concerning literature or philosophy or politics. He instantly embarked on an impeccably phrased, beautifully organized and marvelously illuminating exposition. It sounded better than if the lecture had been prepared a week in advance.

He spent a day with us in the autumn of 1938, when Jacques Maritain with his wife and sister-in-law were our houseguests. On that occasion he delivered in French an unforgettable lecture on "Munich." The surrender of the French and British under Daladier and Chamberlain horrified him. In his peroration he kept repeating "Oh, Jacques, comme c'est lache!" (Oh how cowardly).

Du Bos' reception in South Bend was unworthy of his gifts. Although he liked Sister Madeleva, and was joined by his wife and daughter for whom he had much affection, hardly anyone else paid him attention. He once announced a course on Pascal. One student registered.

When at my suggestion Hutchins tried to get him a post on the University of Chicago faculty, he was vetoed by the dean of the Humanities. This was among many experiences I had during the thirties which led me in the forties, after Du Bos was gone, to found the Committee on Social Thought. I hoped to be able to make appointments like Du Bos through such a department. In spite of his rejection by American scholarship he has come to be recognized in France since his death as worthy of a small but definite niche in the history of literary criticism.

23. THE FRIENDLY ARENSBERGS

My contract with the University of Chicago called for residence, at a reduced salary, during the autumn and spring quarters. This arrangement, made possible by the Economics Department, enabled me to undertake research and writing six months each year wherever we found it desirable to be and to carry on student and faculty business by correspondence. Our annual sojourn in southern California lasted from three weeks to three months.

In Los Angeles we were without our pictures. This gave us a strange feeling, something like missing members of a closely knit, harmonious family. The pictures always seemed an indispensable part of my life as a teacher, for we received many students in our Chicago apartment and believed in the influence of surroundings.

We would have missed the pictures and foreign visitors more had it not been for our friendship with Louise and Walter Arensberg, to whom Elinor's mother introduced us. They had a collection of contemporary paintings and other works of art which was becoming famous and is now part of the Philadelphia Museum of Art. The four of us were drawn to one another from the start. Two childless couples, we were deeply concerned—in different ways but with a similar intensity which makes for fruitful discussion—with the artistic manifestations of our times.

This friendship began early in the thirties, before the period when such eminent Europeans as Schoenberg, Stravinsky, Thomas Mann and Aldous Huxley settled in southern California. The Arensberg house in Hollywood provided an oasis of escape from publicity and motion picture activities. Many magical paintings were crowded into various positions in the entrance hall and on the large closed-in veranda; the bedrooms and bathrooms were stuffed with them; so was Walter's study and they were also to be found along every stairway and corridor.

The Arensberg oasis offered a chance to meet artists; persons such as Man Ray, who had already done some fine photographs of Elinor in Paris, and Salvador Dali, who has incredible facility with paint but rather little to communicate.

I continued working and reading seven or eight hours each day in my mother-in-law's house, a small, rather plain but comfortable dwelling in a working class quarter of Los Angeles. Each year in Chicago I packed huge bundles of notes into a large Vuitton suitcase specially made to hold them, so I would never lack materials.

This small house also gave us a place to return the Arensberg hospitality, which was endless, and to introduce them to friends, such as Artur Schnabel, Dallas Phemister, Hamlin Garland and Edwin F. Gay. Gay has been called the father of economic history in the United States. He was a much travelled man who joined the staff of the nearby Huntington Library upon his retirement from Harvard.

At the Arensberg's house conditions of easy communication prevailed. Cézannes, Picasso abstractions, a Chagall and a remarkable painting by De la Fresnaye were present as one talked. The works that the Arensbergs had assembled were an intimate part of the family life of those two simple and modest art lovers. Louise Arensberg was an accomplished pianist, and their enthusiasm extended to music, poetry and letters. They often invited poets like Witter Bynner to dinner and to spend the evening. But Walter had little time for reading compared with us, for he was heavily occupied in an effort to master what he called the Francis Bacon cipher, a means he imagined of proving once and for all that Bacon was the author of all Shakespeare. He had been working on this since his youth, but never finished in spite of a long life of almost eighty years. He was restrained about inflicting these activities on his friends, although he once showed me that the last letter in three consecutive lines of Shakespeare spelled P-I-G!

I have never found it easy to converse with a masculine type of woman. The two most famous that we met in America during the thirties were Gertrude Stein and Frieda Lawrence, D. H. Lawrence's German widow. Gertrude Stein spent several days in Chicago with Alice B. Toklas and Emily Chadbourne under the roof of Frank and Frances Lillie. We were constantly invited to their parties, but I was never sufficiently at home with Miss Stein to make even a small effort at conversation. Perhaps this was because, as Pierre Sickel in his *Life of Modigliani* has written, "Gertrude was a prude, a bourgeoise at heart; essentially humorless, she took herself very seriously." But that is not a full explanation of *my* shyness. Miss Stein had unusual gifts of exposition as I recognized in a lecture she gave about England. If I had met her not at the Lillie's but in a cozier setting we might have got on better.

Frieda Lawrence used to come for a part of the winter to Hollywood from New Mexico with her lover, an Italian named Luigi Ravagli, whom she later married. At the first Arensberg dinner that they attended with us, he was placed next to my mother-in-law. Having no idea of his identity, Mabel Castle asked pleasantly, "What do you do?" The loud, firm answer came promptly, "I leeve with Freeda."

It is easy to imagine this was a strenuous occupation. His answer could have broken the ice. But I held back that evening, partly I think because Frieda was smoking cigars. Perhaps I had acquired the notion at Harvard that cigarettes were more ladylike. President Abbott Lawrence Lowell was reputed to have remarked, "Nobody smokes cigarettes except women and effeminate men." All the young dons who had academic aspirations took note of the remark to the extent of struggling with immense cigars whenever they smoked at Lowell's house!

Later at another Arensberg party I sought Frieda Lawrence out after dinner and started a conversation. It went well. She spoke of intimate things naturally. I was fascinated by what she told me about three writers whose work interested me, Lawrence himself, and John Middleton Murry and Katherine Mansfield who had lived with the Lawrences for a time in Cornwall. What impressed me most was Frieda's enthusiasm for Lawrence. "He smelt good!" she said triumphantly.

Of all the paintings the Arensbergs possessed there was one in particular for which I developed a weakness. It was by Henri Matisse, painted in 1914. It portrays a life-sized transparent woman in blue—Yvonne Landsberg. This is the most striking Matisse I have ever seen. I have seen many, including two of the most famous ones, the very large canvas at the Barnes Foundation and the one from Russia's Hermitage in Leningrad when it was loaned for exhibition in Bordeaux.

Whenever I was in the Arensberg living room, where that Matisse picture used to hang, I found my eyes turning towards it even in the midst of the most absorbing conversation.

Years before at the Duncan Phillips Gallery we had been much taken by a small Matisse done about ten years after the blue lady. This presented a woman reclining on a couch and apparently the Phillips sold it, for it seems to be no longer in their collection. That work made me regret we had not acquired an oil by this excellent artist when we were living in Paris.

We consoled ourselves with several Matisse lithographs. The first, a woman reclining on her elbow on a beautiful couch and contemplating a bowl of fruit and vase of flowers, was close in subject to the painting in the Phillips Gallery. That was why I bought it from Alice Roullier the minute we saw it at New Year's 1927, on vacation from the Brookings School. Later we bought five more Matisse lithographs. Two are charming heads of women, a third is a nude lying on a sofa. The fourth is another woman's head in a more classical style. We acquired the fifth in Vence in 1949, before the Matisse chapel was officially opened, a woman's portrait in the spare, sure single line style of a sculptor's drawing. We bought this from the beautiful nun who had been the master's nurse during the Second World War when he underwent a serious operation in Lyon. He is said to have attributed his recovery to her. They lost touch, but she later persuaded him to design the chapel in Vence. When she came on her mission to Nice in her nun's habit, Matisse is supposed to have exclaimed, "What a waste." He designed the chapel for nothing.

When we saw her she was selling his lithographs in an effort to cover the expenses of building. She was then much concerned over these costs. But not long thereafter paying visitors came in hordes. The financial problem dissolved, but the traffic congestion provided a different problem for Marc Chagall whose house and studio were then across the road from the chapel. Autobuses threatened to run over him on his daily walks and tourists wanted his autograph. Eventually he and his wife built a quiet retreat and moved near St. Paul de Vence.[1]

Having rejoiced so often in that ethereal blue Matisse in those familiar surroundings at the Arensbergs, I was eager to renew my friendship with it after their deaths. I saw it with Evelyn at the Chicago Art Institute, where it was recently on loan, and again in 1968 when, as hosts to the Chagalls, we were invited with them to visit the Philadelphia Museum of Art. On both occasions the effect was disappointing. The magic seemed to have gone. But I see it still as it enlightened those family parties in the thirties.

One day along about 1938 I was surprised to have Walter Arensberg telephone and ask me to lunch at the Brown Derby Restaurant. Our relations had always been à quatre (a foursome), or, if my mother-in-law came along, à cinq. Walter did not reveal his purpose until the desert. Then he began to hem and haw and, after many stops, said he and Lou had no heirs and in consequence the matter of disposing of their collection was of much concern. He went on with many more stops. They had considered ("Although nothing is decided, nothing at all") forming a group of trustees to handle the matter. In this connection they had thought ("Although nothing is decided, nothing at all") that they might ask me to be one of the trustees. I naturally said, "You must not think of dying, Walter, neither you nor Lou." He then asked, "Would you consider (although nothing is decided . . .) being a trustee?" I repeated that they must not dwell on thoughts of death, but of course if they wanted me to serve in any capacity I would. He also asked me to sound out Bob Hutchins as to whether the University of Chicago might be interested in having their pictures.

This last inquiry too was accompanied by much "ifing," to use a word the late Franklin D. Roosevelt favored. Nevertheless I asked Hutchins. He said that the university *would* be "interested." This news was reported back to Walter by mail.

After Pearl Harbor, our visits to Los Angeles ceased; Elinor's mother joined us at Dorchester Avenue and we never again spent much time in California. For a number of years we heard nothing directly about the Arensbergs' intentions concerning their collection. There were lots of rumors.

Doubtless there was little fact behind most of these, but we learned later from the Arensbergs that their collection had been temporarily "given" to the University of California and then taken back because they were not satisfied with the plans of the President. We saw them on our way to Honolulu early in 1948 and they told us they had considered leaving their pictures to the Los Angeles Museum, but had been disillusioned by the want of understanding they encountered. They later told us that Katharine Kuh, then associated with the Chicago Art Institute, had been sent to catalog the collection. The Art Institute seems to have had a serious interest in acquiring it, and the Arensbergs agreed to lend most of their pictures for exhibition in Chicago in the autumn of 1949.

Leaving Hollywood was difficult for them. I think they had never gone away during the many years we knew them. Rumors of their coming to the exhibition spread in Chicago, but for some time did not materialize. Then eventually some time *after* the opening, they came. Sam Marx, the Chicago architect and collector, who seems to have been acting for Daniel Catton Rich, then Director of the Art Institute, telephoned an invitation to dinner. Mrs. Marx told Elinor the Arensbergs wanted to be with their closest Chicago friends, ourselves. We arranged for them to dine informally with us the night before their departure. They asked to bring Marcel Duchamp who had come from the east to be with them. Their purchase of his "Nude Descending the Stairs," at the Armory Show in New York in 1913, had caused a sensation.

A couple of hours before dinner Lou called to explain she would have to stay in their room at the Blackstone Hotel although Walter and Marcel Duchamp were coming. Walter and she had gone to the Art Institute that afternoon to have a last look at the exhibition. They were alone and left the building to find rain pouring. Since they had no umbrella and no one had thought to provide them with transportation they were soaked. She was wearing the only dress she had brought and could only go to bed.

Our friendship had long reached the stage where we could come together after long absence without having to "catch up." Marcel Duchamp, who was then about sixty, turned out to be a human and delightful guest. He visited my mother-in-law lying sick in her bedroom. He fascinated her. She was a lady of eighty-five and never survived the illness that kept her from the dinner party. The conversation at that was full of those important matters which seldom get into the accounts of museum exhibitions or the chit-chat about the purchases of art dealers. What were some of the possible influences of great paintings and works of sculpture upon history? I asked. Were artists generally motivated in their work by the good as such? Maritain, Waldemar Gurian and Mortimer Adler all took part in the discussion. And however much one might have disagreed with them, they all raised real issues.

The meetings with officials and representatives from the Board of the Art Institute, meetings in which we had no part, led the Arensbergs to decide against Chicago as the home for their pictures. The soaking they received on their last day could hardly have helped.

When we next saw them two years later on the way to Hawaii again, they had decided on Philadelphia, because of visits paid them by Fiske Kimball. The book about him—*Triumph on Fairmount*—suggests that one of Kimball's chief claims on posterity consists in his role in assembling, as director, pictures for the Philadelphia Museum of Art, in particular his "capture" of the Arensberg collection.

I met Kimball twice. The first time was at a meeting at Wildenstein's gallery and house in New York around 1946. A number of museum directors had been invited to discuss the exchange of

students between France and the United States. I was included because of my close relations with France and with the French in the
United States during their wartime exile, particularly with the
Ecole des Hautes Etudes which functioned in New York. The second
time was on the steamship "Liberté" not long before Kimball died.
In the salon of the ship he remarked with emphasis that there was
nothing of much value in the work of a museum director. "All you
do," he suggested, "is fight to get pictures for *your* gallery at the
expense of other museum directors or of picture collectors." This
did not add to the number or quality of great pictures.

Museums and good museum directors have made, and can continue to make, important contributions to the world's artistic future. Artists have been stimulated by the increasing prospect of having some of the works they create on permanent public exhibition.
And the increase in the number of museums has also helped in the
dissemination of knowledge of the visual arts and their history. In
every country, now that travel has become so rapid and so easy,
accessible collections of art make masterpieces available, and it is
possible to document specific works with a facility and a precision
formerly hardly dreamed of.

Nevertheless Kimball's remarks, along with our experiences at
the Arensberg's, lead one to question the presumption that the love
of beauty (and still more love itself) is a function of the multiplication of large museums and of the collections for which their directors and boards of trustees compete. Such an assumption inflates
the importance of multi-millionaire collectors, picture dealers and
museum directors. It deflates the search for beauty as an end, the
end that must always animate artists (including writers) whose
work endures. Ultimately artists themselves are the source of the
material on which artistic middlemen and consumers flourish.

The place of the museum in the world of the future is not
threatened today, save in the sense that everything humans have
created and humankind itself are for the first time threatened with
extinction. But there is a danger that the multiplication of museums,
with their caretakers, may become a partial substitute for the beauty
and delight that art alone can bring to the individual who appreciates
it, whose inner life is changed by it. In Saint-Exupéry's last book
Citadel, left unfinished at his death, he wrote: "Good taste is the
virtue of caretakers in museums. If you abolish bad taste, you will

have neither paintings nor dances, neither palaces nor gardens."

Collections in museums can be helpful to "bad taste," in the sense Saint-Exupéry used the phrase, when they are frequently visited. We were able to strengthen our love of beauty through our leisurely excursions to both the Camondo Collection in the Louvre and the Phillips Collection in Washington. But that was partly because in those days of the twenties few people visited these collections. It was almost like having works of art in one's home or in the nearby houses of friends. But later, after years of community with the Arensberg pictures in their home, I felt something of the icy touch of the caretaker, and of the museum director who employs him, when I saw on public display the same pictures, first and foremost that blue Matisse which had so captured my heart.

In the age we have entered, continual communication with works of art provides a better world than the one covered by newspapers, motion pictures and the usual radio and television programs. To come on a picture when one is relaxed and thinking of other things, can be a creative experience frequently missing from a visit to a gallery. Such a personal encounter bears an analogy to those thoughts which sometimes dart in a mind lying fallow. It offers the artistic temperament an element of surprise which is a stimulus to originality. It also helps beauty to enter the consciousness of the simple amateur.

Such experiences are threatened in the contemporary world. This is why there seems to be no threat in the two initiatives that I felt called upon to take since the thirties. First, the attempt to bring art and artists into the haven I set out to build, separate from and yet part of academic life. Secondly, the decision reached since I met Evelyn about our pictures: the decision not to follow the Arensbergs in seeking a resting place in a museum for our small assortment. Instead we hope to maintain these works as part of our Georgetown house where a few scholars and artists can live surrounded by our inconspicuous treasures.[2] One thing seems sure. The kind of haven we are offering is never likely to be in oversupply.

PART IV

Enduring Values

24. UNITY AND PURPOSE IN EDUCATION

During the summer of 1940, when Great Britain was fighting a lone battle for life, Americans were divided by many rival opinions concerning the war. These ranged from those of the William Allen White Committee in favor of supplying Britain with "aid and comfort," to those of the America Firsters who expressed determination to stay out. Speakers on both sides were solicited by lecture bureaus after the pattern that prevailed in connection with Fascism vs anti-Fascism when Salvemini first visited the United States.

Running parallel to martial concerns were those of my own over the directions in which scholarly research and education generally were moving. They were expressed in sketches for a book later published as *The United States and Civilization.* I found myself almost alone among American scholars in disagreeing with most of our academic aims and many of our methods. However my colleagues might differ on issues concerning the wars in Europe and Asia, they seemed united in the assurance that the trends in research, the increasing specialization of subject matter and of scholarly jargons, were basically sufficient for the future of knowledge. The trends were regarded as inevitable. Even the rare scholar who recognized that the increasing fragmentation of knowledge might eventually multiply difficulties for the application of learned results to the attainment of good ends, felt nothing could be done to meet these difficulties. As long as the country remained at peace, scholars in the social, humanistic and scientific disciplines had only to push farther in the directions they were moving. They should welcome and even solicit increasing funds for such research as the scholarly trends might provoke.

The reluctance to consider reforms in graduate education struck me as no less defeatist than the resignation of the democracies to the forward march of Fascism, Naziism and Japanese Imperialism. Among the ideas Robert Park and I often discussed on our summer walks in northern Michigan was a plan for the thorough reading of a few books that had endured. This might reveal common purposes in different specialties and lay foundations for a new general culture. The idea went back to the kind of teaching I tried out at Swarthmore in 1927.

Reading enduring works came into considerable prominence at Chicago after 1929, with the "great books" course that President Hutchins, in collaboration with Mortimer Adler, introduced to a select group of college students. A proposal was underway in the summer of 1940 to expand this instruction by organizing an additional four or five groups of readers recruited outside the University—a species of adult education. I agreed to share responsibility for one of the groups. The books for the year 1940-41 were to be Greek and Latin classics. Reading them with care provided a new understanding of Mediterranean thought and history from Homer to St. Augustine, subjects long a part of the lectures I had introduced into the Economics Department.

A few weeks before the autumn term began a telegram came from the Social Science Division of the Rockefeller Foundation. Would I spend a day in New York with a few other scholars interested in economic history? Edwin F. Gay counted on my presence.

My relations with Gay went back to 1926-27 when he had returned to Harvard after some years editing the *New York Post*, a distinguished newspaper during and just after the First World War. Moulton introduced us in Washington and Gay became interested enough in my coal book to read the manuscript. Our relations ripened into friendship when we met with our wives in England during the summer of 1933 after that book appeared. When Gay joined the staff of the Huntington Library, our meetings became much more frequent.

Putting a copy of Homer's *Odyssey* into my bag, I caught the Twentieth Century Limited with a reservation back the next night in order to miss only a day of work. Going east I felt carefree and read with relish half of that wonderful book. It had already made me aware as a child of the great winds which blow in Greek waters, winds I was to experience a generation later during my honeymoon with Evelyn.[1] Until I met and married her in 1964 New York, her birthplace, had always been for me a nervously exhausting city. This occasion was no exception. As the visit was short there was no time for the recovery that usually followed the tense arrival.

At the Rockefeller Foundation I was confronted, unexpectedly but inescapably, with a conflict within me that had been hatching for more than a decade, between the comfortable career of economic historian and the pursuit of those plans for educational reform that had taken hold of me strongly since our return to Chicago in 1928-29. I was as attached to the special field of economic history as the most ardently committed scholar. Yet I found that the purposes which had impelled me to become a professor were placed in jeopardy by the specialization that economic history exemplified.

I was disposed to move in a different direction from the specialists, partly because of the devaluation of an enthusiasm for bigness that had filled my childhood imaginings. I had "invented" a ship as big as London (then the biggest city in the world), with the support of a childless couple who lived in the flat above my parents looking out into Jackson Park. For building such a ship, the husband, named Mygatt, supplied imaginary steel in endless quantities from the flaming factories at Gary which lit the Chicago skies over the Park at night.

Our European experiences from 1921 to 1926 had changed the nature of my hopes. I now wanted to defy the winds that were blowing scholars with Homeric force towards specialization, to fashion a world in the image of a much more persistent dream of beauty. Under the influence of our experiences with both past and contemporary art, I came to recognize that the achievement of beauty rests with the right limits and the right refusals rather than with expansion and multiplication as good things in themselves.

Art and scholarship were becoming inseparable in my adult thoughts. Only in their fusion, in a broadening of the scholarly horizon to include art, could I see a possible solution of the issues in graduate education that troubled me.

Shot up sixty floors in a speedy elevator of a new skyscraper, the dozen or so participants in the conference were shortly seated around a long table. Seven or eight were economic historians; the others Foundation scholars and administrators, including the president and chairman of the board of trustees. The director of the social sciences presided. He suggested that the Foundation was toying with a project to develop economic history, although nothing was decided (for a moment he sounded like Walter Arensberg). How should a grant be spent *if* one were made? Each of us was asked to give an opinion and exhorted "to take his hair down."

It emerged that the main idea was to organize a committee, presumably from those present, to supervise inquiries which would be conducted by a number of juniors in connection with some specific subject. This was a device to increase the numbers working in the field. What should the subject be? The only suggestion I remember (it was the one eventually adopted) was that the grant be made for a series of inquiries, conducted piecemeal, into the interrelations between industry and government as these had developed in various parts of the United States. While it might be desirable in the interest of completeness to include Europe, that was impracticable because Europe was at war.

Unknown to the others, I had in proof my book entitled *Industry and Government* comparing those interrelations as they had developed in France and in England from about 1540 to 1640. Looking back I see I might have been expected, in consequence, to embrace the suggestion as the person perhaps best prepared to direct the proposed studies. But that thought never flickered. If it had it would have conflicted with a program of historical inquiry that had already taken form in my mind. Having dealt with interrelations between industry and government, the next scheduled step was interrelations between industry and war.

I had been increasingly concerned over the light-hearted attitude encountered in the academic profession concerning genuine intellectual commitment. Older professors often regarded research, at any rate in the social sciences and the humanities, as a matter of expediency. Would it fit into the particular needs which the senior members defined for their department? was the question usually asked. This outlook became evident, after our return from Europe when banker Frank Vanderlip out of a perhaps misplaced enthusiasm for my academic promise, had written in 1927 to Nicholas Murray Butler that he had unearthed a "find" for Columbia University. Butler sent Vanderlip's letter to Professor Seligman of the Economics Department. Seligman advised the President that if the young man in question wanted to prepare for a faculty position as economic historian at Columbia, he would be well-advised to shift from European to United States economic history.

My inevitable judgment about my colleagues' proposal on that September day in 1940 was that Rockefeller money was *not required* to get a person who was genuinely excited to work at economic history hard and long, and that the best scholars could work more effectively *without* supervision by the proposed *committee*. To use research funds as bait to attract young persons into economic history seemed a dubious means of expanding the field. As envisaged the grant was likely to move inquiries in particular directions determined by the facility with which scholars could obtain financial support. At the same time such a grant might threaten further to fragmentize the fields of "industry and government." Moreover if the subject was divided, as proposed, among many different young scholars each working on a separate area within *the United States,* the results would be mainly factual. General principles of political theory were unlikely to be explored, as seemed desirable, in the light of new evidence. The course taken by the inquiries would set an uninspiring example. The grant would thus become a means of paying men for scholarly activities, only slightly more disinterested than a study of the coal industry might have been if John L. Lewis had financed it, or if I had accepted an invitation, later tendered me by the President of the Standard Oil Company of Indiana to write the history of that enterprise. I saw no prospect that the proposed Rockefeller grant would contribute to a unification of academic disciplines based on the perennial philosophy which was now claiming my allegiance.

Harold Innis, whom I met on this occasion and whose turn to speak came just before mine, said something along these general lines with tact. When I followed I was, alas, hardly tactful. My suggestion was that the urgent need at this juncture in economic history was less for the subsidizing of special factual inquiries, of which there were already so many, than for an effort to use and unite the findings from divers disciplines in their relations to philosophical principles. If the Rockefeller Foundation wanted to break new ground it could support new *kinds* of graduate study and research designed to serve the whole human being instead of a small facet. Some of the pronouncements made by President Hutchins at the University of Chicago were aimed in this direction. Why not then make him a grant for experimenting? This suggestion proved an unwelcome bombshell.

Practical politics has never been my long suit. The meeting precipitated an important choice. That was to disassociate myself from the development of economic history along the lines that were being staked out, and to use whatever resources I possessed as an historian on behalf of graduate study that aimed to unify rather than to fragmentize work of the mind. This seemed the best way to serve the purpose which had originally drawn me into the profession.

While I disqualified myself as a participant in the large grant that the Rockefeller Foundation made a day or two later, not all my col-

leagues were in disagreement with the position I took. My communion
with Innis, who agreed with me in the main, began at that meeting.
A decade later he actually resigned from the University of Toronto,
in spite of patriotic loyalty to Canada, to join the "Committee on
Social Thought," only to be lured to remain at Toronto by the offer of
a deanship.

The decision made at the meeting seemed inevitable, but it was
bound to raise new problems. How could an individual stimulate the
unification of graduate studies so as to encourage a *few* dedicated
individuals to direct their lives towards more constructive goals?
Could a graduate faculty be formed with interdisciplinary unification
as a central objective?

A group of high school teachers gathered in a department store in
the Chicago "loop" not long before the Japanese attack on Hawaii, to
hear proposals for such a faculty. They were skeptical, but the objec-
tions they voiced bore only on the project's *feasibility*. One woman
summed up their doubts as the meeting adjourned: "Well," she said,
"you're against the trend!"

That was the usual response in all quarters, the universities included.
Colleagues invariably invoked technical barriers. Some contended, for
example, that state laws would prevent persons trained in an interdisciplinary curriculum from qualifying for teaching positions.

In *The United States and Civilization,* published in January 1942,
I tried to define the goals of scholarship and of graduate education, indeed of all education and creative work. As a result several headmistresses, a headmaster or two and a college president engaged me as
commencement speaker. The principles of reform in graduate study
which seemed necessary were embodied a little later in a pamphlet
"The Universities Look for Unity," which a distinguished publisher of
German origin, Kurt Wolff, the refugee who founded Pantheon Books,
eagerly published. He had come to the conclusion that my writings
could be the basis of a movement which might sweep the country
and influence many parts of the world after the war. A respected
innovator in American education of the previous generation, Alexander
Meikeljohn, welcomed the proposals in reviewing this pamphlet. He
considered them superior to the more limited recommendations for unification that were published at the same time by a leading English
educationist, Sir Richard Livingston. Several years afterwards a small
college in Mexico City, then directed by two United States citizens,

brought me south with a view to remaking their curriculum along the
lines suggested in the pamphlet.

What could be done administratively at the University of Chicago,
then the chief center of discussions concerning academic reforms?
It was not simply by introducing more enduring books into the curriculum that the higher learning could alter the objectives of specialization in the direction of general understanding and a unification of works
of the mind. Reading classics, from a list drawn up by a committee,
and discussing them in groups of twenty-five or so, might help to form a
public for serious works of the past, whose importance was being lost
sight of in the avalanche of cheap newspapers and pulp magazines,
thriller motion pictures, radio and television programs. But such
reading could make, at best, a limited contribution to intellectual
discrimination and aesthetic taste. Both would have to be newly
kindled if there were to be "common readers" of the kind to whom
Virginia Woolf had addressed herself in two of her most instructive
and delightful volumes. An intellectual and spiritual ferment was
wanted, directed towards discovering the meaning of fresh knowledge
for the future—a ferment such as might lead to new kinds of learned
compositions related to common philosophical goals and to social and
religious reforms which would utilize material improvement for good
ends. What was needed was a faculty in the higher learning to draw
together willing graduate students, professors with broad interests and
even artists, and direct them towards a widening rather than a narrow-
ing culture. They would concentrate on special subjects, but would aim
to relate these subjects to the welfare of the whole human being. This
training would enable disinterested individuals to choose *for themselves*
the tools they needed for a more meaningful use of fresh discoveries in
special disciplines.

Discrimination and taste, and the application of fresh knowledge to
good and to delightful ends, are difficult if not impossible to inculcate
by teaching. There can be no substitute for the individual's love of the
work to be done. Inclinations, even convictions, must be strong in the
young who come for guidance. Havens should be provided, therefore,
where good ends are respected and honored and where persons seeking
them are encouraged to find their own way. A group of individuals,
among them artists and scholars who treat their juniors working for
degrees as young colleagues and cultural participants, should be re-

cruited from those who wish to relate their intellectual inquiries to the
highest norms of human endeavor.

After a year's experience as leader of one of the groups of adults who
read "great books," I wanted to start a new kind of graduate seminar.
Its purpose would be to explore, one by one, with the help of enduring
books, the subjects of historical inquiry that were arresting my own
widening interests. Furthermore, as enthusiasm for interdisciplinary
initiatives seemed to come almost altogether from colleagues who were
not members of the history or economics departments, and from artists
who had no university affiliation, some of whom were European
refugees, the idea was born for a group that would transcend all the
divisions established in universities which separated works of the mind.

With my admiration for Hutchins and his educational pronouncements, I felt bound to ask him at the beginning of 1941 whether he
would prefer to have me continue helping with the "great books" or
undertake within the University of Chicago these initiatives in graduate
study and research. Without hesitation he said he preferred many
times over to have me move in the directions my inclinations were leading. And for the next several years he generously gave me, despite his
overwhelmingly busy life, such help as he could.

The idea took form in a small institute, with its own faculty and
students, cutting across not only departmental but also divisional
lines, and devoted to experiment and reform. In addition to its staff, this
institute drew in, as participants, distinguished artists and scientists.

It may seem curious that Chicago should have become the seat of
such a faculty, the first introduced in any university in the world. And
it was. How can one account for it?

A decade after the founding I had the honor of being invited to
lecture for several months in the Collège de France, as will be explained
in a later chapter. The Collège, despite the name, has no connection
with a "college" either in the American or the French sense of the word.
It has no regular students and awards no degrees. Founded early in the
sixteenth century, in the reign of François I, it became the French
academic Walhalla. It has a permanent faculty limited now to about
fifty, all of whom, like members of the Academie Française, are French
citizens. There is a special room where each member signs his name in
a large book and awaits a huissier (an usher) in uniform, who conducts

him most formally to a lecture hall every time he faces a public.

I was strengthened when I used to sign by finding the signature of Paul Valéry who had been a member for some years before his death. I never knew whether his brother, once dean of the Law School at Montpellier, was still alive when he was elected.

One is free to profess in one's lectures subjects of one's choosing, on condition that the lectures last an hour, no more no less. On one occasion Ernest Renan, who was not only a member but the administrative head of the Collège de France, chose to lecture on an obscure subject relating to Sanskrit. He had few auditors and for his final lecture only one. The great man found himself absorbed by what he was discovering, and as the hour was drawing to a close asked the single auditor if he would allow some extra minutes. "Take as long as you like, Professor," came the reply. "I am your coachman."

During the difficult half year that followed the death of my first wife in 1953, the Collège de France presented me with a community of colleagues and friends such as I had always longed to join. There was creative communication between them.

Among my colleagues was an expert on medieval viticulture, Roger Dion. Like a number of others at the Collège de France, Dion was seriously interested in my publications. He understood the evolution of my historical ideas better than they were understood at home. One day we met casually in the sanctum where professors go to await the huissier. At the time Dion was giving a series of lectures for the Archives Nationales on the history of wine: "Le Vin de France dans l'histoire." He confided a piece of history that he saw might fit into one of my theses. My previous lecture had been concerned with geographical factors in the origin of industrial civilization. I had spoken of medieval times, when vines had been cultivated in Scotland, despite the Scot Adam Smith saying much later in his famous book that an attempt to grow grapes in *Scotland* was the height of economic folly. "My dear fellow," Dion said, "do you realize that the medieval innovators who created the great Burgundy vineyards [vineyards that have produced both red and white wines second to none] chose that area because the soil was regarded as most ungrateful for the raising of grapes?" The challenge of conquering the impossible, of making something out of nothing, galvanized their efforts.

It was partly ungrateful soil that led to the establishment of this new kind of faculty in the midwestern United States. Where the challenge is fiercest the strength of heart and mind necessary to meet it can often be most effectively aroused. Chicago was a testing ground partly because there was so little comprehension of the needs that commanded my allegiance. There more than elsewhere these needs were blatant and compelling. One reflected that, if it should prove feasible to cultivate in Chicago the exotic and hitherto almost nonexistent kinds of grapes which seemed essential to help in fostering a civilized future, this would demonstrate that such grapes can be grown anywhere.

At the same time special conditions in the faculty and the administration made the University of Chicago paradoxically the ideal place for this innovation. At its founding in 1892-93 that university had provided exceptional opportunities for individual professors to develop their work as they saw fit. Frank Lillie used to tell, for example, of a colleague during the first decade who prided himself on the fact that he had never given a lecture or offered a course. After forty years the University of Chicago retained some of that flexibility.

Hutchins was well aware of this and he was deeply concerned with reform. Among the band of professors who resented *his* initiatives, it used to be complained unfairly that he wished to force on them reorganizations which would curtail *their* initiative and violate the charter of faculty independence which was the university's pride.

My desire as an individual to introduce a new kind of department offered Hutchins a unique opportunity, not least because of my background. I was not his appointee, as were other different kinds of reformers, such as Scott Buchanan, Stringfellow Barr and Mortimer Adler. All my family connections were with faculty elements opposed to the proposals attributed to this brilliant and attractive young president. Considerable opposition in the beginning had originated in the scientific faculties, and here was I the son of the founder of the Chemistry Department. The fiercest opposition had come from the Philosophy Department. Most prominent in this opposition at the beginning of Hutchins' term of office was George Mead, once acting chairman of that department, who in protest accepted a temporary appointment at Columbia on the eve of his death in 1931. He was my guardian. How therefore could Hutchins oppose *my* initiatives? Especially when he agreed with some of them?

In view of my age and human mortality, it was now or never in 1941-42. It was also Chicago or nowhere. I doubt that the kind of graduate institute that emerged could have been established in any other university. Our objectives were warmly applauded in 1952 by colleagues from Yale, Harvard, Stanford and other academies, assembled in Pasadena at the behest of the Ford Foundation to discuss reforms in higher learning. But when asked why *they* didn't start similar graduate facilities, they said this could not be done.

It was a very complicated set of circumstances and personalities (most of them favorable and unfavorable at the same time) that interacted to give birth to what came to be called, under duress, the "Committee on Social Thought." [2] It is hardly possible to disentangle a satisfactory explanation. Hutchins' support was indispensable. Yet, it offended many members of the faculty. Some detected a plot to reform, and even to make over, the entire graduate structure of the University of Chicago. The Chairman of the Anthropology Department, Fay Cooper Cole, who had one out of the seven or so votes needed to get us set up as part of the University administrative structure, made a revealing comment to my wife. "If Hutchins hadn't been a member of the group," he said, "no one would have thought of opposing John's plan."

Like virtually all the faculty, including several who briefly associated themselves with us, this professor did not know what the plan was. This was not because of any devious calculations to conceal the intentions. I was almost as incapable as my colleagues of recognizing fully at that time the potential meaning of our innovations. Mine was a case of learning by doing.

The seemingly inconsequential nature of the proposals for a small committee made them viable. Had they been recognized for what they were—a revolutionary effort to make over the basic thinking of modern men and women, to give the heart and the search for delight a plenary place in learning—the effort would probably have encountered fiercer opposition. It was partly my obscurity, and my classification as an economic historian or more frequently and erroneously as an "economist," that permitted the formation of a new kind of academic enterprise. "One reason you are able to say the things you say," an astute Latin-American friend recently told me, "is because no one knows how revolutionary they are."

In 1942 the Committee gained authority to recommend doctors and masters degrees. Four years later we were given the authority to recommend appointments. We became a department of the University of Chicago, at a time when departments had much independence to develop according to their needs as the members saw these needs. We differed from other departments in that there were no departmental or even divisional lines to limit our inquiries. The only frontiers were self-imposed, those required to produce solid creative work and to train students in disciplined habits.

We began to build a permanent faculty in the so-called humanities and the social sciences, and eventually in the field of letters. At the same time we brought for short periods of participation, leading experimental scientists, musicians, a great painter and a great writer. The scope of inquiries by Chagall and Eliot was both more penetrating and wider than that of most professors in the social sciences and the humanities, including professors of art. It was much more imaginative. Our efforts had a special need for the participation of practicing artists of the highest stature.

Soon after the war ended we offered the series of public lectures *The Works of the Mind,* first published in 1947 and now in paperback, in which eminent figures in the arts, the sciences and in administration participated. (Among the men of action were young Senator Fulbright and the pre-Hitlerian German chancellor, Heinrich Brüning). The series demonstrated that a community exists between all works of the mind and heart. Those of the architect, the sculptor, the painter and the musician have a common focus in their efforts to edge closer to beauty and truth; the search for these ends becomes valid only when subjective experiences conform to an objectivity beyond the self.

We encouraged fuller, richer and more independent student participation in university scholarship than is usually achieved. This was accomplished partly by limiting the number of students admitted and selecting them with a care—based on personal interviews and the reading of their compositions—seldom exercised in graduate departments. "True or false" questions were never introduced as tests either for entrance or for graduation. There were no course requirements. Decisions concerning the success or failure of each applicant or student were reached on the basis of all the work done, after discussions by our small faculty as a whole at regular luncheon meetings. At these meetings administrative issues concerning the Committee and its relation to the university were ironed out.

At the beginning of each year—and sometimes twice a year—a meeting, with collation, of all students and faculty members was held in my Dorchester Avenue home with a view to clarifying our procedures and answering student questions. Monthly dinner meetings of our faculty lasted sometimes into the night. They were devoted to the discussion of general intellectual and aesthetic issues, and guests were invited. For instance, persons such as T. S. Eliot, Paul Tillich, and Sir Julian Huxley participated.

We devised methods to train students—by elected readings, tutorial and seminar meetings—in an understanding of basic principles of philosophy (including political philosophy), of history (as created by great historians) and of various arts (as demonstrated by master-pieces). Required lectures were replaced by seminars. In *every one* of these, students were invited to take part; in some they became the organizers and leaders. When he could get the special guidance he needed outside the Committee—or even outside the university or the country—a student was farmed out to an appropriate master, some-times for years. A good example was the late Marshall Hodgson, who succeeded me briefly as chairman of the Committee. As a stu-dent he spent three or four years in Islamic languages and culture under the tutelage of Professor von Grünebaum then of the Oriental Institute at Chicago.

We hoped that the independent work done by students and faculty would be concerned with truths at the interstices between fields of scholarship or of art or of both, because we were in search of a com-mon language relating to all work of the mind that would facilitate general dialogue. As part of the fulfillment of study for the doctor's degree, the student was asked to deliver a public lecture. In it he was expected to demonstrate the contribution that his particular dis-coveries could make to the unification of knowledge.

An impression of the range and caliber of the example this faculty offers, can be conveyed by naming some of the distinguished persons who participated either as visitors or as regular members:

Hannah Arendt, Montgomery Belgion, Saul Bellow, H. S. Bennett, D. J. Boorstin, Jacques de Bourbon-Busset, Avery Craven, Alfred Cobban, Marc Chagall, Louis Chevalier, Colin Clark, Alesander Passerin d'Entreves, Mircea Eliade, T. S. Eliot, Alfeo Faggi, Justino Fernandez, David Grene, Waldemar Gurian, Friedrich von Hayek, Erich Hel-ler, Marshall Hodgson, Robert Hutchins, Harold Innis, Ernst Kantorowitz, Wil-bur Katz, Frank Knight, Ernst Krenek, Olivier Lacombe, Louis Leprince-Rin-guet, C. H. McIlwain, Jacques Maritain, Louis Massignon, F. O. Mathiesson, Mil-ton Mayer, Ralph Mills, B. Mirkine-Guetzévitch, Charles Morazé, James Hastings Nichols, Henri Peyre, Bruce Phemister, Michael Polanyi, Maurice Powicke, James Redfield, Robert Red-field, Richard Rees, Kurt Riezler, Harold Rosenberg, Jean Sarrailh, Artur Schnabel, Arnold Schoenberg, André Siegfried, Edward Shils, Yves Simon, Otto von Simson, Robert Speaight, Theodore Spencer, Igor Stravinsky, Mar-shall Stone, R. H. Tawney, Frederick Tomlin, Arnold Toynbee, Ralph Tyler, Henry N. Wieman, Amos Wilder, and Edgar Wind.

It was one thing to hold to the ideals that led to the founding of the Committee on Social Thought and another to ask others to share them. They can be espoused only by persons who discover them on their own and want to commit themselves. Every man or woman who recognizes the divine fire has to find his own way of kindling it. A teacher can only recognize the formation of ideals in a younger person and encourage him by suggesting that he is on the right track. That is true of colleagues as well as pupils. Many years after we were established as an interdisciplinary department, I served a two year term on the visiting committee for the humanities of the Massachusetts Institute of Technology. James Phinney Baxter, who had long been President of Williams College, was then chairman of that committee. We were acquainted and he knew something about the Committee on Social Thought. When he asked pointedly whether I told the members what they should do, I was able to assure him I did not. If I had we should never have survived. Did I define the areas of inquiry where colleagues should be appointed? Baxter asked. "'Never." Anyone with original disinterested ideas was encouraged and helped with his problems as much as possible. That was all. These were answers Baxter wanted.

They are, it seems, the right answers if the possibilities in individualism and "civilization" are to be fulfilled. Telling the few creative scholars who appear within the universities what to do with their gifts, regardless of their inclinations and beliefs, reminds one of the publishers and dealers who try to reform writers and other artists so their work will suit the markets as salesmen see the markets. On the contrary the secret is to provide promising individuals with conditions that enable them to develop work in which they have a passionate interest. Here we had some success. It was in no small measure the freedom and encouragement our small institute provided, and which would have been partly denied him in an art department, that enabled the art historian Otto Simson to complete two unconventional and illuminating books—*Sacred Fortress* and *The Gothic Cathedral*. They have an appeal for a general public.

Many of the attempts made during the last generation to introduce the "humanities" into scientific curricula, in colleges throughout the United States and no doubt elsewhere, have paid only superficial attention to the human spirit. That is partly because the best students have been obliged (in order to obtain degrees) to pursue a curriculum which fails to arouse their deeper interests and to engage their hearts. It is also partly because young scholars have been obliged to devote their energies to teaching for which they often have little or no concern. This has prevented them from throwing themselves wholeheartedly into the kinds of synthesis that teaching in many colleges, with wide liberal arts courses, has come to require.

Even the favorable conditions for reform that Hutchins valiantly cultivated at Chicago were more frequently resented than welcomed. One of my economics colleagues, who was by no means hostile, where many were, remarked that "The real question is how to get back to the old system under the new plan."

Habits of teaching and research are usually strong. It was difficult to find persons who were willing and able to break with them creatively. One of the chief tasks for the chairman of this first interdisciplinary department was to prevent the establishment of fixed rules which facilitate a return to the old system. Keeping open fresh roads towards the unknown is an administrative task in itself.

When the object was to find persons willing to experiment in new methods, we had usually to turn to older persons with exceptional imaginative gifts, who had already achieved recognition as specialists and who recognized the limitations of their special fields. Whitehead, Schroedinger, Polanyi, Eliot and Chagall are good examples. In addition to their achievements, they were at once qualified and eager to reveal the general in the particular. The average professor who is advanced in years is committed to his special field for its own and especially for his own sake. He lacks both energy and time to follow the new kind of career the Committee was established to facilitate. Yet younger persons who have the energy and who could find the time almost invariably lack the flair and the independence, combined with the scholarly competence, which are indispensable. The change in outlook necessary if they are to fulfill the purposes of this interdisciplinary faculty is rendered the more difficult because there is almost no recognition in the universities, the learned societies, the foundations, or the press of the new kinds of concentration that the Committee encourages. Our work cannot be classified, and almost everywhere existence is denied to the unclassifiable.

The very frustrations and defeats, which seemed sometimes overwhelming, testify to the need for such an effort. Despite obstacles our influence has been considerable. We had inconspicuous but definite success in placing young persons, trained in unorthodox ways, in

useful positions in many departments of knowledge, most significant-
ly in departments of art, literature, classical and oriental studies.
Many of our students have attained professorships. We invented,
developed and maintained for all our students a general training
in the basic principles of philosophy, and in basic matters connected
with art and with great historical writing. We established direct relationships, on an individual basis, between particular professors and
also between our faculty as a group and our students as a group.

This made it possible for one familiar with the Committee on Social Thought to spot its graduates. In 1961 a supporter, former Senator
William Benton, and his very charming wife gave a small dinner to
enable me to explain the nature of our work. At cocktail time I found
myself in conversation with a distinguished lady[3] whose husband,
also present, was then chairman of the board of trustees of Columbia
University. She began to talk about their son who had been at
Columbia. She said he had been inspired by a young associate professor in classics whose outlook was completely independent of that
usual in a faculty member. This professor had changed the direction
of her son's life. As she described this teacher, I felt prompted to ask
her if he was Charles Kahn? She was astonished that I should know;
so I explained, what she did not know, that he was one of the first
students to take his masters degree with the Committee on Social
Thought. The episode provided an entirely unexpected introduction
to the subject for which the dinner had been arranged, a first hand
demonstration of the kind of training we were able to offer.

Although we limited ourselves to teaching thirty students or less at
a time, our pupils have come from every part of this planet. All
sections of the United States have been represented. We also
attracted Japanese and Chinese, Arabs and Israelis, Latin and North
Americans of different colors and sects, as well as persons from almost
every European country. From the beginning we had the good fortune
to develop with the cultural relations division of the French foreign
office, thanks to its originator Jean Marx, an agreement for the exchange of one or two young scholars each year. A number of the
French scholars who came to the Committee—among them Henri
Mendras, Eric de Dampierre and Jean Pierre Faye—are making
careers of distinction in academic life.

Another now at the University of Toulouse, Lucien Mandeville,
appealed to me recently. He asked me to bring to the attention of
the French minister of education, who was then Edgar Faure, the

close relations we cultivated between professors and young scholars. This he counted the most valuable part of his experience with us in Chicago. He saw in our example a partial solution for the French student revolts. Former President Faure and his distinguished wife Lucy were already friends of Evelyn's and mine. He not only responded favorably to the suggestions in my letter, he said he admired the efforts we had made on behalf of the higher learning, that he was finding them useful in his attempt to reform the French universities and graduate institutes.

With almost no notice in the conventional organs of publicity, and without substantial financial support save from the University of Chicago and from a small group of friends, our innovations have spread, as it seems, by a mysterious osmosis. We have affected the methods of teaching and research in France and Japan and no doubt in some other countries perhaps more than in the United States. What we advocated has made a mark on persons the vast majority of whom do not know of our existence.

25. THE HUNGER TO ENDURE

On entering our Dorchester Avenue apartment, a beautifully balanced Queen Anne commode Elinor had bought in an antique shop confronted the visitor. On it, usually, was a thin volume containing Chagall reproductions Paul Eluard had chosen to illustrate his verse. The book's title, *Le dur Désir de Durer*, impressed me. The exacting desire to endure, to leave one's trace, has been a compelling force behind artistic expression. It is often stronger than the desire to have children, really part of the same hunger.

The possibility of enduring as a scholar first came to my attention at Harvard early in 1921, at Haskins' seminar on historical bibliography and criticism. He was comparing the nature of the monograph, which treats a limited subject and time, with a larger work of synthesis. He suggested that, unlike a synthesis, a monograph, if done thoroughly and well, would have a long life expectancy.

This judgment had considerable influence on the choice I made of a working subject at the beginning of our European sojourn. While still at Harvard the importance of coal as a factor in history had been aroused by reading Adam Smith's great book. At the time of our arrival in London in the autumn of 1922 what could seem more limited than the coal mining industry of Great Britain *before* the eighteenth century? I chose that as the subject for an essay I had to submit in a hurry because I was invited to enter a prize competition, from which I soon withdrew on the ground that, in view of our independent income, it might be unethical to accept prize money. The essay had been sent to Amherst professor Walton Hamilton, a member of the prize committee, who later invited me to work at Brookings.

In 1922 scholars supposed that the coal industry had hardly existed until the period of the so-called "industrial revolution." Arnold Toynbee, who had died prematurely in 1883 (uncle of the now famous Arnold J. Toynbee) had delivered at Oxford some lectures which, when published posthumously a year later, had an immense influence in dating that revolution from about 1760, when George III acceded to the British throne.[1]

R. H. Tawney suggested before our arrival in London, in a letter which led to our friendship, that a monograph on the British coal industry was much needed. It might be desirable he wrote, to begin with "an introductory chapter" before the eighteenth century.

In exploring available materials in the British Museum and the Public Record Office, I found to my astonishment that a large quantity of manuscript data existed concerning that early history. This discovery, combined with a vivid memory of Haskins' judgment, led deep into the early coal mines. As this labor took much more time than expected, I actually worried frequently and sometimes worked with undue haste, lest someone should get out a monograph on that subject before mine was ready.

The repercussions of the early coal industry on British and European history turned out to be wider and more important than any of our contemporaries supposed. The problem of research became not one of *finding* data but of selecting what was important from masses of interesting and hitherto unexamined materials in European archives. When the book emerged into print ten years afterwards, it was rewarded by favorable recognition from Haskins himself and also from the dean of English economic historians, Sir John Clapham, who wrote that he thought it would last a long time.

The fateful choice in 1940 at the Rockefeller Foundation, involved not only the creation of an interdisciplinary faculty but also a shift in the nature of my efforts to produce enduring work. The two de-

velopments—towards educational reform and towards a new historical
conception—were interdependent.

My effort as a member of the new faculty took the shape, not of
seeking to illuminate a special subject as had been the original object
of the monograph on the coal industry, but of exploring interrelations
between many branches of history that were being erected into
special and separate fields of scholarly inquiry. The object was to discover and reveal the interdependence between the various sides of
human endeavor and thus contribute to unification of knowledge.

This was a tremendous leap. It involved an attempt to master the
meaning of monographs and documents in many fields and their
implication for other fields, rather than an attempt to dig deeper into
the archives bearing on special subjects. The move had been long in
preparation. I had turned in this direction in the "Conclusion," written in 1931, to *The Rise of the British Coal Industry*. I found myself
sketching possible reciprocal relationships between the coming of a
coal economy and other sides of history. These were the history of
price movements, of land tenure and agricultural technology, of invention and the natural sciences, of religious foundations and religious
thought and of parliamentary government. The scope of this conclusion was dismaying to a younger English colleague, F. J. Fisher
(now Professor Fisher), who kindly helped with the revision after that
book was in proof. He pointed out how unconventional, even un-
suitable, such an approach would appear to contemporary scholars.

My lectures and publications at the University of Chicago had also
prepared me for the leap. I was working on historical interrelations.
My various comparisons of French with English development began
to be published in 1937, in an essay on connections between price
movements and industrial changes, and in 1940 my comparative study
of industry and government first appeared.

The need to produce something enduring became more compelling
than ever, no doubt partly because the trace left by a successful
monograph seemed discouragingly minute. Discoveries concerned with
interrelations might have a much wider significance than monographs,
I hoped, with no sacrifice of permanence. It might be possible to construct new kinds of historical compositions of lasting substance despite the vast oceans of material relevant to the subjects.

Plenty of general histories were being published, but not the kind
I envisaged. The scholars responsible either resorted as individuals to
what in France was appropriately called "vulgarization," or organized

themselves into teams of specialists to cope with some large subject in a more scholarly way. The first alternative seldom produced a result of substantial, let alone of enduring, quality. The second inevitably produced a series of largely disconnected monographs of very uneven interest. As a solution for the problem of reaching a general audience, or of coaxing one into existence, the first alternative was distasteful. The second was unsatisfactory because the kind of élan that gives life to general history does not come from a group, but from an individual.

Large sweeps of history had once been the subject of enduring works by such masters as Voltaire, Gibbon and Ranke. They found their counterparts in the United States in Prescott, Parkman and Henry Adams, none of whom fitted into a conventional university career despite President Eliot's effort to capture Adams permanently for Harvard. More recently the scope of historical research has been widened piecemeal.

Could not the valuable new material, so conscientiously assembled in minute doses by so many workers, concerning so many sides of history: the economic, the social, the domestic, the military, the technological sides, the events political and individual, the evolution of thought—religious, philosophical, political, economic, social, medical and scientific—the evolution of major institutions, political, ecclesiastical and social, the course taken by the arts from literature to painting, sculpture, music and architecture; could not essentials of all these developments be brought into a meaningful unity?

A hope that it could lead me in composition, as in educational reform, to move against the trends. The trends in fields such as sociology, psychology, demography, human ecology were leading towards the more *scientific* treatment of vast quantities of new data, which archeologists and anthropologists as well as historical researchers had been finding during and since the nineteenth century. These data concerned earlier societies as well as the expansive Western European peoples since Romanesque times. But were *scientific* methods appropriate for handling these data if the object were to reveal connections between historical evolution in different spheres of human endeavor? Did the example of the scientist provide the best road towards the general truths an iconoclast historian should seek?

The mathematical treatment of factors in historical causation, attempted by scholars like Pareto and Simiand, had brought grotesque caricatures of past evolution. The actors in the story of humankind have not been algebraic abstractions. One cannot build a comprehensible structure representing historical evolution with mathematical symbols as both Pareto and Simiand tried to do.[2]

For enduring general histories the relevant facts must be ascertained with scrupulous accuracy. Here the handling of documents, monuments and excavated materials and of the evidence they offer, as sought by the masters of historical *science* since the early nineteenth century, is of much value. But scientific methods alone hardly provide the historian with a means of dealing adequately with problems of interrelations, any more than mathematical methods provide adequate means of handling the closely allied problems of causation.

In his essay on genius as personified by Shakespeare, Victor Hugo drew a distinction between science and art which subsequent thought —including the thought of a few philosophers and men of science at least as far back as Erasmus and down through William Temple and Werner Heisenberg—seems mainly to support. One essential objective of the modern scientist has been to measure. Another has been to correct and even to replace his predecessors. Both objectives help to explain why the works of the greatest scientists cannot endure in the same way as those of the greatest artists, whether their medium be poetry, painting, music, sculpture or architecture. Works of art can be unique and timeless to an extent that scientific statements cannot.

Methods derived from the experimental sciences have obtained an ever increasing prestige in connection with the study of history during the past two centuries. This has meant that the collection of facts and their frequent conversion into statistics, satisfying the passions for the tangible and especially the measurable, have become increasingly common. Partly as a consequence, confidence in the *durability* of any historical edifice erected by the scholar has diminished, as the available facts have multiplied and ways of measuring have been refined. Pirenne was beset by an almost tragic fear that nothing would remain of his constructions. He felt far less secure in these than had Ranke,[3] whom he greatly respected and who was two generations his senior. Emile Coornaert reports that Pirenne (1862-1935) once said to him "Nothing will be left of my work in twenty-five years." It was not uncommon by the time he completed his *Histoire de Belgique* in 1932 to claim that each generation writes its own history. My guardian, George Mead, often said just that. One thing that impeded him from publishing as a philosopher was a strong belief that anything he wrote would no longer seem true by the time it got into print. (His disciples have taken a less pessimistic view of the value of his thought.)

More recently still a fashion has developed to seek a reputation mainly by pulverizing the works of predecessors, particularly the most eminent. Even the best works are vulnerable factually in the light of new found facts and quantitative investigations. Scientific judgment, as Temple pointed out, would be more stable than it is (and this is the case with the scientific treatment of historical materials) if the data could be complete, which they never can be.

In realizing something of his dream the artist like the lover, as Erasmus suggested, "no longer lives in himself but in whatever he loves." In this "state of . . . madness," what the artist does, in his quest for perfection, is to isolate and individualize the subject he treats. He lifts that out of the actual world to such an extent, and so convincingly that judgment on the work he creates, as Temple expresses it, "is free from disturbance on objective grounds." This is why a Cézanne or a Monet can be more avant garde, even in an abstract sense, than the most recent abstract painting. Fashions, however tyrannical, cannot destroy beauty. The artist has the opportunity to define his moment so that an increasingly numerous audience through time can find theirs in what he leaves behind. That is why art can achieve a finality science lacks.

The attempt to establish historical interrelationships is inviting to the artistic mind. The whole idea of such relationships is artificial. In one sense they are not history at all. But if they are successfully established by art, nourished with accurately handled materials, they can help us to understand the broad course history has taken better than factual accounts of particular aspects. Thus the artistically-oriented historian should be capable of creating a world corresponding to the realities of past evolution, just as a great painting or a great concerto corresponds to realities which are recognized by others only because the artist reveals them. In creating such a world an historian can derive much help from examples provided by architecture and music as well as by painting and literature.

Self-education predisposed me to approach history in the light of such examples. A need for artistic expression pressed increasingly during the twenties and thirties, a need similar perhaps to the need which filled the lives of Derain and Chagall, Maillol and Lehmbruck, Schoenberg and Schnabel, Valéry and Eliot. The only medium open was historical writing. For that I had been trained and had continued to train myself since I was seventeen. I had learned the technique. In view of my experiences it was natural to want to apply to it something of the love which had come into my life.

Some may ask how one could hope to draw history into the realm of beauty and delight, when history is so vile? The notion that it is vile is derived partly from the fact that historians whose approach was more general and artistic than is now common—Thucydides, Tacitus and Gibbon for instance—dealt with wars and other struggles for power, which are by their nature, evil and messy, and therefore revolting to the finest human aspirations. The new materials now available for discovering interrelationships, and through these for reexamining the nature of causation, can bring less base motives—for instance the search for the beautiful and the good—into new constructions as neglected factors in history.

It is true also that the sculptor, the painter or the musician is often tainted with the same foul characteristics which tarnish the actors in political history. If those artists, in spite of this tarnish, have the power to purify the subject matter they use in the interest of delight, why should a similar power be denied the historian?

The examples provided by the visual and literary arts and the art of music have at least three interrelated characteristics that are neglected in the scientific treatment accorded historical subjects. Of compelling importance to artistic presentation are the order and the elegance of the parts, the chapters and the paragraphs, the sentences and the words with their cadences and their sounds. To achieve something of this order and elegance, the historian is impelled to follow the example of the artist in building his major work out of abundant sketches, as Degas built his Belletti family portrait and as Seurat built his "Grande Jatte." In our home I have had an example for nearly fifty years in a drawing Pascin used as the basis for several of his paintings.[4]

If a commitment to order and elegance could enable the historian to reach towards permanence, the same is true of a commitment to moral principles, to a hierarchy of ethical values, which inevitably guides the greatest artists in their work. Virtue therefore would be a stabilizing force, like beauty, in any artistic historical construction. At the beginning of my teaching at Chicago, I drew moral judgments in connection with history, and a bright student from the history department detected and pointed out that this approach differed basically from that of my colleagues who had espoused the "scientific" outlook of never appraising historical developments of any kind in terms of good or bad.

Thirdly the variety of interpretations, which (as we shall see in a later chapter) T. S. Eliot told the Committee on Social Thought makes for richness in a line of poetry,[5] can also contribute to permanence. In studying the cultural foundations of industrial civilization, I discovered an example of the varieties of historical truth in connection with the conversion, at the end of the sixteenth century, to Roman Catholicism of Chablais, a district stretching southwest along Lake Geneva in the shadow of Mont Blanc between the outskirts of Evian and what is now the Swiss frontier. From the point of view of documentary evidence, the notion that St. Francois de Sales won this territory back from Protestantism without any use of force is only a pious legend. Nevertheless the *belief* that he had done so was widespread, and this belief was possibly a more powerful factor in history than the truths later derived from historical facts.[6] Thus the "artistic" historian who discovers a variety of truths has an opportunity to build a more permanent structure than the seeker after small bits of truth. He can present several interpretations and give them unity and irreplaceability by revealing their interdependence. And by relating these interpretations to a hierarchy of values he can give his account a sufficiently elevated meaning to make more difficult than it has been (as the Tempter tells Thomas in *Murder in the Cathedral*) for men to

". . . declare that there is no mystery
About this man who played a certain part in history."

The new structures artistically-oriented historians might build could provide more human stories than any "scientific" accounts concerned with a particular branch of evolution. Consequently a masterpiece of artistically inspired history could become largely self-sufficient. It could be invulnerable to the multiplication of data, much as any genuine work of art can be free from disturbance "on objective grounds."

If the historian's aim is to draw the various strands of partial truth, discovered separately in connection with many different sides of development, into a unity, his hope of a convincing result depends on his capacity to isolate, to individualize and to humanize his subject. This *ideal* fortified me in my first full-fledged attempt at integral history, *War and Human Progress*.[7] That undertaking gave a unity to life during the nineteen forties, especially after the Second World War, just as the very different *Rise of the British Coal Industry* had given a unity to life after the First.

At the turning point around 1939-1942 in my work I was drawn to traditional sources of our heritage in philosophy and religion. My commitment in contemporary painting and sculpture to the work of Derain, Chagall and Maillol, and in contemporary letters to the work of Eliot, my steady reading since childhood of classics of Western literature, all led towards the most noble traditional concepts and values in religion and moral philosophy as well as in art. I was also impelled towards a stocktaking of the divisive and the unifying forces in the contemporary world, and to a declaration of faith in the latter.

The goals I thought should be sought in the society of the future were embodied in *The United States and Civilization*. It was first written in the form of lectures beginning in 1940, and published within a month of the Japanese bombardment of Oahu and the German declaration of war on the United States at the end of 1941. The book was composed in haste and expressed strong convictions. Fortune has enabled me to revise it all and to write much afresh a quarter of a century later, an opportunity seldom granted an author. The goals defined are intended not only for scholars and academics but for society as a whole, for the individuals who make it up, and not only for American society but for world society.

When the book appeared it had a mixed reception. It cemented some old and very precious friendships: with James Douglas, about to join the Air Transport Command and later to become Secretary of the United States Air Force and Deputy Secretary of Defense after a distinguished career in the law; with Alfeo Faggi, the Italian-born sculptor, and with Artur Schnabel, a Central European who became the most deeply engaged of all these friends. He gave comfort by saying "I think it will live."

Notwithstanding its scope (possibly in part because of that), the number of persons who came to know of its existence was small. Kurt Wolff, a recent émigré with a career behind him before the war as a leading German publisher, soon after his arrival in America stumbled on the book without knowing me. He was so excited that one late spring day in 1942 he walked the streets of New York, his new home, from morning till night in search of a copy. He visited some seventy-five bookshops in vain. No salesman had heard of the book.

According to prevalent attitudes among popular and academic publishers and dealers, books have to be classified. *The United States and Civilization* was unclassifiable. The treatment of subject matter was not that appropriate to an "economist" or an "economic historian." The book was not "history" or "sociology." It *specialized* in the general and so was not treated as a popular work. A few scholarly

journals (from several disciplines, especially philosophy and theology),
did in fact review it, usually with amiable approval, but according to
the mores of American publishing houses and public relations men it
did not fit anywhere. Concerned with the goals of all disciplines and
even of all endeavor, it fell outside the boundaries each of the multiplying specialities were drawing for their recruits.

It raised an especially embarrassing problem for workers in economic history. With the exception of Harold Innis, the leading scholars
in that field had been troubled by the nature of my intervention at the
Rockefeller Foundation. A new journal, *The Journal of Economic
History*, was started in the United States soon afterwards. As was
appropriate, the editor, E. A. J. Johnson, struggled with the question
of what could be properly included under the rubric. Quite rightly he
saw that *The United States and Civilization* should not be reviewed
even though its author had a respectable reputation in the field. But
he not only admired my work in economic history, he had a friendly
personal regard. He apparently thought I might take it amiss if he
did not notice the book, which for aught I know he may have liked.
At any rate he hit on a formula that deftly killed three birds with one
stone. He got me invited to deliver the "Laurel Hill" address at
Stockbridge, Massachusetts on a subject treated in the book. This was
an occasion when a person of eminence was expected to inspire a
socially acceptable audience in that Edith Wharton country where my
father had been raised. The Laurel Hill sponsors wanted Sigrid Undset.
But that would have meant a fee of a thousand dollars, no mean sum
in 1942. So the editor had the happy thought of inviting her to sit on
the platform, while I spoke for nothing, and *The United States and
Civilization*, cited in Johnson's introduction to the speech, received a
decent burial so far as economic history was concerned.

With the founding of the Committee on Social Thought in 1942, I
became involved in its administrative problems. These consumed
much time and energy. I was worried about how to carry out these
extensive new duties without entrenching on the hours usually spent
in reading, study and writing.

I remember talking the matter over with Charles McIlwain, when
he came to speak in Chicago for "The Historian" in the series of
the Committee on "The Works of The Mind." During my youth at
Harvard he had stimulated my interest in Roman law, and since the
publication of *Industry and Government in France and England*

1540-1640 we had been on terms of easy friendship. He explained how he had managed to keep from drowning in administrative duties and university politics. "I soon learned," said he, "when I was put on a committee to do the work as badly as I could, so that I wouldn't be asked to serve again." Sensing vividly the burdens that my chairmanship of the Social Thought Committee were bound to impose, he spoke with vigorous affection: "John, fight for your mornings!"

The matter of committee work largely took care of itself. My administrative actions, together with my unorthodox writings, isolated me increasingly from the conventional channels of professional engagement. I was gradually dropped from the committees which had appointed me before 1942. I seldom served on new ones. The exception was my appointment in 1952 as vice-chairman of the American Council of Learned Societies.

That stemmed from the sympathetic interest the first director of the Council, Waldo Leland, had taken in the Committee on Social Thought at the time of its founding. In order to learn about it, he had joined the small faculty at one of our monthly dinners. He recognized its importance as a pioneering effort and as concerned with problems common to many branches of the Humanities—the area to which he had devoted his life.

This association with the Council of Learned Societies was brought to an abrupt halt after Elinor's death early in 1953. I was writing *La Naissance de la Civilisation Industrielle* as part of my assignment at the Collège de France, and also editing for publication a volume which she had left unfinished. A cable came in Paris asking me to represent the Council at a meeting in the Low Countries, but still depressed and in mourning I was unable to do so.

It is stultifying for professors to offer the same course of lectures year after year until their retirement. So we made it one of the requisites for members of our interdisciplinary faculty to choose their own methods of instructing students, to give any course they liked or no course at all, but, if possible, *never to repeat* a course. So at the end of the nineteen-forties I ceased giving the course for which the Economics Department, by requiring it for graduate students, had provided an audience. It had come to involve each year the training of a hundred students specializing in economics, to whose papers and problems much time had to be devoted.

The success of Committee students was dependent on different kinds of instruction; to no small degree on the example of research we set as members of the faculty. My unfashionable habit of devoting mornings to writing became familiar to most of the young who joined the Committee. And also my addiction to reading "great" books, many of which could be studied and utilized by candidates for passing our general examination in philosophy, history and in some art usually literature.

Soon I was free to explore in one seminar after another subjects related to my growing preoccupation with philosophy and art as part of my view of historical interrelations. The attendance in these seminars was small, partly perhaps because the classics explored had no direct relation to the granting of higher degrees in other departments, and because the graduate students in Social Thought were free to choose the subjects and books on which they would concentrate and require tutorial help. Nevertheless I usually managed to have good students, and always more than Charles Du Bos had for his seminar at Notre Dame University on Pascal.

In the seminar on historians for instance, one student, Bonham Carter, reported on Macaulay and another, William Clark, on Clarendon. In this way it was possible to instruct myself as well as others in past historians, from Herodotus, Thucydides and Tacitus to Bede, Gibbon, Taine, Tocqueville, Ranke, Michelet, Froude, Gardiner, Guizot, Fustel de Coulanges, Prescott, Parkman, Adams and many more. By the same process of joint study with pupils, I worked my way into classics of theology, political and economic thought, into classics of medicine, science, and technology, such as those of Hippocrates, Agricola, Biringuccio, Gilbert, Harvey, Kepler, Galileo and Newton, and into great poetry, plays and novels. I was doing what I love to do and enjoying this hugely.

Instead of diverting me from writing these new teaching obligations strengthened my desire to pursue it. Time came my way to absorb in preparation for my seminars vast literary depositories of historical information, such as Saint Simon's *Mémoirs* (which we are now told seethes with misinformation), Madame de Sévigné's letters and the seemingly innumerable volumes of Sainte-Beuve including his history of the seventeenth-century Jansenist monastery of Port-Royal. Later I acquired from the nine volumes of the Goncourt *Journal* a more personal impression of the nineteenth century than second-hand histories provide. The diminution of conventional committee obligations made room for the new administrative responsibilities which could not be evaded if the Committee were to live. In the end I was left with rather more than less time for reading and writing and my published output increased. The battle for the mornings ended in victory!

Members of university faculties were frequently visited by representatives of publishing houses eager to obtain new textbooks in special subjects. During the thirties several invitations of this kind came in connection with economic history. One was most flattering. A publisher's agent reported that my old friend, R. H. Tawney, and another distinguished English economic historian, a woman of great charm, Eileen Power, had persuaded him that I was the ideal scholar to write a textbook on European economic history. The publisher ended his visit with the offer of a contract.

Ever since our return to the United States I had opposed the practice of teaching from textbooks. In connection with the graduate study carried on within the Committee, such teaching seemed indefensible. The best students should, I felt, find their own way in their subjects with the help of books that had endured. This prejudice went back to my first teaching at Swarthmore.[8] Much as I yearned for a larger audience I could not desert the principles which animated my career by contributing to the "vulgarization" I hoped my new books might avoid. I was not out to summarize the present and fleeting state of knowledge of a special subject, but to conceive works that might prove of perennial concern.

"My dear fellow," I said to my visitor, "I appreciate your and their confidence, but I wouldn't sign a contract to write a textbook for any amount of money." "Wait a bit," he interposed, "what do you mean by 'any amount of money?'" "Well," said I, naming a sum which had substance, "not for a million dollars."

The notion, though it was a fact, that I was writing for the general public, for Virginia Woolf's "common reader," was incomprehensible in the publishing business except for the Harvard publisher of *War and Human Progress,* the late Thomas Wilson. It occurred to me that this very book, which ranged over nearly five centuries of recent history, might be offered to college students as reading in the increasingly numerous liberal arts curricula. But when I suggested this to another agent, who called looking for new texts in economic history, he was horrified.

In the years that followed, the concepts of what makes good reading for students have been altered by the introduction and astonishing spread of the paperback. Four of my books on historical interrelations, among them *War and Human Progress,* have been published as paperbacks. Lately, my excursions into historical interrelations have been finding translators and publishers in several tongues, ranging from Japanese through Arabic, French and Italian, Polish and German to Spanish.[9] The audience for these books is nowhere large but is scattered over a considerable part of the earth.

It is not clear that these publishing efforts at home and abroad will lead to a long-term future for my books, but they suggest that a need exists for this kind of general history. If my efforts leave no trace, others aimed in the same direction will. There is comfort in the thought.

26. SCHNABEL'S HOPES AND DISILLUSIONMENTS

The view is popular that the artist's desire for fame is simply a matter of ambition. His desire is further confused with the pursuit of money. About 25 years ago, in commandeering a porter at the railroad station in Chicago to carry Igor Stravinsky's bags, I sought to enlist his interest by telling him the musician he would be serving was perhaps the greatest living composer. Back came the cynical observation: "The richer they are, the less they tip."

Ambition is undoubtedly present in varying degrees in all artists. When controlled it can be a stimulus. But, if unchecked, ambition for success and prominence is fatal to achievement of lasting beauty.

Eliot and others have suggested that when an artist releases a work it acquires an independent life. And that life can last only when the individual, in creating it, establishes a relationship with a *reality* beyond himself. There is a sense in which the artist creates this reality, but it is equally true, and more important, that the reality was already potential. In finding it the artist has discovered an entity that exists, has recovered something universal which would otherwise have been lost. That is why the greatest works of art are not subject to ordinary laws of mortality.

Artur Schnabel used to compare our efforts at composition, his in music, mine in history. He would have preferred to be remembered for the music he wrote than as the interpreter of great masterpieces of piano composition which he played divinely. But his energies were limited. In his later years especially they were absorbed by the extensive demands for money to take care of his family. As the work of composition paid nothing he had to meet those obligations by concerts and teaching. His free time was further reduced by hearty recurring needs for leisure-consuming diversions beyond these careers. Women (or perhaps one should say Woman) had an immense attraction. They adored *him*. He was almost as successful with them as with the music he played.

Yet, along with his friends Schoenberg and Krenek, he wrote good music in the twelve-tone idiom. His symphony was given a splendid performance by Dmitri Metropolis in Minneapolis in 1947. Elinor and I went to be with him and Therese, his wife, at the last rehearsal and the concert. The work is dedicated to Samuel Courtauld, a man of wealth and a patron of the arts who occupied a place of immense financial and social prominence in the London of the thirties and forties. He wrote Schnabel that this dedication was the greatest honor ever done him. Artur honored me by a gift of a manuscript copy of the symphony now in the University of Chicago archives.

The performances of that symphony still live in my heart. It was given in a hall seating many thousands. At the last rehearsal about twelve persons were in the audience. I sat with Artur. The program began with Mozart's overture to Don Giovanni, to be followed by the fourth piano concerto of Beethoven, with Schnabel as the soloist, and then the hour long symphony he had written. As the orchestra began the opening bars of the wonderful overture, Artur whispered loudly in my ear "Dot iss not my music. Dot iss also good music!"

As a concert artist Schnabel could not give the art of musical composition anything like the single-minded devotion that characterized both Schoenberg and Krenek, neither of whom were concert performers. But he practiced the art with enough talent and imagination to feel sometimes the mysterious overwhelming pleasure that creative fulfillment can bring. Once in the middle forties over lunch in a downtown hotel, when he had come to Chicago to lecture for the Committee on Social Thought, he described the unique effect of the reality beyond time he sometimes touched in composing. He compared this to the exaltation achieved in the most perfect physical union between a woman and a man. And, though a religious nonbeliever, he wondered whether the moments of fulfillment he had experienced in writing music bore some relation to the love of God. He asked whether there might not be an association between the euphoria of the Christian mystic and that experienced by the greatest musical composers—such as Beethoven, Mozart, Bach and Schubert— whose works alone he played from choice.

What aroused these reflections was our discussion of my efforts in the medium of historical writing. During the last decade of his life, which ended in 1951, Artur read with increasing intensity every-thing I published. We agreed that only through discipline and effort could beauty be achieved and then only if the pursuer found the strength to move upstream. That was what led him to call "absolute" music "the Line of Most Resistance."

We met in 1932 at the home of a Chicago friend who had been his pupil in Berlin, a young pianist named Hilda Oldberg.

Part of my fancies, during the years of oncoming adolescence, had been concert programs comprising only the best compositions of the greatest composers. My first meeting with such programs in real life came when I read of Schnabel in the columns of *The New Statesman.* Its musical critic the late W. J. Turner, a man of letters, devoted many articles to the astonishing character and sublime beauty of the music Schnabel created with the piano. Schnabel's program choices resembled those I had made as a child twenty years before.

I confided this to Mrs. Oldberg and her husband. When Schnabel came to play in Chicago and stayed with them they asked us to meet him at a small reception. I thought I recognized, by the way he extended his hands in greeting and by the expression of his face, that his hostess had relayed my program story. Immediately we became friends and our friendship never ceased to grow during the twenty years that followed. With Elinor, who shared my enthusiasms and made them a part of our union, I went to every concert of Artur's on that Chicago visit, and thereafter wherever our paths crossed we went not only to his concerts but to his rehearsals where one could concentrate more completely on the music.

My introduction to Schnabel's playing on the occasion of our meet-ing in 1932, contained a surprise. He played twice with the Chicago Symphony Orchestra. The first time he played the fourth concerto of Beethoven in G Major, a performance for which he was especially famous. My anticipation had been so terrific that I felt vaguely dis-appointed. I soon discovered that this came from the fact that I had already heard the work performed several times by other soloists and had been conditioned for the music by the impressions I retained.

The next day he played the beautiful Schumann piano concerto in A minor. I had never heard it before. Coming fresh the effect was so overwhelming that for the moment Schumann seemed greater than Beethoven. I had the same surprise a day or two later when he played a solo concert. He chose a Beethoven, a Mozart and two Schubert sonatas. What momentarily captured my total allegiance were the Schubert works which I was hearing, like the Schumann concerto, for the first time.

Familiarity with great music as *he* presented it grew through the years. He sought after perfection in the few compositions that he found it "impossible to perform as well as they ought to be performed." Beethoven and Mozart, as they emerged from his inner understanding, fulfilled the impossible standard of perfection created by my childhood dreams. At his hands, these works acquired a meaning no one else had revealed.

I will always remember the words he told me Richard Strauss, then over eighty, addressed to him at Lucerne after one of his last performances of Beethoven's Fourth Piano Concerto. As a young man he had sometimes played as a soloist when Strauss conducted. And now the old musician, who had been in the audience, came backstage because he wanted to exchange with Artur his thoughts about the transition Schnabel had made that evening from the second to the third movement. This had revealed to him for the first time, Strauss observed, the true meaning of the whole work. "Now," the old composer said in taking leave of Artur, "I am ready to die."

Flashes of the kind of insight, approaching revelation, that Strauss had received from Schnabel's playing that night, were my guides. Our friendship and the continual opportunities I had, not only to hear Schnabel play, but equally important to talk with him at leisure about all the matters for which we had an appetite, strengthened my sense of kinship with art.

The idea of bringing creative artists into the scholarly world of the University of Chicago had occurred to me some years before the founding of the Committee on Social Thought. My conversations with Hutchins, which became increasingly frequent from 1936, made him aware of my commitment to art. He also knew of Elinor's and my close friendship with Schnabel, who spent much time with us early that year, when he came to Los Angeles both to play a Brahms concerto with the local orchestra, then led by Klemperer, and some sonatas with Huberman the distinguished violinist. That Los Angeles visit was a continual festival, with meals at Elinor's mother's house, picnics and excursions in our car through the mountains to La Quinta and Palm Springs, and also to Santa Barbara where Artur played four Beethoven piano sonatas, in spite of his distress over the piano assigned him. On touching the keys, he described it as a box of assorted cigars.

Hutchins' query whether Schnabel could take over the music department at the University of Chicago was nevertheless unexpected. The possibility excited me. Hutchins decided to explore it through the good offices of the well-known German singer, Claire Dux, who had married Charles Swift, one of the University's trustees who might be expected to contribute support. The Swifts called on the Schnabels at their summer retreat on Lake Como.

Nothing came of these overtures, although as I learned from Schnabel later, his response had not been intentionally negative, though possibly equivocal because the idea of a university job was new and strange. A couple of years later he agreed to deliver a series of *lectures* at Hutchins invitation, for which Elinor and I provided material support. As we met some difficulties with the University of Chicago Press, the work was published by Princeton.

Schnabel had learned English in his own way after the age of forty. He made delightful puns, not a few of them creative, like the renaming of Alice Longworth's prominent newspaper column "What Malice Thinks." Knowing English was not Artur's native tongue a humorless manuscript reader of "Music, or the Line of Most Resistance" crossed out "Most" and substituted "Least."

With the founding of the Committee, Schnabel became an enthusiastic participant. Whenever he was in Chicago he came to our seminars and he met informally on frequent occasions with students in our Dorchester Avenue apartment. He also had a few students to tête à tête luncheons to discuss their work and their future. It was Schnabel who brought both Krenek and Schoenberg into the orbit of the Committee. Krenek had me speak at the college which then employed him, Hameline in Saint Paul, and my "Hameline speech," as mimeographed for distribution, became for a short time a staple handed to any student who thought of applying for admittance to the Committee. Schoenberg, with his wife, came to the University as Alexander White Professor in connection with our series on *The Works of the Mind,* in which he represented "The Musician." He stayed for other lectures and also gave a concert of his own works with a small orchestra. He and his wife formed a warm friendship with Elinor and me lasting until their deaths. One of his unexpected gifts towards the end of his life was an inscribed copy of his treatise on harmony. He felt my spiritual kinship for art, which to him as to me was a matter of the heart even more than of the mind. And he thought I was working too hard! "What do you do for recreation?" he once asked me. When I could only mutter "administration," he suggested it might be better to set up a manual workshop as he had done to rest *his* mind from composition.

Schnabel himself accepted an official assignment with the Committee as White Professor. The donor of that chair had placed it at the exclusive disposal of the President, and Hutchins generously used it to support the appointment not only of musicians, but also of Eliot and of the physicist von Weizsächer, enabling them to work with our small faculty. Our lectures and seminars were always open to any students or members of the faculty, so this was a way of making felt the presence of men who would not otherwise have been interested in coming to the University of Chicago. On one occasion a member of the music department asked me to invite Pablo Casals. He said the great cellist could only be lured to the United States, whose Spanish policy he then resented, by this "extraterritorial" unit.

When Schnabel came as White Visiting Professor he chose an account of his career as the topic for his seminar. Before each session we would discuss, over luncheon, episodes he was about to relate; and he would jot down on a small bit of paper a score of bywords to guide him. He never considered writing out what he was about to say. But Elinor had the foresight to hire from a local agency a man who came with a tape recorder. He took down not only the story Schnabel told, but the questions and answers which followed each recital. The agency delivered two copies of the rather imperfect version transcribed from their recording machine. Elinor and I kept one which is now in the University of Chicago archives. We gave Schnabel the other. He later told me of the unsuccessful overtures he made to various publishers who complained about his "English" and made other annoying comments. So he set aside the matter of publishing this autobiographical material.

Years after his death a version of what he had said was edited and published in England, without my knowledge and without any acknowledgment of the source. No one would know that an interdisciplinary faculty existed, that this was what drew Schnabel to the University of Chicago, that Elinor's foresight alone was responsible for the existence of a text. But the sound of his voice, the wit of his reflections, the comments and queries of the students remain in my memory as part of the history of the Committee. Thus Schnabel brought "living" music in his own way into the instruction provided by this new "institute," as he liked to call it. His was the way of a nonconformist provided with an extracurricular platform by another nonconformist.

He also helped to nourish roots which eventually grew into a Center for Human Understanding. When the first atomic bomb was dropped on Japan I was in northern Michigan. Before the news, at about the time the explosion occurred, I had a premonition as I was walking cross-country with Elinor. With the reality of this new form of destruction, a sense of the possible doom of our race settled heavily on me. I was unable to feel in the victory over Japan any of the exaltation that took hold of me as a soldier at Camp Lee Virginia when we learned of the Armistice ending the First World War.

In the weeks following Hiroshima and Nagasaki the feeling overwhelmed me that humanity was henceforth confronted by a choice of putting an end to war or of putting an end to itself, or at least to all hope of civilization. Returning to Chicago for the autumn term at the university, I found myself wanting to rally humankind to an awareness of the necessity for world community, suddenly imposed on us all. I jotted down some paragraphs and sent them to Schnabel. He felt they must be published and that signatures should be solicited on a wide scale. He thought this summons should become the basis for a worldwide movement independent of and superior to all particular allegiances—professional, racial, religious or national. We had difficulty in finding others to share our views, but a number of persons, among them several members of the Committee on Social Thought, signed the manifesto. In 1947 the Chicago publisher Henry Regnery printed at his expense several thousand copies with the title "Above All Nations is Humanity," and these were circulated as widely as our connections permitted.

The movement towards good will and love among human beings progressed little during the rest of Artur's lifetime. The four years that intervened and ended in 1951 with his death in Switzerland were filled with disillusionments and critical illness.

With the coming to power of the Nazis in Germany, indeed since that threat became serious during the Depression of 1929-32, Schnabel had turned with special hope to the United States. A product of Central Europe, with a Viennese childhood as a musical prodigy partly financed by the Rothchilds, he might perhaps in spite of his Jewish origin have remained after Hitler came to power. His wife Therese, a lieder singer five years his senior, was a "pure Aryan"; she had in fact relatives in good standing with the Nazi party. She was devoted to her husband and could perhaps have arranged for him to stay if they had been willing to make the necessary compromises. The most grievous would have been to compromise themselves.

His musical achievements were not only highly esteemed but celebrated in the Germanic countries, where he was not thought of primarily as a Jew. Two stories he told illustrate *his* extraterritoriality. Both are about receptions held after his concerts. It was customary for him to dine after playing, and hosts or hostesses vied for the honor of arranging midnight suppers.

On such an occasion shortly after the First World War in Oslo Artur was entertained by the leading Maecenas of the city. It was a large party. A small man, Artur was seated on his host's right with his head alone visible. The host held his guests attention as he explained that everywhere men were faced by a Jewish plot to dominate the world. The Norwegian warmed to this subject, inventing bloodcurdling evidence as he went along.

After listening for some time Artur looked up smilingly at his host high above him and said quietly but audibly, "I am a Chew." That stopped the Maecenas dead. "It isn't true," he exclaimed, "you're joking." "No, it's true," said Artur, "I am a Chew." Dead silence. The man stood up. "Come with me," he sputtered and, leaving his guests, took Artur into a smaller room. "Look here," he said, "I don't believe you." "Yes," Artur said, "I *am* a Chew." The man almost shouted: "Then you are a *noble* Jew." "No," said Artur more quietly than ever, "Chust a Chew."

Another time after a concert Artur gave in Berlin, Walter Rathenau, the rich Jewish owner of one of the world's largest industrial combines and already Foreign Minister of the Reich, was a guest at the reception that followed. He singled Artur out and drew him into a private conversation in a small room. There he demonstrated by drawing graphs what a disaster it would be if, as threatened, Germany should go socialist and nationalize all enterprise. Artur returned to Vienna and at a lunch given by one of his rich gentile patrons, his hostess said, "Dear Mr. Schnabel, you are just back from Berlin, give us the political news, please tell us above all what the Jewish-communist Rathenau is plotting."

Not very long after this episode, Elinor and I had heard Rathenau's moving appeal at the last plenary session of the Genoa Conference.[1] He ended by repeating the Latin word "Pace, pace, pace." As if to deny that peace could represent German policy, Rathenau was assassinated two months later as he was being driven from his house in the suburbs of Berlin to the Foreign Office.

Little in the life of pre-Nazi Germany recommended itself to Artur. But Berlin had become his home. Even after he left in protest he retained in some cases the opinions of a patriotic German. While he was with us in Los Angeles in March 1936 Hitler ordered the German troops to occupy the Rhineland, Artur had been rehearsing the D Minor Brahms piano concerto with Klemperer, and after the rehearsal they both climbed into our Buick car to come to lunch at Elinor's mother's house. Artur was in the back seat with Elinor; Klemperer's vast frame towered above and beside the driver. He bought a newspaper announcing the German entry into territory across the Rhine, contrary to the terms of the Locarno Treaty negotiated freely long after Versailles by a successor of Rathenau, Foreign Minister Stresemann. Seeing the headlines, Klemperer gave an immense sigh of relief. "At last," he said turning to Artur, "that is it. The French will defend their rights, and that will be the end of Hitler." To my surprise Artur entered a mild demurrer. "After all," he suggested, "the area they are entering *is* German."

The war came three years later and the odds for a French victory had changed. When we saw Schnabel in September 1939 he was returning with Therese from a concert tour in Australia. They decided to stay in the United States. Actually they had little choice. Soon afterwards they settled into a New York hotel suite.

Artur's enthusiasm for our "institute," as for my other work, and his admiration for President Roosevelt's conduct of the war mounted together. When news came of the incineration of his mother and other relatives by the Nazis, his last link with Germany snapped. He determined never to go back. Once in my presence in 1950 at Lucerne, Karajan, then a rising star, invited him to play as soloist with the Vienna Philharmonic Orchestra. Moved by the invitation, Schnabel said, "I never go to Germany." Whereupon Karajan with much graciousness and understanding said, "Then I will bring the [Vienna] orchestra to Paris so we can play with you."

Artur had become a citizen of the United States before the war ended. When the judge who naturalized him did not even shake his hand or recognize him as a person of distinction, Artur's disillusionment with his new country began. He suffered from the lack of dignity, generally accorded him in Europe, to which he felt he was entitled.

What dealt his hopes a decisive blow was the changing political scene in the United States. His letters in longhand, written from Switzerland and Italy where he began to go again in the summers, are now in the archives of the University of Chicago. They tell a part of the story of his disappointments. Instead of the new and better America he had hoped for, there came the cold war and the McCarthy era. He feared the United States might become another Nazi-Germany. He felt he was being morally ousted from his new country as he had been from his old. Already ill, he went to Europe with Therese at the end of spring 1951 with no intention of returning.

Elinor and I were with the Schnabels in London for almost two weeks in June, all staying at the Hyde Park Hotel until they left for Switzerland. He no longer was able to enjoy food, and couldn't bear to sit down to a meal in the hotel he had frequented with pleasure for many years. So we used to walk together a hundred yards or so along Knightsbridge to a rather wretched little restaurant he had picked out, where the four of us nevertheless had the comfort of good conversation and of communion in the ideals we shared.

Shortly before he died he is said to have cried "It is enough!" meaning his time had come. Depressed because of his illness he feared the worst for America, with reason as it then seemed.[2] Fortunately what he feared hasn't happened. One price of keeping that worst at bay henceforth is some approach to that world community we sought in the Manifesto of 1946-47.

27. MARITAIN'S CREATIVE INTUITION

Jacques Maritain is thought of mainly as an ardent religious believer whose life, from the time of his conversion in his early twenties, has been intimately and continuously linked with the Roman Catholic Church. Together with his wife Raissa, with whom he was converted, he has been regarded as a proselytizer. His numerous contributions to philosophy are usually treated exclusively as those of a *Catholic* philosopher. Such views are incomplete. They neglect several aspects of his personality which were the basis of our friendship and related to my work in educational reform and history.

For many believers, whether they are Roman Catholic or profess any creed Christian or other, the heights touched by the artist and the man of faith have something in common. Schnabel felt transfigured in the process of musical composition. A man of faith links himself to God (in a sense he creates God) by striving towards what the late William Temple, once Archbishop of Canterbury, called "ultimate reality." By this he meant the world beyond matter, space and time, which according to *his* faith is the Source of all matter, space and time: "there in the beginning, is now, and ever shall be." To the extent that the man of faith, in his inner life, approaches "ultimate reality," he is moving in the realm whence an artist from his darting inner thoughts derives his inventions. But the religious believer cannot share his revelation with others in the same way as the artist. The artist does not have to *prove* their *existence*; his creations can be seen, heard or read.

In Maritain's case the connections between art and faith have always been close. As a youth he thought of becoming a painter and later, during the courtship of his wife, pictures of Rembrandt especially played a spiritual part in their conversion. Later the subject of his Mellon Lectures at the Library of Congress in Washington dealt with art as the fruit of "Creative Intuition."

Maritain had a gift for sharing his artistic insights with me and for grasping mine. Art was a fountain from which we both drank—an inexhaustible source of refreshment in our friendship.

My introduction to Maritain resulted from my regular reading of the *Criterion*. In an issue of that review, T. S. Eliot wrote of him as one of the meaningful contemporary French thinkers. Around 1930 Eliot's comments led me to Maritain's *Art et Scholastique*. That helped me to convey to students at the University of Chicago the nature and meaning of medieval art as part of the history of European society. Like Stravinsky I was struck by Maritain's emphasis on the distinction between the servile arts, where results depend on changes in matter, and the liberal arts, which are mainly constructions of the mind. This distinction revealed contrasts between reality as it appeared to medieval and to modern people. Generally speaking moderns find it more difficult than their medieval predecessors to envisage what their senses cannot detect—what cannot be touched, seen or heard.

I am trying to embody these contrasts in a book which I may call *Roots of the Mechanized World*. Its object is to draw into a unity the major aspects of European evolution in their bearing on the recent "triumph" of man over matter. Religious history has an important place, as does the history of the arts both liberal and servile, and the crafts which in medieval terms belonged to the latter category. So I approach religious history, like other subjects, not as a man of faith but as an artistically-oriented historian. In attaining that orientation Maritain's influence, like Schnabel's, was considerable.

Maritain's influence was also philosophical. Most of his followers as well as his opponents, identify his religion with his philosophy. It was true that for him, as a leading lay member of the Roman Catholic Church, any divorce between philosophy and Catholic philosophy was meaningless. All his adult life he has been a *philosophical* disciple of Thomas Aquinas but he never considered himself a theologian, and in his writings he sought to serve philosophy. He aimed to master not only Catholic but all major philosophers from the Greeks of classical antiquity to Hegel and Bergson. Through his friend and pupil, Olivier Lacombe (who lectured also for the Committee on Social Thought), he extended his attention to Indian and far-eastern philosophers.

What first arrested me philosophically in Maritain was a small essay of his on liberty. That was delivered as a lecture at the University of Chicago during the winter of 1933 while Elinor and I were in Los Angeles. Frances Little, who financed his visit to Chicago and paid for the publication of the lecture, sent us a copy.

I was searching for a solid philosophical basis for my own thinking. Ever since our return to the United States, and before hearing of Maritain, I had been dismayed by the absence of firm goals among American philosophers. I had associated with many of them, both because my guardian George Mead was a leading pragmatist and because, when I joined the University of Chicago, it was the foremost center for the study of pragmatism. I found this an alien creed.

On many occasions while we lived in Washington and Swarthmore I took issue in amiably conducted controversy with elders in philosophy whom I had known since childhood. They usually held that the trends in American living and thought, if left to themselves, would inevitably lead to "the best of all possible worlds." But it became my conviction

that unless American thought arrived freely at firm goals, other than
quantity production, we would, at least, lose sight of the ideals of
the Founding Fathers and, at worst, approach the mechanized night-
mare towards which the trends seemed to be leading. I remember
pointing this out to Frank Aydelotte in 1927.

Maritain's philosophical thought concerning liberty helped to
strengthen my position. Liberty consists in freedom to choose the right
slavery and it is the obligation of ethics to help each of us to recognize
the right slavery so that we can choose it of our free will. That is a
theme of Aristotle's *Ethics,* a work that influenced me profoundly
before I began to read Maritain. For me liberty was a philosophical
not a religious problem. Maritain's moral philosophy helped me to
understand the problem.

At no stage have I identified what I call the right slavery with the
dogma, still less with the rules, of the Roman *Church.* Like Elinor, I
had been brought up an atheist by both my parents and my guardian.
She and I were far from *hostile* to Maritain's religion. As I have explained, my purpose in becoming a professor was to contribute to
human happiness. And unlike pragmatism, Maritain's philosophy
seemed useful in the search for human *improvement* which led to the
writing of my book *The United States and Civilization.*

Learning of my interest in Maritain's thought, Frances Lillie gave
us a letter of introduction when we embarked for our 1933 summer
abroad. The Maritains then lived in Meudon, the Paris suburb.
Their Sunday afternoon receptions were famous. When she received
the Lillie letter Madame Maritain wrote that her husband was vaca-
tioning in the Jura, but suggested we come the following Sunday to get
acquainted with her and her sister, who lived with them throughout
the Maritains' married life.

In my enthusiasm for Maritain's moral philosophy I had thought he
might possibly be persuaded to revisit Chicago. I was delighted
therefore when his wife confided to me that he would be susceptible to
a short term *annual* appointment. "He thinks there is work for him to
do in Chicago," she volunteered. I understood her to mean work on
behalf of moral philosophy.

Maritain had long been teaching in the Institut Catholique in Paris,
and also more recently for shorter spells at the Pontifical Institute of
Medieval Studies, part of St. Michael's College, an affiliate of the University of Toronto. The idea of his joining the Chicago faculty part

time was appealing in the light of my own four good years there. It would be stimulating to have the case for a firmer philosophy than that of the pragmatists put forward by a contemporary scholar. But though Hutchins tried on three separate occasions during the next ten years, to arrange a connection for Maritain with the philosophy department, he was never able to bring it about.

The third attempt deserves mention. The incident recalls Hamlin Garland's stricture on the Middle West as a cultural desert. It was followed not long afterwards by Maritain's appointment to a permanent post in the Philosophy Department at Princeton.

In the winter of 1943 Maritain and Stravinsky were visitors at the same time to the newly formed Committee on Social Thought. I had met Stravinsky at Maritain's house in Meudon in 1936. He had been urged to come to the Committee in Chicago by my staunch friend Nadia Boulanger, to whom music is much indebted. One day during Stravinsky's stay he and Maritain came with Hutchins for luncheon in a private room at the University Club in the Chicago loop. It was a stimulating occasion for Hutchins and me. In the afterglow Hutchins offered them both posts at the university.

Stravinsky declined on the ground that he had to live in Los Angeles because of what he called its "ozone." (That was before the smog from the oil wells arrived.) But Maritain was receptive if a part time arrangement could be made after the war. The Committee on Social Thought had not yet obtained authority to recommend appointments. So Hutchins suggested to the Philosophy Department that they furnish Maritain with a complimentary post, without entrenching on their departmental budget, and on the understanding that all his work would be for the Committee. Two emissaries, a Vice President of the university and the Dean of the Social Sciences, made the proposition to the Chairman of the Philosophy Department. Both were refused. Each asked the Chairman why. Both received the answer: "because Maritain is not a good philosopher." Both asked whether there was a good philosopher in the Department of Philosophy. To this the engaging reply was made, "No, but we know what a good philosopher is."

Some years later we acquired authority to recommend appointments. Yet, curiously enough, it would then have been hardly less difficult to persuade the Committee than it had been to get the Philosophy Department to recommend Maritain's appointment. And this despite the fact that one of his two favorite pupils, Yves Simon, had been made a regular member of our faculty by unanimous choice. Simon was a more dogmatic Roman Catholic than Maritain and lacked his flair for art and his immense personal charm.

Opposition to Maritain within the Committee never reached the point of denying him periodic visits if these were financed outside the university budget. An arrangement was worked out whereby he came as a visiting professor for a few days each year, sometimes twice a year, during the period 1948-1958. In his seminars he tried out some of the ideas that he later incorporated in various books. For me the most moving of these occasions was the autumn of 1956. Maritain frequently consulted me in advance concerning the subject he would treat. This time he suggested he *ought* to devote himself to Hegel, whose philosophy he had been studying with assiduity. But his letter betrayed his preference for a subject that he had only flirted with, namely the views he had derived of the United States from his frequent residences. I urged him to follow his inclinations and *Reflections on America* was the result. That book contains much of delight.[1] Its preparation did not interfere with a sober treatment of Hegel on a later occasion.

Before the Second World War Maritain had made another trip from Toronto to Chicago in the fall of 1934. Alone and with the Lillies, with whom he then stayed, he came frequently to the Dorchester Avenue apartment. Thereafter, whenever he visited Chicago, whether alone or with his wife and sister-in-law, he always stayed with us. Among the pictures we had assembled, some by artists who were his friends, he felt at home.

Raissa Maritain was of Jewish origin. This forced Maritain, when the war broke out and the Nazis invaded France, to settle in the United States. Before that we had several Sunday afternoons with them at Meudon, and meetings at dinner and the theatre in Paris. It was at Meudon that we met Jean Hugo (from whom we bought our watercolor) and Gino Severini (the Italian painter who later occupied the Maritain's house during the war). There Stravinsky told us an unforgettable story. After Italy had joined the Allies in the First World War he had gone to Rome where Picasso had drawn his portrait. Stravinsky put the drawing in his luggage when he took the train back to Paris. At the frontier an Italian customs official opened his bags and pounced on the picture. "What's this?" he demanded. "It's my portrait," Stravinsky answered. "You lie through the teeth," came the instant response. "It's a plan of fortifications!"

Maritain's delight in music and the theatre, as well as in painting, was a part of a commitment to all the arts, and this commitment provided us with inexhaustible materials for conversation and reflection. Two years later, in the autumn of 1938 at the time of Munich, he came with his ladies for a three-week stay in our Chicago flat, while he gave some lectures at the university and in the neighborhood. The three repeated their visit in April 1940, on the eve of the fall of France. On both occasions it was the Chagalls and the Rouaults among our pictures that evoked the most conversation because of the long friendships the Maritains had had with those two artists.

Some time before these Maritain visits, we had bought six etchings by Rouault of street scenes,[2] and also a remarkable self-portrait—a colored lithograph. The success of a lithograph depends to some extent on the way the picture is pulled from the stone. The Maritains were so impressed by the quality of this particular example that Raissa asked to have it reproduced as the frontispiece to the first volume of her book of recollections, *Les grandes Amitiés*.

In that book she gives an account of the lifelong friendship she and Jacques had with Rouault. But there were several stories they told us in the intimacy of their visits which are not in the book. One is especially touching.

Georges Rouault came from a poverty stricken family and was apprenticed to a master glazier. According to custom an apprentice was fed and lodged but not given a cent in hand. Rouault had a consuming desire to paint but no means of obtaining a canvas, brush and colors. He suffered from the want and found out how much money he would need to acquire them. How was he to raise the sum?

Every day his master sent him on an errand to another quarter of Paris and supplied the fare needed to take the tram there and back. Rouault began to calculate and realized that if he could pocket the fare for two months he would have the means for starting to paint.

The idea of robbing his master was unthinkable. So he hit on a plan that provided absolution. When he was released each day for his errand he raced all the way across Paris and back beside the tram he was expected to take.

The same firm moral principles, exemplified by this childhood beginning of Rouault's art, had been part of my own early youth, although there was no need in my case for the physical exertion demanded of Rouault! I owed the principles partly to my upbringing, but the idea of practicing them scrupulously came from Elinor for when we first met she believed in them more firmly than I. Both sources were agnostic. As time went on, especially with the help of Aristotle's *Ethics,* the application of these principles was a great help in my work. I recognized that right conduct was indispensable in the handling of the vast quantities of historical materials that came my way. At first I was inclined to begrudge the time required to make it so. And then I saw that in the matter of accuracy there is no turning sharp corners; there can be no short cuts in the pursuit of truth.

During and after the war Maritain became a strong supporter of the Committee and of my book, *The United States and Civilization.* He was impressed by the possibilities he found in both for turning American leadership, with the coming of peace, in the direction of *Integral Humanism,* the title of one of his books published in the middle thirties. His moral scruples then had led him, at no small cost among his religious associates, to side with the Spanish loyalists against the revolt of General Franco. So the matter of natural law, which is independent of revelation and depends on the keen sense of what is right, loomed large in his philosophy. It was the basis of mine. Maritain's dedication to me of his book on natural law was a rational tribute.

After the Maritains settled in New York for the duration of the war, Maritain was active in the French *Ecole Libre des Hautes Etudes,* a species of non-sectarian university in exile. He was chosen as its president upon the death of Henri Focillon, the art historian, and the relations between this institution and the Committee on Social Thought became close. I lectured at the school in New York and Maritain sent us a delegation of visitors from its faculty. The delegation consisted of Jacques Hadamard, the distinguished mathematician, Alexandre Koyré, the historian of science, Roman Jakobson, the famous linguist, and Louis Marlio, an industrialist who had been president of the French aluminum combine. None were religious communicants, and the first three have been recognized as among the leading scholars of our times.

Nevertheless my association with Maritain seems to have contributed to the suspicion and dislike which existed in some American academic circles for the Committee on Social Thought as a Roman Catholic oriented institute. During the thirties and at the beginning of the forties, on the eve of the founding of the Committee, the philosophy of Thomas Aquinas was popularly supposed to be supplanting that of John Dewey at the University of Chicago. To a considerable extent this was because of the publicity given to Mortimer Adler who came to be frequently regarded (not with complete accuracy) as the intellectual mentor of President Hutchins, and who for some years had espoused and taught Aquinas' philosophy. The suspicion of "guilt by association" reached such a pitch that Beardsley Ruml, formerly dean at Chicago, who had become an officer of R. H. Macy and Company, used waggishly to describe "a Thomist" as a person "in favor of Hutchins." The definition was broad enough to include me.

Adler's connection with the Committee was slight and brief; he left the University of Chicago soon afterward. Before he joined in 1945, his allegedly blind devotion to Aquinas and to Roman Catholicism had already been compromised. During the Second World War he prepared an article for the Maritain issue of the Roman Catholic journal *The Thomist*. He argued that Aquinas had not *proved* the existence of God; so it was up to some contemporary or future philosopher to *prove* this. At the one seminar he conducted while with the Committee, Adler spoke further of Aquinas' limitations. Schnabel had brought Bruno Walter to dinner at our home, and later at the university Adler had Walter on one side and Schnabel on the other. The subject was slavery and Aquinas. In his peroration Adler almost shouted, striking his fist on the table, "Saint Thomas was wrong about slavery; I don't care if he was a saint, he was *wrong*." Whereupon Schnabel peered up with an almost beatific smile and enquired, "Vus he a saint ven he vus alive?"

Looking back a generation I recognize, better than when we paid our first call at Meudon in 1933, what an important factor in attracting the Maritains to Chicago was the prominence Adler then gave to the Thomist philosophy. That philosophy cannot be divorced from the Christian religion as promulgated by the Roman Catholic Church. Notwithstanding Aquinas' own allegedly narrow escape from excommunication when *he* was alive, that Church rests its intellectual foundations on his theology.

A belief in Christ and participation in the Roman Church have always seemed to me to be independent allegiances, though I have come to realize that in spiritual issues so highly charged with emotions, it is frequently impossible to maintain the separation in practice as Charles Péguy did.[3] Nevertheless for the future of humanity the distinction may be important. Christ's offer of love is to every human being. For Him all humans are brothers and sisters. But all churches are exclusive.

I gave the public lectures that were to become *The United States and Civilization* under the Walgreen Foundation of the University of Chicago. One of my auditors was the pastor of the local Unitarian Church, von Ogden Vogt, an older man whom we had known pleasantly for years. He heard the lecture that became a chapter on religion in the book. He had previously told me that, feeling as I did about religion, I should join a church. It didn't really matter which; "some church" would do.

I hadn't realized that my remarks concerning the divinity of Christ would shock Vogt. "You are so out of date, John," he told me, "If Christ were divine we should have had some manifestation of this over the last two thousand years. No religion of the future can be effectively based on that belief."

In view of the declaration in my book on behalf of what Vogt regarded as an outworn belief, it was not surprising that I should have been approached by representatives of the two churches in the United States whose dogmas are least flexible concerning the virgin birth and Christ's divinity: the Roman Catholic and the high Episcopalian. Not long after my book was published a telephone call came from a medical faculty colleague. He asked if I would receive his pastor. He called him "father." (There are in fact several catholic churches in the world, not just one as many Americans used to think, and so there are "fathers" with different church allegiances.) "He is in Chicago on a visit and wants to talk about your book," my colleague continued. "He is very enthusiastic." That afternoon the "father" arrived for tea at Dorchester Avenue. After a brisk, but brief, compliment concerning the book, he asked, "What is your church?" In informing him I hadn't one, I used the word "Catholic." A mystified expression covered his face, followed by belated understanding. "Oh," he said, "you mean *Roman*." He went on to instruct me why the Anglicans were the lineal descendants of Christ and the real Catholics.

Then I received a flattering letter from a lay representative of the Roman "branch." After an agreeable salute to my book this man invited me to have my voice tried out as a possible participant in "The Catholic Hour," a radio program. He mentioned that another candidate was Fulton Sheen. For the sake of avoiding a misunderstanding, I asked my correspondent whether he knew that I was not a member of his Church. He answered with some embarrassment that he hadn't realized this, and did not renew the invitation. I was surprised.

From the point of view of one who is a non-"joiner" and committed to "humanity" for whom Christ died, it is puzzling that this information should have brought automatic disqualification. If my Roman Catholic correspondent really believed what I had written was suited to his audience, he might have waived formalities and given my *voice* a try-out! At least so I reflected.

When a small boy I had been warned by my father that grown people were not infrequently approached, as he had been, by persons offering to "put one right with God." "Beware of such persons," was my father's counsel. How far his advice influenced me in the forties is difficult to say. After an atheistic interlude during adolescence and early manhood, my faith in Christ increased. One factor was no doubt Maritain's friendship, and particularly the close relationship in his mind between the search for firm principles and the Christian religion. Thanks to his good taste, he never approached me in the terms used by the Unitarian, the Anglo-Catholic, or the Roman Catholic who was recruiting for "The Catholic Hour." His religious beliefs seemed to be intermingled with a wider view of humanity that he then expressed in many of his works and lectures. Here we had a common cause, the one in which Schnabel had joined me shortly after Hiroshima when Maritain had left the United States to become French Ambassador to the Vatican.

Other important factors in what I hope I am not blasphemous in calling my Christian belief came before I met or even heard of Maritain. As a child my Presbyterian grandmother transmitted the idea of Christ's divinity, making an immense impression. That led me to ask my mother if I could pray. My mother not only permitted this but used to kneel and help with the prayers. My grandmother survived my mother by over three years and died in 1912 when eighty-six. She begged me when I grew up and became independent to be baptized. That would be sufficient for her purpose, she suggested. That purpose, I suppose, was to have me do the right thing. My grandmother also said we were descended from Gilbert Sheldon, Archbishop of Canterbury under Charles II. A Sheldon had come over to America in the eighteenth century, had settled in what became the state of New York, and my great grandmother, Submit Sheldon, had married Joseph Garlinghouse of Dutch descent by whom she had many children of whom my grandmother was the youngest.[4]

Two experiences during Elinor's and my years abroad drew me again to Christ. One was reading Renan's *Vie de Jesus*. Renan had left the Roman Church when he was at Saint-Sulpice, a seminarian preparing for the priesthood. He is therefore a thorn in the flesh of Roman Catholics. His account of Christ convinced me anew, however, of the Saviour's existence after my guardian had inadvertently provided me with a notion that it was historically unlikely that a man named Jesus Christ had ever lived. It was a kind of revelation for me to learn from Renan's beautiful French prose that he was a real and, in a lay sense, a divine person even to one who did not happen to consider him the Son of God.

The other experience was listening to Bach's St. Matthew Passion as directed by Vincent d'Indy in Paris. On that occasion my growing devotion to the great works of music merged with my childhood recollections. The message received from Bach's music was of compelling moment: Christ was martyred for those very virtues for which all humans of good will and honor and compassion have been persecuted in varying degrees and ways at all times and places, whether or not they were members of a Christian church or of any church. His tragedy is a human tragedy; one which our race may have to surmount to survive. The music accented as nothing else has ever done this participation in the Lord's suffering. It is difficult not to believe that He came to give hope, not only to the poor and maimed and for remission of sins, but to those who are ignored, if not persecuted, for striving to serve truth.

Much later Elinor used to attend Roman Catholic mass and have me join her because of her conviction—a component of her mental illness—that our presence would protect us from those who wanted to do us in. If we appeared as possible *candidates* for conversion, our lives would be spared. She was *not* a Christian in the sense of believing in Christ's divinity, and, as long as she lived, there was never any possibility of a connection with any church.

This did not, however, prevent me from being classified as a "Roman," long before her death in 1953, perhaps (although evidence is lacking) because of Maritain's association with my academic initiatives and his tributes to my historical work. "I hate John Nef," an American scholar now long dead (who never met me) is reported to have said. The report came from a long time French friend, Charles Morazé. During the early years of UNESCO Morazé (without my knowledge) brought my name into discussions as a possible participant. "Why do you hate him?" Morazé asked. "Because he is a Roman Catholic," the man replied. Not knowing this was then untrue, and being from a country where most citizens are at least nominally Roman Catholics, Morazé, who can hardly be thought of as devout, answered "So am I," "Yes," this American sputtered, "but you were born so."

I had a very imperfect conception even later, when Elinor died, of the meaning of membership in the Roman Church. I did not realize the extent to which the act of joining was prompted by the desire to save oneself and how little connection that act had with the service of humankind which commands my allegiance. Nor had I realized the prominent place given to the dogma (shared by some other churches) according to which God, the source of forgiveness of sins, is made the cause for the creation of the species which has been for thousands of years a principal source of the very evils He abhors. The Devil had no reality and it had been impossible for me to locate that Garden of Eden from which the first woman excluded her descendants by picking forbidden fruit. Elinor's unions with me did not fit the story.

I thought of membership in the Roman Church as primarily a testimonial to belief in Christ's suffering for the right and the compassionate in a world for which He was not responsible, and as a refuge for those who try to follow Him in serving the right. I thought of it as a testimonial of belief in the Christian virtues exemplified by Rouault's resolve not to rob his master. I believed in those connections between the coming of Christianity and a higher human morality that Tocqueville, who was not an active communicant, explained so convincingly in his correspondence with Gobineau.[5]

Everything I believed in was suddenly and terribly threatened by Elinor's death. The light lit that morning in New York just after our marriage, when she lifted the last veil, was extinguished when she died. The loss seemed to place all my principles in jeopardy. I felt defenseless, with a desperate need for something firm to take her place. I shall always be grateful for what was done for me, during the period that intervened between her death and my meeting with Evelyn, by a French priest, the Père A.M. Carré, to whom Nadia Boulanger introduced me. He baptized and took care of me for more than a decade.

An English Roman Catholic once compared the Roman Church to a club. The price of membership is to observe the regulations. In Evelyn I married an agnostic as unlikely to commit herself to a church as my first wife or my parents. As a non-believer, who has found herself on the opposite shore on every detail of its dogma, she refused to be married in the Roman Church. I was thereby automatically disqualified, as had been the case when two decades earlier the invitation had come to be tried out for the "Catholic Hour."

Maritain is a subtle and very impulsive man, in some respects even more naive than I in the practical world, less capable of managing his material affairs. His commitment to Roman Catholicism differs widely from mine. It would not help to discharge my debt to him or to serve the cause of accuracy, if I set about interpreting him or *his* career. What unites us is our friendship, the discoveries which we share in the realm where art and faith meet, and our mutual love for each others countries.

My impression is that he grew disillusioned after the Second War by the disappointing responses that followed in his own country and in mine to the integral humanism he had invoked. And then he too suffered a shattering blow in the death of his wife. In a way his blow was more shattering than mine, partly because it came later in his life. Some have supposed that his preoccupation with the Roman Church was intensified because of his wife's devotion to it. However that may be, his dependence on the Church and his loyalty to its dogma seem rather to have increased than to have diminished since she died. She had compelling confidence in his genius. Some attribute partly to her enthusiasm his tremendously large published output. Certain it is that he had virtually completed what he set out to do as a philosopher before her death, that he has been little occupied with philosophy since and that he is abundantly entitled to every attenuation of suffering which the Church has been able to provide.

The controversy aroused by his book *Le Paysan de la Garonne*— a treatise touching on modern tendencies in the Roman Catholic faith—lies outside the scope of this autobiography. From my long association with him as a friend, and what I learned from that friendship of his married life, I was not surprised by the conservative religious positions he has recently taken. He had prepared me, moreover, for the book. Evelyn and I journeyed to Princeton to lunch with him on his last visit to the U. S. in 1966. He came over to say farewell to his American friends; he was then 84 years old.

28. REEXPLORING EUROPE

In the autumn of 1944, after the allied recovery of Paris when victory seemed near, the State Department contemplated extending to Europe an experiment started in Latin America. This was the appointment of cultural attachés to United States embassies, thereby making "culture" a special branch of foreign relations. The French Foreign Office had had a separate cultural relations program for a generation beginning in 1922-23 when it was called the "Service des Oeuvres." Not unnaturally, therefore, the late Howland Shaw, as the Assistant Secretary of State charged with cultural matters, decided to begin in Europe by appointing an attaché in Paris, where the United States Embassy was being reestablished. Jacques Maritain recommended me to his friend Shaw, who offered me the post.

In the light of reason (easily put to flight by the enthusiasm born of war in a good cause), this proliferation of the foreign service was ill-suited to my objectives because it involved increasing specialization at a time when sight of the general—the universal—was being lost. It provided, furthermore, evidence of multiplying government activity on behalf of nationalism, at a time when the needs I represented required an international approach.

The policy of expanding *cultural* activities was based on a theory that, as I was charmingly informed in a pleasant southern drawl by the gentleman then in charge of the program under Shaw, "culture has no enemies." That theory attracted me. Yet, as envisaged for France, the extension required concern with *quantitatively* impressive "cultural" activities—such as rehabilitation of libraries and museums —labor for the administration of which I had no training. In short the work ran in many ways counter to the purposes of my life.

There was an urgent call for the functions that cultural officials were now asked to perform. It is valuable that these functions should be performed well and in as generous a spirit as possible. But performing them, as French experience also showed,[1] contributed little or nothing to a very different movement independent of governments (which might prove to be complementary) towards a strengthening of individualism, internationalism and universalism. There was a need for persons whose working lives were devoted to these ends, persons devoted to the cause of humanity.

"Activism" is no doubt a necessity, but there is a danger that it will be pushed so far as to obliterate basic thought and to deny the heart a role in life now more needed than ever. In the end the value of activism depends on the nature of the goals on behalf of which men and women are active. It was up to me to help define these goals. The acceptance of this Paris post in 1944 would have meant deserting indefinitely the Committee on Social Thought, before it had reached a point where it could continue by itself. As for the books in progress or planned for the future, there would be no possibility in this new government post of having my mornings.

In retrospect this all seems clear. Yet at the time such considerations were partly obscured by the euphoria accompanying the end of one of the most inhuman dictatorships in history, the Nazi dictatorship. Part of the euphoria was produced by the emotions aroused at the prospect of returning to France. With Dufy's picture of the "Blue Train" and the harbor of Antibes looking down on us in our Dorchester Avenue apartment, I had described French Riviera beaches evening after evening to a sympathetic representative of the United States naval intelligence. The only witness of these deliberations my first wife, with her partiality for her husband, decided he was responsible for the successful invasion of the Riviera. However that may be the experience with naval intelligence had whetted my desire to get to France. Night after night the strain of that martial song of the First World War, "Over There," sounded in my ears.

Though Elinor shared the desire to return, the fears aroused by her mental illness had reached an extreme during the war. She believed we were everywhere surrounded by persons plotting our deaths; first hers, in order to get rid of me with impunity. This made the change of habitat involved in the State Department offer seem impracticable as well as unwise for her. And to leave her alone in Chicago was unthinkable.

What clinched matters was an hour's conversation in Washington with her much older first cousin, William R. Castle, who knew nothing of her condition. He strongly downgraded the opportunity this particular new post would offer. He had been in the American foreign service for some fifteen years from 1918 to 1933, and had ended as Under-Secretary of State in the Hoover Administration. He knew the State Department from within as few others did. He knew most of the leading American diplomats and said quite simply that the newly chosen United States Ambassador to France, Jefferson Caffery, had a good opinion of *himself* as a man of culture.

My negative decision turned into a great blessing. When a man grasps at an opportunity likely to prove disillusioning, if he is given the grace to wait, a better opportunity sometimes falls into his lap without the original obstacles. So it proved more than once in my life and never more so than in our return to Europe after the war.

At the time my appointment as cultural attaché was considered, Maritain went to France to consult about matters concerning the Vatican Embassy with de Gaulle's Foreign Minister, Georges Bidault, whom he had known before the war. He established direct contacts with representatives of the French intellectual world who had remained in France during the German occupation. They were glad to have firsthand news of American conditions.

Among Maritain's friends there had been hope that it might be possible to install him, with his artistic tastes and imaginative outlook, in the Collège de France. Maritain's Vatican Embassy got in the way of this project. But he had conversations with the "Administrateur," or head, of the Collège de France, a learned medievalist named Edmond Faral. Maritain seized the occasion to tell Faral about the new reform movement emanating from Chicago and also about my historical books. Faral was an old-fashioned French type. For him mere economic productivity provided no passport to human happiness; like me he found alien the conception that industrial growth is *the* barometer of progress. He attributed these conceptions to the Americans and refused to believe that any *American*, of even the smallest reputation, could possibly share his views concerning the limitations of the technological revolution the world was undergoing.

However the information Maritain imparted did not count against me. Faral had considerable influence over appointments and he remembered what Maritain had told him when, years later, a prominent member of the Collège faculty and an old friend of ours, André Siegfried, rounded up support for installing me as a visiting lecturer.

Meanwhile another French invitation came my way. Its acceptance was to plant me in the midst of Parisian scholarly life, whose broad antenna extended into the entire country, and to prepare me for my later participation in the Collège de France, whose antenna were even more penetrating than those of the Sorbonne. In the autumn of 1948, I was asked by the Institut d'Etudes Politiques, administratively part of the University of Paris since the war, to join its faculty for the second semester of the academic year, starting in February 1949.

By this time the Committee on Social Thought was firmly established with powers to recommend appointments, with a faculty and a small body of promising graduate students. It had the seasoned services of an extraordinarily efficient secretary broken in since 1944, Mrs. Adam Armour. A chairman could leave for limited but extended periods without relinquishing the decision-making authority or risking the dissolution of the enterprise. Also Elinor's "fears," for which the Nazi conspiracy had become a focus, were slightly less acute during the decade that followed the war and preceded her death.

The Paris invitation was sparked by several young French scholars —Georges Friedmann, François Perroux, Louis Chevalier, Jean Meynaud, and Charles Morazé. Morazé, Friedmann and Perroux had visited the U. S. since the war; Perroux once engaged us in a most moving conversation about Bergson and Roman Catholicism.

All these men knew my work, partly through the older French historians Marc Bloch and especially Henri Hauser. After 1932 Hauser spread knowledge of its significance. He published in the *Revue Historique* during the war a French version of my *Industry and Government in France and England, 1540-1640.*

Both Hauser and Bloch were dead when we returned to France, so the invitation to the Institut was arranged through André Siegfried, whose father had been one of the founders of its ancestor the Ecole Libre des Sciences Politiques. That had been set up at the beginning of the Third Republic in 1874, independently of the State, for the purpose of training government officials and diplomats. In spite of its new connection with the University of Paris under the Fourth Republic, the school retained much of its self sufficiency. Siegfried was now its grand older statesman; he continued to teach every year until he reached the age of eighty. He was also President of the Fondation Nationale des Sciences Politiques, which sponsored its publications. In addition he wrote a column for the *Figaro*, the leading morning paper. It was there that he introduced my work to the French public. His interest and generosity never flagged during the decade that followed and ended with his death in 1959.

So I went to France, not for the State Department, but as a part of the French academic establishment, chosen by French scholars to teach French students. The value of this sponsorship for my mission would be difficult to exaggerate. It opened all academic and many social doors. The French scholars received me almost as "one of their own" and largely without the jealousies bred by close faculty relationships.

The subject of my lectures at the Institut d'Etudes Politiques, derived from my nearly finished book *War and Human Progress,* was "The Road to Total War," an analysis of the course of history from the eighteenth to the twentieth century, culminating in two World Wars. A repetition of that "road" seemed at least as disastrous to me as to the French. I wrote my Paris lectures with the help of a French colleague, Alfred Canu, then visiting the University of Chicago, and delivered them in successive weeks. Afterwards I rewrote them as chapters of a book—*La Route de la guerre totale*—published by the Fondation Nationale des Sciences Politiques as one of its "Cahiers."

At the end of the first lecture a veteran of the First World War, with one leg and half an arm, hobbled down the aisle past the groups of students. He told me that, reading the title of the lectures, he felt he must come. In 1917 he had lain long in "no man's land" with his wounds. The slogan of President Wilson that the allies were fighting "a war to end war" had meant much to him. He was not disappointed by what he heard me say.

Before this inaugural lecture rumors had been circulated among the left-wing students to the effect that, along with two other Americans, I was being imposed on the school by the State Department in the interest of a bellicose United States foreign policy. As the lecture hall was filling for my maiden appearance, several students brandished the clenched fist. They were neither seen nor heard again during my four months of lecturing, teaching and direct conversations with my pupils. What scotched the rumors even before I started to talk was the appearance as chairman at this inaugural lecture of the leading French historian, Lucien Febvre, a member of the august faculty of the Collège de France. He introduced me with a full and accurate account of my work.[2]

Febvre was greatly respected. He was known for his independence of thought and politics and for his devotion to a wide view of history, expressed in the title and contents of a collection of his articles called *Combats pour l'histoire.* His contributions to the kind of historical perspective I admired most were found in many illuminating works, in *Philippe II et la Franche Comté, La Religion de Rabelais* and also in *La Terre et l'Evolution humaine.* An English translation of that book on historical geography had been made part of the students' reading program in my general history course at Chicago.

I came to France, therefore, not as a functionary and nationalist but as a disinterested historian and educational reformer, whose ideas for the reform of history writing Febvre partly shared and even acclaimed.

In mid-winter 1949 I boarded the "Queen Mary" with Elinor in New York to take up this assignment after twelve years at home, my longest absence from Europe in a long life. We spent our first night in Caen. Little remained of its gracious looking sixteenth and seventeenth century houses as we knew them from visits during the 'twenties and 'thirties. It had been battered by the allies when German troops held it for a month after the allied debarkation in 1944. In this old university town, we found no sign of a university. All but one of the pre-war hotels had been obliterated. At an improvised bookshop, where the proprietor sold us a recent edition in two thick volumes of Chateaubriand's *Mémoires d'outre tombe,* he advised us to put up for the night in a renovated building converted into a *meublé,* a hotel without restaurant.

After unloading our automobile at Cherbourg, and a slow drive along the wet, snowy winding road bordering the coast where the initial allied landings had been made, once in our room we were too tired to go out. The hotel was patronized mainly by Frenchmen who, for a variety of reasons of business or pleasure or both, came in after the evening and left before the morning meal. But the manager showed the sympathy and the gifts for improvisation that we had frequently appreciated during French motor trips in the 'thirties. He arranged to have our meal served in the bedroom. Dinner cooked in a restaurant some doors away was carried up three flights of stairs by a waiter, who laid two complete *couverts* on the dressing table. Never did a sole taste better. There was no private bathroom, but the bedroom had hot and cold running water. There was a radiator which banged as it gave off traces of heat.

Our room had also a small wooden chair without arms, on which I sat at dinner while Elinor sat on the bed. At the time of her gall bladder operation of 1924 in London, we had found relief from enforced continence by discovering the delights of having her settle down astride. This had led us sometimes to meet that way after her recovery, for on occasions this seemed to draw us closest as it enabled us almost to embrace simultaneously from the rear and the front. The old wooden chair suggested this could be such an occasion.

It provided the firm base we both longed for that first night in
France. And the drama of being there after twelve years, with the
country freed from four years of Nazi occupation, added to the joy
of our total commitment to one another.

Never had life seemed so secure as in this tiny modestly warmed
room, devoid of other furniture, in the midst of a ruined city returning
to life, reaffirming the old layout of its streets, the old ways of living,
the old ways of dining, the old ways of loving. Whatever place the evil
furies that are in man chose to attack that night, it could not be
Caen. The city had proved indestructible.

Paris received us with the affection we felt for her. It was not
long before the secretary general of the Fondation Nationale des
Sciences Politiques, Jean Meynaud, gave a luncheon in his small
apartment on the long rue de Vaugirard. He had recently married
one of his students, a lovely young Greek girl who was destined later,
when her uncle died, to bring him one of those fortunes to which a
few Greeks seem to have secret access. But in 1948 the Meynauds
were still poor. His bride cooked and served everything herself. The
crowning feature was the cake she baked in the form of Volume I of
my *Rise of the British Coal Industry*.

On this occasion I met and began an enduring friendship with the
Jean Fourastiés. Like so many men of his age, he had been retarded
in his distinguished career by the war. In 1949 he had just published
his first book which caught the public imagination, *Le grand Espoir
du XXeme siècle*. It proved prophetic for France as she developed
during the two decades that followed.

Fourastié's "great hope" was economic growth. He has often
explained that his idea of multiplying production as *the* goal was designed for the *French*—a counterweight to conservative tendencies
peculiar to France. "If I were an American, I would be questioning
the value of economic growth as an ultimate goal just as you are,"
he used to say. And now many years later Fourastié has come to
doubt whether economic progress derived from technological efficiency
is enough for France. With the passage of time our positions, in the
beginning at opposite poles, have drawn increasingly close. Now we
both believe what the world needs is a humanizing of economic growth
in the interest of civilization.

The four-month appointment to the faculty in the Institut d'Etudes

Politiques gave Elinor and me the opportunity to make friends outside the immediate academic circle. Shortly before we left for France an annual exchange of students and a scholar had been negotiated by Jean Marx, who was one of Maritain's oldest friends and who had built up between the two World Wars what became after the Second the Cultural Relations Division of the Foreign Office. He came to see me in Chicago in the autumn of 1948, and we established this exchange between the Committee on Social Thought and the University of Paris. It lasted until my retirement in 1965.

In view of this new agreement we were welcomed in France with dinners, not only by the Institut, but on behalf of the Foreign Office by Louis Joxe who had recently succeeded Henri Laugier as director of the Cultural Relations Division and who was on the threshold of his career as ambassador and cabinet minister. We were also welcomed on behalf of the University of Paris by its President, Jean Sarrailh. He had previously headed the Universities of Grenoble and Montpellier. Soon after reaching Paris, he and his wife made an effort to strengthen French friendship with Great Britain and the United States by inviting the British and American ambassadors to a splendid banquet. In the midst of the festivity, Madame Sarrailh told me, one of those diplomats had observed, "If France can provide a feast like this, why should she ask for economic aid?"

Sarrailh was impressed by the message brought in the lectures I gave at the Institut and referred to them in his annual report. Soon after he was chosen as the first president of the new International Union of Universities, that he had helped to establish. He invited me to contribute an article for a small brochure brought out, under the auspices of UNESCO, a kind of manifesto on behalf of this worldwide scholarly group. The article was called "The Universities and World Community."[3] It suggested a new unifying role for universities in the nuclear era.

Some years before Sarrailh's presidency the University of Paris had been given a wooded property of several hundred acres outside the tiny town of Richelieu, south of Chinon in Touraine. Like the town, the estate had belonged to the Cardinal when he governed France under Louis XIII. He had never found time to visit these places, but the properties remained in the family for one of his brothers, Francois de Vignerot du Plessis, was a layman. The title of duke, which the Cardinal held, was conferred on this brother's heir. Generations later, when the male Richelieu branch died out early in the nineteenth century, the title and the property passed through a female descendant who had married the marquis de Jumilhac (1766-1826). Their grandson, who married the rich heiress Marie Alice Heine (later Princess of Monaco), died prematurely in 1880 after renovating the property with her help. It was their son who, as the last duc de Richelieu (1875-1952), gave the vast estate to the University of Paris.[4] He conceived of it as a Chequers for the head of this Paris Academy.

The office of "Recteur" had become in Jean Sarrailh's time an overwhelmingly exhausting burden. It involved not only the operation of the enormous University of Paris, continually growing in complexity and in number of students, but also the supervision of secondary education in the area of the Ile-de-France. Beyond those official duties there was seemingly endless diplomatic and academic entertaining to be done. These demands were at least as backbreaking as those of a British prime minister, and the Rector had need for a retreat such as Richelieu provided. It was far enough from Paris to be out of range of calls from colleagues and students.

The large rambling house which the Sarrailhs occupied was built when the Heine family allied with the Jumilhac to replace the vast old seventeenth-century chateau which had been demolished. The servants rooms on the third and top floor far outnumbered the master bedrooms, but the Sarrailhs always left the servants rooms empty. On more than one occasion the Sarrailhs received me for long weekends. The three of us celebrated with lukewarm champagne in a bistro, the peace Mendès-France managed finally to negotiate ending the war in Vietnam. Here too Jean helped me with the proofs of the French translation of *War and Human Progress,* and I had the honor and pleasure of reading in proof his monumental volume on the Enlightenment in Spain, *L'Espagne éclairée de la seconde moitié du xviii eme siècle.* It was at Richelieu also that we talked over plans for his visit to the United States on behalf of the International Union of Universities. During that visit in 1954 he spent a week in Chicago as guest of the Committee on Social Thought, staying in my Dorchester Avenue apartment and delivering a lecture on the Spanish Enlightenment which was published in *The Journal of Modern History.*

The first of the French scholars to visit the Committee under the exchange agreement with the Ministry of Foreign Affairs was Louis

Leprince-Ringuet. He came in 1950 when he was a rising star among French physicists and a professor in the Ecole Polytechnique. (Later he became a member of the Collège de France and of the French Academy.) His visit helped the Committee to extend its relations to the Physics Department and the Medical School of the University of Chicago. Thanks to the mutual interests of Enrico Fermi and Leprince-Ringuet, we met on several occasions with the Chicago scientists. In exchange for Leprince-Ringuet, my friend Dallas Phemister the great Chicago surgeon, not long before his death late in 1951, went to the Paris School of Medicine representing the Committee on Social Thought. In Chicago Leprince-Ringuet lectured on "religion and science" and "philosophy and science." But what surprised me and drew us into ever closer relations, was his enthusiasm for beauty. He has painted all his life and has recently had a one-man show in Paris. His love of art extended to music and provided us with a meeting ground essential to the development of our friendship. He joined the Center for Human Understanding,[5] and three times came to Washington to participate in its meetings, the last time in 1964 just after my engagement to Evelyn.

One of the earliest exchange students from the Sorbonne to the Committee was Eric de Dampierre, of a famous old French family. His parents gave a dinner for Elinor and me in 1951 to meet the Pange-Broglie, who virtually "adopted" me during the years of my widower-hood. Jean de Pange was a distinguished medievalist outside the academic establishment. The family ramifications were extensive and extraordinary in the fields of both letters and sciences. The Comtesse de Pange was the sister of the late Duc de Broglie. Every year after Elinor's death the Panges and their son Victor (who had paid us a visit in Chicago in 1952) invited me to the family chateau in Normandy. The owner Maurice de Broglie was, like his younger brother Louis (who won the Nobel prize), a great physicist. It was to this older brother that Leprince-Ringuet owed his profession and schooling. The two had established a relationship of master and pupil similar to the kind we sought within the Committee on Social Thought, a kind the more needed now that it has become so rare. The Duke presided over the rambling chateau at Broglie with its scores of rooms, its magnificent library, and no private bathroom! His sister Pauline has since become famous for her three fascinating volumes of reminiscences of this old family during the Third Re-public. The Broglie are descendants of Madame de Stael, whose daughter became Duchesse de Broglie. Madame de Pange and Victor maintain the artistic tradition of letters thus brought into the family.

Two years after Elinor's death Victor married the beautiful older daughter of our friends the Henri Costa de Beauregards. Their chateau of Beauregard is on the Lake of Geneva in upper Savoy, and Evelyn and I have often visited there. With the help of his wife, Victor de Pange has carried on his late father's lifelong interest in a single Europe, by working for the Conseil d'Europe in Strasbourg, an authentic organization looking towards unity.

These relationships have been and are precious. Since I married Evelyn the meetings and discussions with the Panges and the Costa de Beauregards have helped to broaden the base of my relations with France and Europe. They have provided insights into French life, thought and culture, to the enrichment of the work begun with my return to Paris in 1949, work which contributed immensely towards what is, I hope, the spreading influence of the Committee on Social Thought and the Center for Human Understanding, an outgrowth of the Committee.[6]

The most decisive event on behalf of this influence was my four-month appointment in the winter and spring of 1953 as lecturer in the Collège de France. André Siegfried, who had taken so personal an interest in my teaching at the Institut d'Etudes Politiques, came to the conclusion that this school did not provide a platform sufficiently broad. He had already retired from the Collège de France. But he retained considerable power over appointments and set about to make a temporary place for me. When he succeeded he redoubled his efforts, through his column in the *Figaro,* to obtain the kind of general audience I was seeking. This led eventually to a small public not only in France but also in Italy, Spain and parts of South America.

Siegfried was supported by another retiring member of the faculty at the Collège, Lucien Febvre, who had already done so much in 1949 to ease my way into the French academic establishment. One of the most moving experiences of my life was the speech of welcome he gave on behalf of the Collège at the reception arranged on the occasion of the honorary degree I received from the University of Paris in 1955.[7] Febvre regarded my *War and Human Progress,* published in 1950, as a work to be compared to Proudhon's *Guerre et Paix.* That was my first full-fledged effort in the medium of integral history. In writing it I put aside a plan which had begun to grow in my mind for a more "total" history. My new assignment at the Collège de

France provided the greatly desired opportunity to make a sketch
for the wider study of historical interrelations that I had postponed.
The lectures I gave were written and then converted into book form
in 1954 as *La Naissance de la civilisation industrielle et le monde
contemporain*[8] under the fearful conditions of Elinor's last illness and
death. Subjects were omitted on which I lay store, such as the history
of manners and of the arts, from literature to painting, music and
architecture.

An invitation from the University of Belfast provided an opportunity to touch on those subjects in another book, written in English,
Cultural Foundations of Industrial Civilization. This is a revised
version of the Wiles lectures founded by an American lady, Mrs.
Janet Boyd, in memory of her father in the hope that they would
contribute to international understanding and world peace. This book
of mine has been translated into Arabic and Spanish, as well as French.
It complements the book that emerged from the Collège de France
lectures, and this was further complemented by an essay on the
interrelations between ecclesiastical and economic history. Thanks
to the Italian statesman, Amintore Fanfani, the essay was published
in Italian in *Economia e Storia* before it found its way into English.
Not inappropriately. A precocious professor in 1933, Fanfani had been
the first to write concerning the implications of a chapter in my coal
book on the growth of private industrial enterprises stimulated by the
confiscation under Henry VIII of ecclesiastical property.

The reception accorded my eleven Collège de France lectures led
Siegfried to suggest that there be a final hour at which the public
would have the opportunity to ask questions. Such a discussion hour
was, we discovered, without precedent insofar as this great French
institute was concerned. As a traditionalist and head of the Collège,
Faral was shocked by the suggestion. Since Siegfried's influence was
powerful he did not like to reject it. He finally agreed, on two conditions: that Siegfried preside, and that the session end, as *lectures*
were expected to, exactly one hour after it began.

Faral had a third reservation of which we were unaware until the
session ended. In spite of several private interviews with me, and his
attendance at my inaugural lecture, he could not quite believe what
Maritain had told him concerning my views of the limitations of
economic growth as a test of progress, and of the need for a more
comprehensive interpretation of the past than a specialist in eco-

nomic history could provide. So he planted his elderly wife with two of her friends in the audience. After the session all three ladies came backstage. Almost in unison, they exclaimed, "Sir, it is a disgrace that it has to be an *American* to tell the French what their own professors should be teaching them."

29. "LET HIM WHO IS WITHOUT SIN . . ."

The appointment at the Institut d'Etudes Politiques, like the later appointment at the Collège de France, led to informal meetings as well as lectures with groups of students, teachers and other adults not connected with either institution. I twice addressed the Société X-Amérique, a dining club of businessmen and civil servants who had graduated from the Ecole Polytechnique, the famous school for training military officers and engineers. And I spoke to the Ecole des Hautes Etudes Militaire for my friend General Olivier Poydenot (nicknamed "Twist") who was in command of that school at the time. My appointments also brought about brief assignments outside Paris, at Toulouse and Caen for instance. During one occasion in 1949 when Elinor and I were motoring to Cap d'Antibes,[1] we paid a call on a French priest, the late Père Lebret, who directed an experiment in humane religious culture which endures, *Economie et Humanism*. We had met in Paris but his headquarters were then in a village a few miles west of Lyons. He had invited us to stop. In the course of conversation over tea he apologized because he was scheduled to speak to a group of nuns and a few civilians at five o'clock. "Only," he cautioned me abruptly, "it is *you*, not I, who will give the talk."

During the 1949 Easter holidays I lectured at the extension school of the University of Birmingham. My visit to England, where I met T. S. Eliot and Friedrick Hayek in London, enabled me to make those two important appointments to the Committee on Social Thought.[2] Hayek accepted a permanent chair he was destined to hold for almost fifteen years. The Economics Department welcomed his connection with Social Thought, although the economists had opposed his appointment in Economics four years before largely because they regarded his *Road to Serfdom* as too popular a work for a respectable scholar to perpetrate. It was all right to have him at the University of Chicago so long as he wasn't identified with the economists.

In an effort to heal Second World War wounds the University of Chicago had established an exchange for faculty members with the University of Frankfort, which bears the illustrious name of the Goethe University. I was invited to take part in the program and agreed to go for a brief visit in midsummer 1949, after the Paris semester at the "Sciences Po" ended. I gave five lectures on successive days, adapting parts of *La Route de la guerre totale* for presentation in German. Otto von Simson, a Prussian by birth whose great grandfather had been the first President of the Reichstag (at the time of the Franco-Prussian War[3]) was for several years executive secretary of the Committee on Social Thought and had taken a leave of absence to teach for an extended period in Frankfort. He was on hand to receive us, to help with my German and to present me to the students and faculty. In opening the series we announced that a question period would follow each lecture. The first was an historical account of conditions leading to the French Revolution and the Napoleonic Wars. Not a word was said about the recent war Germany had declared against the United States. But its scars were displayed in the very building that enclosed the amphitheatre where I spoke. As the lecture ended a German student rose from the high reaches at the back. Without preamble he spoke four words, and halted: "Wir sind nicht schuldig."

The silence was stunning. I had no desire to enter into the war guilt controversy and decided to emphasize a theme that runs through *War and Human Progress*, that the ultimate causes of war are in man's nature, in the Evil to which humans are subject. I found myself saying, "Before God we are all guilty."

As that student's remark was irrelevant to the lecture's subject matter, it suggests a bad conscience. The dominant feelings of Germans amid the devastation that still prevailed in most large German cities, more than four years after peace had come, were difficult to decipher. On our way to Frankfort from northern France and Belgium, we had motored through the Rhineland to Cologne in our rather worn De Soto car, bought in 1941 just before the United States went to war. Though seldom directed at us, the expressions of the inhabitants among the rubble portrayed a disgust and hatred for which our bombing was no doubt partly responsible. When after bumping over unrepaired roads we entered devastated Cologne, we were almost out of gas. Seeing an improvised shack with petrol pumps, I drove over and explained to the proprietor that, having no German currency, it would be necessary to pay in American money. That seemed to be the least of his worries. "Talk to me in English," he insisted while his employee had begun to fill our tank, "I speak it very well." He drew us out of earshot and said "I want you to know that ninety-five percent of the people in Cologne are still Nazis."

During the week with German colleagues and students that followed in the "Chicago house" of occupied Frankfort, one impression prevailed. Whatever the political complexion of the interlocutors, the experience of the Committee on Social Thought and the messages of peace, educational reform, integral history and a single humanity (that I brought) were of little interest to our hosts. Their outlook was various. Most were concerned, not unnaturally, with rehabilitation. Almost as many expressed a fierce dislike of the Russians. This took the form of recounting alleged barbarities committed against West Germans in communistically-governed East German cities.

What impressed one of the American exchange students then at Goethe University was the remarkable mechanical know-how of the local people. He had been sent by the Department of Art at the University of Chicago to spend a year in "Chicago house." He was attracted to Frankfort by his German descent and was well satisfied with what he found. He remarked that the chauffeur at "Chicago house," who drove the scholars about the city, was a remarkably "constructive" person because he knew how to take an automobile apart. "That is a great man," this student suggested on one occasion. It took the edge off the recommendation to discover that the chauffeur had a local reputation for having run over chickens, cats and dogs, that he had narrowly escaped crushing more than one pedestrian. Efficiency whatever the cost was apparently the ideal that appealed to the visiting student from Chicago.

Seldom did one hear from the professors a good word about the Russians. Their conduct seemed to have become a kind of King Charles' head. Whether the diatribes against the Russians were partly camouflage for feelings of dislike for the occupying conquerors from the United States (which had so many soldiers stationed in Frankfort) and for the devastation of our bombing, it was impossible to determine. Hatred for the Russians seemed to be authentic but how far it was justified is another matter. It seemed to be a kind of naziism converted into anti-communism. I was reminded of an occasion on the eve of the Second War when, driving back in a taxi from the French National Archives through the Paris streets, we encountered a parade of cars moving in the opposite direction, with their occupants in tight-fitting sweaters standing aloft and brandishing clenched fists. "Did you see those guys?" the driver asked as he deposited me at a hotel on the left bank. "Today it's the clenched fist; tomorrow the stiff arm. It's all the same."

As we crossed the frontier on our way back from Frankfort to Strasbourg we encountered a different outlook. The German customs officer glanced perfunctorily at our automobile papers and passport. Handing them back, he asked, without preamble, "What do you think of the Russians?" I explained we hadn't seen any. "I'll tell you what I think," he volunteered. "They're not so bad. I got to know them during the war. They spit into their hands and wash their faces with the saliva. That seems strange. But it's only because our habits are different." His reaction seemed less emotional and totalitarian than those to which learned Germans had accustomed us.

Reflecting on these experiences and on the anti-communism manifested in Frankfort, I found myself reverting to my response to that German student at my first lecture: "Before God we are all guilty." How far were my failures to strike sympathetic chords, failures which also occurred in other countries, the fault of the United States?

Some time before the Second World War was decisively won, at a time when the Russian troops were taking the offensive against the German invaders, and when the allies, after sweeping the Axis out of Africa and part of the Italian peninsula, were about to land in Normandy, I attended a lecture at Northwestern University. The subject was some aspect of abstract economic theory. My colleague and host, who sat next to me in the audience, apparently got bored listening. Knowing that I was starting an interdisciplinary faculty at the University of Chicago, he slipped me a note: "Have you any graduate student who's competent in Russian language and history?" As a matter of fact, somewhat surprisingly (since there were then only a handful of students working with the Committee on Social Thought) we did have a remarkably intelligent young woman, Shirley Robin, only eighteen, who had just mastered Russian. After marrying another of our students William Letwin, she was to get her doctor's degree with us years later for brilliant work in certain broad aspects of English philosophical thought during the eighteenth and nineteenth centuries.[4] Before suggesting her as a candidate, however, I thought it wise to ask my colleague for what purpose a Russian "expert" was wanted. "Frankly," he answered, "to help prepare war against Russia."

I had been shocked by the mass murder of political opponents perpetrated under Stalin, news of which came through to us before the end of the thirties. I had been horrified by the cynical alliance entered into by the Russian communist government with the Nazis at the outset of the Second World War. Yet it was profoundly disturbing to discover early in 1944 (if it was true) that we were preparing to fight a country which, at the time, was no threat to the existence of the United States, a country actually helping the Americans to defeat a power which *was* a threat.

In *The United States and Civilization* I had written in 1941, "If it ever comes to the United States, communism would be even worse than in Russia . . . We shall renounce all hope of a future American civilization worthy of the name if we guide the ship of state to the port of Leningrad." Let the words stand. But the way to avoid communism in the United States has never seemed to rest with a crusade to wipe it off the face of the earth by armed force. This was not an uncommon state of mind following the Second War, in places of power as well as in the streets, before, during and especially immediately after this visit to Germany. It led to wonder whether Americans were not encouraging the attitude of total hostility towards the Russians displayed by Germans.

No doubt this attitude was in no small measure provoked by the brutal and wanton takeover of Hungary in 1947 and of Czechoslovakia in 1948, and by the threat to the Berlin "peace" settlement that was being met in 1949 by the American air-lift from Frankfort. Yet fear is seldom one-sided. The Russians were not exempt from fear of the United States. It is not impossible that preparations our country was making to fight Russia, apparently even when we were still allies, contributed to what seemed to many simply the shocking belligerency of the Moscow government. And that belligerency may have seemed to a frightened Russian people, used to invasions and now threatened by the rattling of the atomic bomb, merely a measure of self-defense.

Two years after our visit to "defeated" Germany, I had the honor of attending at Arden House near Tuxedo, New York, the first meeting of the American Assembly, a group organized originally under the direction of General Eisenhower after he had been made president of Columbia University. The subject announced for discussion was "How to improve United States relations with Europe." Although Eisenhower was at SHAPE and unable to attend, a number of leading American figures—from Averill Harriman and John D. Rockefeller III to Henry Luce and Arthur Hays Sulzberger—were delegates. There were nearly a hundred participants. I had asked the French consul general in Chicago, Francois Brière, who had become a friend, what could be done to improve our relations with his country. He gave me a list of several American policies which troubled the French. When I read his statement aloud at one of the meetings, it aroused no interest. The policies it evoked were not discussed. The sessions were hardly concerned with the matter of improving our relations with Western Europe. They were preoccupied with problems of containing or pushing back the Russians.

The mentality I met in high places had its counterpart in the labor world. An outspoken New York taxi driver volunteered one day: "Do you know what I'd do if I were President? I'd drop a few of them eggs on those men in the Kremlin." No doubt all this was anticommunist rather than anti-Russian sentiment. But how could the Russians feel sure that the eggs would fall only on the communists and leave intact the lives of the two hundred million people ruled, often most brutally, by Stalin and his sycophants?

Violence seemed to be gaining the American scene. Were these manifestations of blind hatred influencing United States culture? Was our culture encouraging these manifestations? What message were Americans carrying to Europe after its years of agony?

There was much that was constructive in the United States aid brought through the Marshall plan for rehabilitation. This financial support administered by American officials was, as some French and other Europeans recognized, unprecedented in the history of international relations. It helped enormously in renewing and fulfilling that twentieth-century hope in economic growth which Fourastié in his book was summoning the French to espouse. Country after country, and not least among them France, has achieved conditions of material well being and hygiene such as had hardly been approached before. The standards of living in European nations (measured in volume of goods produced) have risen during the last two decades to levels far above those known in times past. Yet almost everywhere today, and not least in the United States, the talk is of a human crisis of unparalleled dimensions.

This may be explained partly by the fact that the American example has been one-sided. When we arrived in devastated France during that winter of 1949, a United States cultural attaché invited me to give an account of the Committee on Social Thought to a group of French high school teachers. In introducing me he rejoiced in being able to demonstrate that just about any darned thing, however crazy and impracticable, could be attempted in the U.S.!

In some ways, and without its much increasing gratitude towards, or understanding of, the United States, Europe soon after the war was beginning to outdo America in Americanization. Before the war we had travelled in our automobile on the back roads and the main highways everywhere in France without encountering a hitchhiker. We had seldom met a bystander who displayed an interest in the mechanics of our Buick. But in the France to which we returned after 1948 hitchhikers were even more numerous, if often less alluring, than they had been in the United States before the war, when Claudette Colbert's gesture in "It Happened One Night" had multiplied *en masse* the number of male drivers who swerved to a halt by the roadside whenever they saw a pretty girl thumbing a ride. Everywhere in French towns, sometimes even in villages, young men would ask permission to examine our parked car, whether it was the delapidated De Soto or the sprucer 1950 Oldsmobile that replaced it. They would inquire the price. Their dreams were of owning cars and using gadgets, of drinking Coca Cola and sampling the *Reader's Digest*, called in its French form *Selections*. Their wants have now created a congestion in French cities and on French highways which frequently outdoes that in the country of Henry Ford. Mass consumption, mass production, mass building have become French motifs, until it is rare anywhere to find workers, like those of older times, sensible of the beauties of the villages and hills which Corot, Courbet and Cézanne and later Signac, Derain and Dufy immortalized in their landscapes.

Multiplying the number of students became the goal in education. Personal guidance even in the graduate schools became almost an impossibility. The professors who tried to have easy and close relations with their students were frustrated. "We can no longer offer a training in scholarship," I heard Pierre Renouvin, the admirable dean of the Faculty of Letters at the Sorbonne, tell Jean Sarrailh soon after he retired as Rector. "There are too many students." Some years before the French cultural attaché in New York, the late Pierre Donzelot,[5] suggested a further fragmentation of teaching in the

French universities. He would have introduced the departmental system. I pointed out how my American experience (which he had applauded) suggested that the indiscriminate application of the departmental system, without some counterweights in general training of the kind offered by the Committee on Social Thought, was destroying the ideal of the complete human being, dear to French tradition.

The Americanization of France extended to art. For the first time Americans are calling the tune for French artists. An American notion that what isn't publicized must be without distinction has been making its way into French life. Publicity has now a subtle, insidious influence on their art, most strikingly perhaps on painting. For at least a century and a half, down to the Second World War, painters born (or nourished as adults) in France created the best and most beautiful among contemporary works of art. This is no longer true. Chagall, Dunoyer de Segonzac and Picasso seem to be the last of a great line which stretches back at least to the beginning of the nineteenth century. And, for all his genius, Picasso sometimes yielded to the weaknesses so evident in younger and lesser artists.

Shortly before I moved to Washington, I loaned two Derain pictures to an exhibition of recent works held at Notre Dame University. The curator was excited over these pictures. As he conducted me about the gallery my eyes lighted on a Dubuffet. There was much merit in the *painting;* I could see how Dubuffet's technique had started a movement. But for me, as I told the curator, it was not a happy movement. It squeezed humanity out of art. The curator agreed. Yet the only other "lender" who came to this *vernissage* was saluted not for his interest in works of art but because he claimed to have collected more varieties of whisky bottles than had ever before been assembled. That visit to Notre Dame, where I used to have many connections when Waldemar Gurian directed *The Review of Politics,* reminded me of an episode involving Dubuffet. He came to Chicago in connection with an exhibition of his pictures at the Arts Club. A Chicago friend of ours, who was the chairman of the exhibition committee, gave a dinner party in his suburban home about twenty miles out of town. We were asked to drive Dubuffet to the party.

We called for him and his wife and manager at their hotel. It was a late autumn night; light freezing snow was falling. I was in the driver's seat concentrating on the slippery roads, with Dubuffet beside me; the others were in the back seat. Elinor led an animated conversation about painting, directing her remarks and questions main-

ly to Dubuffet. Most of her opening observations concerned the
Middle Ages and the Renaissance, and Dubuffet responded pleasantly
but perfunctorily. When Elinor moved to recent artists, to Matisse,
Chagall and Picasso, Dubuffet lapsed into silence. After some
minutes he turned around, no longer able to bear his disappointment.
"Madam," he said with emphasis, "don't talk to a painter about
other painters. That's like talking to Mohammed about Christ."

"The McCarthy era" that began at the time Elinor and I reached
Europe, did much to mar the favorable image of the United States,
formed during and after the Liberation of France. Fears that our
country might follow the roads to totalitarianism were aroused by
news of character assassination in America and the treatment sometimes accorded Europeans who were invited to visit the U. S. In three
cases of potential mistreatment, I helped to prevent the worst.

In 1950 the Committee on Social Thought recommended the
appointment for membership on permanent tenure of Michael Polanyi.
Of Hungarian origin, he was a refugee from Germany, where he had
been a member of the scientific Walhalla, the Kaiser Wilhelm's Institut in Berlin. Polanyi obtained asylum in Great Britain before
and during the Second World War and visited the United States on at
least one occasion soon afterwards. He was a fine example of a person who had constructively gone beyond his specialty, and therefore
of particular value to the Committee. He had turned from an exclusive career as a scientist to the study and profession first of economics and then of philosophy. He was an outstanding opponent of
totalitarianism in all forms, not least in the communistic form which
had invaded his native Hungary.

In 1950 we came over to Europe partly because of an invitation to
lead a session on the history of war at the World Conference of
Historians in Paris. Arnold Toynbee honored me by participating in
that, preoccupied as we both were with the problem of avoiding a
third world war. The conference also offered me, at Pierre Renouvin's
session, an opportunity to expand my point of view concerning the
importance of writing history in the light of enduring moral standards.
My unconventional position found support from an Italian historian,
Professor F. Ghisalberti, whom we met for the first time. This
visit to the Conference was the occasion for bringing Michael
Polanyi, also in Paris, the invitation of the Committee on Social
Thought. We spent many hours together. He talked much of the

news he had of the communist tyranny in Hungary from escaping
relatives and friends. We discussed the future of the Committee on
Social Thought and he agreed to throw in his lot with that enterprise.
He resigned from the University of Manchester where he was professor, and prepared to move to Chicago. But when he applied for a
visa to enter the United States, the American consulate in Liverpool
would not grant it. It was never refused, but time passed and it never
arrived. The new Chancellor of the University of Chicago Lawrence
Kimpton, tried to help by bringing the matter to the attention of the
then Secretary of State, the late Dean Acheson, but this led nowhere.
So we lost Michael Polanyi. Finally when it was too late, not long
after the advent of a republican administration in 1953, he was
given a visa. Although he has now passed the retiring age, he frequently comes to the United States and to the Committee on Social
Thought as a visiting professor.

In 1951 another case occurred, much more charged with potential
damage to United States relations with Europe. About to return to
Chicago in September on the "Queen Mary" from Cherbourg, I delivered at Jean Sarrailh's house in Paris the text of my essay "The
Universities and World Community," for which he had asked as
President of the new International Union of Universities.[6] Sarrailh
was temporarily at the Sorbonne out of season because he was about to
sail on the "De Grasse" en route to Mexico. He was to be the
principal speaker and the recipient of an honorary degree on the
occasion of the four hundredth anniversary of the founding of the
University of Mexico, the first university in America.

Not knowing this and supposing he was still at his native town of
Monein, near Pau, I was astonished to receive a telephone call a couple
of hours after delivering my typescript. I thought he must want to
suggest a revision. As a matter of fact he was calling to tell me that,
had he known we were sailing on the "Queen Mary" two days after
the slower "De Grasse," he would have taken passage with us.
Naturally pleased I asked, "Can I arrange to change your ticket?"
"Oh, it must be too late," he replied, "but, of course, try." So I began negotiating with the Cunard Line.

Later in the afternoon the Rector telephoned again; he was very
angry. "An unimaginable thing has happened, Mr. Nef," he said.
"The United States has refused me a visa." "May I come and see
you now?" I asked and left immediately. On reaching the Rector's
office at the Sorbonne, I called the United States Embassy. The

Ambassador was away but I got through to someone who seemed vaguely familiar with this matter. I asked if the Embassy realized what it would mean to French opinion if the head of the University of Paris, who had, unofficially at least, a position equal to that of a French Ambassador, were refused passage through New York en route thence by plane to Mexico City. Finally an official who was in charge in the Ambassador's absence, came to the phone. He said "You don't know the circumstances fully or the difficulties they present." "Where are you now?" he asked. "In the Rector's study at the Sorbonne," I explained. "Where are you going to dinner?" "If the Rector can be persuaded," I told him, "we are taking him to Drouant's." "I will try to telephone you there," he said.

Luck played into our hands. The Rector loved oysters. Drouant has wonderful seafood and the first oysters of the season had just arrived. But when we parted later that evening no message had come from the American Embassy and the prospects of resolving the impasse seemed small. The next morning the "De Grasse" boat train took off without the Rector. The Mexican Ambassador, who had gone to the station to pay his respects, had no one to greet, and so, as Sarrailh put it on the telephone, an unprecedented insult had been directed to the leading French university.

At this point the man at the Embassy phoned to my hotel. He had the visa. Then Louis Joxe, who was still the Director of Cultural Relations in the French Foreign Office, called and said, "Please get the Rector to accept the visa and go on the 'Queen Mary' with you. You have great influence with him. That is the only way he can reach Mexico in time for the ceremonies." I telephoned to the gentleman at the Embassy and asked him please to go to the Sorbonne and call upon Sarrailh. I explained I had a place on the "Queen Mary," "If necessary, get down on your knees and plead with the Rector to go with us." "This isn't the eighteenth century Mr. Nef," he observed. "Pretend it is," I suggested.

An hour later the Rector called, "I'm coming with you John!" The man from the Embassy had done his work. Just how I never knew. And I never knew what the Rector had done to disqualify himself, beyond the knowledge that his name was found on some appeal which had many signatures, one of them a communist's.

Later difficulties arose in getting a visa for Marc Chagall. Thanks to the financial support of my friend William Wood-Prince, then the President of Armour and Company, Chagall was invited with his wife to spend three weeks with the Committee on Social Thought in March 1958, as is explained in the next chapter. Chagall's disillusionment with the communist government of Russia had been known since his flight from his native country in the early twenties. He is as opposed to communism and to all kinds of totalitarianism as anyone I know. He became a French citizen, at the suggestion of Edouard Herriot. Had he gone back to Russia in Stalin's time he would have been at the very least banished to Siberia. Nevertheless, in view of previous experiences, we thought best to begin negotiations for a visitor's visa in the late autumn of 1957. Chagall's Russian wife, who never had any trouble with her visa, could get nowhere with her request for his. So another Chicago friend of the Committee, Hermon Dunlap Smith (President of the large insurance firm, Marsh & McLennan) began negotiations on Chagall's behalf via the State Department and the American Ambassador in Paris, Amory Houghton. Matters dragged along without result and the time for the Chagall departure from France drew near. At the eleventh hour a visa was granted thanks to Billy Prince's telephone call to the White House, and his talk with the secretary to the Cabinet. When Billy finally reached me he said. "Mr. Rabb tells me they are granting the visa. Marc Chagall is too important a person to be left to the State Department."

It should be reiterated that none of these three distinguished men were communists or fellow-travellers. All were persons of the highest character; Polanyi and Chagall ardent *anti*-communists. Indeed, it was once suggested by one of my younger Chicago friends (speaking not as a wag but in all seriousness) that it may have been "communists in the State Department" who were responsible for preventing Polanyi from joining the Committee on Social Thought.

Comedy and tragedy mingled during the cold war. The treatment of suspicious characters, not a few of whom should have been above suspicion, did little to improve United States relations with Europe. While the Europeans were adopting so many American devices, stimulated by our financial aid, they seldom (except in West Germany) swallowed whole the State Department's cold war attitude.

As time went on the worst features of the McCarthy era faded. The experimental Committee on Social Thought grew and flourished. Perhaps the most important factor in its survival and eventual respectability was my return to Europe. There the purpose of this adventure was better understood than in the U. S.; in France especially it was enthusiastically supported by influential opinion.

Yet even in France it would have been impossible to start a Committee on Social Thought. When I set about, as will be related in its place, to form a Center for Human Understanding, my friend Jean Sarrailh (under the erroneous impression that the project was an extension of our interdepartmental faculty to the University of Paris) warned me privately not to try. Opposition to such an interdepartmental faculty was directed not against the ideas and practices inaugurated at Chicago by our faculty. It was prompted by the belief that these ideas and practices were already represented adequately in the French higher learning. On two occasions when I was the dinner speaker at the Club X-Amérique, the group cheered me on the ground that I was encouraging the kind of general culture for specialists which they believed had been inculcated by this engineering school ever since its inauguration at the time of the French Revolution and Napoleon. The American image abroad gained considerably because knowledge spread in France, and eventually in some other European countries, of these efforts by an American on behalf of the whole human being. Many learned Europeans felt that the efforts were needed in the United States. Over-specialization and materialism were considered American deviations from which Europeans often supposed they were immune.

There *was* less need abroad for an interdisciplinary faculty. In the United States, to a greater degree than in Europe, all has to be classified, departmentalized, catalogued. When I became the recipient of an honorary degree from the University of Paris and later from the University of Strasbourg, the first question many American friends asked me was what kind of degree had been awarded. They did not realize that these French universities grant only one degree "honoris causa," and that all who are honored have a common bond. In the United States the disposition to categorize has become almost a universal habit, to the point of supplanting a general outlook! For an unclassifiable book aimed at a general public a special category must be found cost what it may. Not long after the first edition of *The United States and Civilization* appeared, a young Chicago publisher was introduced to me by Alice Roullier who told me the man was interested in my work. He came with a portfolio full of pictures a friend of his had done of American houses. Laying them on the table at my university office, he asked if I would write a book, or at least an introduction, about houses in the United States. When

I inquired why he thought me competent to treat this subject, he said he admired my recent book on the United States! He apparently imagined because of the title that I must possess some special knowledge of American history.

In contrast after my return to Europe, a French businessman, Jean Faye, President of the Non-Ferrous Metal Combine, without any academic or editorial qualifications, paid attention to the actual subject matter of my books which he read with care. He used to tell me that on his automobile and railroad trips through France he was frequently reminded, when he looked out upon old waterwheels along the streams, of passages I had written describing them and their place in industrial history. A knowledge of what I was about as an historian spread much more easily in France than in the U. S.

I sometimes receive from American owned encyclopedias, whose editors no doubt classify me as an "economist," requests for articles. Invariably they are on special and minute subjects concerning which I have no knowledge. It remained for a new French encyclopedia[7] to ask me in the person of the interdisciplinarian I have become, to write an historical account of the coming of "industrial civilization."

In mid-June 1949, after four strenuous months with the Institut d'Etudes Politiques, we motored south for a ten-day breathing spell at Cap d'Antibes. It would be difficult to exaggerate the beauty of the hilly coasts behind as they burst on us the first morning of our stay, through the big window of an attic bedroom in the hotel— a room as small as the one in Caen, though luxuriously appointed. This was before the erection of the skyscrapers which now mar the landscape. All the wonders of the Mediterranean and Maillol, remembered across thirty years of time, were confirmed and multiplied during our brief holiday, drenched as that turned out with endless sunshine. It was so long since we had been abroad that André Sella had forgotten us. I saw him surreptitiously peering through the door the night we arrived, as we were dining in the old restaurant of the hotel where "table d'hôte" used to be served while his father made the rounds from table to table. We passed his son's inspection as successfully as on the earlier occasion in 1922 when we drove out from Cannes in a horse-drawn carriage to claim the royal suite. He actually offered that later but we could not afford it.

Those few bright days of cold salt water swimming in June 1949 were followed by the spate of strenuous lecturing and instructing in

Paris, London and Frankfort. We needed a breathing spell even more than before, but hotels everywhere were booked solid in that warm August which proved so good for wine. There seemed only one way of resting before returning to Chicago. When I sent Sella a telegram he contrived to fit us in, in spite of his crowded season which was reaching its height. We began at once helping Sella to renew the cultural traditions of the hotel which went back to the visits of Anatole France in the winter seasons before and during the First World War. Sella long ago placed a white stone in the garden, with a quotation from *Sur La Pierre Blanche,* to commemorate this alliance with letters and art. I have since done more than *commemorate* the alliance. In the fifties the Siegfrieds came regularly for the day, also later Jean Désy the retiring Canadian ambassador to France and his wife, and the Chagalls. We formed a small group which Sella welcomed as a contribution to the varied clientele he had been seeking. For more than twenty years, Cap d'Antibes has provided my work with a base abroad.

In all these ways my initiative, as well as my publications, got a hearing in continental Europe. It was perhaps symptomatic of the greater separation of callings that I found myself much less at home, not only with scholars but with professional artists and writers, in my own country than abroad. During the 'fifties and early 'sixties the communion I sought was supplied especially by Chagall and Eliot.

30. STRENGTHENING TIES WITH CHAGALL

Marc Chagall came back to Chicago only a few months after his first visit, this time accompanied by his daughter Ida. It was autumn 1946 and the Art Institute, under its director Daniel Catton Rich, put on an exhibition of his work. At the dinner Rich gave at the Tavern Club before the opening, Chagall fixed on me to accompany him about the exhibition. As usual, he would stand in front of one after another of his canvasses and repeat in his charming pixie voice, "Je ne comprends pas cet homme" (I don't understand that man.) And, also as usual, whenever anyone addressed him as "Maitre," he would respond *"Je ne suis pas Maitre, je suis centimetre."* These responses are as characteristic as his signature.

A day or two later, before Chagall lunched with us in our Dorchester Avenue apartment, an East European immigrant to France,
who had taught at the Sorbonne and come to the United States as
a refugee, telephoned and asked to see me. I had heard of but never
met him. So I suggested we have a conversation in my room at the
university the following Monday. He sounded disappointed and
said, "I know Chagall is lunching with you tomorrow and would
like to call to your attention that I am a good friend of his *("je suis très
bien avec Chagall")*. Being of a charitable nature and not wanting
to hurt him, I invited him to lunch. He monopolized the conversation
on a single theme: All great men are slimy characters. *("Tous les
grands hommes sont des salauds.")* He illustrated this thesis with
two examples, one Lenine, the other Bergson. I had not met either,
but to combine them in such a context struck me as droll, not to say
grotesque. Having known Bergson through his books, I felt it was
inappropriate to attribute bad character to that great philosopher
out of hand.

Our self-invited guest had not come to listen. I have always hoped,
however, that he heard the comment Chagall managed to squeeze into
an all too brief pause. "In my experience," Marc observed, "any one
with a genuine claim to be called 'great' is usually graced with a
minimum of decency." These words confirm my belief that the
decency and integrity of an artist's life are not handicaps but contributions to his art.

Not long after this visit, Chagall returned to France. Before settling at Vence in 1950 he rented briefly a villa on Cap Ferrat and for
a longer spell a country cottage in Orgeval, a small village close to the
Seine northwest of Paris. It was there that we saw him for the first
time in Europe, when I came in 1949 to teach at the Institut d'Etudes
Politiques. He asked us to lunch and we spent the afternoon together.
When Chagall settled at Vence he bought a large double house, one
part of which became his studio. Vence is close to Cap d'Antibes and
beginning in the summer of 1950, he used to come down for swims
and luncheons. The first time he went into the water from the
steep rocks that surround the swimming cove (which had been a
tiny harbor for sail boats in 1922 before the summer season got
going), Marc manifested some trepidation. It was only partly simu-
lated. When Marcel, the lifeguard who with his wife took care of the
cabins for André Sella's guests, finally got him (buoyed by a life
preserver) into the clear salt water, he cried joyously *"L'eau n'est pas*

seulement bonne; c'est sucrée" (the water's not just pleasant, it's sugar coated.) He has come back innumerable times since, and the adventure of entering the sea has not lost any of its excitement.

We used to return these visits in Vence where we could enjoy looking at his paintings and strolling in the garden of his newly acquired house. We also spent a long afternoon with him in September, 1951, at Gordes in the Vaucluse, in the tumbled down old chateau with many rooms that he and his first wife Bella bought before the Nazi occupation of southern France. It was the first time he had returned there since the "liberation." His purpose in coming was to spread out and sign copies of the new luxury edition of La Fontaine's Fables that he had illustrated with beautiful prints. He needed more space than was available in his residence at Vence. He was touched that, in response to a letter, Elinor and I had driven out of our way (returning from Antibes to Paris) to see him and spent the night in the nearby town of Apt without benefit of luxury such as the Cap provided. Not a few of our most complete unions were without that. The night in Apt and another later on the same trip at Tournus were of this kind. The large brass beds in those hotel rooms resembled one John Sloan preserved in an etching of 1905, "Turning out the light." [1] They provided a solid foundation which helped link Elinor and me to the mystique of childhood, the only time in our lives when we had not known each other.

She had played an intense role in all the early meetings with Chagall. But before the next trip to France she died, leaving me alone as Chagall had been left by Bella. Neither he nor I support unhappiness well. Like him, perhaps even more, I found the emptiness difficult. Work without love deprived me of daily bread.

I left Chicago almost immediately in February 1953 to lecture at the Collège de France. I stayed, as was then usual when in Paris, at the Pont Royal Hotel, where the director of the Institut d'Etudes Politiques had installed us four years before. Many of the rooms look on the famous old rue du Bac with its tall seventeenth-century mansions, one of them once the residence of Samuel Bernard, Louis XIV's most influential financier. The Pont Royal had one of those open-grill lifts not uncommon in Paris that provide a view of each floor as they descend. On the ground floor waiting to ride up was Chagall. Neither of us spoke but he seemed to know of my loss. We embraced with the unspoken understanding that, as fellow guests in the hotel, we would meet again.

I walked into the gray rain of a Paris winter's day and headed for a modest restaurant not far down the rue du Bac towards the river. It was called the Restaurant des Ministères. For Paris it was large and barren, almost unappetizing, somehow appropriate for a man whose wife had just died. Sitting at a vacant table, before a waiter came to take my order, I thought about the unexpected encounter at the hotel. As we had learned from Maritain, less than a year before Chagall had married Valentina Brodski, a Russian lady he had known a few weeks. I found myself wondering what she could be like. At that moment the revolving door of the restaurant started to turn, and a beautiful dark haired woman appeared. Our glances met. She seemed to look straight at me, as I looked straight at her. Instinctively I knew it was Madame Chagall. As the door continued to turn he followed. I arose and went to meet her. No introduction was needed. We three lunched together and from then on were friends. I was drawn to them that first day, in my widowerhood, and the feeling of communion grew as our meetings multiplied. Chagall helped me feel we belonged in the same world. His wife, whom all her friends call Vava, is an essential part of that world, of all Chagall is and has become since their marriage. I have drawn strength from being included in their family circle and from being permitted to take part in many of Marc's moments of triumph.

The Chagalls were ever kinder throughout the sad period of my life. In the south of France every summer they would join me for swims and meals and I would return the visits at Vence. We also met frequently in Paris. They were in the audience for the ceremony when I received an honorary degree from the Sorbonne. They also came to the reception given on this occasion by the Collège de France when Lucien Febvre spoke about my work. In this way I helped introduce the Chagalls to the French scholarly world as they helped introduce me to the world of art—small steps in lifting barriers between those two worlds.

Starting from different homelands and backgrounds, Chagall and I had a common concern with the creative life in relation to our time. This concern and Chagall's enthusiasm brought him to the Committee on Social Thought again in 1958. Following in the path of Schnabel, Maritain, Schoenberg and Eliot, he came as visiting professor and took part in the everyday life of the group. He and Vava spent three weeks in the old Dorchester Avenue apartment where I then lived alone. He delivered a lecture and conducted a student seminar; simultaneously the Renaissance Society at the University of Chicago arranged a small exhibition of his work. He became a familiar figure on Dorchester Avenue and Fifty-seventh Street and on the campus. When he would go out alone or accompanied by Vava or me students followed him as if he were the Pied Piper of Hamlin.

Each morning he sketched for several hours, or worked with water-colors, while I wrote in another part of the flat. In the evenings and at lunch colleagues, students, or friends from the city who had taken part in the life of the Committee, would join us. We often visited the seminar room at the University where the faculty held discussions with the students. When this visit was mentioned to faculty members from other universities or from other departments of the University of Chicago, it was difficult to persuade them that Chagall had done any work. They had no idea of the informal methods of instruction, of the learning by doing, which had always given this interdisciplinary group independent life.

One of my wittiest American friends, who had a long experience with university administration in several academies, was fond of telling his intimates that one reason professors spend so much time in committee meetings is to escape their wives. They can always return home in the late afternoon, in the evening or even in the small hours of morning, claiming they have been busy over important matters. At least that is what they tell their wives, and in repeating the story they come to believe it.

Such colleagues were not in a position to understand the constructive life we aimed to generate, a life in which Chagall's wife and other student and faculty wives of the Committee took part as listeners and animators. The nearest approach to a working life of the kind we sought was in the scientific laboratories. But there was a difference between these often expensively equipped settings and our casual working quarters. The artist needs more time at work not less than most scientists, and he needs, more than most scientists, connections between the rooms where he works and those where he relaxes. He needs a woman who keeps house and defends his interests. The surroundings that animate him are not those of the clinically clean laboratory or of the carefully swept library or museum. The artist flourishes on what the French call a *beau désordre* (beautiful disorder), a disorder where the materials he most needs are ready at hand. Marc Chagall found such disorder, as did our students, in that Dorchester Avenue apartment. The disorder can be contagious. No formal instruction can take its place.

The Chagalls took a friendly interest in my activities when I organized the Center for Human Understanding in Paris in 1958 and 1959.[2] Imagine my happy surprise when, lunching together in July 1962 on the tenth anniversary of their marriage in a restaurant on the Left Bank, Marc said he wanted to join. He said he shared some of my hopes of overcoming the ills of the nuclear age. So he and Vava visited Washington a year later for the 1963 spring meeting of the Center at which he made the principal address: "Why have we become so anxious?" It forms part of a book *Bridges of Human Understanding*,[3] published in New York the following year by Francis Bellamy of University Publishers. Out of his experience Chagall tells us "It is childish to repeat the truth, which has been known so long. In all its aspects the world can be saved only by love . . ."

31. THE GIFT OF T. S. ELIOT'S FRIENDSHIP

The art closest to an historian is that of letters. The *story's* the thing and great histories, from ancient Greek times onwards, have been notable works of literature.

I have suggested that a contemporary historian, seeking to enter the tradition of historical writing that begins with Herodotus and Thucydides, can find inspiration in arts such as music or painting which offer him no temptation to imitate directly. They provide examples of the form, the elegance and the concrete subject matter becoming to descriptions of historical interrelations and of historical causation. The same can be true of poetry if, as in my case, the historian is devoid of the slightest talent for writing verse, but has an inner life enchanted no less by "The Ode to a Nightingale" than by an opera such as "Don Giovanni" or Vermeer's "View of Delft."

Among contemporary writers no one has mastered both effective prose and inspiring poetry better than T. S. Eliot. The unmatchable excellence of some of his critical essays and some of his poems made me less subject with these to the dangers of imitation than was the case with Fielding's novels, for Eliot tells *his* stories not in prose but in verse. Moreover Eliot has been, at least for me, the most appealing and helpful model in modern literature, probably because much of his poetry as well as his criticism is based on varied and extensive scholarly learning. Before throwing in his lot with England he studied for the doctors degree in the philosophy department at Harvard and wrote a thesis published just before his death.[1]

As a young historian I was greatly, though almost unconsciously, influenced by Proust. Proust, however poetical his story, hardly wrote any poetry. Nor did I meet him. Whereas in the case of Eliot, the influence eventually came as much from his friendship as from what he wrote. So much so that it is impossible to separate the two and decide where one influence began and the other ended. Eliot's friendship was a gift that arrived a quarter of a century after I first read and appreciated his poetry and his criticism. We met only after the Committee on Social Thought had been established.

While Eliot had close relations for years with William R. Castle, it is not clear when or how their friendship began. Castle was a young member of the Harvard faculty when Eliot was a student, and both belonged to the Fox Club. Yet, looking back on his undergraduate days, Eliot did not remember knowing Bill. In the thirties they were close friends, however, and after the Second World War Eliot always stayed with the Castles in their house on S Street when he visited Washington. Bill Castle had developed an enthusiasm for my work at Chicago following the publication of *The United States and Civilization*. He told Eliot about it and interested him in it too. In May 1947 I began to exchange letters with Eliot in the hope that he might contribute to and counsel us concerning the review *Measure* that we were about to launch as a contribution to the Committee on Social Thought, with Eliot's *Criterion* as our model. A subsidy was provided by the Regnery family, and Henry Regnery, the Chicago publisher with whom I had many conversations, became a member of our editorial board. With Robert M. Hutchins' approval I organized the board and chose Otto von Simson to be editor.

I met Eliot for the first time in May 1949, in London. An English friend Robert Speaight who had been caught in America at Notre Dame University when the Second World War broke out and who had been Elinor's and my luncheon guest frequently in Chicago, arranged a meeting at the Garrick Club. Laryngitis had attacked and for one of the few times in my life I was without a voice. Nevertheless I was able to communicate sufficiently for Eliot to agree to visit the Committee for an extended period of at least two months. Some weeks later, during a second brief visit we made to London to participate in the annual Anglo-American historical meetings, he came to dinner at the Connaught Hotel with his sister-in-law, Mrs. Henry Eliot, with whom he usually stayed when he went to Cambridge, Mass.

At about this time *Notes Towards the Definition of Culture* was published. I read it on the steamer returning to the States in September. This tract was the main subject of a luncheon conversation with Robert Hutchins soon after my arrival in Chicago. Before we parted Hutchins bought a copy at the university bookstore. *Measure* was soon to appear and, as chairman of its editorial board, Hutchins had agreed to contribute the leading article in the first issue. He took off from Eliot's tract, arguing that Eliot was essentially misguided in the emphasis he laid on higher learning as suited for a distinguished few. The higher learning, at least at the college level, should be for all. The issue was of special concern to me, as will appear more fully in the next chapter. If the individual of unusual talent is to develop his powers to the full, the opportunities we have been trying to offer through the Committee on Social Thought are essential. But in my view they are suited only to a very few whose work is not what we ordinarily associate with undergraduates, though not all undergraduates are too young for such work.

One education for all was a question on which Hutchins and I differed, as became plain to both of us ten years earlier when he read *The United States and Civilization* in typescript. Ours was I have always felt an example of disinterested and constructive disagreement.

Upon joining the Committee on Social Thought for the autumn term of 1950, after the first issue of *Measure* with Hutchins article had been published, Eliot chose to speak on the "Aims of Education" in order to state his position clearly and to discuss its implications for the future of learning. His four lectures were published in successive numbers of *Measure*.[2] Fourteen years later, after Eliot's death, Mrs. Eliot published them in *To Criticize the Critic* (1965).

The opportunities for quiet discussion offered by Eliot's two months in Chicago were an immense boon. We met almost daily. He also paid me two short visits later. The first was in 1956, when he was still a widower. The second was in 1959, after Valerie Fletcher (who had met him several months after I had in 1949) married him

and introduced the great happiness which illuminated his last eight
years.

Eliot's life is instructive in connection with the complexities confronting an innovator in the arts. The achievements of an artist may
eventually obtain a considerable—even a large—circulation, as have
now the publications of Eliot; they may bring many wealthy clients
and widespread publicity, as have now the pictures of Chagall. But if
the contribution is to be a serious one of enduring value, the creator
will always be confronted in his beginnings, as both these artists were,
by what strikes the contemporary advertising mentality as a pitifully
small audience. Nor can the great artist gain the "success" which may
one day be accorded his achievements by *seeking fame*. A large public
must never be, to the smallest degree, his master. His only slavery is
to his mission. And the results he achieves, even after he becomes
famous, are in an important sense for the few. Only a few have inner
experiences and personal knowledge that enables them to participate
creatively in what the true artist creates. This in no way diminishes
the importance of making his works accessible to as many as possible
among the young for it is not possible to select with certainty those
who will become the few.

For a long time the response to Eliot's work was small. Elinor
and I had the idea it would benefit the University of Chicago to bring
him there twenty years before he came. She had actually written him
a letter to explore the possibility as far back as 1932. Although in
1956 fifteen thousand people managed to squeeze into a hall in
Minneapolis when he lectured at the University of Minnesota, back
in 1932 Hutchins dismissed the suggestion that he be invited to the
University of Chicago. "Oh," Hutchins said, "he wouldn't get an
audience."

For many years Eliot had difficulty in finding publishers for his
poems. Leonard Woolf has given a fascinating account of early
achievements of the Hogarth Press that he and Virginia Woolf founded.
They had met Eliot in London as early as 1917, even 1916, and they
themselves printed and bound his *Poems* in May 1919. This was
the fourth Hogarth Press publication; two of the four were works of
the Woolfs, the other was Katherine Mansfield's *Preludes*. Of Eliot's
Poems the Woolfs published rather fewer than 250 copies at 2s. 6d. each,
and the book went out of print in 1920. *Prufrock and Other Observations* had been published in 1917 in England by The Egoist Ltd., at

1*s.* a copy; yet it was three years before all the 500 copies printed were
sold. Leonard Woolf had bought one which Eliot later inscribed as
follows, on the eve of the Woolfs' publication of his *Poems:*

> "*. . . for Leonard Woolf my*
> *next* ⎫ *publisher,*
> *second* ⎭
> *with gratitude and affection*" [3]

In the 'twenties and 'thirties Eliot's books of criticism also had
only a small sale. And this was true of the wonderful magazine,
The Criterion, which he edited with extraordinary enterprise and
fidelity for eighteen years, from 1922 to 1939. In the innocence of
my admiration for it, I was once under the impression that it had
thousands, if not tens of thousands, of subscribers. On the occasion
of Eliot's second visit to Chicago in 1956, a project was on foot to
revive the publication of *Measure,* which had been discontinued after
two years. Eliot attended the monthly dinner of the Committee on
Social Thought, partly for the purpose of discussing the proposal. The
impression stuck in my mind as the discussion began that he had once
told me the sale of *The Criterion* had seldom exceeded a thousand
copies. Thinking it would be useful to know exactly, I asked him
whether my memory was correct. "John," he said, "we never sold a
thousand copies."

Measure was not comparable in depth or in unity of purpose to
The Criterion, but it was of considerable distinction and it covered
almost as many serious subjects as the Committee on Social Thought
itself was covering. A service might have been done for culture if
Measure had been kept afloat. A pity therefore that the Chicagoans
who had backed it should have "measured" its value in quantitative
terms. It was discontinued in 1952 because even with the help of Eliot's
four contributions, the average sale reached only about 2,500 copies
in its second year of publication.

Eliot was already famous enough in 1950 to fill a large hall in
Chicago when he gave his four lectures. Although they appealed strongly to those Chicagoans who had welcomed the initiative of the Committee on Social Thought in bringing him, the lectures were hardly
popular at the university, in spite of the audience of more than a
thousand that they drew. This was partly because it was regarded in
some quarters as undemocratic to offer special educational opportunities for a select few, as Eliot advocated, and partly because a poet
who stepped out of his specialty to criticize education was ipso facto

unwelcome. Moreover some particular members of the faculty may
have felt threatened by Eliot's suggestion that the numbers in the
higher learning as a whole were too large. Others still were almost
certainly troubled by Eliot's "Catholicism." It was even rumored at
the time that he was about to become—had indeed already become—
a "Roman." Grumbling was heard. One graduate student from some
east European country (who had no connection with the Committee)
felt it his duty to seek an interview so that he could tell me how bad
the lectures had been and what a disservice to the university. I
thanked him for the information and assured him he could probably
have lectured better himself.

Eliot's success at Chicago was in small seminars with faculty and
students of the Committee. Perhaps the most moving experience in
connection with these was a seminar devoted to his *Four Quartets*.
Each of four students was assigned the task of discussing one of those
poems. They put much zest into their preparation and delivery. An
exciting conversation followed in which others among the twenty-
five or so persons present participated as they sat round a large
oval table. Views were freely expressed. We were confronted at one
point with several different and seemingly conflicting interpretations
of the same line from one of the poems.

At his own desire Eliot was presiding. So the audience appealed
to him. What had he meant by these words? "I have really forgotten," he answered. Then he added, "All of you are right, I think
I meant every one of the things that have been suggested." And
he went on to remark that the strength of poetry is in the richness,
the diversity of its possible meaning.

Isn't this true of all works of art? I have heard a few great musical
compositions over and over again; they have never sounded quite
the same; each hearing has been a new experience, even the hearing
of the same recording. Great pictures which have captured me "for
keeps" have never moved me twice in quite the same way. This is true
even of the small pictures I have lived with at home.

I once visited a kind couple for several days. The walls of the
bedroom and bathroom they provided were covered with pictures
mainly of nude women, by a painter who had been the husband's
friend. They all tired me after the first day for they were all alike and
always looked the same. Herein was a striking contrast to the effect
produced by Derain's "Buste de femme" which I have seen almost
daily for more than forty years. Reference has been made already to

the extraordinary realization Derain managed to achieve in her breasts. They seem to change expression continually with the changing expression of the face and the rest of the body. An art critic from Switzerland, who came to see me in Chicago, was captivated when he sat watching this canvas during luncheon. His enthusiasm over the "living" qualities of the picture were such that I was prompted to tell him about a young couple who had lunched with me soon after their marriage. I had overheard the wife—a lovely looking girl— whisper to her husband, "Do mine look like that?" On hearing the words my Swiss visitor remarked, "It must have caused him very great embarrassment to answer!"

In the contrast between the living effects produced by Derain's woman and the dead nature of the nudes in the house of my friend lies one of the important differences between art and counterfeit, between the "living" and the dead. These differences are difficult, for many persons they are impossible, to understand. And they need to be understood. That is why I have always been an advocate of small groups in the higher reaches of graduate instruction.

Even the few students accepted by the Committee fail often to respond to the opportunities offered. It was only by heroic efforts that Elinor Nef was able to recruit four or five auditors for each of three lectures Harold Innis gave some years before his death in 1952, under the intriguing title "Minerva's Owl," a study which is being published posthumously. Yet Innis was even then considered a great scholar, and the implications of such work as this, for the study of what has become the popular field of communications, was already beginning to be recognized.

Our effort to create a refuge for the exceptionally gifted few is not segregation. The many, no less than the few, find it to their advantage to have a training suited to their inclinations. As a matter of fact the nature of the inclinations of many were revealed on another occasion in the life of the Committee a couple of years before Eliot's visit. Tawney had come to us for a term as visiting professor. He offered several lectures open to the public. He asked me whether it would be suitable for him, in addition, to be at home one day every week in his room at the university for two hours, so that students could drop in and talk. He then announced this intention to an audience of several hundred who attended his first public lecture. But although he kept the appointment in his room for the ten weeks that followed, only three students appeared. Meanwhile an instructor in the graduate school was offering a course for credit on the historical work of R. H. Tawney. Forty to fifty students attended her class.

Is it not important nevertheless in the cause of reform, one will ask, to expose many directly to greatness? Of course it is. For as has been just suggested one cannot determine by any kind of test which students will rise to creative distinction. This depends on the nature of their future lives and science is incapable of predicting that. My old friend Marcel Moye, of the University of Montpellier law school, believed he could select among the students whose work he supervised the ten percent or so who were *capable* of attaining distinction. But, among these he could never be sure who would land among the one percent.

That is why a group like the Committee on Social Thought should accept a larger number than might be thought desirable. As the need for creative distinction has never been so urgent perhaps as now, the way should somehow be opened for more to rise to creative heights. Ways will have to be found to nourish the best in quiet community and to provide the gifted with great examples. In principle no one should be excluded who does not exclude himself. This principle is not unrealistic. No one in the university was excluded from the seminar Eliot conducted, yet only about twenty-five students came. Most of the others didn't choose to participate; they wanted to be told. It is perhaps significant that a representative of *Time* visited this seminar, but no report ever found its way into the magazine.

One of the cultural institutions of Chicago that survives two world wars is *Poetry* magazine. Its founder, Harriet Monroe, died sometime before the Committee started. *Poetry* had come on difficult times financially and Eliot's last visit to Chicago in 1959 had been undertaken to raise money to insure its survival. Almost a decade earlier Marion Stroebel Mitchell, who had worked with Miss Monroe, offered me the presidency of the Modern Poetry Association, then the publisher of *Poetry*. She also suggested immediately after Eliot's 1950 visit to the Committee on Social Thought that the two enterprises merge.

She and her doctor husband had long been kind friends and I wanted to help her. The barriers to acceptance lay not simply in my limited capacities for assuming administrative burdens. The objectives of the two institutions were basically different. The Committee's concern was with art, scholarship and graduate education in *all* realms. *Poetry* while concerned with *one* of the principal arts was being led by current trends into the position of making verse another specialty, and of counting its success as a magazine (as was perhaps inevitable) in terms of numbers of subscribers and even in terms of numbers of contributors. Naturally in its quest for means to continue, *Poetry* made the most of earlier contributors who had become illustrious. Eliot was an outstanding ornament of *Poetry's* past. *Poetry* was the first to print "Prufrock," in June 1915, four years after that revolutionary poem had been written.

Eliot was intense in his loyalties. In the forefront of these was a sense of his responsibilities to the United States, the land of his birth, childhood and early youth. That accounts to no small extent for his participation in the fund raising celebration in 1959. Among a host of items auctioned on that occasion, were two empty bottles of Chateau Lafite 1945, which he signed after Valerie, he and I had drunk them during this visit. Someone paid $50 for his signatures.

Not the least of Eliot's loyalties was to Ezra Pound, for whose literary gifts he had great respect, independently of their friendship. Pound's work is likely to remain an outstanding contribution to letters. Long before meeting Eliot I used to quote each year in my opening lecture on economic history from *The A.B.C. of Reading*, where Pound draws an illuminating distinction between the abstract nature of Western compared with the concrete nature of Oriental thought. The distinction has an important bearing on the rise of modern science and its consequences.[4]

Following the Second World War, when Pound was shut up for some years at St. Elizabeth's Hospital in Washington, Eliot's visits to the Castles were partly connected with Pound's near presence. Eliot used to see him regularly, spending considerable time with his friend. This association with Pound had a bearing on the misconceptions which circulated concerning Eliot's political views. It had a bearing on his unpopularity in certain quarters, like those of the graduate student who protested about the lectures he gave at Chicago. Pound's enthusiasm for Mussolini, his almost treasonous position concerning the outcome of the Second World War in which he espoused the Italian fascist cause against that of his native land, were made a blot on the characters of his friends. In Eliot's case the cavilers were unaware, or they forgot, that it was Pound who persuaded Harriet Monroe to publish "Prufrock" in 1915, and that Pound seems to have played a most constructive critical part in editing "The Waste Land," which is dedicated to him. Those contributions Eliot could not forget. They brought him to the side of his friend in trouble. Through guilt by association, it came to be loudly whispered that Eliot too was a totalitarian.

Eliot's choice of the Castles as his Washington hosts may also have contributed to the false rumors. Bill Castle was a friend of Lindbergh and an opponent of Roosevelt. By the time I knew Eliot there was nothing to support this view of him. He was much more "liberal" politically, in the best sense of the word, than is supposed. He so staunchly opposed some of Bill's ideas concerning United States policy after the war that this might, but for Eliot's tact and Bill's good manners, have led to a rupture.

Rumors concerning Eliot's politics went back a long way. During the years that immediately followed the First World War he had in fact found congenial some right-wing journalists who were also devoted to letters. In the early twenties he and Jacques Maritain briefly belonged to the circle in Paris that was based on the royalist newspaper *L'Action Francaise* of which Charles Maurras and Léon Daudet (son of the celebrated author) were editors. Both Eliot and Maritain abandoned the group in the late twenties, a defection that in Maritain's case was hardly forgiven.

In the preface to the small collection of essays entitled *For Lancelot Andrewes* (1927), Eliot had a sentence to the effect that he was a classicist in literature, a royalist in politics and an Anglo-Catholic in religion. But when years later Simson asked him to give this declaration substance in an article for *Measure,* he replied that he was no longer in the frame of mind that had impelled him to write the sentence.[5] It is traditionally supposed that young men sow wild oats as "leftists" and then become sober hardheaded conservatives in maturity. It is also true that some fresher spirits, like Eliot, tend to move away from right-wing rigidity and with years grow younger in spirit.

I am less informed about a turn, if there was one, in Eliot's last years in the matter of "catholicism," beyond the certainty that in his later life he never seriously contemplated joining the Roman Church. As his host in Chicago I was brought into increasing touch with a cleric whom I had come to know pretty well independently, Bernard Iddings Bell. On one occasion years before, Bell contributed an article to *The Criterion;* he was enormously enthusiastic about Eliot and, as the "Anglican priest" he considered himself, felt that Eliot as a com-

municant belonged under his tutelage. In the course of the poet's 1956
visit to Chicago Bell had organized a meeting in a small room,
part of an Episcopalian church on "the North Side." An audience of
parishioners crowded into the room, and Eliot was provided with a
flimsy, shaky lectern inadequately lit. He had agreed in advance that
the auditors could call the tunes. They kept asking him to read his
graver poems, especially one and then another of his *Four Quartets,*
three of them composed in England in the shadow of the German Blitz.
Unable to see easily in the dim light, Eliot labored valiantly and
finally broke off. Without an invitation he recited with astonishing
gusto and felicity two or three selections from *Old Possum's Book of
Practical Cats.* Never did I hear him read so delightfully.

After he finished we escaped in a hired car to the comfort of
Dorchester Avenue. "Tom," I said, "you were wonderful in the
Practical Cats." "Yes," he said, "I did rather bring that off."

The ill founded charges surreptitiously noised about concerning
Eliot's allegedly totalitarian tendencies pained him deeply. When he
and Valerie were at Dorchester Avenue in 1959, a press conference
was held in the drawing room, lit up on a dingy autumn morning by
three large Dufy watercolors and two Chagall gouaches. One of the
correspondents opened fire with: "You're anti-semitic, aren't you
Mr. Eliot?" Eliot's face showed he was wounded, as a grossly unfair
charge wounds a sensitive person. After a short pause he made a
moving reply: "I am a Christian. I should think I was *pro*-semitic."

Soon after Elinor died in 1953 and I was in Paris starting to lecture
at the Collège de France, I received Eliot's letter of condolence which
I cannot read even twenty years later without very deep emotion.
I had agreed to deliver a lecture at the newly founded university in
Nottingham late in April, and Tom invited me to dinner at the Garrick Club the night I was to spend in London. Between Paris and
London I lectured at the University of Lille, adapting one of the
lectures I had already given at the Collège de France. I made what
proved to be an ill-advised assumption that it would be simple to
translate myself from French into English. As no one could possibly
be in Nottingham who had heard me either in Paris or Lille, I planned
to prepare my Lille lecture for delivery in Nottingham during my
hour on the channel boat from Calais to Dover.

Alas the going, like the sea, proved heavy. The real trouble was not
the sea. It was my mind which was incapable of rendering my French

into intelligible English. When over dinner, I told Eliot of this predicament, he said, "You cannot possibly *translate*. You will have to rethink the whole thing." He spoke from firsthand knowledge for he had written both poetry and prose in French.

After Eliot died I was much intrigued to meet at a dinner St. Jean Perse, *nom de plume* of the distinguished French diplomat and ambassador, Alexis Léger. Léger came from Martinique; his temperament was ardent; and that evening he was marvelously sparkling in conversation for at least four consecutive hours. He spoke of the way Eliot had patiently come to him again and again in the interest of precision, when translating into English Léger's great poem, *Anabase*, based on his knowledge of the ancient East and its history. Léger derived much amusement from a point that had led to more than one conversation with the translator in Léger's office at the Quai d'Orsay; how to render *"caleçons d'or"* into English. Léger roared as he told us Eliot had finally fixed on "knickerbockers;" Léger having forgotten his own exact words, *"ces caleçons de filles aux fenêtres,"* which Eliot actually translates "girls' camiknickers hanging at the windows."

Eliot's observation at the Garrick Club taught me a lesson useful ever since. The problem of translation is almost insoluble. How can a similar total impression be found in another tongue for a line of great poetry if that contains a variety of meanings? When rendering another's words as Eliot was doing in his *Anabasis,* even the finest and most loyal translation becomes inevitably a kind of labored imitation. Eliot's equivalent in English verse for Perse's poem, while beautiful, is a kind of copy nevertheless. *Anabasis* never acquired the rugged warmth or passion conveyed by *Anabase.* The only rethinking that can improve on the original is essentially a fresh idiom, and here the form, cadence and choice of subjects can be best aided by examples from artistic media that do not permit direct translation.

This matter of translation leads to reflections upon the overwhelming difficulties of communicating in our crowded interdependent world. For understanding the great need is to bring harmony, in its bearing on great issues that threaten to divide humankind, to a number of relevant meanings which are different and often appear to conflict. This is essentially an artistic problem much more difficult to handle linguistically than the translation of scientific or logical propositions or of technical "know-how" relating to our increasingly mechanized economy. That is why, even in ordinary conversation, it is not enough to have just a working knowledge of a foreign tongue. Moreover language is only one way of communicating and an addiction to language for its own sake is likely to get in the way of the universal understanding for which sensitive human beings now long.

Eliot's help with the problem of writing history was mainly in the confirmation he provided for prejudices I had acquired. One was of the need the writer has to reserve his strength for the work of composition and to make time for those "visions and revisions" of which Eliot sang in "Prufrock." In order to permit this the writer who lectures must make the lecture a major effort, and never undertake more lectures than he can prepare fully without damage and if possible with benefit to his career as a writer. Eliot confirmed my long-felt conviction that in prose any approach to the richness poetry alone is capable of providing is through the clarity, precision and simplicity of statement which can come only after much meditation and many rewritings. That he was a master here does not require laboring.

Eliot's second marriage, unlike his first, was a masterpiece of happiness. When he and Valerie stayed with me in Chicago they wanted to be as quiet as possible. Consequently we invited almost no one to share our frequent collations. These provided an opportunity for sustained conversations that were continued at the next sitting. We talked much of literary reputations. They described a recent occasion when they had gone to Paris and stopped at the Pont Royal Hotel in order to participate in the meeting of a small and distinguished academy, the Academie Septentrionale. That has only one English member and Eliot has been recently elected in place of the late Rudyard Kipling. In speaking of his predecessor he gave one of those literary revaluations for which he had a genial wisdom, so that his essay not only reappraised the writer under discussion but did this in the light of Eliot's evolution as a writer from youth to maturity.

We also talked of poor Charles Morgan who had come in 1942 to Chicago with a letter of introduction to Elinor and me, and who had died recently a victim of his own pretensions to literary glory. He was one of a dozen writers whose lives and work were clarified by our conversations during the Eliots' stay. And I also learned of the circumstances that had brought the two together. Faber and Faber advertised for a new secretary for Tom in 1949. Having always felt for him as a contemporary writer a unique admiration, Valerie Fletcher applied. There were at least thirty candidates so her appointment was by no means certain. How different would have been Eliot's last years if she had been rejected.

Our meetings on that last visit to Chicago were interrupted for an afternoon and evening by a trip to which I had committed myself long in advance to lecture in Moline, on the Mississippi, for a convention of Illinois high school teachers. This was Eliot territory for he had been brought up not much farther south along the river at St. Louis, and two nights later in Chicago he spoke to some other high school teachers at the Art Institute most movingly, mentioning connotations that the Mississippi had for him in connection with the authentic enthusiasm for poetry so difficult to arouse in the young.

Some years before, when I first knew Eliot, I remember telling Osbert Sitwell how American he seemed. Sitwell couldn't have been more emphatic in his agreement. Yet as I have suggested in an earlier chapter, Eliot needed Europe and above all England for both his life and his career. The French have a waggish saying that journalism can lead you to any heights provided you escape. Since Mark Twain's time the saying might perhaps be applied to the role of the Middle West in the creation of beauty.

I must return briefly to the occasion with Eliot at the Garrick Club in 1953. The principal subject of our conversation was Elinor's life and death. As we talked I discovered that in a strange way, Eliot out of an unhappy and I out of a happy marriage, had a common experience of tragedy which brought us closer, through the mental illnesses of our first wives.

In 1964 almost on the eve of Tom's death, I had the joy of introducing Evelyn to him and to Valerie. Shortly after our marriage we had an afternoon with them in June at their apartment in Kensington and then they drove us to Hampstead where we both had engagements. Ours was with Julian Huxley—a celebration of his seventy-fifth birthday. But discretion forbad our telling Eliot where we were going or Huxley with whom we had come.

The Eliots took to Evelyn and we arranged to dine together at the Hyde Park Hotel late in September (Tom had often come to that hotel to dine with me when we were both widowers.) It turned out to be the evening before his seventy-sixth and last birthday. In the afternoon he had gone to receive the United States Medal of Freedom from the American Ambassador, because his health was already too frail to allow a trip to Washington. At the Embassy he had struggled up many steps. With his shortness of breath this was terribly exhausting. On top of the climb he had unexpectedly to face television lights and cameras, and newsmen. It was sad, but not surprising after this ordeal, that we had to rest more than once on our way from the street to the restaurant overlooking Hyde Park at nightfall.

He loved good claret and a share in a bottle of one of his favorites, Chateau Cheval Blanc 1953, restored him. All four of us had a memorable visit, with good conversation about poetry and poets, ending with Robert Frost.

Evelyn tells me I have omitted a story about an earlier meeting with Eliot. Not long after his marriage to Valerie, which took place in January 1957, I was in London and arranged to meet him for tea in his small room at Faber and Faber. The Eliots were just back from an American journey while I had been again in Paris. In conferring over the telephone about our meeting I asked how his trip to the United States had gone. His answer, "It was a success," puzzled me for this was not a word he commonly used about himself.

He was in the habit of visiting the United States almost every year, invariably lecturing just enough to cover expenses of the journey for owing to British travel regulations he could take very little money out of England. The day after our telephone conversation I was with him in his small office. This was hardly big enough for four, just right for two. I was in a chair facing the large photograph Paul Valéry had inscribed to him many years before. I started the conversation by asking what he had meant when he spoke of the American journey as "a success." The answer he returned in a mild voice was made as I was looking, not at him, but straight at that photograph. "Introducing Valéry to the United States," he said. "And how did you do that," I asked absentmindedly, "by lectures or readings?"

Then my eye caught his. He had said Valerie and I heard Valéry. I realized my mistake, which he understood. We both rose and he gave me the accolade saying "John, I know what you think of marriage and I know what you think of success."

32. ON BEHALF OF THE HUMAN PERSON

About fifteen correspondents came to the press conference arranged for Eliot upon his arrival in Chicago for the *Poetry* auction. The collation provided by my housekeeper helped ease their morning—as well as Eliot's.

Among the visitors was an extraordinarily dashing black man named James Stricklin, who turned out to be—in the tradition of Stieglitz and Man Ray—an artistic photographer of much promise. With his camera Stricklin met the train that brought the Eliots in the early morning to the old Englewood Station, where, incredibly, I encountered the same porter who served the Stravinskys seventeen years before. During the session in our drawing room Stricklin confined himself to taking a few pictures so discreetly that there was no sense of intrusion. In fact his presence was reassuring in the midst of a barrage of often ill-considered and in some cases ill-mannered questions. When the correspondents departed, Stricklin was the only one to say good bye and thank you for the food and drink.

About a week after the Eliots left, in the gloom of an empty apartment on a dreary Saturday afternoon, the door bell rang. There was Stricklin with the gift of a fine set of photographs he had taken in our drawing room that morning and at the dinner-auction for *Poetry* at the Arts Club two nights later. He gave me a second set for the Eliots. His pictures helped to recapture and illuminate their visit and the light he brought has not faded. After Stricklin's Saturday afternoon appearance he and I established a firm friendship since strengthened by our marriages.

In considering the nature of the influence the Committee on Social Thought may have upon the future of the higher learning and upon creative achievement, especially in the arts, the problem Eliot's visit helped to define—the problem of who ought to have advantages of the kind we try to provide both students and faculty—is of basic importance. Jim Stricklin's connection with the Committee and still more that of Frank Brown (a black man of letters who began working for a degree with us shortly before his premature death) suggest the nature of the individuals whose careers we should foster.

When Stricklin came to lunch for the first time on a cold, harsh winter's day, he set the key in which applications for participation in such small groups should be examined. Warmed by food and a chateau-bottled claret, he sensed our mutual delight in the good things humans have invented; he showed his pleasure in everything he found. *"Here I can breathe,"* he murmured. "It is as if I were in France." He served with the United States army for a couple of years and had encountered for the first time the "equality" he thrived upon. In

France he had the experience of being received not as a black but as a human being. Whatever the color of those with whom he associated, he was accepted for what he was and even more for what he was trying to become. Neither the dark nor the light people had classified him as a black. He was a man.

On the eve of his marriage to his beautiful girl Joyce, the couple and the best man accepted my invitation to dine in the Dorchester Avenue apartment. It was a hot summer day. Robert Buron, the French parliamentarian who had been for a time Minister of Transportation during De Gaulle's presidency, was in town briefly with his wife and daughter on their way home to Paris from a trip round the world. We had already met in 1952 when Buron headed a French parliamentary delegation and, with several other deputies, came to dinner where he found Maritain a fellow guest. (After that Buron was fond of saying, "In order to meet Maritain you have to go to the Committee on Social Thought in Chicago.") In view of Jim's earlier discovery of himself in France, I asked the three Burons to share this bridal dinner.

Joyce arrived on time. But Jim and his best man had gone in his old Mercedes to a distant country village to carry back and install in the bridal apartment a vast iron bed that had been long in his family, the kind of bed Elinor and I had shared at Apt and Tournus. The two men arrived only shortly before midnight. I kept wondering how the Burons were able to stay on for Jean Béliard, the French consul general who had brought them, left around eleven. I discovered that in order to experience American life to the full they were taking a bus from Chicago to New York before flying home. The bus left at three in the morning. So we continued the party for two hours after the bridegroom arrived.

Jim Stricklin's associations with the Committee on Social Thought, and later with the Center for Human Understanding, were always informal. He believed in our aims and wanted to declare his allegiance to them. He kept a photographic record of the members of both groups and of the meetings of the Center. As a result a graphic account exists of the two institutions that approaches high art as the best photography can.

The Committee had an even closer relationship with Frank Brown. He became a student and was on the way to getting his doctor's degree when he died. Brown was an outstanding hero among Chicago blacks before he joined us. He had risked his life by walking into a quarter of the city where the local white population had threatened to kill any black "invader."

A gifted writer, Brown had already completed and published a novel, *Trumbull Park,* when David Grene and I encouraged him to apply for admission. Another—a kind of *Crime and Punishment* with a South Side Chicago background—was written under our tutelage. *The Myth Maker* has now been published. More perhaps than his first novel it has touches of greatness. Like Stricklin, Brown was no longer concerned when we met, if he ever had been, with becoming a black artist. He aspired to be an artist. In the Committee he found this was a valid aspiration and that he was welcome as a person potentially touched by genius. As do many promising persons, he possessed an innate modesty that recognition did not alter.

We often lunched together and talked about his work, his life and his aims. Like Stricklin, Brown was at home with himself. He came to me full of quiet courage the day his doctor had diagnosed leukemia. I advised him to tell no one, because I did not think it would help to have people gossiping over his doom, and his tragedy became our secret. We were in touch frequently during the year that followed. The day Frank died his widow, who had sometimes come with him to lunch, telephoned to ask if I would speak at the services in a Chicago funeral parlor. It was a moving event with a couple of hundred people massed in a small space. I hadn't realized that apart from a dark woman poet, Gwendolyn Brooks, who read some of her verses, I would be the only speaker. The mourners were all black.

Years before when the Committee on Social Thought was starting, a letter had come from a black man asking whether he would be admitted if he applied. In replying I tried to make clear that his color had no significance but that the work we offered was suited for only a very few. The Committee was exclusive but not on the basis of color, only on the basis of quality, and a kind of *quality* which is very rare. It is not black quality or white quality. It transcends both blacks and whites and all the classes, races, sexes and nations into which humanity is now divided to its peril.

By the time I was fourteen some local boys on the Chicago South Side had filled me with anti-Jewish prejudices. A few days after meeting Elinor I hinted at these and she stopped me by declaring. "I am Jewish." She meant that one of her first cousins was married to a half-Jew. Her words put an end once and for all at fourteen to a budding prejudice. Like my former black housekeeper in Chicago,

Agnes Thornton, I am as dismayed by the "Black Power" movement as by claims made by white people to white supremacy. I am equally dismayed by claims to Jewish supremacy. This is no time for segregation. It is as human beings that all need to unite. The dream of the late Martin Luther King cannot accomplish its purpose if it is only for black Americans, if it excludes Aryans or Jews or Orientals. And the pursuit of excellence, as Stricklin and Brown have pursued it, contributes to the dream. I would like to think the policies of the Committee on Social Thought are small instruments in its service. Our aims are positive. We were not founded simply as a protest against overspecialization. The task of cultivating the general requires specialization very different from that habitual in the higher learning, but nonetheless concentration of an intense kind. Among those who enter graduate study—and that study is appropriate for only a small minority—few are suited to such work as ours set out to be. The pursuit of special knowledge in particular fields of enquiry has been yielding important and in some cases epoch-making results. The creative advance of inquiries in connection with those learned specialties should be the main but not the exclusive purpose of university research and graduate instruction. It is to be hoped that the new kind of specialization we have introduced may help give direction to these older specialties, may help define the goals for which it is desirable to carry out investigations, and may help also to limit the number of such investigations in the interest of quality.

In any event the opportunities our faculty was founded to offer—the cultivation of the arts in particular—are happily desired by only a minute portion of the population. No one who is genuinely eager to embark on such a career, and who has acceptable qualifications, should be refused a trial. But not all who feel called can succeed. Failure should be no disgrace. Nor should it constitute a handicap to the pursuit of other kinds of graduate inquiry or to still other kinds of training. Artur Schnabel was fond of saying, "No one is obliged to be a genius." And, needless to say, being a genius is far from a guarantee of happiness.

During the nineteen-fifties the Committee on Social Thought was faced with new problems. After the resignation of Hutchins as Chancellor of the University of Chicago at the end of 1950, the disposition manifested long before by one of my colleagues to "get back to the old system under the new plan," became more effective throughout the university than during the previous fifteen years or so. There was a disposition to dismantle those innovations with which Hutchins name and personality were identified. The disposition found support from an impression that the financial position of the university had been worsening for years—to a point some trustees thought a threat to the existence of this comparatively young institution, founded in 1892. A drive for economy began. One of the guideposts adopted was to slough off, whenever possible, units and practices without an equivalent in other universities.

By that criterion the Committee on Social Thought should have been the first of the innovations to disappear. Two factors enabled it to hold its own and to continue without the support sometimes forthcoming until 1951 from additional university funds, particularly the White visiting professorship that Eliot, Schoenberg and Schnabel had held. One was the distinguished character of our faculty. The other was the partial financial and the strong moral and spiritual support granted by several of Chicago's citizens who had been my friends for years, several among them trustees of the university. These friends, including Margaret Castle in Washington, were particularly enthusiastic about the visitors from abroad who came to us as a result of my European journeys.

Among the Chicago friends no one perhaps gave more heartening encouragement than a young man fifteen years my junior whom I met after he retired from service at the end of the Second World War. Born William Wood, he was adopted as William Wood-Prince by the late Frederick Prince and given control of the vast business empire, including the Chicago stockyards, the elder Prince had built at the end of the last century. Frederick Prince did not overrate the business gifts of his ward, whom he had known from infancy. Billy Prince is a constructive innovator such as one rarely finds in any calling. As President and later as Chairman of the Board of Armour and Company, he extended its operations, after the elder Prince died at 93 in 1953, into new fields and new areas all over the world. Through an allied enterprise he introduced a cheaper kind of fuel for freighters. He was one of the earliest American financiers to seek trade with Soviet Russia.

The original and imaginative approach he brought to business was grounded in a love of art and literature. He introduced me to the great Spanish writer, Unamuno, and once lent me a volume of his essays. On the flyleaves were compositions of Billy's that he had taken pains to ink out so successfully that no line of the verse he had written could be deciphered. Our friendship was strengthened when *War and Human Progress* appeared, a book he has championed ever since. What brought us closest was the kind of setting the Committee aimed to provide its faculty and students. One day when we were lunching in his private room at the Saddle and Sirloin Club, he told me of his Princeton experience. He found the formal academic work there painfully boring. Towards the end of his junior year in the mid-1930's, when he was having a drink by himself in the bar of a New York hotel, he began a conversation with an older man at an adjoining table. He explained how Princeton disappointed him and mentioned his love for poetry. "Look here," said the stranger to Billy's astonishment, "I am a professor at Princeton and I share your predicament. I give a kind of private seminar at my house once a week in the evening. Half a dozen or so students come. We read poetry aloud and discuss it over the refreshments my wife provides. Why don't you join us?"

Billy did. This transformed his senior year into an interesting one, the kind he had hoped a university could offer. He saw not incorrectly that the Committee on Social Thought offered conditions for exceptional students similar to those he had encountered during his last year at Princeton. He became our enthusiastic supporter. When representatives of the University of Chicago "development office" would come to see him about other matters, he would tell them it was the Committee alone that interested him. No doubt that was a convenient financial tactic, but it was also true. He became the chairman of a group we called "Associates" of the Committee and later of a Center for Human Understanding. We had other distinguished Associates, foremost among them in support Leola Epstein, and also James Douglas, Hermon Smith, William Benton, Margaret Farwell, Marshall and Kay Field,[1] Alfred and Rue Shaw, Margaret Castle,[2] Thomas Alcock and Hugo Anderson, each from a different background but all united in their belief in this academic innovation.

The effort to treat students as adult junior colleagues, which so attracted Billy Prince, was helpful to the most promising young persons who came to us for training. The non-conformist discipline we are able to offer has helped graduates, now recognized for their contributions in many fields, to bring influences we have stressed and results we have achieved into new environments. Robert Hartwell, a researcher of prodigious energy in the field of Chinese history, is speculating about the cultural influences that produced an early Chinese industrial revolution in the eleventh century and those that hindered this revolution, unlike the one in Elizabethan and Stuart England, from leading to the introduction of heat energy as the source of power for driving machinery. Philipp Fehl has achieved an established position in the art departments, first of the University of North Carolina and now of Illinois. He lays a novel emphasis on the *moral* significance of works of art. Shirley Letwin, instead of specializing in Russian studies, has established with her husband William Letwin, another of our graduates (now on the faculty of the London School of Economics), a frequented "salon" where values can be humanized.

Threats to the purposes the Committee had been founded to champion came, in a way, as much from within as from without. The inclination to get back to the old system under the new plan was ever present, in varying degrees, among my colleagues. It was also encouraged by some of the students, especially by those who had few inventive gifts, the sort who wanted to be told rather than encouraged to be themselves. In the early days one young woman used to break down and cry for a tutor who could explain exactly what Plato meant. She appealed successfully to the president of the university for personal tutoring on one occasion. But if Eliot was incapable of explaining precisely a great line of his own, how could we expect a twentieth-century professor (or even a university president) to be sure what that ancient Greek artist meant by a passage in the *Dialogues?*

Many students were seeking a gospel. There is nothing wrong with that search but it was not our responsibility to supply one in the form of intellectual capsules. We hoped we could help some students to find one for themselves. And, in spite of difficulties, we managed to retain the possibility for inventiveness among both faculty and students. We kept open opportunities for inquiries designed to bring different fields into a unity. One of our graduates, who served the cabinet secretariat of the United States under Eisenhower, found the instruction offered in historical interrelations of value in his work. He could apply the principles to the policies formulated by particular government departments, revealing their interdependence and helping to evaluate what weight should be attached to the recommendations of each department.

We managed to resist pressure from within and from without to specialize dogmatically in the particular. We preserved in a few scholars an appetite, nourished by the visits of great contemporary artists, for an imaginative approach to the so-called social, behavioral and humanistic sciences. We kept the way open for the poet and the man of letters. The chairman who has succeeded me, Saul Bellow, is among the most gifted contemporary men of letters.

Kenneth Boulding is one of the most ingenious and broadest of contemporary economic thinkers. In a letter written from Japan in February 1964 (a most important month in my life), he suggested that the initiative taken by the Committee was too important to be cornered by any particular university. He is right. The freedom and the opportunities introduced into graduate studies could lead to the formation of small groups at various universities throughout the world. They should be started only when there is a deeply felt desire among scholars or artists or both—persons of outstanding reputation and promise—to unite for the sake of the work they are attempting as individuals. Such groups should not be mere copies of the Committee on Social Thought, any more than the Committee on Social Thought under the chairmanship of Bellow should be a replica of what it was under me. It is desirable that graduates of such groups be granted a new kind of higher degree now that Ph.D.'s have been devalued by the overwhelming increase in the number awarded.

The leadership that might help bring students out of the wilderness of controversy, in which they are burying themselves with the help of many faculties, calls for fresh ideas suited to particular circumstances. Though even the genius has a need for models, mere imitation is never creative. It was partly to avoid having students memorize notes taken from my lectures that I was prompted in 1940 to move away from conventional instruction in the field of economic history.

Example can provide creative kinds of stimuli. The fresh instruction and research undertaken by the Committee are relevant to most aspects of education. They suggest the value of innovation and of student participation in universities and even in some colleges and high schools. But neither innovation nor participation is an end in itself. Neither can be justified unless it helps to raise the quality and the moral value of the work done by individuals. A move that might contribute to such improvement would be a break away (by those few scholars and students who feel the urge as I had felt it in 1939-42) from the localism that pervades academic communities. Local loyalties are often inconsequential, invariably time-consuming and sometimes dangerously racial or nationalistic. These loyalties need to be re-placed by a dedication to permanent values in teaching, learning and research which can rally the noblest aspirations of the individual's inner life.[3] These values can never be finally achieved but they are renewed in striving to serve them. These values are related to our common humanity, the subject of the next chapter.

33. NEW HORIZONS

Louis Joxe had negotiated the agreement with the French Foreign Office for exchanges between the University of Paris and the Com-mittee on Social Thought. By the time of my Collège de France assignment in 1953 he had become ambassador in Moscow. He was succeeded as director of cultural relations by a younger colleague, Jacques de Bourbon-Busset. Bearer of an illustrious name, Bourbon-Busset is descended not only from the great thirteenth-century king Louis IX (Saint Louis), as all surviving Bourbons are, he is de-scended also from the family of Louis XIV's famous and influential minister Colbert, who was of merchant origin. A less celebrated ancestor, a Bragelongne, awoke fond memories of my childhood enthusiasm for Alexandre Dumas' *Three Musketeers* one of whom is called Bragelonne.

Bourbon-Busset had risen through many ranks of a diplomatic career and had a promising future. He had been *chef de cabinet* to the late Robert Schuman when Jean Monnet joined with that dis-tinguished statesman in fathering the European common market. Already before his studies as a youth at the Ecole Normale Supérieure, Bourbon-Busset had a passion (known to only his boyhood intimates) for letters. The passion never lapsed though few opportunities came his way to exercise it. In the forties he published under a *nom de plume* a short novel, *Le Sel de la terre*.

We had never met. But when I arrived in France to carry out my assignment as a visiting lecturer at the Collège he and his fascinating wife welcomed me with generous understanding. During the years of my widowerhood they took me into their family circle and treated me with compassion of a kind that confirmed my faith and hope in the human adventure. They and others like them provided me with some of the protection I had lost and for which I felt the need. Laurence de Bourbon-Busset had a deep sympathy for my lack of family because like me she was an only child. Her father had been killed in action early in the First World War when she was an infant. Until she met Jacques she lived in solitary womanhood with her mother, who was little more socially inclined than my father.

Soon after my arrival in Paris the Bourbon-Bussets gave a luncheon for me in their apartment on the Boulevard Saint Germain. My Collège de France lecture was to begin at three. Sensing my concern lest I arrive late Laurence offered to take me in their car. We left the lunch party and this tiny bundle of feminine drive slid into the chauffeur's seat of the small Peugeot. The traffic problem in Paris was far less desperate then than now and as she drove she talked about her four children—three of them little boys—and her devotion to the seventeenth-century chateau thirty miles south of Paris in the Gatinais, "Le Saussay," inherited by her husband from the Colbert side of his family. She said she wished she could leave the city and live there altogether. She promised they would soon ask me to visit and the prospect filled some of the emptiness that Elinor's going had left. As we took leave I was so consoled that I barely noticed Laurence had mistaken for the Collège de France the Ecole de Droit and had deposited me there. The distance separating the two was short and I arrived in time for my lecture.

The Bourbon-Bussets fulfilled her promise beyond my hope. A few weeks later Jacques took me to the chateau for a weekend. As we were approaching it in the beauty of spring I endeared myself to them by remarking that I didn't see how they could bear to live anywhere else. After that they often invited me for extended stays.

Jacques is a complicated person and it has never been clear whether he and Laurence befriended me because of my interest in art or because of my historical scholarship. Before my visits to "Le Saussay" I learned, from one of his schoolboy friends, of his preoccupation with letters. This man lent me *Le Sel de la terre* after exacting the promise I would not reveal the authorship, a promise I kept until the author himself gave away the secret. Whatever the origin of Bourbon-Busset's friendly feeling for me, mine for him and his wife was aroused in no small measure by his gift for writing and her's for painting, a pursuit she carried on regularly as an amateur. Two years after becoming director of cultural relations he resigned from the Foreign Office to devote himself wholly to literature and to his wife.

Their life together was rich. She had been trained in economics and she took upon herself the running of what they made a considerable agricultural enterprise by consolidating several neighboring tenant farms that they owned around Ballancourt, the site of "Le Saussay." They then worked the whole estate directly as a single farm. When someone asked Jacques if he enjoyed farming he answered a trifle evasively, declaring with emphasis "my *wife* is crazy about it." Nothing could have been truer and, thanks to Laurence's enthusiasm, energy and brains they made a go of farming in this age of revolutionary agricultural mechanization.

When the Bourbon-Bussets came in 1957 to the Committee on Social Thought in Chicago for three weeks they stayed with me in the Dorchester Avenue apartment. Laurence was studying with zest scientific pasturage and horticulture. At her behest I arranged a number of visits to pasture farms in the Chicago neighborhood and consultations with learned authorities concerning the cultivation of flowers. She absorbed the technological knowledge that was imparted by the landed proprietors and the professors with a speed and resourcefulness I had not encountered before and was not to encounter again until I married Evelyn.

The hopes Artur Schnabel and I shared for world community during 1945 and 1946 were revived in a different form before that visit of the Bourbon-Bussets. During their stay in Chicago the three of us talked frequently about the feasibility of forming a small group whose allegiance would be simply to humanity. How had this conception come into my mind? How has it since evolved with the Bourbon-Bussets' help?

In 1948 I had the idea of forming a small international group of persons of reputation who wished for and were able to represent a world point of view, independent of the conflicts that were dividing peoples after the war. During a visit to Mexico City College in the spring I was advised to call on a distinguished poet and diplomat who had been Mexican minister to France and to the Argentine, the late Alfonso Reyes. We agreed on the need for finding persons willing and able to work together as friends in the name of humanity, some of whose findings would be published. This idea played about in my mind as I was finishing *War and Human Progress*. *The Oregonian* of Portland devoted a long editorial to the meaning of that book in 1953, three years after its publication. The editor detected my conviction that a world-wide authority of a few disinterested persons of the highest integrity might be vital in building the peaceful unity without which few may survive. He said the book showed that such a Council could be modeled "after the Royal Society under Newton and rising superior to governments." As I have since recognized, the concepts which my historical work has embodied lay emphasis too exclusively on the West. In reading the copy of Chateaubriand's *Mémoires d'outre tombe*, bought in Caen the first night of Elinor's and my return to Europe in 1949, I became aware of the possibility Chateaubriand had recognized more than a century before for all the nations and races and religious sects of the earth to merge. The mission was unfulfilled. Could there be any higher temporal goal for mankind than the creation of a universal patriotism represented by a small dedicated group of humans unattached to any cause less general than humanity's future on earth?

One of the recent British Ambassadors to the United States John Freeman, who reviewed *War and Human Progress* for *The New Statesman*, recognized this implication. Assuming mankind is not bent on suicide, historical forces are pressing for a new devotion to the eternal verities and to the charity, compassion and love towards which the noblest aspirations of men and women have always been directed, in China and Russia as well as in ancient Greece and Western Europe, among Buddhists no less than among followers of Christ.

In the fifties these historical forces were little in evidence. Nor could a professor hope to muster the authority that would empower an independent group of the kind the editor of *The Oregonian* wrote about. The last thing I felt entitled to claim was the wisdom that should be inherent in the "worldwide organization of best minds." Nevertheless a beginning had to be made, a call had to be issued for such a Council.

A world point of view would involve no dilution of nationality but only of the uglier sides of nationalism; the alternative is too awful for a compassionate individual to contemplate, unless he approaches mankind as a "two hundred percent American" who hates the "whole damned human race." If the nations continue to build ever more expensive arsenals of increasingly destructive weapons, absorbing a greater proportion of their national incomes, the consequence will be what the late Edwin Hubble called "the war that must not happen." Such a war could destroy all the beauty that men and women have managed to create across several millenia. Such a war could destroy all the knowledge that scholars have acquired, and that is now stored in archives and libraries as well as in their heads. It is not only men and women who would disappear in vastly greater numbers than ever before; it is the power they have demonstrated to surmount their limitations through the arts as well as the sciences. "When old age shalt *this* generation waste" *naught* will perhaps remain.

In my youth—in the midst of the grim despair expressed in "The Waste Land," "The Love Song of J. Alfred Prufrock" and "The Hollow Men"—new approaches were being made to world history. The most compelling version that attended me during early days of private happiness in Vienna was the version of Oswald Spengler. An English translation of the introduction to *Untergang des Abendlandes,* by the young American writer Kenneth Burke, appeared in *The Dial* about the time that magazine published its portfolio of fine artistic reproductions. The despair of Spengler's book was most persuasive for Europeans and for some Americans who survived the First World War. In the tradition of Gobineau, forsaking the original meaning of the eighteenth-century word "civilization," Spengler saw industrialism as just another civilization destined to die and eventually be superceded by other societies with similar life spans and patterns of achievement and degeneration. As the First World War ended the idea that "civilizations" are mortal was expressed also in 1919 by Paul Valéry in a famous sentence: "Nous autres, civilisations, nous savons maintenant que nous sommes mortelles."

Like Valéry and Spengler, my generation missed a new and different truth accessible to an historian of "industrialism." It is not just "civilizations" which are mortal; it is "civilization," the whole human effort towards beauty and truth, the love, the tender manners, the decency and seemliness that give form and substance to virtue. In that sense the word "civilization" seems to have been coined in Europe in the mid-eighteenth century.[1] It expressed a new hope: That the powers humans were achieving over nature could be used to raise humanity to a higher level of dignity and harmony than had ever existed. This gave both men and women a new and inspiring ideal.

The abandonment of this original meaning of the word during the nineteenth and twentieth centuries, the substitution of "civilisations" for "civilisation," were symptoms of the weakening of that ideal. It seems vital for mankind to renew it, to return to the original meaning as understood when the word was introduced into the French and English languages.

One source that helped me to recognize the limitations of the "cycle historians," was the letters Tocqueville wrote to Gobineau more than a hundred years ago. My French friends, the Maurice Bayens, were lunching with me in Paris at the beginning of the sixties. That was before Bayen had been chosen to head the University of Strasbourg. He is a modest quiet man who had come to me in Chicago and had given me unobtrusively a small volume of verse he had published. As Rector of French Fellowships we met annually for several years to discuss the exchange of students between the University of Paris and the Committee on Social Thought. These meetings led to a friendship with his family, particularly with his remarkable wife, who as Françoise Lorrain wrote an account (*La Colonne de Cendres*) of the French tragedy of Vietnam which she witnessed as a trained physician when her husband was Rector of the University of Saigon.

The day after our last Paris luncheon together, when I was about to leave by plane for New York, Madame Bayen sent a copy of the Tocqueville-Gobineau correspondence. In reading that book during the seven-hour flight my conviction was strengthened that the whole conception of the human race as divided into competing societies was spiritually retrogressive, that it stood in the way of the merging of the races and nations to which Chateaubriand had looked forward before Gobineau's book—*Essai sur l'inégalité des races humaines*—was written. As Tocqueville feared, humanity has been moving in the direction of its own destruction, partly under Gobineau's influence.

In 1931 or 1932 in the midst of the great depression, a Chicago colleague invited me to a faculty lunch for Arnold J. Toynbee, who was lecturing at Northwestern University. The name Toynbee was then known to scholars largely because it had belonged to his uncle, long since dead. The so-called English "industrial revolution," which bewitched many who instructed students, was associated with *that* Arnold Toynbee.[2] Presumably this was why my University of Chicago colleague, Quincy Wright, seated me next to his nephew at lunch. As a budding economic historian I was classed in the uncle's field. Before the luncheon guests dispersed, Toynbee in a tête à tête asked how his uncle's thesis stood up after a half century. The question was embarrassing, for my historical investigations during the previous decade suggested there had been in England at least two industrial revolutions. During the reigns of Elizabeth I and the early Stuart kings a speeding up of industrial and (as we now know) of agricultural development pointed in the direction of our contemporary mechanized world· In the changes wrought in ways of living and working that development was an indispensable preparation for the speeding up emphasized by Toynbee the First.

The later Industrial Revolution actually got going not, as he supposed, in the *mid*-eighteenth century but at the very end. The earlier English speeding up in rates of economic growth was accompanied in continental Europe (where except for Holland there was no such leap in volume of output as in England) by innovations in many lines of endeavor, among them the natural sciences, which contributed mightily to the later speeding up. Innovations in intellectual and cultural history were partly responsible for the mechanized world we live in, with heat energy as the source of power. For the *roots* of mechanization and the civilization that encouraged mechanization one needed to study Medieval and Renaissance Europe and especially the century following the Reformation (1540-1640). In fact the study of European and American history during some two hundred years and more prior to the rapid spread of steam power after the 1780's, seemed hardly less indispensable than the study of the British Industrial Revolution, for meeting the human plight that began to confront mankind at the time of the great depression.

On the occasion long ago when these ideas were germinating, but had not yet been thought out or published, I did not know that my luncheon partner was engaged on a magnum opus in the field of world history, a field already tilled by H. G. Wells and more apocalyptically by Spengler. The first three volume installment of *A Study of History* appeared in 1934. It caused no stir at the time in the United States popular press but made an immense impression on a few of Toynbee's colleagues and friends. In London in the summer of 1934 R. H· Tawney (who was later much less enthusiastic about this book as a whole) told Conyers Read and me over dinner in a Bloomsbury restaurant that in historical writing *A Study of History* seemed to him the only work of genius that had appeared in the twentieth century. I read the book with great interest and was struck by certain poetical passages of description, particularly by the paragraphs (that appeared only later in 1939 in Volume IV) where Toynbee compares the decline of the Roman Empire to a beautiful New England autumn such as I had savored at Harvard. What struck me even more was the resemblance of Toynbee's historical pattern to Spengler's. And indeed a couple of decades later, when Toynbee lectured for the Committee on Social Thought (the second of the visits he paid us), a questioner asked him what he thought of Spengler. He replied most candidly: Spengler was an historian of genius; when he—Toynbee—had come on *The Decline of The West* at the time he was embarking on his *Study*, his first instinct had been to abandon the project. Momentarily he felt he was setting out to do what had already been done.

My lectures in history at the University of Chicago began in 1929. I felt it would help the students to compare the coming of industrialism in Europe with the evolution of Greco-Roman societies. At the time Spengler's Introduction to the *Decline of The West* seemed the best means of presenting a world view of history that would help in such a comparison. Finding Toynbee's pattern similar to Spengler's (and somewhat less fatalistic and pessimistic) I offered students after 1934 their choice of Spengler or Toynbee.

My inquiry into historical development was a different venture from either. It led me later to question the validity of the Spengler-Toynbee thesis. Toynbee was not concerned, any more than Spengler, with the kind of history pure and simple towards which I have been drawn across the past forty years. The specialization of historical investigations that has gone on since the early nineteenth century has provided extraordinarily extensive new information concerning many particular subjects besides economic history. I was more and more engaged with interrelations between developments in many fields of history which other academics treated separately. The more I studied the interplay between various aspects of historical evolution in Western Europe, and compared this evolution with that of other societies, past as well as contemporary, the more I became impressed with the *novelty* of the problems that confront all of us today. Ours is not the repetition of an old story, as the cycle historians have assumed. Our minds and hearts now have a new human condition to contend with. Only a new human dedication can meet it.

As the editor of *The Oregonian* observed in his discussion of *War and Human Progress*, my conception of contemporary society and its historical origins is independent of the theories of Marx, Spengler and even Toynbee. My conception summons humans everywhere to reestablish the spirit of "civilization," with its eighteenth-century meaning, and with the inspiring hopes in the individual and in humanity which account for the existence of the word.

Nevertheless certain scholars felt there was a resemblance to Toynbee (and there was) in the fact that we had both moved away from the kinds of historical specialization which enjoyed respectability in the academies. He too was concerned with interrelations and like him I was increasingly preoccupied with wide sweeps of history. Evidence of a disposition to link me with Toynbee turned up after my return to Europe following the Second World War. By that time his fame in the United States had become immense. To my astonishment I was asked to introduce him to the audience at one of the annual conferences of Anglo-American historians in his native country.

Toynbee's *Study*, despite its huge sale, did not command the applause of most historical scholars either in Great Britain or the United States. They were baffled by its sweep. When the first three volumes were sent for review by Bernadotte Schmitt, as editor of the *Journal of Modern History*, to one of the most prominent American professors of history, he returned it saying he did not care to review it. It covered too much ground. This very comment had been made by an editor of *The New Yorker* when I described to him the book the Committee on Social Thought had brought out in 1947, *The Works of the Mind*, containing chapters by some of the most eminent men of our time. My own books, after *The Rise of the British Coal Industry*, have been occasionally subjected to similar criticism. In fact it has sometimes seemed that I share Toynbee's unpopularity among scholars without sharing his vast public. My artistically-oriented historical writings have a different meaning from his. More and more mine have come to emphasize the view that individual initiative can be of greater importance than any "cycle" in determining the course of history.

A generation ago *United States and Civilization* was reviewed in two Jesuit periodicals, in each case by a priest. Both admired the book. One thanked God the author was a pessimist, the other that he was an optimist! Both were right.

While writing *War and Human Progress* I gradually became aware that the stakes the world has in building upon eighteenth-century "civilization" are overwhelming. The only response which could overcome the widespread pessimism about human nature now rampant in the United States, even more than in Europe, is a greater optimism. That is a faith that human capacities for compassion and love could become more influential than ever before.

Holding this faith accounts for my effort to establish a Center for Human Understanding. I discussed the idea of forming such a group in the forties with Schnabel, and also, after he returned in 1948 to the United States following his service at the Vatican, with Maritain, when he began his regular visits to the Committee on Social Thought. In the Walgreen lectures he gave at the University of Chicago in 1949 (which were published in 1951 under the title *Man and The State*) Maritain called for the formation of a group of wise men. Bourbon-Busset took up the idea later in a brochure published in France as a testimonial to Maritain. Late in the summer of 1957 Bourbon-Busset and I attended a conference on Atlantic Community sponsored by several American foundations and held at Bruges. Proposals for a group of the kind the editor of *The Oregonian* saw foreshadowed in *War and Human Progress* were in the paper I prepared.[3] At the behest of the late Adriano Olivetti, the Italian industrialist who presided over the section of the conference in which Bourbon-Busset and I participated, that section devoted most of its sessions to a discussion of these proposals. Olivetti encouraged my hope that the organizers of the conference might go beyond its agenda and set up a world group of the kind we sought. But in fact the concern of the organizers was only to strengthen *Atlantic* community by founding an Atlantic Institute.

I could not abandon my idea. It seemed to grow naturally out of the Committee on Social Thought. I was encouraged to pursue the venture by growing adhesion to that body of students from all over the world and representative of many different races and creeds. Our efforts were often impeded by the provincialism of the rules and customs connected with a particular university. Perhaps there would be more freedom for spiritual growth with a fresh unit less dependent on the structure and organization of the University of Chicago. The notion that the Committee was "extra-territorial" was not false and some concrete move into international territory seemed imperative.

It was surprising that the group of Associates, almost all of them from Chicago, followed me into the wilderness. It was more surprising still, at least at first sight, that the chief executive officials of the University of Chicago gave us their blessing and welcomed our use of the university's name in connection with the group, when many of our members had no affiliation with the university. We were certainly helped by my promise not to ask for financial help beyond the valuable facilities the university was willing to furnish by handling any sums we were able to raise. Nor is it impossible that some of those officials, whose enthusiasm for the Committee on Social Thought was lukewarm, saw in the Center for Human Understanding a convenient means of diverting my interests in the direction of Europe and particularly France. My reputation there had come to be recognized by the administration of the University of Chicago as an asset.

Whatever the explanation, the plan for a Center was approved at the end of 1957 by the trustees. The following April I set out to consult my French friends. Our group was formed in Paris at a luncheon held in Calvet's restaurant on the Left Bank, a few days before the Algerian crisis which some weeks later brought General de Gaulle to power. Chicago was also represented at our luncheon by my architect friend, Alfred Shaw, who was lecturing in Paris on architecture and civilization as exchange professor from the Committee on Social Thought. Two officials in the French Foreign Office— Roger Seydoux, later French Ambassador to Russia, and Joxe, who was then *Secrétaire Géneral* (a post equivlent to permanent Undersecretary of State)—gave me enthusiastic support in the midst of the dramatic events which brought the changeover in French government inaugurating the Fifth Republic. To begin with the group included Siegfried, Sarrailh, Maritain (as honorary member), Bourbon-Busset and Charles Morazé. Before summer we added the retiring Canadian Ambassador to France, Jean Désy.

The first plenary meeting was held in Washington in 1962 in Meridian House through an arrangement with Robert Richman's Society for the Contemporary Arts. Before that meeting we were joined by a number of other distinguished men, among them Leprince-Ringuet. As a scientist strongly drawn to the arts his adherence was especially valuable. At the first meeting he was sitting beside me. As I glanced at his pad I recognized in a sketch he was making, while he talked about France becoming a nuclear power, a perfect resemblance to a young woman I knew very well. It was a drawing of Sara di Bonaventura,[4] who looks increasingly like her grandmother Eleanor Roosevelt. This was the first inkling I had that she had come to our meeting. Leprince-Ringuet had never seen her but was struck by her bearing and her face.

Another of our scientist members was Herbert Anderson, Fermi's younger associate, who for a time was director of the Fermi Institute of Nuclear Physics. One of the most creative administrators who joined us was Thomas Carroll, the President of George Washington University. His premature death soon after our third meeting in 1964 was a heavy personal as well as professional blow. An association with the Committee on Social Thought was maintained by the Center for Human Understanding through the double membership of Hayek and Eliade and also of my young collaborator Ralph J. Mills, who with his wife took an active part in preparing the Washington meetings. Bruce Phemister, who had also been associated with the Committee, became executive secretary. Several of the Committee Associates—James Douglas, Leola Epstein, Hermon Smith, Charles Benton, Kenneth Dam and William Wood-Prince —became participating Center members and helped to extend our discussions to include business, publishing and the law. We aimed to draw in representatives from many professions and fields of creative endeavor and to represent all parts of the world. With the help of Guy de Commines, a rising figure in the French diplomatic service and a descendant of the fifteenth-century historian Philippe de Commynes, African embassies participated and also some delegates representing Latin America, India and Japan.

These new relationships helped overcome my exclusive concern as an historian with Western Europe. They emphasized the world setting occupied by contemporary history. In one of my earlier historical essays, still unpublished,[5] I had attempted to distinguish modern from medieval reality, as that existed among our Western ancestors. Experience in starting the Center for Human Understanding showed the need for distinguishing also Oriental, Near Eastern, Russian, Japanese, Latin American and African reality. In the future I would like to extend my historical inquiry to include these realities and the problem of reconciling them. That attempt is not unrelated to the small problem that confronted me as far back as 1923 at the Bibliothèque Nationale in Paris, when I discovered that the methods of cataloging books were so different from those of the United States.[6]

For the first plenary meeting of the Center in Washington my friends, the James Douglases and the William Wood-Princes came on from Chicago, and gave a dinner for the delegates and members. This was the first of a series of dinners in Washington, Chicago and

Paris where our future was discussed informally. The conference cemented the group and its friends. That was how this small offshoot of the University of Chicago came to be established in Washington, where three annual conferences were held. These were followed, in 1966, by a fourth in Chicago. As a result of that meeting we published (under the auspices of Stuart Mudd, chairman of the publications committee of the World Academy of Art and Science) our second and final book, *Towards World Community*.

If the future should demonstrate that the Center has been a small creative force on behalf of the world community (which Schnabel helped me to evoke as early as 1945-46) that will be because its activities have been largely limited to persons with similar aims who came to know each other well, to feel confidence in one another, and to have continuous relations and discussions on an individual basis. The last conference, which produced *Towards World Community*, was carefully prepared and the questions to be discussed formulated over a period of eighteen months, through several meetings Evelyn and I had with the Bourbon-Bussets and the Morazés in Paris and Le Saussay. I corresponded at some length with other participants— among them James Douglas, the late Marshall Hodgson, Herbert Anderson, Marshall Stone, William Wood-Prince and the late Lord Boyd Orr—and Evelyn and I had more than one preliminary meeting in Chicago over dinner with the Associates.

Through the volumes, *Towards World Community* and *Bridges of Human Understanding*, the fruits of these meetings are being slowly disseminated in many countries. For some years I have represented the United States as a foreign correspondent of the "Fédération pour le Respect de l'Homme et de l'Humanité." This body, established in Paris, has aims resembling those of our Center. It was started by an old friend of mine, the late Gaston Berger, once director of higher education in France, who was influenced in his administrative work by the Committee on Social Thought. It has operated under the leadership of a highly gifted French businessman, Dr. Edmund Gros, who has now been succeeded by Joseph Foray. At Foray's suggestion I sent *Towards World Community* to fellow foreign correspondents in many countries.

Whether or not these correspondents share the belief expressed by Chagall (in *Bridges of Human Understanding*) that humanity "can be saved only by love," all are animated by a world point of view. It would be constructive to have the particular issues, now dividing the nations, the creeds and the races, faced from that point of view by an authoritative group of persons whose pronouncements could obtain world-wide authority. If, moreover, as is suggested in the previous chapter, other small faculties are formed with goals similar to those of the Committee on Social Thought, all could be bound together to the advantage of our aims in an informal union of the kind foreshadowed by the ten year existence of the Center for Human Understanding. This would be the kind of union hoped for but never realized in connection with the International Union of Universities. One of its chief animators and its first president was Jean Sarrailh.

The core of such a body would be a small disinterested council which could develop into a world supreme court, no larger than the Supreme Court of the United States, chosen perhaps by the holders of the Nobel Peace Prize. This council should be independent of all existing international organizations, for in these each delegate represents some particular interest, usually a nationalistic interest. The new council would represent, and would help to nourish, the interest of humanity. Its authority would not be political, but moral and spiritual. Supported by several extraterritorial faculties, which will we hope be formed in numerous places, the new council might, by persuasion, bring about reforms in the organization of the United Nations such as could make it eventually a truly international body, devoted to the purpose for which, like the earlier League of Nations, it was founded. That purpose is to prevent wars between nations. Such a purpose needs the inspiration that could be derived from those universal values that many humans of all colors, nations and persuasions share. Such values are alone capable of rallying the noblest aspirations in the professions, in business, in the arts, in craftsmanship and even in routine mechanized labor, and above all in politics and international statesmanship, where they are alas sometimes little in evidence.

PART V

Renewal

34. ROAD TOWARDS FULFILLMENT

The Committee on Social Thought had a monthly seminar of its faculty and students. We always met around the huge oblong table in the Social Science Building at the University of Chicago. In mid-January 1953, just before the installation in Washington of the Eisenhower administration, we had a small dinner in our Dorchester Avenue apartment preceeding the seminar which was to be chaired by Fritz Hayek. He and his wife came and also Elinor and James Douglas, who had been offered the office of Under Secretary of the Air Force in the new administration. It was the last dinner Elinor Nef gave. She was already too ill with cancer to go out.

That day she had received a letter from our good friend Nadia Boulanger, introducing a young American couple. They were contemplating marriage and were in Chicago to see the woman's parents. The man was Mario di Bonaventura, whose musical gifts Nadia had detected, encouraged and enlarged. He has since demonstrated them brilliantly and prominently as performer, conductor and organizer at Dartmouth College, where he has made music at the Hopkins Center a matter of international importance. The problem was that he and his girl were held back from marrying because Mario was a Roman Catholic. She was an agnostic whose mother was against the marriage.

They spent the evening with Elinor who vigorously advised them to marry. She was remarkably persuasive on behalf of any cause in which she believed. The di Bonaventuras have always felt that her advice was the decisive factor in bringing their union about. In the sadness of Elinor's death less than a month later, the two were convinced they owed her a debt. They wanted to repair my loss. It took a long time.

Not many months after this first meeting the di Bonaventuras came to see me in Paris. Later they used to drop in at the Dorchester Avenue apartment on the rare occasions when they were in

Chicago. Our paths also crossed in the New York area where they lived for several years. Mario comes from an extraordinary musical family. He and his brothers and sister all have absolute pitch. So Mario supposed everybody had perfect pitch, until he went to school and found it wanting in most of his playmates. After his superb training under Nadia Boulanger he approached his profession with dedication and determination. But for some time these qualities were of small help to his career. He had to eke out an existence for himself and his wife, even after their first child was born, playing jazz in a New York nightclub. A younger brother Anthony, a concert pianist, had married Sara, the elder daughter of the former Betsy Cushing Roosevelt. She remarried and, on his marriage to Sara, Anthony di Bonaventura became the son-in-law of John Hay Whitney, who became Eisenhower's ambassador to Great Britain.

In his effort to find a more dignified musical position than that of nightclub entertainer, Mario di Bonaventura sought a connection with the music department of a university. But long in vain. I would hear from him occasionally when he used my name or Mr. Whitney's or both as reference. But no one in the specialized world apparently regarded either name as a recommendation for a musician. I was never consulted. What could an "economist" know about the musical art? Mr. Whitney's name was apparently hardly more helpful. University men live in innumerable separate compartments. For university purposes an ambassador and art collector could not possibly offer advice to a music department. Nor could an educational reformer.

Indeed the family connection of the two di Bonaventuras was ironically a handicap to their musical careers. Not long before Mr. Whitney's resignation as ambassador to Great Britain, Anthony was invited to play the two last Beethoven concertos as soloist with Klemperer and the London Philharmonic Orchestra. Klemperer had chosen him on the advice of a musician friend in Central Europe who had heard a concert Tony had given. Klemperer was more than satisfied with the result and distressed when the London newspaper notices were inadequate. He expressed this disappointment in performing circles and learned a rumor had been spread that the American Ambassador had *purchased* this assignment as soloist.

My recommendation of Anthony as a gifted pianist was equally fruitless. As I have related, the Eric Oldbergs introduced me to Schnabel. Eric had later become chairman of the board of trustees of the Chicago Orchestral Association. A well-known brain surgeon, he had been a pupil of the great Harvey Cushing, Sara di Bonaventura's maternal grandfather. When she and Anthony asked me to spend a family Sunday with them on her stepfather's Long Island estate, I listened with delight to Anthony playing the piano for his children, and appealed to Oldberg to give him a tryout as soloist with the orchestra.

Nothing came of this suggestion. Although the handsome young man with a glamorous wife and many children had assignments in Europe, and although he played with more than one reputable American orchestra, he wasn't good enough for Chicago. The Orchestral Association was not interested in the opinion of a Chicagoan who was no specialist in the field. Did they know that the Committee on Social Thought had been responsible for bringing Stravinsky, Schoenberg and Krenek, as well as Schnabel, to the university? If they did, they gave no sign.

For several years Mario's wife Dorothy di Bonaventura had been suggesting that I meet Sara with whom she thought I would have much in common. So it proved. The meeting was an essential link in the adventure that made possible a last beginning. The meeting was arranged for a Sunday evening supper in a New York suburb, in a rather bleak flat that Mario and Dorothy were occupying with Lorenzo, their first born. It was late summer 1958. Before we had been together fifteen minutes Sara and I found a common bond in Eliot's poetry, and from our mutual interest in the poet each of us discovered the other was reading Simone Weil, I in the original French, she in an English translation published posthumously with a preface by Eliot.

We were both impressed by the deep religious feeling Simone Weil's words conveyed, by her total commitment to Christ and by the internal drama which kept her as a Jewess from joining the Roman Church. We were moved by her reflections on the meaning of life in revolutionary times, lived in her case in the tragedy of the Nazi German invasion of her country. She had been brought to England but had felt guilty in being there. As a young Frenchwoman she thought it her duty to share the privations suffered by those who remained in occupied France. So she confined herself in England to the rations she understood would have been available to her at home. She was tubercular and is said to have starved herself to death in this zeal, leaving behind an extensive number of compositions.

The di Bonaventura family were as Catholic, in the conventional

Roman Church meaning of the word, as they were musical. Adherence to the rules of that Church came to them as effortlessly as absolute pitch. Sara had not been brought up a Roman Catholic; she had not joined on her marriage, but she adhered, with the loyalty she felt towards marriage, to all the regulations that obliged her to bring up her five children as members. She often accompanied Anthony and the children to mass. Her religious affiliation was Episcopalian and she shared my belief in the divinity of Christ. Our spiritual positions were such as to make Simone Weil's religious faith seem relevant to both of us though I am not suggesting that we possessed that remarkable woman's ardor. On one occasion Sara asked my opinion as to whether she should join the Roman Church. We turned the matter over in our conversations, and aware of the rigorous enforcement of regulations by some elements in the clergy, I could not conscientiously advise her to do so. Our greatest bond was in the importance we attached, out of different childhood experiences, to faithful conjugal and family relations. As a small girl and until her marriage to Anthony, Sara had suffered not a little from having been born a Roosevelt during times when venomous comments at the expense of her paternal grandfather, the President, were casual small talk in the schools she frequented. She suffered even more from the refusal of her father to return to his family and take care of her and of her younger sister Kate.

Feeling great sympathy for my problem as a widower, no one perhaps would have recognized better than Sara the implications of Eliot's remark that day at Faber and Faber concerning my views of "marriage" and of "success." For Sara, as for me, success was through marriage. She and Anthony read some of my books and attended a lecture I gave at Cooper Union in New York. She was in sympathy with most of my efforts towards educational reform. The three of us used to meet for lunch or dinner, sometimes at a restaurant, sometimes in their New York house where Sara did all the very good cooking herself, and where she provided Tony with a marvelous studio for practicing. Almost from the outset of our friendship she sensed the necessity of finding me a wife. She became even more concerned about the matter than Mario and Dorothy.

Sara had gone to Milton Academy where she established a deep and enduring friendship with a remarkable young woman named Mary Wilde. Miss Wilde has made her way without help from her family, who through her mother inherited the immense landed property of the

Fields in Lenox, where the parents operate a farm for cattle.

Both Sara and Mary have a firm sense of loyalty and dignity that is sometimes wrongly supposed to have become extinct. Their companionship grew with the years, especially after both settled as young married women in New York, where Mary married a brilliant young lawyer, Robert Carswell, now a partner in the firm of Shearman and Sterling. The two couples long had houses in the same city block with entrances on adjacent streets so that continual informal meetings and conversations were possible.

At about the time the Center for Human Understanding began to hold plenary meetings, Robert Carswell was chosen by the new Secretary of the Treasury, Douglas Dillon, to be his special assistant. The Carswells moved temporarily to Washington, retaining their New York house. Interested as she was in social work and trained for that, Mary Carswell found a temporary though not entirely satisfactory job helping foreign students for the Washington International Center. Its office was in Meridian House where, by arrangement with the Society for the Contemporary Arts, I obtained occasional secretarial help in transacting Center business. On my way to or from this labor my eye would sometimes light upon a very beautiful and well dressed young woman sitting at a desk in the large entrance hall. Who could she be? I wondered. On the occasion of the second plenary meeting of the Center in 1963, when the Chagalls and several other French members were in town, she introduced herself. To my surprise and delight I discovered she was a friend of Sara's, for Sara had been interested in the work of the Center and had surprised me happily by coming with Tony to the first plenary meeting where I had recognized her in Leprince-Ringuet's sketch.

I had increasingly fruitful relations with the Carswells. They frequently came to small dinners in the tiny apartment I had taken in California House, an old fashioned building where a generation earlier Elinor and I had supper on more than one occasion with Justice Brandeis and his wife, in the days when I was working for my doctor's degree at the Brookings School. Bob Carswell's duties at the Treasury were of an exacting nature and he took his work seriously. He seldom arrived home before nine or ten at night. He would then finish the evenings with us. On these occasions there were often other persons whose acquaintance I was making through my new work, for example Jacques Kuoh-Moukouri, then Ambassador of Cameroon, and Godwin Onyegbula, then Counselor of the Nigerian Embassy. Both spoke for their countries at the second meeting of our Center and contributed to *Bridges of Human Understanding.*

Late in the autumn of 1963, soon after President Kennedy's assassination, came a letter from Mario di Bonaventura, who had been settling into his work at Dartmouth. While we had long been friends, we never maintained a correspondence. This was the longest letter he had ever written me. Its subject was the widow of the famous explorer, Vilhjalmur Stefansson, who had died rather more than a year before. Mario explained that she had recently come to live in Washington and that he would like us to meet. But he sent no address and no letter of introduction. He suggested that if Sara's younger sister, Kate Haddad, were still in town, she would arrange a meeting. Otherwise, he wrote, "trust to the Washington whirl."

The letter gave me no idea of the age of its subject; it told next to nothing about her save that she was liked in Hanover, New Hampshire, where she had lived with her famous husband. His name was not strange and I was later to recollect that in my youth, when I had operated the Harvard Union, Stefansson had come as a participant in the lecture series I organized to bring that student hall out of the red. What he conveyed in his lecture was astonishing news. Contrary to what we were brought up to suppose, the Arctic was not necessarily an uncomfortable region to visit. This is the theme of his *Friendly Arctic.*

These recollections came later. At the time of receiving Mario di Bonaventura's letter I was arrested only by the thought of the Widow. I was terribly in need of a wife and I knew that the di Bonaventuras were anxious to provide one. The prospects of meeting Mrs. Stefansson however, seemed slim. Any "whirling" was connected with work for the Center. Sometime after the letter came I walked into Meridian House carrying it in my pocket. At her desk Mrs. Carswell gave me that happy smile of greeting that always made my going easier. The impulse to confide the letter to her proved irresistible. She studied it with the pains that can be aroused only by love of the subject, a care documents rarely receive amid the avalanche of papers which descends upon us, papers we sometimes retrieve and file for a future reference that seldom materializes.

"John," she said, "I will take care of this." She reminded me that Tony di Bonaventura had a recital in Carnegie Hall in February, and that we were asked by Sara not only to attend the concert but to go afterwards to a reception that the Whitneys were helping her sister Kate Haddad to give in their apartment off Central Park West. Mary Carswell explained that she and her husband would open their New York house for the weekend and give a small dinner (Mary is a marvelous cook and Bob a lover of good wine) on Sunday evening before the concert. She would invite "the widow Stefansson."

I had no idea whether Mary would succeed in persuading Mrs. Stefansson to make the trip to New York. But I went on the chance and stayed Saturday night at the old Drake Hotel, where the French manager was making me especially welcome because I had brought the Chagalls there on their way to and from the Center for Human Understanding the year before. Early Sunday morning I telephoned the Carswells. Mary answered the phone. "John," she said, "the Widow is coming!" The time set for the dinner party was 6:15, but she suggested that we confer at their house a quarter of an hour before. Somehow Providence filled me with a confidence that is rare in my experience but that has been vouchsafed me on a few great occasions. Intuition told me this was one. So I walked into the Carswell house full of hope just at six for a preparatory discussion of our plans. "If the Widow's a pill," Mary said, "we won't ask her to the Haddad party."

Fifteen minutes later she appeared. We sat down on the sofa in the drawing room. A stream of precious thoughts and ideas, at once accurate, imaginative and in spirit close to my preoccupations and tastes, poured from her. Except for ten days from the following Thursday, when I had to go to Chicago for Committee on Social Thought business, we have never been long separated. Blessedly we kept in touch during those days and nights by telephone.

Two other couples the Carswell's age arrived. They were not going to the Haddad's after the concert, but the idea of not inviting the Widow never crossed our minds again. After an animated dinner party, the four of us climbed into a taxi outside the Carswell home. In order to insure a continuing relationship with the Widow I asked all three, on our way to Carnegie Hall, to dine in Washington in my apartment in California House on Leap Year Day, then hardly three weeks away. At the back of my mind was the faith that here was my wife, and that, if this hadn't become a certainty by February 29th, that date might be propitious to obtain a final commitment.

The promise of those first minutes of her conversation has been not only fulfilled, but doubled and redoubled with every new beginning, and lovers make endless new beginnings. Our mutual love of art found expression in the conversation we carried on in the box at the concert. Tony played Beethoven's sonata, opus 101. It was unfamiliar for it was not one I had heard Schnabel perform. Tony played it beautifully. In the glow that followed, the Widow seems to have made a statement which she has never completely confirmed since. It was to the effect that she was carried to the heights by the music of Bach, Beethoven, Mozart and Schubert. As for the others, she seemed to imply, their music never quite reached the altitudes these composers achieved. Whether she really said this or not, such was the interpretation I put on her words.

At the Haddads' large party we found not only the Anthony but the Mario di Bonaventuras. Dorothy said something to the Widow to the effect that she had wanted to keep me for her or had wanted to keep her for me. It's not certain which, and I learned of her remark only later. But as we both found we were going back to work in Washington the next day, I managed to persuade her to give up the shuttle she planned to take and accept a breakfast flight with me at 8:30 on American Airlines. I should have insisted on picking her up early at her brother's where she was spending the night, for when I reached La Guardia airport in time for the breakfast flight she wasn't there. It never occurred to me she wouldn't come. I let my baggage fly off with the 8:30 plane and sat down to wait. Sure enough, not very long afterwards she appeared in her white lambskin coat, which had already shed some of its hairs on to my black woolen one. She was surprised I had stayed, although for me it would have been inconceivable to leave.

The confidence that had taken hold the day before had not flown away with my bags. We went off with great joy to breakfast at an airport restaurant. For we were overwhelmingly glad to be together after the danger of missing one another. Somehow I believe neither of us has ever wanted to be separated since. On the plane back she agreed to come that night to my apartment and act as hostess. The occasion was a small dinner for the Ambassador of Uruguay and his wife. I persuaded Evelyn to come early. The picture by Vanessa Bell caught her eye as by an artist she did not know. She asked who had done it. When she learned it was Virginia Woolf's sister, my stock rose for Virginia Woolf is one of her favorite writers.

I had to be in Chicago Friday morning. Evelyn invited me to lunch on Thursday at the Brookings Institution. She had come to Washington six months before to help run the American Sociological

Association. The Association had taken offices at the Brookings Institution Annex, while she lived in a new apartment building across Dupont Circle on Twentieth Street. As administrative officer of the Sociological Association, she had entertainment privileges in the private dining rooms that sedate Brookings Institution possesses. Although Mary Carswell had counseled me the day before at Meridian House not to jeopardize by undue haste the result she wanted hardly less than I, I found myself asking the Widow to marry me and to her overwhelming astonishment she found herself saying she would. Neither of us was able to eat a morsel, to the distress of the waitress. We found ourselves wanting to have a plaque put up in the staid room for others to see saying, "Something wonderful happened to us here. It might happen to you." Our presence was no contribution to statistics. But this newly hallowed place resurrected past memories of the Brookings, of Salvemini and also of Harold Moulton who had been partly responsible for bringing me so long before to the now defunct Graduate School.

During the ten days that followed our fondness developed in long telephone conversations. I got back in time to keep the Leap Year date with our benefactors. And at that dinner, perhaps a little to Mary's surprise, Bob Carswell fully approved of our haste, if it were haste, for there never seemed to me anything hasty about it. It had the inevitability of a work of art. And it was art—particularly the musical art which has played so strong a part in both our lives— that contributed to the web of friendly connections which brought me to the Carswells and through the Carswells to Evelyn. Mary felt that our engagement was a triumph of match-making for her, and so it was. An old Chicago friend, the late John Nuveen, had taken to wine only after the age of 55 and thereafter acquired one of the most extensive cellars in the Middle West. He had recently given me a case of fabulous old bottles. I selected the best of these, a Romanée Conti 1934 and we four drank it with pheasants at this Leap Year supper. By that time Evelyn and I had our appetites restored, and for my part nothing I have ever drunk in a fairly long experience has approached the perfection of this wine. Mary has kept the empty bottle as a lamp base and reminder in the secluded country house she and Bob have built near Lenox.

Not long afterwards the Carswells gave the bridal dinner for us in their rented Georgetown apartment with the James Douglas, the Anthony di Bonaventuras and Evelyn's sister and brother-in-law, the Max Fellers. Judge Youngdahl, who had been governor of Minnesota, married us the next day, April 21. We all met in his chambers and he made a little speech none of us will forget on the tenderness of marriage. Before and after that day I moved everything I could cram into Evelyn's apartment on Twentieth Street, where we stayed until we left for a five month honeymoon in Europe. We spent it especially in the Mediterranean world which began at Cap d'Antibes and stretched through Florence to the Greece neither of us had ever visited. This voyage united my new life with that of the summer of 1922 when I had first felt the warmth the Riviera breathes in July and August.

35. A COMPLETE WOMAN

I love to look at a photograph in my study taken in 1914 or 1915 before Evelyn was two. It shows her seated on her mother's lap beside her two older sisters. She is looking out upon the world with her typical eager, searching and enquiring look, quick to seize the essentials of any interesting impression. Her parents were immigrants from Hungary. Her father died suddenly in a doctor's office when she was fourteen. Her mother was never able thereafter to adapt herself to the outside world, preferring her own inner world of mental illness. Although she lived on for some thirty years, she never again functioned as a mother or a person. So the four children, including a boy born after Evelyn, had to bring themselves up. Evelyn found a kind of foster mother in a teacher at the Washington Irving High School in New York to whom she feels she owes her life. When she had a burst appendix and would certainly have died of it, this teacher got her to the hospital for an emergency operation. In addition to that act of mercy, her teacher managed to impart to the adolescent girl an enthusiasm for great reading and music.

After that early help Evelyn was left on her own to discover the world and herself. She made herself at home in a world that her mother had rejected.

I don't know how she came by the natural gift of song and memory which distinguishes her from any other human being I have known who is not a professional musician. And her incredibly sure memory extends to a multitude of subjects that musicians leave aside. She combines these gifts with an extraordinary rapidity and clarity of mind, nimble and sure, witty and graceful. Most sensitive people recognize how unique is this combination. Not long after our engagement, Bernadotte Schmitt and his wife came with Constance Green to meet my fiancée. Schmitt, who had been my colleague at the University of Chicago, grew aware as Evelyn conversed over lunch, of some of the extraordinary talents with which she has endowed herself. "John," he burst out, "this is the best thing you have ever done!" I now know even better than I did then how true these words were. "There's a solution to every problem," she is prone to say. It is through this genius in meeting immediately and effectively the daily problems of existence—however small or large—that my end is being turned into a beginning.

Before she embarked on her twenties her remarkable possibilities were recognized by three distinguished Americans, all considerably older than she. The three were Buckminster Fuller, Christopher Morley and Vilhjalmur Stefansson, whom she eventually married. She never went to college. With her father dead and her mother ill, the matter was not even considered. All her relationships were established during a career as a working girl. For more than a year she sold books in the rather famous Gotham Book Mart in New York, a position she was given at the suggestion of Morley.[1] And not infrequently she went to the celebrated Romany Marie's in Greenwich Village where no alcoholic beverages were ever sold.

The recognition from distinguished men came almost without her knowing what was happening. And indeed, she has always less than recognized her own gifts of mind and body. Later she was to become a full-fledged member of the faculty of Dartmouth College, not only without a doctor's but without a bachelor's degree. And this in an ivy league place that didn't admit women as students! It must be a unique achievement, although those are not words Evelyn would use about that experience of hers in this degree-ridden world.

For part of her early years she lived in a small room of her own on the top story (the attic) of the home in Brooklyn where her family moved from New York. She was always feeling overlooked, and when her older sisters would go into town or out on dates she used to ask plaintively, "Can I come too?"

A set of complicated circumstances difficult to relate accurately, even if she were to tell them herself, led her to make at nineteen what turned out to be an unworkable marriage with Bill Baird, the famous puppeteer. He was remarkably gifted, has since reached the top of his profession, and his book on puppeteering has been translated into French and perhaps other foreign languages. But these were not the interests towards which Evelyn's life moved, although when they lived together she worked as a puppeteer under his direction with considerable success.

Stef had met her, apparently before she left high school; she does not remember exactly the circumstances. He was thirty-four years her senior, one of the most famous explorers of the modern age. In college he had lost a friend from a burst appendix and happened to come on the scene again at just the time when Evelyn was recovering from her almost fatal attack, which occurred while she was married to Baird. Because of Stef's earlier experience in losing his friend, he went to see her in the hospital. Not many years afterwards, when she had left Baird, she met him on the street and he asked what she was doing. When he found she was unemployed he suggested that she might, if she wished, come and work for him. By this time, in the later thirties he had given up active exploration and was a scholar and author, a field which he cultivated with immense results, publishing more than a score of books. Though a delight to many women, he had never married. In addition to his writing, he collected through the years what became the most comprehensive polar library in the western hemisphere, rivalled only by one in Russia. This library was to become Evelyn's province. She married Stef in 1941 when she was twenty-seven, on the eve of the United States entry into the Second World War. The library was then housed in their offices in New York on Morton Street and later at St. Luke's Place. They moved to Hanover, New Hampshire, because of an arrangement with Dartmouth College to acquire the library. The College made Evelyn librarian when the Stefansson Collection became a separate division of the Baker Library.

She had already started on a new career, without formal preparation, the career of author. Astonishing natural talents, marvelously husbanded, were the teachers.

With her almost incredible gifts of memory, she remembers every song that attracted her, songs going back to the Middle Ages and coming down to the latest jazz. She even remembers and can hum many of the great compositions of Beethoven, Bach, Mozart, Schubert, Handel and Gluck. She once performed, before her marriage to Stef, in a nightclub where she sang songs in French. The audience mistook her for a French girl, although she then knew not a word of the language, but sang the songs perfectly as she heard them, largely from records, with their French words and accent. It was only much later, after our marriage, that she learned to *speak* French in 1965, in five days in a Berlitz "Total Immersion" course she took in order to be at home with the friends and the life I had already made.

She has an enthusiasm for all the visual arts that began in her youth in New York. We find ourselves in essential agreement where this enthusiasm is concerned and the agreement has deep roots in both of us. Early in her life she had come on that Picasso etching of a woman's head that had arrested me in the Photiadès apartment in Paris in 1923 or 1924. Like me, she had the impression when *she* first saw it—unsigned as it is—that it must be by an old master.

I have never known her to be totally wrong about anything she set out to explain and her gifts of sure memory and clear perception were the basis of her career as author. The chance came just after her marriage to Stef when he turned down an offer from a publisher for a book about Alaska. He suggested that she write it instead. This seemed to her an overwhelming assignment, but she has never been one to refuse anybody for whom she cares very much. Fortunately she was not yet thirty—I mention this because I have said elsewhere that some qualified authorities hold you cannot learn to write books after that age. Her first book was published before the end of the Second World War. It is called *Here is Alaska* and it has kept afloat during the three decades that have followed. When many years after its first appearance her publishers—Scribners—became aware that Alaska would soon be made a state, they suggested she revise the book for an edition that could be brought out when statehood was granted. So she decided to visit Alaska, a detail which up to that time she had neglected. Earlier she had become a rather stunning professional photographer, and many, perhaps half, the illustrations in the new edition are photographs that she took herself. *Here is Alaska* has sold already more than 106,000 copies.[2] Nevertheless, it is a very good book.

After finishing the first edition Evelyn wrote two other books on the Arctic which have also had a considerable circulation: *Within the Circle* and *Here is the Far North*. She retained a diffidence about her gifts as a writer. When she finished the manuscript of *Within the Circle,* she asked Stef to go over the text and make suggestions. He rewrote parts extensively, although she had already submitted her version to Scribners. So she sent the new version to the editor suggesting it be substituted for the original. Somewhat to her surprise Alice Dagleish said she much preferred the book as Evelyn had written it. And that is the way it was published. Actually Stef never learned this. He did not read the book in print and she never told him what had happened.

Stef was a gifted linguist. He could handle more than half a dozen languages. But he did not know Russian and during the forties at his suggestion Evelyn decided she had better learn that tongue as the Russians published a great deal relating to the lands about the Arctic Circle. Accordingly she spent two summers at Middlebury, Vermont, where special courses were given in Russian as well as in other languages. She mastered Russian to a rather remarkable extent. When I introduced her to Marc Chagall after our marriage, it was the only language they had in common and she startled both him and Vava by her vocabulary and her good accent. Now she can offer Chagall a choice of Russian or French.

Scribners became ever more enthusiastic about Evelyn's books. In 1959 they suggested she bring out one on Russia. They sent her there and she travelled alone for six weeks in Siberia without any help except her knowledge of the language.

She combined all these activities with the very exacting social demands made on her by her marriage to Stef, who was always having to entertain "visiting firemen" and even "firewomen." She took part after 1951 in a new course of studies offered by the Dartmouth faculty, an Arctic seminar, which was enthusiastically attended by a number of Dartmouth College men. Meanwhile—I don't know how she ever managed so much—she acted as an amateur in plays at Dartmouth, did as much folksinging as she could, sang madrigals and baroque music especially through her growing friendship with Ellen Griswold (whose husband was professor in the Tuck Business School), and studied sculpturing and wood carving. Several exquisite little pieces emerged from this, although she had only a very small amount of time to give to the plastics arts. These examples are part of our Georgetown house—the subject of the next chapter.

After Stef's death in 1962, she decided to leave Hanover temporarily for a year. A member of the Dartmouth Sociology Department who was about to become director of the American Sociological Association, asked her to come to Washington to assist him in the administration of that rapidly expanding organization. He had met Evelyn in Hanover and was skillful enough to recognize how much she would be able to accomplish. She set up the offices, hired a staff of some eight or nine people, and helped plan the whole enterprise with great efficiency, mastering at the same time all the administrative and a good many of the technical sides of sociological studies in the United States. Her skill as an academic administrator in sociology reached a climax in 1964, when just before our marriage the president-elect of the Association made a trip from Cambridge to settle the annual meeting program for the coming year. He arrived in Washington in the morning, having reserved a room for two nights. Evelyn presented him with her draft of the program which with staff help she had quickly but carefully prepared. By lunch time his work was completed and in the afternoon he was on his way back to Harvard. I got the benefit because the two evenings this freed for her were ours.

Since marriage she has embarked on a new career (or more accurately careers) that moves in many directions outside the home, but is also combined with an absolutely amazing gift for handling small, mechanical matters connected with housekeeping. She can fix the electrical connections when lights go off, lay her hands magically on missing books and other objects that no one else can find, clear off a dinner table, make an omelet which reminds me of my first gastronomic experience in Paris at Larue's in 1921—all without fuss so that you are scarcely aware it's being done. Many of her gifts (particularly the electrical skill), out of my mechanical ignorance seem almost uncanny.

The first thing she turned to after completing, with a closing chapter, Stef's autobiography left almost but not quite finished at his death, was the editorship of the Great Explorer Series of books. It runs to several volumes. The series was conceived in Stef's mind but never took form in his lifetime. The plan is to describe the discovery of the major regions of the earth's surface through the accounts of the explorers. Each volume is assigned to a scholar of reputation in the area, who is enjoined to tell as much of the story as possible in the original words of the discoverers. Five volumes have appeared. Evelyn chooses the authors, edits the volumes and writes the prefaces. It is a testimonial of the recognition that is accorded her achievements that the National Archives have asked for her papers to retain as part of their Polar Archives collections. She is busy sorting out these papers and preparing them for preservation. It is another testimonial that she has been elected for a three year term as president of the Society of Woman Geographers.

At the same time the house is all torn up by workmen who are installing a small studio for Evelyn, part of a storeroom never used before, encased in great glass windows which bring the outdoors of Georgetown indoors. In this studio Evelyn is renewing her art as a sculptress and woodcarver. The pieces she manages to fashion add to the charm of the house. Her first work of renewal was a head of little Kate Carswell.

Towards the end of 1967 the Carswells embarked on the adventure of adopting what is turning out to be a most adorable and responsive baby girl, then hardly two weeks old. They have done Evelyn and me an honor most precious by making us not only Kate's godparents along with Sara Wilford, but by "adopting" us as her grandparents. Kate's adopted grandmother knits her clothes, sculpts her smiling little face and seizes any pretext to fly to New York to see her. Like me, Evelyn would have liked to be a parent; she has been as devoted and loving, and at the same time as discreet, a grandmother as any child or any parent of an exceptionally attractive child could desire.

Some twenty years ago I came on a sentence that intrigued me. It was taken by *The New Statesman* from *Hornsey Journal*: "The atomic energy latent in women, if released for construction, would save the world." Evelyn has helped me to understand the meaning. Through her I know that it could be true. For me she is a constant Source of Delight and Peace. I have begun to be as interested in her life as I have been in mine.

Now it is I who ask *her* "Can I come too?"

36. HAVEN IN WASHINGTON

If one seeks to begin life anew, a change of scene can help. It can be especially helpful when one loses by death a partner of thirty-one years. When Evelyn decided to marry me, I told her I would live anywhere so long as I could live with her. The choice should be hers, but I hoped she would not choose Chicago, where my career had its base for thirty-five years. During our five months honeymoon— in London, Yorkshire, Paris, Provence, Tuscany and Greece—we con-

sidered other possibilities. Before our return we had settled on Washington, where Evelyn had retained her comfortable, modern but very
small apartment off Dupont Circle.

After visits to Hanover and to Chicago, where I was soon to be
relieved by retirement from administrative burdens as chairman of
the Committee on Social Thought, we returned to that apartment.
We immediately set about house hunting. We decided tentatively
we did *not* want to live in Georgetown. It was too fashionable and
the prices of good houses would be beyond our range. But no sooner
had we begun to look than our amiable house agent insisted on
bringing us there in his car. He drew up alongside the place from
which we have since decided we never want to move. It was a
dreary afternoon in early November; the house was barren and cold;
being fond of warmth I was slightly repelled. I almost muffed what
turned out to be an extraordinary opportunity. Evelyn sensed from
the start the charm of this house but did not want to settle unless I
was equally pleased. So the agent showed us several other possibilities outside Georgetown. One was most spic and span and only
just constructed. I fell for it and we actually made a bid, only to be
told that the property had been sold. This proved to be inexact. A
couple of weeks later the deal our agent had thought consummated
fell through and we were again offered that newly built house. But
by this time we already owned the house we had first rejected,
an old house built between 1790 and 1810.

Failing to get the new place we had returned to Georgetown two
days later to have another look, this time with Mary Carswell. There
are few people whose imaginations are more constructive than
Evelyn's and Mary's. Before the afternoon was over they had recognized the opportunities this house would provide for our work, pictures,
books, rugs and furniture, for Evelyn's sculpture and carvings and
for the collection of objects relating to the polar regions she has
acquired over the years.

The place we decided on was under a cloud. But like the miracle
that had brought us together in New York, this worked in our favor.
Our agent felt it his duty to tell that the difficulty the owner was
having in disposing of this house arose from the fact that there had
been some eighteen months before two violent deaths. Both occupants, a childless couple, had committed suicide, one a few weeks
after the other. This was depressing the price. So we made a bid and
within a few hours, after telegraphing the owner who lived in another

town and after a little haggling, our agent got the house. Now we are forever meeting people who say how much they regret they did not buy it. Some seem to hold us responsible.

My rebirth came about under the auspices of a generation unborn when I had first lived in Europe. Through the Carswells especially my ties with this oncoming generation and with Evelyn's (for in years she is much less far removed from them than I) have multiplied and strengthened. Mary Carswell has brought us a new group of young friends. The most remarkable are Congressman James Symington and his wife Sylvia. I discovered to my surprise that both Symingtons felt as I did about serving the good and the beautiful through one's profession, a belief I missed among most of my contemporaries when Elinor and I lived in Washington almost fifty years ago.

At the time of our engagement Evelyn and I met a young couple from the Argentine, the Rafael Squirrus, who had come only recently to Washington for the Pan American Union. Through contacts established with the Argentine Embassy, he was suggested as a possible participant in the third Washington meeting of the Center for Human Understanding. A distinguished poet, with discriminating eyes for the visual arts combined with the world wide point of view the Center was seeking, he has been a staunch ally ever since the spring of 1964. Evelyn and I share the outlook of Rafael and Mary Squirru as we share the very different outlook of Robert and Mary Carswell. In the case of the Squirru new windows have been opened on a part of the world—Latin America—whose charm captured me during my brief journey to Mexico in 1948.

At the same time Washington made possible continuous contacts with the Europe to which so much of my life is linked. The arrival in 1965 of the Charles Lucets in the French Embassy was providential. He had been with Joxe and Bourbon-Busset in the direction of French cultural relations at the time I had developed those associations between the University of Paris and the Committee on Social Thought so fruitful for the international mission to which I was summoned. With the Lucets I have been able, thanks to Evelyn's support and fresh understanding of French, to take up that mission where it left off when I retired from the University of Chicago and dissolved the Center for Human Understanding. Lucet and I have decided our common concern with letters should draw us together for the rest of our lives.

Not long after the Lucets arrived I was sought out by the Irish ambassador William Fay, an admirer of Maritain, because two of Maritain's books are dedicated to me. With his wife Fay had spent years in Paris as ambassador to France. Their links to French civilization were second only to mine. Our friendship grew ever stronger in 1968 and 1969 with the help of that warmth of which the Irish at their best have the secret, only to be broken in two by Bill's sudden tragic death after a gall bladder operation when these recollections were being written. It speaks for the ease Evelyn always felt in the Fays' company, that she was never repulsed by her impression Bill's friendly feelings were enhanced by a hope he could convert her.

The England that I as a youth so much admired and had come to miss, has been brought back by Evelyn, who knew it through Stef. It has been represented wonderfully so far as we are concerned not only by former Ambassador John Freeman and his young wife, but by the Richard Scotts and the young Huxleys. Grandson of "C.P.," Scott not only revives my memory of the *Manchester Guardian* that played an important part in my European education when we read it daily from 1922 to 1926; he is also the grandson of J. A. Hobson, who impressed me so much by his words at the time of the General Strike of 1926, and whose unorthodox books on economic subjects I began to read at Cap d'Antibes in summer 1922. That was when I had *Crome Yellow* for lighter reading. Matthew Huxley is Aldous' only child. While most of his life has been spent in the United States of which he is a citizen, and several of his earlier years in the South of France, Matthew is as English for me as T. S. Eliot was American! At any rate both he and Judy his second wife, like Anna and Richard Scott, have immensely enriched the circle of a younger generation rediscovered since Evelyn and I settled in Georgetown. And this is true of several other couples not named in these "souvenirs," but to whom we have drawn close. They are part of the New Year's eve party we give each year for the Carswells.

Here in Georgetown I have only to stroll down the streets with their many trees, their old houses and their friendly neighbors to catch a glimpse of Degas' "La repasseuse" (painted in 1869) reproduced in the window of a laundry shop. The picture carries me back to the Paris streets I knew more than a generation ago when the adventures in beauty and delight that led into this search for meaning began. Few persons so late in life, whatever their condition and outlook, have been offered such an opportunity for beginning.

In the course of its near two hundred years existence our house seems to have undergone a number of transformations, though we know too little about their history. After a long period in the late nineteenth and early twentieth centuries when Georgetown residences generally were not kept up, it was substantially renovated at the time of the Second World War by Wilmarth Lewis the Yale Walpole scholar. He bought it, apparently from Ellen Lamotte (who Elinor and I knew through Emily Chadbourne) and lived here with his wife during his war service. He also bought the adjacent house, a part of this one long ago. It now belongs to our neighbors former Congressman Robert Hale and his wife. Their generous welcome when we moved in brought multiplying links with an older generation of Georgetown. In what is now the Hale house Lewis installed for a brief spell an English man of letters, Sir Herbert Read. At about that time Elinor Douglas, before her marriage to Jim, landscaped our small garden for Lewis and planted the magnolia tree which has become an essential part of the enchanting scene from our back windows now illuminated by a great Chagall mosaic.

Since we took possession at the end of 1964, Evelyn has continually had fresh ideas for developing the small property.

Except for a short, frustrating week she has never employed a decorator. She has managed almost to rebuild the interior around the pictures and other objects of art (some associated with her knowledge of the polar regions) that have come to us across half a century. The spacious high-ceilinged living room— which occupies the entire main floor and (with its two fireplaces) must once have been two separate rooms—has been turned into a home for four Derains, four Dufys, two Signacs and the classical Picasso gouache of a seated woman.[1] Years in a Chicago flat had soiled the Derains sadly, especially the "Buste de femme" on canvas. Our New York friend from whom we bought the Maillol had all four paintings cleaned by an expert, Alain G. Boissonnas, in the summer of 1968. His work has brought out the varied qualities of "Buste de femme" and of "Vase de Fleurs," with discretion that we like to think would have accorded with the idea Derain might have had for them if I had responded to his invitation in 1928 to reconsider these works in his studio.[2] At any rate Boissonnas has come as near to doing what was needed as is possible without taking liberties that no one except the artist could legitimately take.

The entrance hall, with two doors opening on this living room,

leads down to the lowest floor with its low ceilinged dining room whose
windows peer through the garden onto the mosaic. The dining room
has been made a home for Segonzac's "Green Trees," for two small
Derain heads, for the large pastel which Pascin himself retouched,
for Dufy's "Morocco" and for the Vanessa Bell painting that made
such a strong emotional impression on Evelyn the first night she came
to my California Street flat. As one is about to turn into the staircase
leading down to this dining room from the ample entrance hall, one
comes upon Bracque's beautiful colored lithograph and a Jacques
Callot etching Evelyn bought for our last anniversary, a picture
of the "Place" where Callot had a house in his native Nancy 350
years ago. Facing these at the top of the stairs is the large drawing,
"The Art Critics," in which George Grosz managed to make a work
of art out of a caricature. As one descends another Grosz is followed by
the colored drawing of Le Corbusier, and by Pascin's large sketch of
two women on a couch, the basis for at least two of his paintings.
Before entering the dining room one sees Vlaminck's colored lithograph of a French village and an oil painting of a Russian temple
by Nicholas Roerich, a picture Elinor bought from that artist in San
Francisco in September 1921 two days before she told me she would
marry me. Roerich was the director of the art school in Russia where
Marc Chagall first went to learn the great art of painting. Roerich
also cooperated with Stravinsky in the "Sacre du Printemps."

The staircase that mounts from the entrance hall to the large
bedrooms on the second floor, is an ascent even more fascinating for
our friends and visitors than the descent to the dining room. There
are two white niches; one of these seemed made for the Pre-Columbian
statue of a girl that Evelyn bought to surprise me one Christmas day;
in the other I have insisted that Evelyn retain the first work of
sculpture she ever did, "Good morning, morning!" The white walls
of the entry and the mounting steps seem designed for the Picasso
1904-05 series of etchings. That is where Evelyn has placed most of
them: "Salome with the head of John the Baptist," "Tête de femme"
(the life-sized one that awakened Evelyn and me to contemporary
art), "Le Repas frugal," "Les pauvres," "Buste d'homme," "Les deux
Saltimbanques," "Tête de femme" (a small one fuller of humanity
even than the large), "Les Saltimbanques," "L'Abreuvoir," "Au
Cirque," "Le Saltimbanque au repos," "Le Bain," "La Toilette de la
mère," "La Danse."

In these etchings are elements of the paintings (a number of which

I have seen in galleries and private collections) that Picasso did from 1903 to 1907 (including his so-called "blue" and "pink" periods), between his emancipation from the spell of Toulouse-Lautrec and his fierce break with artistic tradition in the "Demoiselles d'Avignon." I am the last person to speak for him, to determine when he found himself. But insofar as I find *myself* in him it is in the early realizations represented in this house by these blacks and whites purchased from Vollard in August 1926. Bob and Mary Carswell occupied the guest room during our absence in Hawaii in April 1965. When he was wakeful, instead of counting the holes he had played recently on a golf course as had been his wont, Bob envisaged these Picasso prints one by one as he came to know them entering the house and climbing the stairs. He found more variety to lure him to sleep than in the eighteen holes of all the golf courses he could remember. These pictures helped him to recuperate from the long and exacting months when he served Dillon at the Treasury.

The guest room they lived in is full of Pascins and leads on to a large sun-flooded bathroom. There one finds two Picasso black and whites mingled with two Rouault etchings finished in 1928,[3] a Dufy etching, an early nineteenth-century Boilly print and an eighteenth-century colored picture of English coal heavers linking me to the the years of research which started a non-conforming historian on his way. Next door to the guest room is our large bedroom with the Chagalls (of which more in the last chapter) and Evelyn's newly done bathroom in blue, from which, thanks to her records and stereo, emerges some of the loveliest music that can be obtained by artificial means. The two ample and separate bedrooms each open onto a hall with the small Léger water color. From this hall another flight of steps leads to the top floor. Evelyn has adapted the staircase and the hall above it to a mélange of our smaller original prints: the Rouault self-portrait of 1928, a Kandinsky, a Renoir, a Picasso and a Laurencin, a Dufy landscape, two Matisse heads and several Segonzacs mingled with the Albright he gave me and a remarkably successful engraving of pears by Galanis.

Meaningful for my earliest recollections are two John Sloans which Elinor had foresight to buy sometime before she died: "Turning out the Light" (1905) and "Reading in the Subway" (1926). Sloan has managed to bring into the bare and inexpensive surroundings he created a kind of tranquility (mostly missing not only from museums but from richly furnished homes) which recalls in a mysterious way a sense of happy release and fulfillment that used to come in manhood, and also in earliest infancy when I was surrounded by my mother's and my grandmother's love unadorned by luxury. "Reading in the Subway" recalls the sense of exaltation I derived endlessly from the novels I absorbed in long snatches on the subway between Cambridge and Boston and later in the London underground on my way to the British Museum, the Record Office or the Guildhall. "Turning out the Light," is one of Sloan's most famous engravings. With its vast iron-railinged bed filling the small room, it seems to connect me with my birth more than seventy years ago in a bed similarly extensive. When this picture was sent by Sloan in 1906, on invitation, to an exhibit of the American Water Color Society, it was returned as too vulgar to exhibit—a kind of rejection unthinkable in the United States today but not uncommon then. Luckily for me I was not rejected when I arrived even earlier than 1906 in the bed of which "Turning out the Light" reminds me. I must have been glad to find myself in the spare mid-western flat in Chicago on Jackson Park; the bed gave me the reassurance only a wanted child experiences, a tender pleasure that I also recapture in the happy Kelly prints left to Evelyn by her foster mother. These Kelly prints complete the cycle of pictures in our Georgetown dining room. Our American works, including an Adolf Dehn engraving, indicate how natural has been the transition from our beginnings to my last beginning.

When we came into this old Georgetown house the top floor was a nondescript clutter of three rooms and bath, where one presumes overnight guests were sometimes stowed away. It was a small apartment the interior decorator who owned the house before us had not troubled to develop. This floor has now been transformed not only to accommodate further pictures and ornaments but also to satisfy our continuous and demanding professional needs. With the help of a promising young architect, Colden Florance, Evelyn planned and completed the remodelling which has provided us with working separate from living quarters. Years ago André Siegfried devoted a column in *The Figaro* to "The Thinking Chair." The idea came from the United States but he consulted a distinguished French physician, his fellow Academician the late Pasteur Valéry-Radot. This grandson of Pasteur agreed that the ideal posture for writing, if one is to employ completely all one's faculties of thought and imagination, is a reclining one; the feet up and the entire body extended and relaxed. In the case of the historian the necessary comforts of the chaise-longue should be augmented by a large, flat movable table where notes and papers can be distributed in a beautiful disorder intelligible to the writer, a table that can be rolled over the chaise-longue and its occupant until he has access to these materials without changing his reposeful position.

Evelyn provided a "Thinking Chair." It is set in an ample study bathed by the sun and with a background of trees and sky above the rooftops. Nearer at hand, in addition to family photographs, the room is lighted by a drawing and several etchings and lithographs by Dunoyer de Segnozac and Henri Matisse. Peeping through the door is Jean Hugo's tiny watercolor of a street in Nimes and a minute lithograph of Marie Laurencin. The study also has a large desk and two further long tables for notes and papers, many shelves full of books, plus a closet and filing cabinets containing ammunition gathered over forty years from archives and books, ammunition now massed for deployment. The occupant of this composer's paradise is protected from interruption and inconvenience by the intervention of two women provided with two other smaller studies, each equipped with typewriters and other indispensables. One belongs to Evelyn; it is there that she does her writing and transacts her business, a good deal pertaining to the Society of Woman Geographers. The other is occupied with discretion and skill by Mrs. Darlene B. Hickey, who saves us both endless time and trouble. In this way I am shielded from my own vulnerability. The *travail à domicile* I lectured about all my life and have always sought to practice is mine more fully than ever before. To go to work I need only walk up one, two or three flights of stairs, depending from which floor I start.

Why have I the temerity at this late date to begin again?

When the prospects for appointments to the Committee on Social Thought were being discussed a couple of decades ago, the distinguished astronomer S. Chandrasekhar (who speaks for the scientist in *The Works of the Mind*) suggested that the qualifications for membership could be found only in seasoned scholars with long careers behind them.[4] One might justify the employment late in life of the author with words Whitehead is said to have used in connection with his appointment at Harvard: "When you can't get a very good man, you get a very old man." Unlike Whitehead the old man is *self-employed*. Since the thirties I had toyed with the idea of writing a new kind of integral history that would revolve not around political events but around the interrelations between developments in various fields of human endeavor, mainly in Europe but with comparisons with America, Asia and other parts of the world. At the beginning of the sixties Roger Shugg, then editor of the University of Chicago Press, suggested I bring together in a book some of my early studies in economic history and allied subjects hitherto available only as articles in learned reviews. I realized when doing this that my ideas concerning historical interrelations had matured considerably since 1934 when my first articles appeared. In the interval my point of view changed. At the second plenary meeting of our Center for Human Understanding I discovered that mechanization (with power derived from heat energy) had become the central concern of the emerging nations of Asia, Africa, the Near East and Latin America, as well as of the countries of Europe, North America and the former British Empire. How fast is it desirable for those nations (sometimes called "underdeveloped") to move towards mechanization and automation? What traditions do they wish to retain even if retaining them involves slower progress in achieving material facilities? Rereading my old articles I found myself not merely revising but in some cases rewriting. After more than a year's labor a new volume appeared, called *The Conquest of the Material World*. It was ready for the printers soon after I met Evelyn and was published at the time of the discovery of our Georgetown house toward the end of 1964. By revealing changes in my own thinking, the process of revising old material turned to be preparation for a new book.

Since we settled in this house the opportunity came to prepare a draft of the book. The administration of the University of Chicago honored me with an invitation to embody my researches in three series of lectures for the Committee on Social Thought in successive years pending my retirement. As a consequence a sketch exists in twelve chapters for the volume I have begun to write. The chapters in embryo are a revised and expanded version of those twelve lectures, based on new material I assembled during the thirties, forties and fifties. Along with these chapters several history books I have published since 1939—*Industry and Government, War and Human Progress* and *Cultural Foundations of Industrial Civilization*—provide scaffolds upon which parts of this new book can be built. My French *La Naissance de la civilisation industrielle et le monde contemporain* is a rough outline of the whole.[5]

Some of Paul Valéry's words have made a strong impression on me, though I never met him. He is reported to have said that for the writer no terror equals the one he experiences when confronted by a blank sheet of paper. For me that terror is now attenuated. Many of the sheets of paper at my disposal are marked up and there are plenty of them! They cannot be copied into the new book. But somewhat after the manner that the many sketches a painter makes for a major picture can help in filling the large empty canvass that attracts him, these papers provide a basis for the fresh story I want more than ever to tell now that I have Evelyn to read it.

Proust's experience as a writer, about which so much has now been unearthed, demonstrates the force of Valéry's remark. Like Valéry, Proust recognized the value of the relaxed state of mind which abundant materials of the writer's own composing can provide. One reason he undertook to translate works of Ruskin (whose outlook on medieval art so closely resembled his that he could rethink him in French without really knowing English) was because of the training this work provided for translating *himself*.[6] As a younger man he had written many essays most of which had not been published. The only work of his own printed before 1913, *Les Plaisirs et les Jours* (1896), had sold so few copies by 1922 that we bought the first edition in Cannes for a few francs before we left that town in July to escape the dipsomaniacs. Proust had even written a longish unpublished novel, *Jean Santeuil*. The scaffolds he found in the pages he had been filling since his youth eased his journey, when nearly forty he embarked in 1909-10 on his great adventure *A la Recherche du Temps Perdu* that was to become a great adventure for many others. While he might have had difficulty before the War of 1914-18[7] in qualifying for a society of professional authors in mid-America, he had rich materials of his own available. His literary life was no blank sheet.

For the attainment of the novel history, visions of which have played about in my mind during the past four decades, a scaffold, perhaps one should say a series of scaffolds, are indispensable. These I have. I don't need to invent the book; it exists; I have only to translate it. But is the necessary time, cash, inspiration and patience forthcoming? One thing is certain. If I never achieve such a history it will not be the fault of physical conditions provided by this Georgetown haven. Here wherever I move I am greeted by small works of the graphic arts which after forty-five years retain a freshness that inspires me with a desire to discover a new freshness in my inner heritage. If I am able to rethink my writings and experiences in the light of art, and build a structure with original materials from manuscripts already at hand and from reading at home and in great libraries, especially the Library of Congress, I shall not have forsaken the childhood dream which started my career.

37. CHAGALL'S FIRST AMERICAN MOSAIC

The day after Evelyn accepted my proposal of marriage I had luncheon in Chicago with young Charles Benton. Unknown to me he had visited the Stefanssons at Dartmouth some years before in connection with an Arctic project for one of his father's firms, Encyclopedia Britannica Films. In Hanover at the Stefansson Collection in Baker Library he encountered the magic of Evelyn's personality. She has a remarkable gift for conveying her widespread knowledge and enthusiasm. That gives her a capacity for teaching the young which no combination of earned degrees could provide. Young Benton became for a brief spell her pupil, an experience he could not forget. He hadn't the faintest inkling I knew Mrs. Stefansson; nor I that he did. The totally unexpected news confided to him that February day in a Chicago restaurant elated him. Although he is of naturally enthusiastic disposition, never had he betrayed to me enthusiasm approaching that aroused by my engagement.

A member of the Center for Human Understanding, Benton had taken part in the first two plenary meetings held in Washington in 1962 and 1963. Knowing Evelyn's amazing gifts, a notion beset him that she might operate the Center for the members in collaboration with me. He made a proposal to that effect at the end of the third plenary meeting held on the eve of our marriage.

There is no infallible recipe for a good marriage; the means of attaining it are as varied as are the two human beings upon whose union any marriage depends. It is possible that a collaboration between wife and husband operating an organization resembling the Center for Human Understanding might have contributed both to the health of the enterprise and the health of the marriage. But intuition, which has guided me on a number of occasions, suggested Benton's proposal would be ill-suited to Evelyn's and my marriage. Everything that has happened since we dissolved the Center as a formal organization in 1968 has confirmed that intuitive judgment.

Evelyn is very much a person in her own right. She has lost none of her freshness and hope. Of all the Americans I have known she is in many ways (although she would never claim nearly so much) the most adult. She has her own career, embarked upon long before we met. She is many years my junior and the directions in which she will move in the times ahead remain to be determined. In the interest of my happiness at least as much as hers, *she* must determine those directions. A friendly acquaintance recently opined that no doubt Evelyn collaborated in my historical research and composition. In a sense this is true but not in the sense this acquaintance was assuming. Freshness and hope are contagious and every day Evelyn's restore mine. The warmth and modest assurance she transmits has buttressed my optimism. And by providing me with conditions as nearly perfect as possible for working, she has made me the greatest gift a wife can make. That bouncy old French professor André Siegfried, with his prolific published output, was fond of repeating a maxim of his invention: "There are three kinds of wives: those who force you to work; those who keep you from working; and there is my wife." If she were classifiable, Evelyn would fit the third category.

The Georgetown house is a haven for her as much as for me. And both of us like to think it is a haven for others we love and want to help, and that it might become one for others whom we can never know but to whose lives we would like to contribute the optimism we feel in each other. The prospect of making such a haven and uniting that endeavor with a similar one in the South of France, we owe to Marc and Vava Chagall. Many friends and acquaintances have helped Evelyn and me to reach the place where we find ourselves after more than eight years together. None have done so much as the Chagalls to teach us how this home might serve the future of humanity. My friendship with Chagall has entered a third stage.

A year before the Carswells introduced me to Evelyn, the two Chagalls and I made a recording. A man named Louis ("Studs") Terkel (who as a student once followed my lectures in "economic history") came on specially to Washington for the second plenary meeting of the Center because Chagall was to participate. Terkel operates a small radio station (WIMT) heard only in the Chicago area. He got the three of us together, after the public sessions had ended, in a private room at the Mayflower Hotel where most of the Center's delegates were staying and recorded our conversation. That was broadcast in Chicago during two successive half-hour periods. In this recording Marc explained a plan he already had for a museum in Nice to house the sketches, colored lithographs and pictures that comprise his "Message Biblique." That message is the work of a lifetime. As a child brought up in Vitebsk, Chagall saw the world through the colors of the Old Testament. Biblical themes absorbed him as they have ever since. He began the works which form the "Message Biblique" at least as early as 1925. After the Second World War, his return to France in 1947 and his marriage to Vava in 1952, he completed illustrations for the Bible between 1952 and 1956.

Towards the end of this period, when he was almost seventy, he began to be fascinated by the possibility of renewing the great traditions of the glaziers art as he had first observed that in the twelfth and thirteenth century windows of Chartres Cathedral. Church windows continued to be works of art for another 250 years as painting on glass developed during an age when painting influenced many media. Then, after the mid-sixteenth century, the arts of fashioning colored glass windows largely disappeared from Europe. The two ceramics Chagall did for the chapel in the Plateau d'Assy in Haute Savoie were a preparation for his work in glass. That began in 1957 in connection with the invitation he received for two stained glass windows in the Cathedral of Metz. In 1959, at the time of the first comprehensive retrospective exhibition of his pictures held in the Louvre, he was persuaded to turn aside from the Metz windows (which he finished after 1962) by the invitation to prepare the now very famous Jerusalem windows. They were completed during 1960-61 and installed in February 1962. Their subject is the twelve tribes of Israel.

Virtually all of Chagall's magnificent glass work is based on themes derived from the Old Testament. It is therefore a continuation of his Message Biblique, although the glass windows themselves he continues to create are not destined principally for the Chagall Museum at Nice. Besides the Jerusalem windows and those at Metz, there are now some most beautiful ones in the Frauen Kirche in Zurich, and an exquisite series which he did for the small Rockefeller chapel near Tarrytown, in addition to the window in memory of Dag Hammarskjold in the United Nations building in New York undertaken in the cause of peace.

The Jerusalem windows were in his mind when the three of us—he, Vava and myself—made the recording for Terkel in 1963. As we are told by Jean Leymarie in his account of those windows published in 1962, Chagall intended them as "an artistic monument" with "a universal religious message . . . transcending the Judaic faith . . . [with the] promise . . . of a new, complete and eternal humanism." [1] It was the search for that by the Center for Human Understanding that led him with Vava, only a few months after installation of his windows in Jerusalem, to suggest himself as a member. In speaking of the Jerusalem windows in the Terkel interview he was anxious to stress that universal meaning. He asked me to translate for the Chicago audience his intention to express a message for all. He had me explain again that the Jerusalem windows are not in any special sense for Israel but for *humanity*. As he declared in his talk to our Center in the spring of 1963, the way towards the eternal city is the way of love. This is what unites us and explains the convergence of our two efforts since 1964.

The Chagall museum at Nice is almost finished. It will provide a permanent resting place for the "Message Biblique." A large mosaic now in preparation will be set in the building and that will contain lecture and seminar rooms. Chagall has frequently asked if I would participate in the work of instruction on behalf of universalism and love that he hopes will be carried on there. I have always assured him that, within the limits of my capacities, I shall be glad to.

We have come to know each other better during the sixties, during and since his 1963 visit to the Center when the three of us were much together not only in Washington but also in New York after I met their boat. Sara di Bonaventura asked with some hesitation whether it would please them to see her parents' private collection of paintings. Sara's hesitation arose because they then had no Chagall. Sara and her husband called at the Drake Hotel and took us to the Whitney house where her mother was waiting. As Marc entered he found himself confronting a Picasso. Turning to me he asked, "What do you think of that Spaniard?" I answered naturally: "I see only Chagall." That got us all off to a good start.

Since our marriage Evelyn has contributed, through the growth of a new and deeper friendship *à quatre*, towards a possible fulfillment of hopes for the future we four share. The Chagalls have adored her from the start. Soon after they first met he said to me, "Thank you for your wife." Chagall's plans for our Georgetown haven are partly a result of our marriage. They are a more constructive contribution to the cause the Center for Human Understanding stands for than

Evelyn could have made if she had been drafted to perpetuate that organization.

Thomas Hoban Alcock of Chicago has become one of the most respected and effective attorneys in the Middle West. He did a great deal to sustain me after Elinor died and he was one of the first friends to whom I confided my engagement. After some altogether logical shock over its haste, he has now become one of Evelyn's foremost admirers. We owe him the genial idea of the John and Evelyn Nef Foundation established in 1965. It absorbs such activities of the Center for Human Understanding as we have been able to maintain. To our great honor the Chagalls have joined with Alcock, Carswell and ourselves to form the board of six directors for this small Foundation. This establishes the link between the Nice Museum and Georgetown both Chagalls and we have been seeking. How was this association brought about?

On the occasion of Evelyn's fifty-fifth birthday in July 1968, the Chagalls joined us for a prolonged sojourn at Cap d'Antibes, that Mediterranean paradise of my youth. There leisurely discussions had often been carried on with friends whose names have appeared in these pages, among them the Chagalls.[2] But the summer of 1968 was the first occasion on which the Chagalls came for a stay. They have come every summer since. It was during the first of these three week sojourns that our common hopes began to take more concrete form. One evening this Riviera retreat flowered into something approaching the Abbaie de Thélème of Rabelais' imagination, enlightened not only by the beauty of Chagall's art, as he sketched and wrote in Russian on his memoirs, but by beautiful music. Elaine Shafer and her husband Efrem Kurtz, the conductor, had been guests at the Cap for two years. One afternoon the cabin "in the woods," that André Sella had for years reserved for me and that the Chagalls now always share with us, became the setting for a "concert champetre."

Elaine Shafer is perhaps the most delicate flutist of our times. She tuned in more and more harmoniously with Evelyn and with Chagall, whose delight in great music, above all that of Mozart, is an unending resource in which he loves to have his friends participate. During the happy hour that ends a July day of swimming at the Cap, where the pine and olive trees draw from the air the dampness of the sea and combine with the dry scent of thyme and of many varieties of flowers, Elaine played her wondrous flute, with the feminine modesty that she feels, to the Master and to his four companions—her husband,

Vava, Evelyn and me. The strains of Mozart, Bach and the most beautiful Gluck—the "dance of the sprites" from Orfeo and Eurydice—diffused outdoors through the garden, were given varied qualities such as cannot be compressed within the confines of a concert hall. Chagall caught them to perfection in the mosaic he later composed.

During this visit of 1968 at the Cap, we planned the trip which brought the Chagalls to New York and Georgetown the following November. We were at Kennedy Airport to meet their plane on a Sunday noon. The festivities began at the Carswells with a party for Kate. The Chagalls had arrived in time for her first birthday and the four of us were chosen to participate in the celebration in the room where Evelyn and I had met.

The Salle Chagall in our Georgetown house contains only his pictures, the first two that I had bought in Paris in 1925, a colored lithograph from his "Arabian Nights" series, further pictures he has given to me and to Evelyn—"Petit Composition pour John (1957)," "Bon Anniversaire, Evelyn Nef (1964)," "Bon Souvenir, Evelyn (1969)," "Bon Anniversaire, Evelyn (1970)," "Pour Evelyn bon anniversaire" (1972), and our wedding announcement on which he sketched his congratulations. And in the living room downstairs are displayed two works in book form which are inscribed to us in the colors of his art: Marc Chagall, *Monotypes 1961-1965*, published by Gerard Cramer in Geneva; and exemplaire no. XVIII of *Vitraux pour Jerusalem*.

The Chagalls came to the United States partly to attend at Pierre Matisse's New York gallery the vernissage of an exhibition of paintings Marc had done during the three previous years. They came also to visit our Georgetown house (where they spent a week in the Salle Chagall) to see how he could improve it. The interior as Evelyn had arranged it with the pictures distributed through the various rooms, along the halls and the walls of the four storied staircases satisfied Chagall. He refused to touch the house but announced that he would do a mosaic as a kind of frame for the small garden, an integral part of the property. He completed the *maquette* in the summer of 1970 and unveiled it in his studio when Evelyn and I came to lunch before leaving Provence. In the following years the mosaic was completed under his direction at Biot (a few miles from the Chagall home at Saint Paul de Vence) by Lino Melano, the Ravenna craftsman Marc employs. The ten parts were then packed and sent by air to our Georgetown garden, where workmen were building a wall

The Chagall mosaic in the garden of the Nef home; Mrs. Evelyn
Stefansson Nef is at the left. (Photo by Joan Davidson)

to receive this work. It brings the notes of Orfeo, the magical colors of the Mediterranean and the soft air of southern France, as Chagall has captured them, to the United States. The Chagalls followed for the unveiling, presided over by the French Ambassador. In a way this great mosaic, Chagall's first in America, is the gift of the France which provided the setting in which our friendship matured.[3] It is a frieze of fantastic beauty inspired by Gluck's music (as played that afternoon beside the cabin in the woods at Cap d'Antibes), by the six year asylum the United States provided Marc during the war, and by Evelyn's and my story as lovers. The refugees are streaming across the Atlantic towards rescue among the skyscrapers, and the work is addressed, in the cause of love, to all humanity.

Like the art of stained glass, mosaic is an artistic medium Marc has perfected since his marriage to Vava. He has chosen this medium partly because he is aiming at the greatest possible permanence for his message on behalf of humanity. As a great Renaissance painter observed, mosaic is the material of Eternity. And in the subject of our mosaic (as in that he had undertaken in 1967 for the Law School of Nice University[4]) Chagall has enlarged the scope of his message to include Greek mythology. Here is Orfeo with his lute, with the three graces and Pegasus the winged horse. This is a further expression of the desire we four share to humanize the technocratic order which has taken possession of the world. It is our mutual hope that this masterpiece will help establish a permanent link between Nice, Washington and Chicago, and that the whole property will be used for purposes foreshadowed in these "souvenirs."

Is it possible to find—in spite of all the violence that defiles mankind, and in the midst of automation, televised commercials, computerized calculations and journeys to outer space—new opportunities for the individuals who are seeking love and tenderness and beauty in the service of the good? Is it possible, as a result of the leadership of a few individuals, to nourish world community? Those questions may have to be answered in the affirmative if the human experiment is to continue, for violence has become a luxury humanity can no longer afford. It is our hope that this house of Evelyn's and mine as eventually owned and administered by the University of Chicago will emphasize the need for affirmative answers. One of the purposes of the Nef Foundation has been to "carry on creative work in literature, the visual arts, music or architecture." The Georgetown house is intended to provide "a place where scholars from any country can pursue the search for truth, unity and justice free from dominating nationalistic traditions and interests."

I have not been able to create the Island that took form in my inner life as a child—an Island where great pictures and works of music and poetry flourish without publicity. Yet by the grace of Evelyn and the Chagalls, I live in a house and garden created in the image of that childhood dream. After we are gone this Georgetown haven could offer a few persons (wisely chosen for terms of residence appropriate to their creative needs) favorable conditions of existence for the pursuit of beauty. The large drawing room on the main floor capable of seating as many as a hundred, and the garden in good weather, could provide a meeting place for groups concerned with the formation of a worldwide realm of general discourse and with the humanization of living for which considerable numbers of persons in the contemporary world are longing and that the Committee on Social Thought was founded to nourish. Here in that drawing room and garden there is sufficient space for meetings of the Supreme Court of Humanity envisaged by the Center for Human Understanding.

REFERENCES

CHAPTER 1

1. See Nef, *The United States and Civilization* (University of Chicago Press), 2nd ed., Chicago, 1967. Cf. William Temple, *Nature, Man and God*, London 1935, pp. 158-64 and *passim*.

CHAPTER 2

1. He worked most of his life on a book about Eleanor of Aquitaine. But, alas, Amy Kelly did a better book on the same subject and it came out at about the same time. 2. See below, Chapter 35. 3. See below, pp. 176-77. 4. See below, pp. 197-98. 5. See below, Chapter 28. 6. See below, p. 290.

CHAPTER 4

1. These facts have been arrived at with help from the memory of the Sella family, particularly of André Sella's brother and of his two sisters, Madame Henry Mercier and Mademoiselle Irene Sella (cf. below, p. 323). It has sometimes been stated incorrectly that the Gerald Murphys came with Picasso and his first wife in the summer of 1922. That was a year later, in 1923, the *second* year that the hotel had a small summer clientele.

2. See below, p. 34.

3. For her experiences after marriage see her *Letters and Notes*, Vol. I (privately printed, Los Angeles, 1953) which I edited. And her papers preserved in the Archives of the University of Chicago.

4. She died within a few months.

5. My rewritten version is now Chapter 3 of *The Conquest of the Material World*, Chicago, 1964.

CHAPTER 5

1. See below, pp. 34-36.

2. We still have it in our Georgetown house, see Chapter 36.

CHAPTER 6

1. See below, pp. 34-36.

2. Edwin Wilson had a distinguished career and became an ambassador himself, although I have not seen him since our meetings in Vienna.

CHAPTER 8

1. These appear as a group in the wonderful mosaic now in our Georgetown garden (see below, pp. 323-25).

2. See the paperback edition of *The Works of the Mind*, Chicago, 1966.

CHAPTER 9

1. See below, Chapters 30 and 37. 2. Below, Chapter 21.

3. Elinor Castle Nef, *Letters and Notes*, Volume I, privately printed, Los Angeles, 1953, p. 120.

4. Cf. below, page 252.

CHAPTER 10

1. We own another imposing Pascin pastel, a bust (a trifle more than life-sized) of a large boned woman. Elinor and I bought that in Los Angeles during the Great Depression of 1929-33, when its owner seems to have been hard up for money. Evelyn

has at last found a frame worthy of the picture. For two other small Pascins which I acquired in 1926 before leaving Europe, see below, p. 93.

CHAPTER 11

1. See below, Chapters 28 and 33.   2. See below, Chapter 13.
3. *Albertine Disparue*, Paris, 1925, vol. ii, pp. 129-33.

CHAPTER 12

1. Cf. below, pp. 283-84, 286-87, for the role which "civilization," in the original meaning of the word, has played in my academic work.

CHAPTER 13

1. Along with a great many other pictures by Derain, this belongs to a Frenchman who lives in Troyes, I am told.

2. I had learned from experience with archivists that it is dangerous to the success of one's search to take "no" for an answer. For example at Newcastle-on-Tyne the town clerk had assured me we had wasted our time in making the trip north from London; there was nothing relevant to my history of coal in the municipal archives. Yet after consoling us over luncheon with a Berncastler Doktor 1921—the finest bottle of Moselle I ever tasted—he discovered, through me, that in those very archives, right under his nose, were some completely fresh manuscripts of coal shipments nowhere else to be found.

3. Nor is the opinion that Guillaume offered in his letter at variance with the view of Marc Chagall concerning these four Derains. Chagall has a high considered opinion of the entire collection of pictures in this Georgetown house. That partly accounts for the mosaic in the garden, the first mosaic he has done for the United States. (See below, Chapter 37).

4. Cf. below, pp. 95 sq.

CHAPTER 14

1. *Cahiers d'Art*, Paris, 1927, no. 6.   2. See below, p. 266.   3. See below, pp. 123-24.

CHAPTER 15

1. I am not clear whether this name was derived from Chagall's painting with that title, done in 1911, now in the Musée d'Art Moderne.

2. See below, pp. 99. Cf. Appendix B. ("French culture in its Relation to the Economic Civilization").

CHAPTER 16

1. *Religion and the Study of Man*, Houston, 1961.   2. See below, Appendix A.

CHAPTER 17

1. T. S. Eliot, *Poems Written in Early Youth*, London, 1967, pp. 34-35, 42-43.

2. As an additional concession, I was accorded the privilege of using Taussig's *Principles of Economics*, instead of Bye, during the other half year!

3. This is no longer true. Part III of my coal book has been partly utilized—to excellent purpose—by Eric Kerridge in *The Agricultural Revolution*, London, 1967.

CHAPTER 18

1. Lord Russell's version is in his autobiography.

CHAPTER 20

1. Published in 1947, and as a Phoenix paperback, with my explanatory prefaces, in 1966 by the University of Chicago Press.

CHAPTER 21

1. I had liked Hoover ever since my Harvard days, when in 1920 I was secretary

of the local Hoover-for-President Club, and was later to do a broadcast with him on Agricola's book *De re Metallica* which he and his wife had translated in London from the Latin edition of 1556 before the 1914 War.

2. *Letters and Notes, Volume I*, privately published, Los Angeles, 1953.

3. See pp. 103-04.

4. The publication of Quentin Bell's biography of Virginia Woolf adds much to our knowledge of her. It rather confirms the comparison I have made between her illness and that of my first wife, whose complex however was an excessive desire, not to die, but to live.

5. See above, p. 61. 6. *The Conquest of the Material World*, 1964. Ch. 4.

CHAPTER 22

1. The lecture was published in *The Review of Politics* (VIII, no. 2, pp. 192-222 (1946)) by the founder of that journal, Russian born Waldemar Gurian. Another refugee from tyranny, first the Communist and then the Nazi, Gurian was a continual guest at meals in our flat on Dorchester Avenue. He regarded our interdisciplinary faculty, the Committee on Social Thought, as the most creative initiative in American higher learning, which was not displeasing. Among the numerous foreign visitors who passed through Chicago to participate in the work of the Committee, I was able to help him find contributors for his review.

2. See Chapter 32.

3. Nef, *The United States and Civilization*, 2nd edit., Chicago, 1967, pp. 359-61.

4. *Ibid.*, pp. 359-61 and *passim*. 5. See Appendix B.

CHAPTER 23

1. See Chapter 37. 2. See Chapter 37.

CHAPTER 24

1. Cf. above p. 27. 2. See above, pp. 8-9.

3. If my memory is correct, she was the celebrated Henry Luce's sister.

CHAPTER 25

1. See below, pp. 285-87.

2. Pareto, *The Mind and Society*, New York, 1935, Vol. IV, pp. 1433-4, 1455, 1460n., F. Simiand, *Recherches anciennes et nouvelles sur le movement* . . *des prix*, 1932, pp. 421, 424 sqq.

3. *History of the Reformation*, Austin trans., London, 1905, p. x.

4. See above, p. 64. 5. See below, p. 261.

6. See Nef, *Cultural Foundations of Industrial Civilization*, Cambridge (Eng.) 1958, pp, 139-145.

7. The late Crane Brinton thought I had partially succeeded. "Mr. Nef," he wrote, "has made a rare combination of what the profession calls 'economic history' and 'intellectual history,' a combination which results, quite obviously, in an enrichment for history pure and simple." (*New York Herald-Tribune*, December 24, 1950).

8. See above, pp. 106-07. 9. See below, Appendix A.

CHAPTER 26

1. See above, p. 35. 2. Cf. below, Chap. 29.

CHAPTER 27

1. Like the English version of his book on natural law (see below, p. 218) *Reflections on America* is generously dedicated to me.

2. We gave one of the etchings to Evelyn's nephew and his bride for their wedding, so there are now only *five* in our house.

3. See below, Appendix A ("Péguy and the Spirit of France").

4. Joseph Garlinghouse was the first sheriff of Ontario County, New York. An older sister of my grandmother married Orville Comstock, who built and owned a famous hotel at Avon Springs, and later moved to Rochester. After his first wife died, he married Mary Garlinghouse, my grandmother. She brought up his two children, one of whom (Mrs. Alice C. Smith) was adopted, while the other (Pinckney) died in adolescence. My mother Louise Bates Comstock, much younger than either, was the only child of Orville Comstock's second marriage. (This information has been verified through Harriet Parsons, of Toronto, Canada, who is Alice Smith's granddaughter, and for whose help I am grateful).

5. See Nef, *The Conquest of the Material World*, Chicago, 1964, Chap. 9.

CHAPTER 28

1. See the discussion of cultural "nationalism" by Jacques de Bourbon-Busset, who once directed the cultural division of the French Foreign Office, in *Towards World Community* (ed. John Nef), The Hague, 1968, pp. 92-95.

2. There is apparently no text for this introduction, but two of Febvre's speeches in a similar vein concerning my work are preserved in the Archives of the University of Chicago (see below, p. 229).

3. See below, Appendix A.

4. For these details I am grateful to Madame Sarrailh, who supplied me with a genealogical chart of the Richelieu family.

5. See below, pp. 282 ff.   6. See below, Chapter 33.

7. The text of this unpublished speech is in the Archives of the University of Chicago, together with my reply and another of Febvre's speeches about my work apparently given in 1953.

8. It has since been published in Japanese and Italian translations, but no American or English publisher has offered to have it rendered into English.

CHAPTER 29

1. See below, p. 250.

2. Regarding Eliot's appointment see Chap. 31.

3. Moritz Busch, *Bismarck: Some Secret Pages of His History*, London, 1898, vol. i, p. 403.

4. Shirley Letwin, *The Pursuit of Certainty*, Cambridge, England, 1965.

5. Before coming to the United States he had been President of the University of Nancy and later Director of Higher Learning in France.

6. See above, p. 232.

7. The Encyclopedia Universalis, a publication started with the help of American money provided through the Encyclopedia Britannica.

CHAPTER 30

1. See below, p. 315.   2. See below, Chapter 33.

3. Out of print, but mimeographed copies can be pruchased from University Microfilms Limited, Ann Arbor, Michigan.

CHAPTER 31

1. T. S. Eliot, *Knowledge and Experience in the Philosophy of F. H. Bradley*, London, 1964.

2. December, 1950, pp. 3-16; Spring, 1951, pp. 191-203; Summer, 1951, pp. 285-297; Fall, 1951, pp. 361-375.

3. Leonard Woolf, *Beginning Again*, Hogarth Press, London, 1964, pp. 241-45.

4. A matter touched on in my *Conquest of the Material World*, chap. 7.

5. In 1961 he explained the circumstances under which he originally wrote it (T. S. Eliot, *To Criticize the Critic*, 1965, p. 15).

CHAPTER 32

1. Later Kay Fanning.   2. Mrs. W. R. Castle.

3. Cf. Nef, *The United States and Civilization*, 2nd ed., Chicago, 1967, part II.

CHAPTER 33

1. Nef, *The United States and Civilization*, 2nd ed., Chicago, 1967, pp. 35-37.

2. See above, p. 190.   3. It is unpublished, see Appendix B.

4. Now Mrs. Ronald Wilford.   5. See below, Appendix B.

6. See above, p. 47.

CHAPTER 35

1. W. G. Rogers, *Wise Men Fish Here*, New York, 1965, p. 195; and see her photograph with Christopher Morley at the Book Mart in the early thirties.

2. She has now rewritten the book for a *third* edition in 1973.

CHAPTER 36

1. See above, p. 91.   2. See above, p. 86.

3. And there are three additional Rouault etchings not hung—all five are from the series "La petite Banlieux."

4. Cf. above, p. 187.   5. Cf. above, p. 236.

6. *Marcel Proust and His Time* (1871-1922), London, 1955, p. 62.

7. The first volume, *Du Coté de chez Swann*, appeared in 1913, but it was not until 1919 that the volumes of *A la Recherche* began to multiply and publication was not completed until 1926, four years after Proust's death.

CHAPTER 37

1. Marc Chagall, *Vitraux pour Jerusalem*, Monte Carlo, 1962, p. 34.

2. See above, p. 251. André Sella died in June 1970 at the age of eighty after selling the property, with the Hotel du Cap and Eden Roc. It had been in the hands of the Sella family for almost a century and they had owned it outright for over half that time. The original proprietors had failed in 1870 with the outbreak of the Franco-Prussian War. The Hotel then languished until in 1887 André Sella's father, Antoine Sella, came from Italy to make a success of the venture. He ran it until 1931 when the management was assumed for the next forty years by André Sella (F, de Caigny, *De la Villa Soleil à l'Hotel du Cap*, privately printed for André Sella in 1969—a short essay which Sella asked me to translate into English for his friends and clients).

3. Evelyn has described the story of its installation, in which she played the principal part, in the *Washington Post Potomac Magazine*, January 23, 1972.

4. *Le Message d'Ulysse*, Antibes, 1969.

A BIBLIOGRAPHY OF THE AUTHOR'S PUBLISHED WORKS

The Rise of the British Coal Industry, 2 Vols. London: Routledge & Sons, 1932; reprinted 1966.

Industry and Government in France and England, 1540-1640. American Philosophical Society Memoirs, Vol. XV. Philadelphia, 1940. (Reprinted by Russell, 1968. Paperback edition by Cornell University Press, 1957.)

The United States and Civilization. University of Chicago Press, 1942. New edition extensively rewritten, 1967.)

The Universities Look for Unity. New York: Pantheon Books, 1943.

La Route de la guerre totale. Cahiers de la Fondation Nationale des Sciences Politiques. Paris; Librairie Armand Colin, 1949.

War and Human Progress. Harvard University Press, 1950, Reprinted Russell 1968. (Paperback edition by Harper Torchbooks, under title *Western Civilization Since the Renaissance,* 1963; reprinted by W. W. Norton under original title in 1968.)

La Naissance de la civilisation industrielle et le monde contemporain. Paris: Librairie Armand Colin, 1954.

Cultural Foundations of Industrial Civilization. Cambridge University Press, 1958. (Paperback edition by Harper Torchbooks, 1960.)

Religion and the Study of Man. Smith Lecture in History, University of St. Thomas, Houston, Texas, 1961.

A la recherche de la civilisation. Paris: Presses Universitaires, 1963. (English version — *A Search for Civilization.* Chicago: Henry Regnery Co., 1962.)

The Conquest of the Material World, Essays on the Coming of Industrialism. University of Chicago Press, 1964. (Paperback edition by Meridian, 1967.)

PAPERBACK EDITIONS

Industry and Government in France and England, 1540-1640. Ithaca, New York: Great Seal Books, Cornell University Press, 1957.

Cultural Foundations of Industrial Civilization. New York: Harper Torchbooks The Academy Library, 1960.

Western Civilization Since the Renaissance: Peace, War, Industry and the Arts. New York: Harper Torchbooks/ The Academy Library, 1963. (Original title — *War and Human Progress*)

The Conquest of the Material World, Essays on the Coming of Industrialism. Cleveland: Meridian Books, 1967.

War and Human Progress. New York: W. W. Norton, 1968.

FOREIGN TRANSLATIONS

La Conquista del Mundo Material. Translated by José Luis Etcheverry. Buenos Aires, Argentina: Editorial Paidos, 1969.

Arabic translation of *Cultural Foundations of Industrial Civilization.* Translated by Dr. Mahmoud Zayed. Beirut, Lebanon: Dar Assakafah, 1962.

Fundamentos Culturales de la Civilizacion Industrial. Translated by Noemi S. Caletti. Buenos Aires, Argentina: Editorial Paidos, 1964.

Les Fondements culturels de la civilisation industrielle. Paris: Payot, 1964.

La Guerre et le progrès humain. Colmar & Paris: Editions Alsatia, 1954. (Contains improvements not in English editions.)

Japanese translation, *Industry and Government in France and England, 1540-1640.* Translated by Professor Tetsuji Sumida, Hiroshima, Japan, 1958.

Japanese translation, *La Naissance de la civilisation industrielle et le monde contemporain.* Editions Mirai Sha a Tokio, 1963.

L'Origine della Civilta Industriale e il Mondo Contemporaneo. Translated by

Maria Luisa de Roberto. Milan: Giuffre Editore, 1968.

Estados Unidos y la Civilizacion, Translated by Eduardo Prieto, Paidos, Buenos Aires, 1972.

BOOKS EDITED BY JOHN U. NEF

Letters and Notes Volume I, by Elinor Castle Nef. Los Angeles: Anderson & Ritchie, 1953.

Bridges of Human Understanding, based on meetings of the Center for Human Understanding held in Washington, D. C., May 2-4, 1963. New York: University Publishers, 1964. (Authorized facsimile produced by microfilm-xerography by University Microfilm, Ann Arbor, Michigan, 1969.)

Towards World Community. World Academy of Art and Science No. 5, The Hague: Dr. W. Junk N.V., 1968.

CONTRIBUTIONS TO BOOKS

"English and French Industrial History After 1540 in Relation to the Constitution," in *The Constitution Reconsidered* (ed. Conyers Read), Columbia University Press, 1938. (Paperback—Revised Edition with a new Preface by Richard B. Morris, New York: Harper Torchbooks, 1968.)

"War and the Early Industrial Revolution," in *Economic Problems of War and Its Aftermath*. Ed. C. W. Wright. Chicago, 1942.

"The 'Industrial Revolution' Reconsidered," *Science, Philosophy and Religion, Third Symposium*, N. Y., 1943.

"Relations Between the Intellect and the Great Peace 1815-1914," in *Approaches to National Unity* (eds. Lyman Bryson, Louis Finkelstein, Robert M. MacIver), New York: Conference on Science, Philosophy and Religion in their Relation to the Democratic Way of Life, 1945.

Preface, *The Works of the Mind* (ed. Robert B. Heywood). University of Chicago Press, 1947. (Paperback— preface and new foreword, *The Works of the Mind*. Phoenix Books, University of Chicago Press, 1966.)

"The Goal of American Education," *Goals for American Education* (eds. Lyman Bryson, Louis Finkelstein, Robert M. MacIver), New York: Conference on Science, Philosophy and Religion in their Relations to the Democratic Way of Life, 1950.

"The Industrial Revolution Reconsidered," *Studi in Onore di Gino Luzzatto*, Milan: Dott. A. Giuffre, Editore, 1949.

"Mining and Metallurgy in Medieval Civilization," Chapter VII, *The Cambridge Economic History*, Vol. II, 1952. (New revised edition in press 1973.)

"The Genesis of Industrialism and of Modern Science, 1560-1640," *Essays in Honor of Conyers Read*, University of Chicago Press, 1952.

"The Industrial Revolution Reconsidered," *The Making of English History*, Book I, New York, 1952.

"The Universities and World Community," *Three Aspects of University Development Today*, Paris: International Universities Bureau, 1953.

"Les Universités et la communauté mondiale," *Trois aspects du développement de l'université d'aujourd'hui*, Paris: Bureau International des Universités, 1953.

"Essence de la civilisation industrielle," *Eventail de l'Histoire Vivante*, Lucien Febvre, I, Paris: Librairie Armand Colin, 1953.

"Prices and Industrial Capitalism in France and England, 1540-1640," *Enterprise and Secular Change*, Lane and Riemersma, Homewood, Ill., 1953.

"Lesson from History," *This I Believe*, Edited by Edward R. Murrow, New York: Simon & Schuster, 1954.

"The Progress of Technology and the Growth of Large-Scale Industry in Great Britain, 1540-1640," and "Prices and Industrial Capitalism in France and England, 1540-1640," *Essays in Economic History*, ed. E. M. Carus-Wilson, Aberdeen, 1954.

"Memoir of Mabel Wing Castle," *My Mother's Reminiscences*, Elinor Castle Nef, Chicago, 1954.

"A History of Coal and Its Relation to

the Development of Technology and Science," *A History of Technology,* Vol. III, ed. Charles Singer, London, 1956.

"L'Amérique du Nord," *L'Encyclopedie Francaise, Tome XI, L'Univers Politique,* 1957.

"Le problème de la guerre: aspects politiques, techniques et culturels," *Centre d'Etudes Culturels de Nice, Science et Technique,* ed. Louis Trotabas, 1958.

"Technology and Civilization," *Studi in Onore di Amintore Fanfani,* Volume V, Milan: Dott. A. Giuffre, Editore, 1962.

"The Historical Unreality of the Cold War," *Conflict Resolution and World Education,* ed. Stuart Mudd, The Hague: Dr. W. Junk Publishers, 1966.

"L'Avenir de la Communauté Atlantique," *Mélanges à la Mémoire de Jean Sarrailh,* Centre de Recherches de l'Institut d'Etudes Hispaniques, Paris, 1966.

"Postep techniczny a rozwoj wielkiego przemyslu w Anglii (1540-1640)" in *Geneza nowozytnej Anglii,* ed. Antoni Maczak. Warszawa: Panstwowe Wydawnictow, 1968.

"World," "Culture and Civilization," "Nation," "Capitalism," "Fatherland," in *Prophetic Voices, Ideas and Words on Revolution,* ed. Ned O'Gorman, New York: Random House, 1969. (Paperback edition).

"Political, Technological, and Cultural Aspects of War," in *The Critique of War,* ed. Robert Ginsberg, Chicago, 1969.

"Industriel: La Civilisation industrielle," *Encyclopaedia Universalis,* Paris, 1971.

"L'Esprit comme cause de la révolution industrielle," chez Denoël, Paris, 1973.

ARTICLES

"Dominance of the Trader in the English Coal Industry in the Seventeenth Century," *Journal of Economic and Business History,* I, 1929.

"The History of an English Village," *Journal of Political Economy,* XL, 1932.

"Richard Carmarden's 'A Caveat for the Quene' (1570)," *ibid.,* XLI, 1933.

"The Progress of Technology and the Growth of Large-Scale Industry in Great Britain, 1540-1640," *Economic History Review,* V, 1934. Reprinted in various anthologies.

"James Laurence Laughlin (1850-1933)," *Journal of Political Economy,* XLII, 1934.

"A Comparison of Industrial Growth in France and England from 1540 to 1640," *Journal of Political Economy,* XLIV, 1936.

"Note on the Progress of Iron Production in England, 1540-1640," *ibid.,* June, 1936.

"Thoughts on the Abdication of King Edward VIII," *The Christian Register,* Jan. 7, 1937.

"Prices and Industrial Capitalism in France and England, 1540-1640," *Economic History Review,* VII, No. 2, May, 1937.

"American Universities and Western Civilization," *The Review of Politics,* I, No. 3, July, 1939.

"In Defense of Democracy," *General Magazine and Historical Chronicle,* Oct., 1939.

"A Social Science Objective," *The University of Chicago Magazine,* Nov., 1939.

"On the Future of American Civilization," *The Review of Politics,* July, 1940.

"L'Industrie et l'Etat en France et en Angleterre, 1540-1640," *Revue Historique,* CXCI (1941). (A French version of the book *Industry and Government in France and England, 1540-1640.*)

"Industrial Europe at the Time of the Reformation (*ca* 1515 *ca* 1540)," *Journal of Political Economy,* XLIX, Nos. 1 and 2, Feb. and April, 1941.

"Civilization at the Crossroads, I," *The Review of Politics,* III, No. 3, July, 1941.

"Silver Production in Central Europe, 1450-1618, *Journal of Political Economy,* XLIX, No. 4, Aug., 1941.

"Civilization at the Crossroads, II," *The Review of Politics,* July, 1941.

"The Responsibility of Economic Historians," *Journal of Economic History*, I, supplement, Dec., 1941.

"War and Economic Progress, 1540-1640," *Economic History Review*, XII, 1942.

"Europe and the United States after the War," *Belgium*, III, Nos. 5-6, June and July, 1942.

"Philosophical Values and American Learning," *The Review of Politics*, IV, No. 3, July, 1942.

"Recent Changes in the Direction of American Education," *The Changing World*, London, 1943.

"Art in France and England, 1540-1640," *The Thomist*, V, Jan., 1943.

"Philosophical Values and the Future of Civilization," *The Review of Politics*, V, No. 2, April, 1943.

"The Industrial Revolution Reconsidered," *Journal of Economic History*, III, No. 1, May, 1943 (a developed version of the same title listed above).

"Péguy and the Spirit of France," *The Review of Politics*, V, No. 3, July, 1943.

"The Meaning of Victory," *The Living Church*, Nov., 21, 1943.

"Wars and the Rise of Industrial Civilization, 1640-1740," *Canadian Journal of Economics and Political Science*, Feb., 1944.

"La Victoire," *La République Francaise*, April-May, 1944.

"Limited Warfare and the Progress of European Civilization, 1640-1740," *The Review of Politics*, July, 1944.

"Historians and Social Scientists, Both Have a Joint Contribution," *Saturday Review of Literature*, Sept. 16, 1944.

"History and the Social Sciences," *Saturday Review of Literature*, Sept. 17, 1944.

"What is Economic History?" *Journal of Economic History* (The Tasks of Economic History), Dec., 1944.

"La Vie de l'esprit et la grande paix, 1815-1914," *La République Francaise*, Nov., and Dec., 1944 and Jan., 1945.

"A Search for Unity," *Human Events*, No. 7, Washington, D. C., 1946.

"Medieval and Modern Reality," *Proceedings of the Catholic Philosophical Society*, March, 1946.

"Architecture and Western Civilization," *The Review of Politics*, April, 1946.

"Realité Moderne," *La République Francaise*, III, No. 5, May, 1946.

"A Movement Toward Educational Reform in the U.S.A.," *Times Educational Supplement*, 1948.

"Warum führt die Menschheit Kriege? *Hamburger Akademische Rundschau*, Dritter Jahrgang 1948-49.

"Die grosse Friede und Seine Ursachen," *Hamburger Akademische Rundschau*, Jahrgang 1949.

"The Chicago Experiment," *Forum*, CXI, No. 1, Jan., 1949.

"The Committee on Social Thought of the University of Chicago," *Universities Quarterly*, London, May, 1949.

"The Future of History," Fortieth Anniversary Celebration of *France-Amérique*, Paris, June, 1949.

"The Economic Road to War," *The Review of Politics*, II, No. 3, July, 1949.

"Les Universités et la formation d'un conscience sociale aux Etats-Unis," *Politique Etrangère*, V, 1949.

"The Enlightenment and the Progress of War: Citizen Soldier," *Measure*, I, 1950.

"The Enlightenment and the Progress of War: The Triumph of Science," *Measure*, II, April, 1950.

"Whither Drifts Mankind? Toward Ruin —Or Renewal?" *The Hindu*, Jan. 26, 1950.

"Un Mouvement humaniste aux Etats-Unis," *L'Age Nouveau*, Nos. 53-54, 1950.

"Rapport sur la guerre," *IXe Congres International des sciences historiques*, Paris, 1950.

"History, World Government and Reform," *Common Cause*, III, No. 12, July, 1950.

"La Guerre prépare-t-elle la paix?" *La Vie Intellectuelle*, March, 1951.

"Ruin or Renewal," *Common Cause*, IV, No. 10, May, 1951.

Transcript of radio discussion by John Nef, Herbert Hoover, Lyman Bryson on "*Agricola's De Re Metallica*," *Invi-*

tation to Learning, Summer 1951, Vol. 1, No. 2.

"Recollection of Artur Schnabel," *Manchester Guardian,* Sept., 1951.

"The University of Chicago and the World, 1929-51," *The Review of Politics,* XIII, No. 4, Oct., 1951.

"La Tâche de l'Histoire: Critique et Programme d'Action," *France-Amérique,* Nos. 1-3, 1952.

"In Quest of Man," *Diogenes,* No. 1, Nov., 1952. (Also available in French).

"La Guerre," *Revue Internationale d'Histoire Militaire,* No. 12, Paris, 1952.

"17th-Century French Political Pamphlets," *The Newberry Library Bulletin,* III, No. 2, April, 1953, Charles H. McIlwain and John U. Nef.

"Communication and Human Welfare," *Journal of Economic History,* XIII, No 1, Winter, 1953.

"L'Art religieux et le progrès economique au moyen age," May 30, 1953, *Association pour l'Histoire de la Civilisation,* 1951-1953, Association Marc Bloch, Toulouse, Nos. 3-4.

"The Significance of 'The Review of Politics,'" *The Review of Politics,* Vol. 7, No. 1, Jan., 1955.

"La Riforma Protestante e L'Origine Della Civiltà Industriale," Estratto dalla Revista *Economia e Storia* Fascicolo II, April-Giugno, 1955.

"Histoire économique et histoire intégrale," *L'Actualité de l'Histoire,* Bulletin trimestriel de l'Institut francais d'Histoire sociale, Juin, 1955.

"L'Universalité française," *The French Review,* April, 1956.

"Man as a Whole: An American Experiment in Criticism and Reform," *The Listener,* Vol. 56, Nov., 1956, London.

"The Universities and Human Community," *Western World,* April, 1958.

"Le Mariage aux Etats Unis," *Revue Dominicaine,* Nov., 1958.

"Art, Science, and Life," *Bulletin of the Atomic Scientists,* Feb. 1959.

"Principles behind Civilized Unity," *Christian Economics,* May (?), 1959.

"André Siegfried m'a fait decouvrir mon pays," France-U.S.A., Paris, June-July, 1960.

"André Siegfried et Les Etats-Unis," *France Amérique,* Paris, 1961.

"Civilization, Industrial Society, and Love," Occasional Papers of the Center for the Study of Democratic Institutions, Santa Barbara, 1961. (Also available in French.)

"Is the Intellectual Life an End in Itself?" *The Review of Politics,* Vol. 24, No. 1, Jan., 1962.

"A New Christian View of History?" *Thought,* Autumn, 1962.

"La Verité, la foi et la civilisation: Tocqueville et Gobineau," *La Table Ronde,* No. 180, Jan., 1963.

"Truth, Belief and Civilization: Tocqueville and Gobineau," *The Review of Politics,* Vol. XXV, No. 4, Oct., 1963.

"Reminiscences of Jules Pascin," *Pascin,* Catalog of Exhibition, 1966/1967. University of California, 1966.

"The Search for Civilization," *The Center Magazine,* May, 1969.

Translation from the French by JUN, *From the Villa Soleil to the Hôtel du Cap* by F. de Caigny, broadside, 1969.

"War and Industrial Civilization, 1640-1740," *The Review of Politics,* n.d.

Speech at the ceremony honoring Maitre and Madame Marc Chagall at the dedication of his mosaic created for the garden of Evelyn and John Nef, November 1, 1971.

"Reform of Graduate Studies," *The Center Magazine,* Vol. VI, No. 1, 1973.

"Peut-on Dégager d'une masse oppressives de connaissances, les grandes lignes d'un ordre et d'une unité?" printed by The Académie des Sciences morales et politiques Paris, 1973.

BOOK REVIEWS

Review of Thomas Southcliffe Ashton and Joseph Sykes, "The Coal Industry of the Eighteenth Century," *Journal of Modern History,* March, 1930.

Review of "The Cotton Trade and Industrial Lancashire, 1600-1780," by Alfred P. Wadsworth & Julie de Lacy Mann, *Journal of Modern History,* Vol. IV, No. 4, Dec., 1932.

Review of Herbert Heaton's "Economic History of Europe, July, 1937.

Review of N. S. B. Gras, "Business and Capitalism: An Introduction to Business History," *The American Historical Review*, Vol. XLV, No. 4, July, 1940.

Review of Charles Wilson, "Anglo-Dutch Trade," *American Economic Review*, June, 1943.

"God Reigns in Changing World," Review of B. I. Bell's "God is Not Dead," *The Living Church*, Nov. 25, 1945.

MISCELLANEOUS

"Above All Nations Is Humanity," a broadside, Chicago, Regnery, 1946.

"Essay on 'Robert Ezra Park'," University of Chicago Press, 1946. (Earlier version published in *Phylon*, 1944.)

Memorial Service for Henry Nattens 1926-1948. (Privately printed).

"Harold Innis: Shapers of the Modern Outlook," *Canadian Forum*, Jan., 1953.

UNPUBLISHED MANUSCRIPTS BY THE AUTHOR

BOOKS

The Genesis of Industrialism — three manuscript volumes and part of a fourth in various stages of competition.

Toward Universalism (various versions).

Roots of the Mechanized World—twelve lectures (one version in the Nef residence and another in the Archives of the University of Chicago). Also more recent preparatory sketches for this book in the Nef residence: "Assault on the Underworld" (1972) ; "The Passion for Rapid Growth: Its Historical Origins and Consequences" (1972) ; "Invention Is of Various Kinds" (1972) ; "Invention and Technological Progress Before the Black Death" (1972); "Towards Quantitative Progress" (1971-72); *The Future of History; Le dur Désir de durer,* projet de livre pour série "Discours de la méthode" Editions Gauthiers-Villars, Paris.

ARTICLES AND PAPERS

FOLDER A

Elizabethan Literature and the Philosophy of Art, talk at Wells College, 1943.

Art and Life (alternate versions), Oct. 20, 1958.

Speech to College Art Society, Moline, Illinois, Oct., 1959.

Art in the Decline of Cosmopolitan Civilization, read for the Literary Society of Washington, D. C., Dec. 10, 1966, and at Duquesne University, April 19, 1967.

Art, Life and Virtue, *c.* 1958.

Art, Science and Life (alternate unpublished version of article in *Bulletin of the Atomic Scientists*).

Art and Civilization: Interrelations Between Art, Life and Virtue, 1959.

The Social Setting Necessary to Achievements in the Creative Life, Swarthmore, 1927 (two similar versions).

Interplay of Literature, Art and Science in the time of Copernicus. International Symposium "The Nature of Scientific Discovery," Washington, 1973.

FOLDER B

Christianity and Warfare.

La Guerre Totale Est-Elle Inevitable? Delivered May 27, 1953 at Ecole des Hautes Etudes Militaire in Paris presided over by General Poydenot ("Twist").

The Causes of War, lecture before the Army War College, Carlisle, Pennsylvania, Feb. 28, 1956.

Ruin or Renewal?

Le Problème de la Guerre.

The Meaning of Victory, College Mount Saint Scholastica.

FOLDER C

The Twilight of Western Civilization, Washington, 1926.

Philosophical Values and the Future of Civilization (unpublished version of article in *Review of Politics*).

Wisdom and Civilization.

The Coming of Civilization and the Birth of Industrialism.

The Human Comedy.

Spiritual Principles Behind Civilized Unity, April 8, 1959.

FOLDER D

The End of the Great Peace.

Relations Between the Intellect and the Great Peace 1815-1914, given at the Fifth Conference on Science, Philosophy and Religion, 1944.

Speech to Headmistresses at Highland Park, Illinois, Oct. 16, 1943.

The Road to Peace, commencement talk at the College of St. Thomas, St. Paul, Minnesota, June, 1942.

Foundations of International Order (also treated in *Universities Look for Unity*, Pantheon Books, 1943).

What Are We Fighting For?

FOLDER E

The University Curriculum and the Future of Western Civilization, 1938.

The Future of American Education, talk given at the University of Notre Dame, South Bend, Indiana, April, 1943.

The Task of the Universities in the United States, speech given to the Harvard Club of Honolulu, 1938 (printed under title "American Universities and Western Civilization").

Mr. Hutchins' Work for Liberal Education.

Education and the War.

Our Common Universe, speech over the Mutual Broadcasting System, Education for Freedom, Inc., Jan. 17, 1944.

Human Minds in the Twentieth Century, 1946.

The Higher Learning at a Turning Point in World History, 1942.

Unity and Purpose in Higher Education, 1972.

FOLDER F

The Unity of French Civilization, speech to American soldiers, University of Chicago, 1943.

French Classical Civilization.

Speech to France Forever, Feb., 1944.

French Culture in Its Relation to the Economic Civilization, Chicago Council on Foreign Relations, March 25, 1947.

French Universalism in Modern Times, Chicago Council on Foreign Relations, April 16, 1947.

France 1949.

The Meaning of France.

The United States and World Community, paper for Alliance Francaise de Chicago, 1958.

FOLDER G

Speech at University of Caen, 1953.

Vers une Synthèse Nouvelle des Hautes Etudes.

L'ideal de l'amour Conjugal aux Etats-Unis (another version published in *Revue Dominicaine*, Nov., 1958).

La Decouverte de la France, talk at the farewell party for the Brières (French Consul Général), Chicago, Dec. 30, 1953.

Un Mouvement de Reforme aux Etats-Unis, talk delivered in Paris in 1949, with supplement.

Sketch for talk given to the students in the Cité Universitaire, Paris, April, 1949.

La Devenir de la Civilisation Industrielle, speech given at the University of Lille, Spring, 1953.

Speech given in Rome at the World Historical Congress, 1955.

Paroles Données pour l'Association Marine Internationale à Bord le Paquebot Liberté, 1954 (English version attached).

Discours pour André Siegfried, May 31, 1960.

Speech at Alliance Francaise de Chicago, April 6, 1972. "L'Esprit comme Cause de la Révolution Industrielle."

FOLDER H

An Age of Social Upheaval "The Many and the Happy Few."

History and the Unification of Knowledge.

History and the Social Sciences.

History, World Government and Reform, Jan., 1950.

Speech to History Department, University of Chicago, 1950.

Summary of "Can There be a New Christian View of History?" c. 1961.

The Future of History.

FOLDER I

Theories of the Origin of Industrialism, Chicago, Feb. 4, 1935.

Discussion at Economic History Meeting, New York, Dec. 26, 1935.

Science and Man, Sept. 20, 1960.

Tradition and the Coming of Industrialism, St. Procopius Monastery, 1960.

Cultural Foundations of Industrial Society, lecture given at the Cooper Union in New York City, Feb. 8, 1960.

The Coming of a New World, three parts.

FOLDER J

Commencement speech at Faulkner School, Chicago.

Foundations of World Community.

Dream of the Infinitely Large, c. 1949.

Renewal (1950).

Lecture at Saint Mary's College, South Bend, Indiana, Oct., 3, 1951.

Speech on the Limitations of Planning given in 1943 or 1944.

Talk to the Renaissance Society, 1934.

FOLDER K

Our Common Purpose, speech at Ferry Hall, Lake Forest, Illinois, 1943.

What Can I Believe?

Lecture given at the University of Michigan July, 1952.

Speech at Seabury-Western Seminary.

Human Minds in the Twentieth Century.

The Cult of the Job.

North America and World Culture, 1957.

FOLDER L

The College Looks Toward Unity, Mexico City College, June, 1948.

World Wars and the Crisis of the Intellect, Mexico City, June, 1948.

Commencement Talk at Mexico City College, 1948.

Talk to the School of Music at Fontainbleau, 1949.

Lectures given at the Institute of Design, 1946: The Historical Foundations of Modern Man, The End of Religious Unity, An Age of Unlimited Warfare.

FOLDER M

Medieval and Modern Reality.

Introduction to lecture on "The Road to Total War" given at the University of Frankfurt in July 1949 and portion of speech.

Die wirtschaftliche Entwicklung zum totalen Krieg.

Der Geistige weg zum Totalen Krieg.

Power and the Scientific Revolution, speech given at History of Science Conference, Providence, Rhode Island, April 4, 1952.

Speech on Science given at the Collège de

Philosophie Paris, Spring, 1949.

Speech at Anglo-American Historical Conference in London, July 8, 1949 (used in *War and Human Progress*).

FOLDER N

Our Common Universe, broadcast, Jan. 17, 1944.

The Method of Historical Comparison in Relation to European History, c. 1540-c. 1640, speech delivered to Economic Historians in Chicago, Feb. 22, 1946.

Broadcast on the Material Road to Total War, 1949.

Talk delivered at 1935 session on economic history at the meeting of the American Economic Association.

World Community and Universalism.

Assault on the Underworld, speech given to Literary Society, Washington, D. C., April 15, 1972.

FOLDER O

English Literature and the Industrial Revolution of Shakespeare's Lifetime.

The Place of the Sixteenth and Seventeenth Centuries in the Rise of Industrialism read at a meeting of the American Historical Association at Urbana, Illinois, Dec. 29, 1933.

Factors in Economic Growth in the Seed Time of Industrial Civilization, given at the Conference on Strategic Factors in Periods of Rapid Economic Growth, New York City, April 9-10, 1954.

Coal and Industrialism.

Higher Education and Human Community, Conference on North Atlantic Community, Bruges, 1957.

FOLDER P

Copy of chapter contributed to *Cambridge Economic History* (Vol. II), second edition in press, 1973.

FOLDER Q

(John U. Nef's Youthful Writings)

The Government of Alsace-Lorraine under French Rule before 1789, History term paper, June 7, 1917.

Crimson-Lampy Hockey, Feb. 15, 1918.

Diary, 1920.

The Vision, 1917.

Helene, Duchess of Aquitaine, written for the elementary history course at the University of Chicago, 1916-17.

The German Government of Alsace-Lorraine and Its Significance, written at Harvard, autumn 1917.

"C'est la Guerre," written at Harvard, March, 1918.

FOLDER R

Paper written presumably in Vienna in Dec., 1924.

Lecture on Early Coal History, Brookings School, Washington, 1926-27.

Shall Europe be Americanized? Paper at Brookings School, 1926-27.

Problem of Wages in the Coal Industry with special relation to Great Britain, written at Swarthmore, Winter, 1928.

Lectures on present day economic problems.

"The Robert Brookings Supreme Court," 1972.

FOLDER S

International Stock Show 1957.

The Mission of a Graduate School.

Changes in Graduate Instruction at the University of Chicago.

The Committee on Social Thought (c. 1945).

Remarks at Committee on Social Thought Faculty-Student Reception, Oct. 9, 1963.

Talk at Annual Committee on Social Thought Party, 1962.

Student-Faculty Meeting of the Committee on Social Thought at John U. Nef's home on Nov. 16, 1961.

The Universities and Human Community, c. 1958.

Man As a Whole: An American Experiment in Criticism and Reform, B.B.C. Broadcast, Third Program, Sept. 3, 1956, Paris.

Speech to X-Amerique, June, 1953.

FOLDER T

The Langevin Plan

Les Universités et la Formation d'une Conscience Sociale aux Etats-Unis.

Remarks at Student-Faculty Meeting, 1953.

Recent Changes in the Direction of American Education.

John U. Nef's participation in Colloquium at University of Denver, May, 1966.

Talk given to the Fulbright Scholars, May 16, 1967.

The Committee on Social Thought of the University of Chicago.

Toward the Foundation of a New Graduate School.

Report of the Chairman of the Committee on Social Thought, May, 1961.

Problems of an Interdisciplinary Faculty as seen in the Light of Historical Interrlationships, Extracts from talk to students and faculty, Oct. 8, 1965.

FOLDER U

Above All Nations is Humanity, II, 1947 (Sequel to "Above All Nations is Humanity" listed in Appendix A).

La Faculté interdisciplinaire de l'Universite de Chicago (talk to France-Amerique, Paris, June, 1949).

An Established Interdisciplinary Faculty, talk to the Visiting Committee of the Humanities of the University of Chicago, Oct. 9, 1970.

The Shortcomings of Specialization, B.B.C. Broadcast, Third Program, Spring, 1949.

The Committee on Social Thought and the University (various versions).

Remarks made to the Panel on Educational Research and Development, Washington, D. C., 1965.

Voice of America Broadcast on the Meaning of the Committee on Social Thought, Washington, D. C., 1960 (?).

FOLDER V
(Introductions)

Bourbon-Busset, Comte Jacques de

Castle, Mabel Wing	Hayek, F. A.
Chagall, Marc	Heaton, Herbert
Chevalier, Louis	Heller, Eric
Coulton, Dr. G. G.	Innis, Donald
Craven, Avery	Lacombe, Olivier
Fehl, Philipp	Leprince-Ringuet, Louis
Fulbright, Senator	Letwin, Mrs. S.

Gourevitch, Mr.
Hartwell, Robert
Moraze, Charles
Ong, Father
Patterson, Bradley
Peyre, Herni
Sarrailh, Jean
Siegfried, André
Simon, Yves

Mahdi, Mushin
Maritain, Jacques
Marlio, Louis
Speaight, Robert
Stravinsky, Igor
Tawney, R H.
Toynbee, Arnold, J.
Warren, Reginald de
Weizacker, Professor von

Introduction as chairman of the Session on the Absolute Monarch at the World Conference of Historians, Rome, 1965.

Introduction to talk given to the Midwestern Writers Association, Evanston, Illinois, summer of 1942.

Introduction at Library Association meeting in Milwaukee, 1942 (?).

Remarks on the occasion of the dinner party for the Italian Ambassador and Madame Ortona, May 30, 1972.

FOLDER W
(Memorial Services)

Brown, Frank L.
Epstein, Leola

Hodgson, Marshall
Park, Robert Ezra

Carroll, Thomas Henry, President of George Washington University — a paper circulated to the Center for Human Understanding, August, 1964.

FOLDER X
(Honors)

John U. Nef's reply to Rector Maurice Bayen on the occasion of receiving the doctor's degree "honoris causa" at the University of Strasbourg, Nov. 22, 1968.

Reply to Lucien Febvre at reception given for John U. Nef at the Collège de France, Nov. 8, 1955.

Remarks of John U. Nef upon his election as Officer of the Legion of Honor

at the French Embassy, Washington, D. C., May 22, 1964 in reply to Ambassador Alphand.

FOLDER Y

Leadership in Higher Education lecture at the Hellenic-American Union, Athens, March, 1967.

Marc Chagall et la Formation Artistique d'un Historien, March, 1968, Washington, and to the Alliance Francaise, Chicago, April 21, 1969.

Educational Reform and the Future of the Human Race—Random Remarks.

Higher Education and Leadership in Human Understanding presented as a paper to the seminar on international education of the Department of Health, Education and Welfare, Dec., 1962.

Toward One Humanity, remarks made at Seminar of the Department of Agriculture, Nov. 3, 1970.

A Supreme Court for Humanity (in French), Nov., 1971.

FOLDER Z

Questions Auxquelles la Science ne peut pas repondre. Vers la formation d'un petit groupe d'amis, Paris, 1958.

Approaches to a Surer Peace.

Letter to Gaston Berger (in French) on the occasion of his founding *Prospective*, March 1, 1960.

A New Conception of Grandeur, report on the first meeting of the Center for Human Understanding, Washington, D. C., Spring, 1962.

Interview with the Columbia University Oral Series concerning the late Adlai Stevenson, 1966. (No transcript available).

INDEX